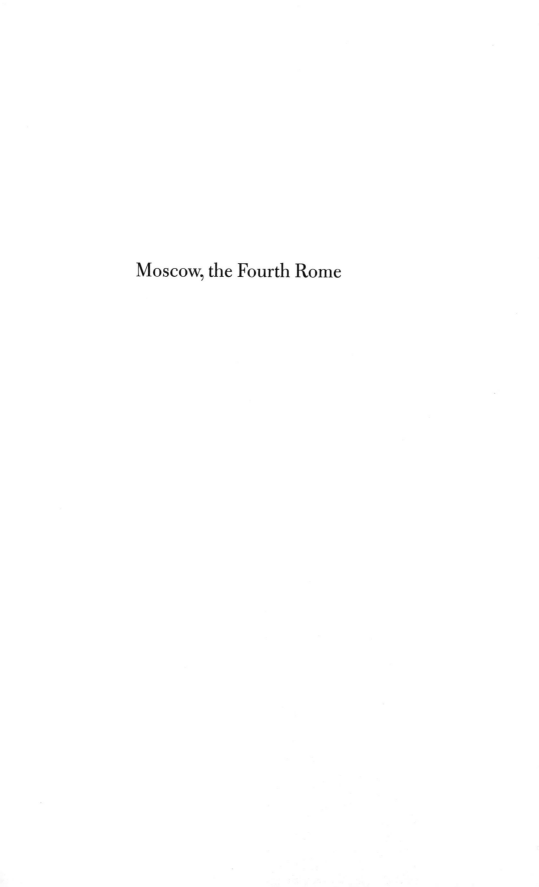

Moscow, the Fourth Rome

Moscow,
the Fourth Rome

STALINISM, COSMOPOLITANISM, AND THE EVOLUTION OF SOVIET CULTURE, 1931–1941

Katerina Clark

Harvard University Press

Cambridge, Massachusetts · London, England

2011

Library of Congress Cataloging-in-Publication Data

Clark, Katerina.

Moscow, the fourth Rome : Stalinism, cosmopolitanism,
and the evolution of Soviet culture, 1931–1941 / Katerina Clark.

p.   cm.

Includes bibliographical references and index.

ISBN 978-0-674-05787-6

1. Moscow (Russia)—History—20th century.   2. Moscow (Russia)—Intellectual life—20th century.   3. Cosmopolitanism—Russia (Federation)—Moscow—History.   4. Popular culture—Russia (Federation)—Moscow—History.   5. Stalin, Joseph, 1879–1953—Influence.   6. Communism—Russia (Federation)—Moscow—History.   7. Social change—Russia (Federation)—Moscow—History.   8. Soviet Union—History—1925–1953.   9. Soviet Union—Intellectual life—1917–1970.   10. Social change—Soviet Union—History.   I. Title.

DK601.2.C55 2011

947'.310842—dc23   2011024709

To
Peter Isaac, Benjamin Michael,
Joshua Applebye, Nicholas Manning,
and Sebastian Holquist

Contents

Moscow, the Fourth Rome

Introduction: The Cultural Turn

IN THE CORONATION SCENE of 1547 that opens part 1 of *Ivan the Terrible* (*Ivan groznyi,* 1943), Eisenstein has the young tsar conclude his speech with the words: "Two Romes have fallen, Moscow is the third, and there will be no fourth! And for that Third Rome the single master will be I ALONE."[1] In Eisenstein's earlier article of 1933 about his film *Moscow* (never shot), he opens with virtually the same words, adding: "this pronouncement by Filofei comes across to us from medieval times through tsarist Muscovy and autocratic Moscow. Moscow as a concept is the concentration of the socialist future of the entire world."[2]

In these two pronouncements about Moscow as a Rome, Eisenstein is invoking a famous statement made four centuries earlier by the Russian monk Filofei of Pskov. In the early sixteenth century during the reign of Ivan's father, Vasilii III, Filofei pronounced in one of his three "Third-Rome" epistles:[3] "so be aware, lover of God and Christ, that all Christian empires have come to an end and are gathered together in the singular empire of our sovereign in accordance to the books of prophecy, and this is the Russian empire: because two Romes have fallen, and a third stands, and a fourth there shall not be."[4] Many have concluded that Filofei was claiming for "the God-protected city of Moscow"[5] the role of center of Christendom, as successor to first Rome itself, and then Constantinople, which had been called "New Rome" or "New Jerusalem" since 381, but had fallen to the Turks in 1453.[6]

Filofei's dictum, made around 1523/1524, did not receive a lot of attention until the second half of the nineteenth century, when it became popular to read his pronouncement of a "third Rome" to mean territorial conquest or imperial dominion as Russia's manifest destiny. Eisenstein's representing Ivan as intoning the dictum has its rationalization in that the reign of Ivan IV ("the Terrible") and his territorial conquests are generally seen as marking the beginning of Moscow (Russia) as an empire. Filofei himself had, however, seen Moscow as the "third Rome" in the sense of center for world Christianity. As such, even in Filofei's own time, and for several centuries to come, Moscow was generally aggrandized as a "new Jerusalem," in other words, more unambiguously as a spiritual center. But as Iurii Lotman and Boris Uspensky have remarked, the idea that Moscow was a "third Rome" "was by its very nature dualistic" and "brings together two tendencies—the religious and the political," in other words, representing on the one hand the spiritual hegemony Russia would enjoy as the center of "true" Christian faith, Russian Orthodoxy, and on the other some form of international dominion.[7]

The implicit reference to Filofei's pronouncement in this book's title is to suggest that Soviet Moscow, as emblem of a new, Bolshevik order, was to be a Rome, an analogy some used in the 1930s. But it was not, as in Filofei's conception, to be a model and center of Christianity. Rather, it was to be the capital of a *different,* post-Christian, belief system. Hence I am calling it the "fourth Rome," though that was not a title given it at the time.

In Eisenstein's script for *Ivan the Terrible,* the main thrust of the claim that Moscow is the "third Rome" is (as also in his *Moscow*) political hegemony. *Ivan* shows how this medieval Russian tsar unified his country by determined might, defeating internal enemies and pushing its borders out to reach the sea. The film has also widely been seen as an apologia for the brutal purges of the 1930s (though this position has been disputed by some leading Eisenstein scholars) and an extravagant allegorical portrait of Stalin, a document in the cult of personality; in my deliberately literal translation of Ivan's words above, Moscow's elevation to being the "third Rome" will be effected by "I ALONE" (capitalized in the scenario).[8]

Eisenstein himself was one of the most sophisticated, cosmopolitan, and polyglot Soviet intellectuals. Was he, in generating such texts in the 1930s, betraying his iconoclastic stance of the previous decade, when he was a player in a transnational avant-garde? Was he "capitulating" or "conforming" under pressure from Stalin, who sent Andrei Zhdanov in 1941 to commission the film from him?[9] Was he falling in line with a general shift over the Soviet 1930s that many scholars have observed, a shift from proletarian internationalism to a revival of prerevolutionary culture and nationalist themes?[10]

Ivan, which, as Yuri Tsivian points out, "some people even think the most complex movie ever made,"[11] cannot be dismissed as an officially endorsed propaganda piece, even though Eisenstein was awarded a Stalin Prize for it. Nor should it be taken, as it has often been, as a prime and unambiguous example of the revival of the national. As I argue in chapter 9 and elsewhere, a pervasive subtext in the film, operating largely at the level of the visual, is the example of the western European Renaissance, with its peripatetic artists such as Holbein (who today would be called "transnationals"), its leaders who were great patrons of the arts (Henry VIII, Elizabeth, Catherine de Medici), and such intellectual giants as Erasmus and Machiavelli. In fact while working on this film Eisenstein wrote an article about this connection between Ivan's Russia and the roughly contemporaneous Renaissance in western Europe. In it he suggests the ineluctability of violence in these famous Renaissance leaders' pursuit of the twin aims of aesthetic and political power.[12] Arguably, Eisenstein produced in this film an allegorical representation of national glory by locating that "terrible" phase of Russian history within a pan-European context that included the Renaissance as a time of extraordinary cultural achievement. From this perspective, though the film is patriotic and inflected by a purge mentality, it could be read as presenting the life of Ivan as the tragedy of an able leader: in a sort of Faustian bargain, he implements the violence that might facilitate a national flowering, but in its misdirected excess that flowering eludes him; instead, in part 3, of which Eisenstein was allowed to film only fragments, Ivan is left to contemplate blood and devastation all around.

One should be wary of conjecturing what Eisenstein "actually thought" or "intended" in making this multivalent film. Even if one accepts the above interpretation, it could be argued that Eisenstein, that voracious reader of Western texts, could not be viewed as typical of the Soviet intellectual of the 1930s. But I am taking his scenario for *Ivan*, the first draft of which was completed in April 1941, just before the Soviet Union was invaded that June and hence a culminating point of this study, as an end case that throws into relief a general phenomenon of the 1930s: the way nationalist or imperialist trends coexisted with, and were often imbricated with, some form of cosmopolitanism.

This book treats cosmopolitan trends in Europe during the 1930s, but it does so from an unusual viewpoint—the evolution of Stalinist culture as seen through Moscow intellectual life. It examines an important moment in the prehistory of key concepts of literary and cultural studies today: "transnationalism," "cosmopolitanism," and "world literature." Contemporary discussions of these terms are largely focused in the present, identifying precedents in figures like Kant or in the French Enlightenment, but seem largely unaware of the extent to which "world literature" and the Enlightenment played an important role in European intellectual, and even political, life during the 1930s. This was especially so in that unlikely place the Soviet Union, which promoted "world literature" both for domestic consumption and as emblem of the antifascist movement. In discussing cosmopolitanism in this context, however, one has to recognize that it coincided, and to some extent overlapped, with another "-ism" that is eerily absent from current discussions of the transnational or cosmopolitan—"internationalism," which was in the past often a euphemism for the cause of Soviet ideological hegemony throughout the world.

Is cosmopolitanism to be seen as an alternative to internationalism? And what of nationalism? These three -isms are not completely separate. Liah Greenfeld in *Nationalism: Five Roads to Modernity* stresses that "the development of national identities . . . was essentially an international process, whose sources . . . lay outside the evolving nations," adding "at the same time, [it was] an indigenous development" born of a "crisis of identity" and dissatisfaction with the status quo.[13] And Pheng Cheah argues in *Spectral Nationality* that such dichotomies as "nationalist particularism versus cosmopolitan universalism and cultural nationalism" "pathologize nationalism," often "opposing it to Enlightenment universalism from which it is allegedly a fall," and failing "to recognize

that nationalism is also a universalism because both it and cosmopolitanism are based on the same normative concept of culture. Many German
philosophers of national *Bildung* (e.g., Herder, Schiller, Humboldt, and
Fichte) were also cosmopolitanists who saw the nation and its culture as
the most effective actualization of universal ethical ideals."[14] Arguably, in
the 1930s the causes of nationalism, internationalism, and even cosmopolitanism were not distinct but to a significant degree imbricated with
each other in a mix peculiar to that decade.[15] In the case of Soviet cosmopolitanism in *this* decade, it was of a distinctive kind, inextricably bound
up with Soviet internationalism and patriotism, and yet not reducible to
either. The cosmopolitans themselves, though not apolitical and of course
also internationalist, were *as cosmopolitans* driven by a desire to interact
with the cultures and intellectuals of the outside world, and especially of
Europe, and to expand their own horizons and those of their compatri-
ots. The people I am calling cosmopolitans did not themselves identify
with that term. In the thirties it was rarely used in the Soviet press and did
not have particularly positive connotations; in the late 1940s, the term
emerged to prominence as *the* pejorative in an official campaign against
things Western in general and Jews in particular, but I am not using it in
that sense.

In this book I look at how Soviet culture evolved during its most "terrible" phase, the 1930s, decade of the Great Purge. But mine will be a
somewhat perverse account. To date Western histories of Soviet culture
have been largely shaped by the master narrative of the twentieth century
dominated by what Kristin Ross has called the "obligatory reference to
the twinned catastrophes of Gulag and Holocaust," which has submerged
much of this era's particularity.[16] In cultural histories of the Soviet Union
one such presumed "catastrophe," generally twinned with the Gulag, has
been the closure of all independent cultural organizations in 1932 and the
introduction of socialist realism as a mandatory "method" for all branches
of the arts, a cultural holocaust, as it were, anticipating the human holocaust to come in the purges. From this perspective, the Soviet Union was
just another "totalitarian" power. Here I hope to provide a more complex
picture, even while showing how the major characters in this book were
involved in the purges and the extreme cultural centralization in one way
or another.

I seek to tell the cultural history of the 1930s without dwelling on the purges, or on some titanic struggle between the regime and the dissidents. I do not dispute that trajectory, but rather want to incorporate it in a broader perspective. I hope to show how over these years the country developed as a singular "civilization" but did so while simultaneously interacting with the outside world, and primarily with continental Europe, in this decade the main sphere of interest for Soviet intellectuals, though with America as well. This enlarged purview allows me to show the simultaneity of different trends, different readings of texts and different lobbies within the Stalinist cultural world, as well as the simultaneity of similar trends in the Soviet Union and the West. I am endeavoring to integrate a rather neglected international dimension into the overall interpretation of Stalinism.

Though this is a limitation, I am not doing a political or institutional history about great power machinations, or about the masses and their tastes or reactions, very hard to gauge in any event, or about what "Stalin" wanted or did. As Mark Mazower has said, "as for Hitler and Stalin, their domination is clear enough. But one can make too much of their character flaws, oddly comforting though they may seem." He continues: "dictator denunciation—in many ways the obverse of hero worship— attempts to ring-fence civilization off from the totalitarian temptation—as indeed from other forms of political violence as well." The "effect is to bracket the phenomenon off from modernity, to preserve civilization's purity"; but "liberalism was on its way out in interwar Europe."[17] As this book will show, there are parallels between developments in the Soviet Union, including the growth of a nationalist culture, with those in other European countries, and especially Popular Front France, with which it was linked for a time in an alliance.

To claim that Soviet culture of the 1930s originated with Stalin is to overpersonalize the forces that drove it, though "Stalin" can be an effective cipher. Stalin, and the Party cultural apparatus, were indisputably extraordinarily powerful and as the decade wore on began more and more to actually commission and monitor cultural products (as seen in the case of *Ivan*) and to implement their pet schemes, but they were not extrasystemic figures, figures from outside the culture system, but rather picked up and mediated, selectively, some of the dominant currents in the thinking of the time. But as is generally true of politicians they had little stomach for the highbrow avant-garde, and this effectively narrowed the purview of Stalinist culture.

The competing claims of nationalism and internationalism were a problem that neither the Soviet leadership nor the intellectuals ever really resolved. Stalin has traditionally been typecast as drawing away from internationalism because of his 1924 theory of "socialism in one country," that is, the doctrine that it is possible to pull off a socialist revolution in a single country, such as Russia, without a broader proletarian revolution. But if you read his writings of the 1920s, such as his classic book *Problems of Leninism* (1926), one finds the dream of some international communist entity is far from abandoned. Some interpreters of Soviet history like Mikhail Agursky have tipped the scales over and contended that the Soviet Union was nationalist from the very start. Agursky argues that, for example, Lenin welcomed the assassination of Rosa Luxembourg and Karl Liebknecht because they were powerful rivals to dominate world communism.[18] To assume that internationalism was just a mask for naked power is to go too far. The 1930s were a posticonoclastic moment, but not a moment when internationalism died.

Evidence in Soviet culture of the 1930s of a weakening of "proletarian internationalism" in favor of Great Russian nationalism, or "national Bolshevism," is not far to seek. But to point this out is not to tell the whole story. As Karl Schlögel has argued in *Terror und Traum: Moskau 1937,* this time cannot be covered in a single narrative. Rather, there was a "simultaneity" of disparate trends and phenomena, different stories that provide different perspectives on the same moment, and they should all be covered.[19] This book hopes to supplement the standard account, which analyzes the decade in terms of a turn to Great Russian nationalism—already well argued and documented—by pointing to a simultaneous, if more precariously flourishing, internationalism. This internationalism was, however, no longer automatically "proletarian," the term "proletarian" having been largely abandoned around 1932. In effect, those in authority in culture dumped "proletarian internationalism" in the interests not of "retreat" but of a grander narrative. This made possible a culture that was not merely internationalist but to a surprising degree cosmopolitan as well.

I prefer to see the revival of pre-Soviet Russian culture in the 1930s as part of a Great Appropriation. In building up its own image, Moscow appropriated both laterally (absorbing contemporary trends in other countries, primarily western European, but also American) and diachronically (appropriating Great Russian and European culture of the past). In one of the more blatant expressions of this, Boris Iofan, the chief Soviet architect of the 1930s and designer of the bombastic Palace of Soviets in Moscow, remarked in *Pravda* after a trip to New York, Chicago, Rome, and Berlin in 1935: "wherever I might travel, whatever I might see, I approached everything from a particular point of view: what of all this has to be 'taken home,' to the Soviet Union."[20] But such Western culture was not just appropriated. In the process it was reworked, reinflected for the specifica of Marxism-Leninism and the Stalinist epoch.[21]

The Great Appropriation might seem to be a hegemonic program, but it also facilitated greater interaction with intellectual life abroad. It would take a stretch of the imagination to see Stalin's entourage as "cosmopolitans"; for a start, they did not command foreign languages. But the intellectuals who were more directly involved in the Appropriation tended to be cosmopolitan by inclination.

This book seeks to chart the evolution of Soviet culture without circumscribing its account with an intellectual iron curtain, that is, by the totally Soviet focus that has characterized most cultural histories to date. No nation can be "an unproblematic limit for cultural histories."[22] As scholars have become fond of pointing out lately, the emergence of comparative literature as an intellectual project coincided with the flowering of European nationalism at the beginning of the nineteenth century.[23] As a distinctive discipline it was

> shaped from [its] inception by the intersection between nation-based paradigms and others that are more transnational and cosmopolitan, exilic and migratory. Hugo Meltzl de Comnitz in the second volume of the first journal of Comparative Literature, *Zeitschrift für vergleichende Literatur,* which he founded in 1877, cites as his motto a quotation from a letter written by Schiller in 1789: "It would be a pitiful, petty ideal to write for *one* nation only: for a philosophical spirit this limitation is absolutely unbearable. This spirit could not

confine itself to such a changeable, accidental, and arbitrary form of humanity, a fragment (and what else is a great nation?)."[24]

Many scholars have also written about the central role played by literature in forming national identity, and most particularly by national poets. At the hands of writers, the "fragment," the arbitrary, becomes the whole and necessary, or at any rate at the hands of those who co-opt literary figures and texts for the national cause. Yet, as Margaret Cohen has pointed out, in the modern period literary geographies are largely "supranational," particularly "in the case of the central genre of the modern period, the novel."[25] In addition, Goethe, the first advocate of "world literature," is one of the "national poets" used to define the nation's identity, though his nation, Germany, did not exist as such when he wrote. This example highlights both the importance of point of view in demarcating what is "national" from what is "inter-" or "trans-national," and the extent to which the two concepts cannot be seen as absolute binary opposites.

Despite the Stalinist regime's hegemonic, authoritarian, and isolationist proclivities its culture did not emerge as an act of parthenogenesis. As Marx and Engels themselves recognized, cultural autarchy is undesirable. In the *Communist Manifesto* (1848) they observe: "in place of the old global and national seclusion and self-sufficiency, we have intercourse in every direction, universal interdependence of nations. And, as in material, so also in intellectual production. The intellectual creations become common property. National one-sidedness and narrow-mindedness become more and more impossible."

We will note here how quickly Marx and Engels move, despite their base/superstructure hierarchy in *The German Ideology* (1845), from "material" to "intellectual" production. The Soviet Union was ostensibly committed to increasing production, to churning out all those tractors, all that pig iron, and to "catching up and surpassing" the West in the economic sphere, and though to be sure a great deal of attention and investment went into that cause, yet culture emerged as the area defining Soviet identity. Symptomatically, within the Politburo for much of this decade, oversight of production was largely relegated to Grigory Ordzhonnikidze and Lazar Kaganovich while Stalin took over stewardship of culture.[26]

In the 1930s, culture, and especially literature, became the Soviet secular surrogate for religion and central to the Soviet Union's claim for international dominance (see Chapter 2). Ideology was in theory of paramount importance and often stressed over material progress, but it was not sufficient. Literature, in concert with the new architecture, provided emblems of the new system of value: aesthetic forms embodied ideology. As we shall see (in Chapter 3), the aesthetic provided a critical interface between politics and mores in systematizing the value system and working out a code of values and behavior.

But the function of culture in the Stalinist 1930s, and of literature in particular, was not purely instrumental. In that decade culture began to take off both as a value for its own sake and as emblem of national glory, achieving a cult status in a cultural turn. This turn took place around 1931–1932, the beginning point of my study.

There are many reasons for this cultural turn. Literacy had been acquired, the populace were more educated, and now Soviet society could move toward a common culture for the educated and the masses alike, one that went beyond (though it still included) the crude poster or ideological skit. As many scholars have pointed out, the era of iconoclasm had ended, and a time of étatism with interest in national aggrandizement had begun, and historically potentates have turned to culture to effect this. The Soviet Union was acquiring industrial and military might but wanted world recognition, so the country appropriated culture, rather as in American history the robber barons evolved into great patrons of scholarship and the arts and started their own cultural foundations. More than the robber barons (though this was often true of them, too) the Soviet purveyors and legislators of culture believed in their mission. They promoted culture to mobilize popular support, but also to attain greatness for their society to be attested in a great architecture and literature.

Arguably Stalin, and many Soviet cultural bureaucrats and intellectuals— themselves inheritors of a messianic tradition—aspired to generate a superior civilization, to make their country a primus inter pares in a cultural confederation within *their* world, continental Europe.[27] Though in time the official platform veered in the direction of "national Bolshevism," there was another possibility, one that was so strongly marked in the 1930s that I would argue the cultural history of the decade should not be told without it—yet it most often is—and that is the possibility of pan-European cosmopolitanism with the Soviet Union as the leading player and exponent. Many, but not all, were particularly taken by the notion of "world literature" and did not want the new Soviet culture to be defined by the vernacular tradition. Here there was a major justification in the Marxist classics. In the *Communist Manifesto* (1848) Marx and Engels went on from their insistence in the paragraph quoted above on the "mutual interdependence of nations" to conclude: "from the numerous national and local literatures, there arises a world literature," as it were the culmination of literary evolution. Not everyone was equally committed to this, but Maksim Gorky, himself long wooed to come back from emigration and embellish Soviet culture with his international reputation, was a powerful advocate. In 1934 he prevailed on the organizers of the First Congress of the Writers Union (where he was titular head) to invite big name authors from foreign countries, and Zhdanov, the Party spokesman there, and others also invoked the object of realizing a "treasure house of world literature."[28] Allegedly the aim of Soviet literature was to "create an art which would form [vospityvalo] the builders of socialism . . . and turn them into the true heirs of all of world culture."[29] Gorky is a huge subject in itself, and I cannot address it here, except to note that he died in 1936 and the shift to greater Russian nationalism became especially marked in 1937, though there were many other factors involved, not the least of which was the specter of war.

In their bid to lead "world culture" the Soviet establishment were not unique. Culture became an area where in the 1930s the rival states and rival world systems of Europe began to compete for the right to be considered the true leader of the continent. Soviet spokesmen tended to establish their superiority over Nazi Germany, and later Franco's Spain, and even England, with claims that *they* paid more attention to culture and also honored the great works of a rival state's culture more than that state did. Thus, for example, the claim was made that Shakespeare was neglected in England but enjoying tremendous attention in Soviet Russia.[30] Central to the Soviet claim of preeminence was its axiom that the Marxist-Leninist system is manifestly superior. But they needed more, especially since the country was not a leader in technology or military might. Its claim was stronger as "world" capital of culture and ideology.

In that the Bolsheviks were representatives of a world system with universalizing aims, potentially Moscow would form the center of a new, transnational imperial formation of some kind, a "Rome." In a reduced sense it already was; it was a version of the land-based empire, and ancient Rome is a paradigm of that formation.[31] Moscow as metropole commanded a large swathe of territory; the press kept boasting that the Soviet Union encompassed "one-sixth of the world," a "sixth" that comprised numerous administrative entities peopled largely by ethnic minorities. Lenin and Stalin were initially opposed, however, to its becoming a traditional empire: in Lenin's "Imperialism: The Highest Stage of Capitalism" (first published in 1917) imperialism was regarded as a capitalist vice. They were committed to what Terry Martin has called an "affirmative action empire," though imperial Rome also allowed heterogeneity and local governance and sought assimilation of non-Roman subjects.[32] The Soviet Union, however, could be seen as aspiring to become an even greater empire, though not as direct ruler of Europe or the transatlantic world but in another sense now often applied to the case of contemporary United States, which is commonly labeled an "empire," but an empire largely characterized by overwhelming economic, political, and cultural dominance rather than by territorial conquest or direct political rule.[33] In the case of the Soviet Union, cultural dominance was particularly pursued. Culture was power.

I am going to argue that culture's function went beyond that. Whether consciously or unconsciously, the ideal that stood before the country in the 1930s was an aesthetic state, a *Kunststadt*.[34] An aesthetic state, as defined by Joseph Chytry in his book of that title, "will stand for a social and political community that accords primacy, although not exclusiveness, to the aesthetic dimension in human consciousness and activity." The connection between the aesthetic and the political can "form values, 'aesthetic morals,' though which such a people sustain and elaborate their social and cultural unity."[35]

The ideal of the aesthetic state, prominent in ancient Athens and Renaissance Florence, was further developed by German thinkers from the mid-eighteenth to the late nineteenth century. It is particularly associated with Friedrich Schiller and his *Aesthetic Letters* of 1794–1795 (and Fichte, Schelling, and others who argued that an aesthetic education is critical for producing exemplary citizens).[36] Schiller saw the nation as becoming whole if it realizes an aesthetic state. In addition, in Hegel particular aesthetic models (the Egyptian, classical, and Gothic) define entire world systems and punctuate the road to man's, and society's, self-perfection.

Schiller and Hegel had a great influence on Russian thinkers of the nineteenth and early twentieth centuries, notably on Vissarion Belinsky, that darling of leftist and Soviet scholarship. Soviet indebtedness to Belinsky and his cohort let the German Romantics in the back door of the "Marxist-Leninist" state. Georgy Lukács and his Moscow coterie helped usher them in, promoting translations of Hegel and Schiller's aesthetic theories. Lukács wrote an extended introduction to a collection of Schiller's writings on aesthetics in translation, which largely comprises a selection of his *Aesthetic Letters*.[37]

The fascists, then, were—pace Benjamin's famous pronouncement in the Epilogue to "The Work of Art in an Age of Mechanical Reproduction" (1936)—not alone in aestheticizing politics. In Nazi Germany, Eric Michaud argues in *Cult of Art in Nazi Germany,* "the legitimation of power through divine right was replaced by legitimation through artistic genius."[38] But there was a difference between the Nazi incorporation of culture and the Soviet that can be caught in the different branches of the arts that they privileged. Whereas Michaud identifies painting, sculpture, and architecture as the paradigmatic Nazi arts, the Stalinist regime of the 1930s favored written texts.[39] The Soviet preference could be seen as a variant on the long-standing trend among European socialists, analyzed by Regis Debray in a recent article, to identify with the printed word in general and with literature in particular.[40] In the Stalinist 1930s, this pattern among socialists is complicated by the fact that textual authority became a major means of legitimization. One got what Debray calls "a totalitarian hijacking of the Enlightenment," but it included an *extra*ordinary reverence for the book, which functioned as a cult object in a secular faith.

In National Socialist rhetoric, according to Michaud, the people or state are "molded by the artist-Führer," or, as Goebbels put it in his novel *Michael* in a quote used by Michaud, "a statesman is also an artist. For him the people are merely what stone is for a sculptor."[41] In Soviet iconography, however, the leader figure, Stalin, is *writing* the nation (see

Chapter 2). The distinction is not a mere matter of aesthetic preference. As Michaud argues, sculpture, particularly of the muscular male body, can be associated with the Nazis' obsession with the "master race" and their program of ethnic cleansing. The sculptor molds the body with clay, or, as Nazi rhetoric emphasized, chips off the dross from his amorphous block of stone, paring away all that is unaesthetic to produce the perfect body.

In Nazi texts, purifying the race (eugenics) is identified with producing a pure art, an achievement in aesthetics. In the Third Reich "the violence of the artist had become a virtue for the statesman."[42] But in some senses the exercise of might in the name of an aesthetic ideal is an incipient danger in any *Kunststadt*. The "aesthetic state" is not free of coercion, for implicit in it is the idea of mandating some consensual (even if minimal) notion of what constitutes the aesthetic, and enforcing its priority. Schiller himself wrote of the need to *purify* in order to achieve the aesthetic state, a need Plato articulated earlier in his *Republic*.

Stalinist culture was centered less around an image of a body that stood for the body politic or the people—a statue—than around a narrative, paradigmatically a biography. But both the Stalin and the Hitler regimes, whether their iconic artifact was a sculpture or a biography, sought to generate an artwork where what they saw as inessential or contingent was eliminated (see the discussion of Lukács in Chapters 1 and 3). The national creative genius, guided by aesthetic ideals, was to seek thereby to realize the necessary and eternal. Certain trends in the avant-garde, such as Surrealism, were inevitably doomed because they privileged the arbitrary and insignificant seeming.

Soviet citizens were to be surrounded by the beautiful and also to be au courant with the greatest achievements of "world culture," both as judged by those in authority. Architecture and urban design, rhetorically linked with the national narrative, played an important role here. In rhetoric and visual imagery they functioned as a mediating interface between physical selfhood (the human body) and the metaphysical space of the political body.

In national narratives, generally, the capital city is represented as isomorphic with the state, and indeed personifies it. Though cities are essentially polyglot in their semiotic systems,[43] such profligacy had for the

Soviet capital to be reduced to a single set of semiotic referents, a single narrative encoded in its very architecture and urban design. Originally, in 1918, the Soviet leaders had been forced to use Moscow as their capital, retreating there from the tsarist capital, Saint Petersburg (called Petrograd at the time), when it was threatened by counterrevolutionary forces. But in the 1930s Moscow's status as the capital became in official rhetoric a matter not of historical accident, but of necessity. Starting in 1933, a cult of Moscow was fostered by the authorities, a cult that became central to the entire culture system. Between 1931 and 1941, a paradigmatically "Stalinist" time, the Soviet government lavished attention and money on rebuilding the city (until projects had to be shelved as the country dealt with the German invasion). Reconstructing Moscow was to modernize the capital but also to provide a guarantee and proof of the preeminence of the Soviet Union with its new system of value. The leadership sought to create what it saw as an aesthetic environment and advanced "new Moscow"—what it would look like when according to new plans it was rebuilt—as the paradigm of Soviet beauty.

Moscow culture became Soviet culture in two senses. First, in that the absolute majority of the commissions and publication outlets and the most privileged housing and living conditions for intellectuals were established there, Moscow became the place where culture was "happening." A steady stream of intellectuals relocated to the capital. Second, culture spread centripetally. Exempla from Moscow (architectural styles, theatrical repertoires, etc.) were mandated for everywhere else. Leningrad, the former capital (as Petersburg) and rival, remained an equal really only in film and ballet; even then the edicts, journals, and critics that set the canon came largely from Moscow.

As a realization of the national aesthetic, the Soviet capital was considered advanced as compared with the rest of the country. Consequently, a cultural history of Moscow captures the evolution of Stalinist culture at large, and, since the state was so centralized, the traffic patterns both within the Stalinist cultural realm and in its interaction with abroad. As Nancy Condee has noted, the metropole is the "center through which the peripheries largely negotiate their relations to each other,"[44] but in a closed society like the Soviet Union it is also the site through which the country negotiates its relationship to the outside world.

Paradoxically, even as the Soviet Union became an increasingly closed society, it simultaneously became more involved with foreign trends. The ways it was closed down are well known. Yet, beginning around 1932–1933, the ostensible date for the narrowing of Soviet cultural horizons with the introduction of internal passports and the abolition of all independent cultural organizations, strong countervailing trends can also be observed. Although, as Terry Martin has shown, in 1932 policies toward the national minorities shifted and Russian was stressed as the national language,[45] at precisely this time the Soviet cultural world became more cosmopolitan, more open to products from the West. The horizon of Soviet culture widened as translation took off.

The huge spate of translations published in the 1930s cannot be ignored by those who write of nationalism tout court. The infamous years 1937 and 1938 produced a harvest of translated works by major western European and American writers. Though we have to recognize that, given the length of time it takes to translate, this harvest was probably sown around 1935, the high point of the Popular Front entente, this does not alter the fact that Western literature was prominent on the horizon of Russians during the purge years.

As Yuri Lotman in *Universe of the Mind* and others have pointed out, some of the great flowering times in Europe occurred as a sequel to a period of intense absorption of another culture or cultures, often through translation and language learning. Lotman's five-stage progression, which begins with the receiver country taking on other cultures through translations and ends with it becoming the transmitter that "issues forth a flood of texts," is perhaps a little schematic.[46] Yet his ideas are useful here because they suggest the importance of translation in cultural evolution and the possibility that an orgy of translation may lead not to a derivative culture and an eclipsing of the national tradition but to a flowering of the "receiving" culture, a reworking of it potentially enabling it to become a "transmitting" culture. This was an ideal that in the Soviet 1930s many shared.

One example of the role translation of foreign texts has played historically in ushering in a cultural renaissance, one that has attracted recent attention, is the decisive shift in German intellectual life associated with the journal *Athenaeum*. This journal was at the center of a wave of translations by figures like Friedrich Schlegel, August Wilhelm Schlegel, Friedrich

Schleiermacher, Friedrich Hölderlin, and Goethe. Translation can be re-garded as a form of intercultural mediation, but as Antoine Berman points out in his account of the intellectuals grouped around the *Athenaeum,* they saw it more as a means of appropriation, and the route to national aggrandizement as well, affording a *Bildung* (cultural formation), that would take the nation to the cultural level necessary for it to become a world leader.[47] Many of *Athenaeum*'s principals saw translation not as fostering a derivative culture but on the contrary as "a durable asset to the German patrimony." They regarded the translator as a sort of a broker of "world literature" (a concept after all introduced by Goethe), one who could enable the Germans to become cultural leaders. Translation could provide in German a treasure house of European literature and a market place where all nations presented their merchandise. This would encour-age others to learn German and vault a not-yet-existing Germany into a position of cultural hegemony.[48]

In the example of the German proselytizers for translation we see how cosmopolitan ideals and national ambitions were inextricably inter-twined. Haun Saussy has said that "too much hospitality to foreign con-tributions signifie[s] a failure to acknowledge the special character and genius of the home language."[49] Yet the intellectuals clustered around the *Athenaeum* saw translations not as foreign imports but actually as "a con-stitutive moment of Germanity [Deutschheit]." They believed their trans-lations gave them access to the "universal" and could thereby provide their ticket to world cultural domination, to a glory that, A. W. Schlegel claimed, "has been reserved for the Germans," while Novalis proposed that "only for us have translations become expansions."[50]

Another example of translation as a route to securing a national iden-tity and aggrandizement, this time in the 1930s, was a state-sponsored campaign in Turkey. The campaign was largely a result of Ataturk's deter-mination to establish a secular, respected state in post-Ottoman Turkey and to resituate it in a "radically different cultural geography" that, as Azade Seyhan comments, "aspired to translate what it saw as the exem-plary representation of Western education into its own discourse of na-tion." Here we see implicit two points that are germane also to the Soviet case. First, Seyhan's "what it saw as" implies selection based on the re-ceiving country's conception of value in what was available for translation (actually in the Turkish case, that was often determined by intellectuals in exile there from Nazi Germany). Second, the process of adaptation and bowdlerization forces these texts into a "discourse of nation." In fact, as Seyhan points out, in Turkey the process was not just one of opening up or broadening; even as under Ataturk Western texts were being introduced, Turkish itself was being purged of words from Arabic and Persian to reclaim the "real" national language.[51] It should come as no surprise to learn that in the Stalinist 1930s there was often considerable textual adjustment in the translations, but that is not our subject here.

Potentially the wave of translations from European literature in the Soviet 1930s might have led to a flowering and ultimately Soviet dominance as this newly translated literature was reworked and incorporated into the national cultural treasury. Consider, for example, how the Russian absorption of English and French writers early in the nineteenth century resulted in the emergence of Aleksandr Pushkin and Mikhail Lermontov, the great national poets who presided over its "golden age" of literature, and how the absorption of western European (primarily French) modernist art early in the twentieth century (Cézanne, Picasso, etc.) resulted in a Russian avant-garde that could lay claim to world preeminence (e.g., Kazimir Malevich).

In the 1930s, commissioned translations provided a livelihood for a lot of writers, such as Boris Pasternak, who were having trouble getting their own works published. But for them the motive was not only material. "By devoting themselves to the preservation of the 'classics of world literature,' observes Brian Baer, "literary translation perpetuated the concepts of timeless 'universal values' and 'world culture' that were in opposition to what they saw as the tendentious, politicized, and class-based official culture of the Soviet Union."[52] While I don't disagree with Baer here, I would like to point out that in the 1930s, for example, several translations of Rabelais's *Gargantua and Pantagruel* were published with large print runs, including a translation into Kazakh and an expurgated version for children by the poet Nikolai Zabolotsky.[53] Rabelais's book then became the ostensible subject of Bakhtin's 1940 dissertation (discussed in Chapter 9), which was, inter alia, a celebration of "world literature." The 1930s were a propitious time for Rabelais because of the Soviet alliance with socialist France. In other words, Rabelais, who was generally cited in

Soviet short lists of the greats of "world literature," was at that time official literature.

I am not going to claim that Soviet cultural dominance happened to any decisive degree as a result of the spate of translations published in the 1930s, but this possibility certainly guided the cultural leadership and many intellectuals. The impact of the translated material is hard to ascertain. It is difficult for example to gauge whether, in practice, this material was absorbed largely by the intellectual elite, though several Russians have told me that their grandparents who were not remotely intellectuals left behind a considerable library of European literature in translation. One can only speculate about what it might have been had not the purges and a draconian censorship prevailed. It might seem that the influence of the translated material was minimal, but there are indications that it was stronger than might appear on the surface. Those writers who show evidence of drawing on the translations range from Osip Mandelstam, incorporating in his last major poem before being consigned to the camps where he died ("Unknown Soldier," written in 1937 during his Voronezh exile) elements from Byron's *Childe Harold,* Hegel's *Aesthetics,* and Joyce's *Ulysses,* all recently issued in translation,[54] to the militantly "proletarian" dramatist Aleksandr Afinogenov, whose diary entries after he was thrown out of the Party in 1937 reveal that by then he was triangulating his identity in terms of Thomas Mann's *Magic Mountain* (1924) and Romain Rolland's *Jean Christophe* (1904–1912), two texts with transnational themes that were translated and heavily promoted in the Soviet 1930s; he was also using as models such multiply translated writers as Shakespeare, Goethe, and Heinrich Heine.[55]

Socialist realist literature is highly parochial, yet in this decade it became less so. In 1938–1940, the most nationalist stretch of 1930s culture, Veniamin Kaverin published a Stalin Prize–winning classic of socialist realism, *The Two Captains* (discussed in Chapter 8), a novel not about production but about Russian and Soviet exploration that is situated in the context of the great world explorers and draws on writers like Wordsworth and Dickens for its basic plot; the narrative is enhanced with recurrent references to Western and Russian classical literature. Even some acclaimed novels about industrial production began to acquire this broader purview.[56]

This book will look less at the impact of translated literature, which is hard to ascertain. It is, for example, difficult to gauge whether in practice, as distinct from intention, this material had an impact largely on the intellectual elite. Rather, this book follows the interactions with the West, the movement to establish a transnational cultural space in which Soviet intellectuals, armed with the new cultural capital afforded by the translations, were expected to lead.

Versions of the idea that Moscow would be a "third Rome" had been popular among Russia's immediately prerevolutionary modernists—the neoRomantic and idealist philosophers of her so-called Silver Age—most seeing her as a mediator between what they viewed as the stagnant 'East' and the materialism, rationalism, and liberalism of the 'West.'[57] Other thinkers from central Europe had similar ideas around this time for their countries, articulated for the case of Germany by Settembrini in Thomas Mann's *Magic Mountain.*[58]

Soviet ideologues often picked up the *Sonderweg* rhetoric of the Silver Age but reinflected it to fit into the standard Marxist-Leninist narrative. As Stalin put it in *Problems of Leninism:* "while shaking imperialism, the October revolution has at the same time created . . . a powerful and open *center* of the world revolutionary movement, . . . around which it now can rally and organize a *united revolutionary front of the proletarians and of the oppressed peoples of all countries against capitalism.*"[59] The Comintern (Communist International) was founded in 1919 to further this.

In the 1930s, Bolshevik messianic proclivities in the cultural sphere were echoed by many intellectuals who were taken by a dream of Moscow's cultural and spiritual dominance in the world. This dream could be seen as a sovietized version of the doctrine of Moscow as a "Third Rome" that had been a favorite of prerevolutionary intellectuals. But precisely what might that precedent mean?

Stalinist Moscow as a Rome?

Imperial Rome and the Rome of the "Third Rome" doctrine are not the same, in that the paradigmatic time of imperial Rome, the rule of Augustus (27 BC to 14 AD), was pre-Christian. Although Moscow of the 1930s aspired to become the "Third Rome" as the center of a world belief system (if a post-Christian one), in many other respects it is more comparable with Rome at the height of the classical era than in its later incarnation as center of Christendom. But identification with imperial Rome is also in the Russian tradition. For example, pace Eisenstein, the historical Ivan the Terrible never pronounced "Moscow the Third Rome," but he did claim that his line was related to that of Augustus Caesar, as did subsequent tsars, including Peter the Great and Catherine, who also never invoked the "Third Rome."[60]

Under Augustus, Rome emerged from being a relatively unremarkable capital of a military power to becoming the center of a great culture whose impact continues to be felt today. But Augustus affected this in no small measure by appropriating the culture of the previous great civilization, the Greek, which became a cultural standard.[61] One sees an analogous dynamic in the Soviet 1930s, though the Soviet "Greece" was largely western Europe. In architecture, for example, under Augustus there was an effort "to rebuild Rome in a style comparable to (but of course, more splendid than) the greatest Greek cities of the eastern Mediterranean. . . . To this end they created a city of huge vistas and planned monumental complexes replete with porticoes, theaters, and huge Hellenistic piazzas."[62] A similar pattern can be seen in the Soviet Union with its ambitious building plans. As in ancient Rome, the new Moscow architecture celebrated power but also provided a material encoding of key values of the new order.

In seeking to aggrandize the capital, Soviet architects drew on what were explicitly precedents from ancient Rome and its putative successor in what was considered the Great Tradition, the Renaissance. In the use of Roman precedents, the Soviet Union was far from unique in Europe of the 1930s. Three particularly ambitious European states—Stalin's Russia, Germany, and Mussolini's Italy—were vying with each other as to who deserved to don the mantle of Rome, and they sought precedents in "Rome" for their "new" states. Whether or not these leaders succeeded in recapitulating Rome, and most would agree that they did not, they were attempting to establish a "Rome" in the present, in the sense that in Augustan Rome, a city that had not been particularly remarkable became the world standard. Mussolini sought specifically to recapture in his capital Augustan Rome. He directed that some of the major monuments of antiquity be excavated or restored and that the architectural clutter that had grown around some of them be cleared away to reveal them in their glory. In 1937, the year after Mussolini declared Italy an empire, he commemorated the two thousandth year from the birth of Augustus as an aesthetic justification for his regime.[63] The attempt to recapture the greatness of Rome in city architecture was not confined to so-called totalitarian regimes. There were also earlier precedents, such as most famously in the mid-nineteenth century when Napoleon III, in commissioning Baron Haussman to redesign Paris, sought to realize Augustan Rome on the Seine.

In the Soviet 1930s, however, an explicit Roman precedent really only applied in architecture, where Rome's Vitruvius became a much-cited authority and his works were published in translation. I see parallels with Rome not so much *literally* as in the way the Soviet Union built up its imperial culture not in isolation but by appropriating the Great Tradition of western Europe. This was in effect the meaning of "world literature" as Soviet spokesmen used the term, a world-historical literature that assimilated the great literature of other nations and developed them further in a new Marxist-inflected canon vaunted as their consummation. In addition, in ancient Rome many of the new "universal" histories extolled the conquests and accomplishments of the Roman leaders by using precedents and authors from Greece; hagiographic texts were written by Greek intellectuals with close connections to Roman leaders.[64] Soviet authorities, somewhat analogously, encouraged European intellectuals to declare allegiance to the Soviet Union and tried to recruit European writers to produce their panegyric narratives. Among many examples of this, Henri Barbusse, rather than a Russian, was chosen to write a life of Stalin, which appeared with big print runs (in 1935 he was placed on the podium for the Red Square May Day parade as a reward).[65] And the leading theoretician of socialist realism's place in "world literature" was Georgy Lukács, a Hungarian Jew closely associated with German intellectual life; he also wrote introductions to several of the translated works of European literature and theory.[66]

What we see in such examples is not just a matter of appropriation in the sense of gathering cultural trinkets or big names to adorn the new state and its metropolitan center. Central to the drive for greatness was a determination to preside over culture and create a great culture as both backbone of the system and guarantee of that greatness.

Literature was at the heart of what I see as a seismic shift to an epic mode (see Chapter 9). As with the epic of ancient Rome, there was a "very solid link" between the new "epics," realized largely in novel form, and power.[67] In the novels themselves this link was mandated to be more than "very solid" and actually ineluctable (this is in effect the meaning of socialist realism's base principle of "party-mindedness [partiinost']").

In literature, classical texts from ancient Greece and Rome were rarely invoked, though several appeared in translation, including the *Aeneid* in 1933 and the *Iliad* and *Odyssey* in 1935.[68] It was, rather, modern European authors who were characteristically cited as icons of "world literature," typically Shakespeare, Cervantes, Goethe, Molière, and Rabelais. Yet, despite classical Rome's marginal influence on Stalinist literature, there are parallels in terms of the functions of literature within the political-cum-cultural system and in the characteristic genres and literary strategies used (including censorship).[69] Rome's central text, Virgil's *Aeneid,* and the series of epics it generated provides a good analogy with Stalinist socialist realism, though not in terms of content except in a very general sense. The *Aeneid* is effectively a political appropriation of Homeric epic that draws on its aesthetic power in glorifying Rome and its alleged past. It incorporates a reworking of classical Greek motifs and stories (especially from the *Iliad*) to realign them to a story beginning in ancient Troy and culminating in the foundation of the metropolitan capital and thereby of the dynasty, leading to Augustus and an empire said to have no end in time. In short, the *Aeneid* had become "enshrined as Rome's national epic and as the ideological prop for the one-man rule of the emperor."[70]

The overall plot of the *Aeneid* became standard for subsequent Roman epics. Through constant semireplication of the motifs, characteristic discourse, and plot functions of this text—gestures of fealty on the part of authors—there evolved a single master plot for the classical epic and a standard lexicon.[71] Socialist realism was not grounded in a single exemplary text but several. But, analogously, from these texts a masterplot emerged that combined elements from each of them and rehearsed the twin themes of national unity and the great line of leaders. The Soviet masterplot did not culminate in the founding of the capital per se but, effectively a functional surrogate, in a crucial moment the hero journeyed to the "new Moscow," a higher order or even semimythical space "founded," as it were, by the nonbiological dynasty of Lenin and Stalin.

Another parallel would be the role the *Aeneid* and its literary progeny in played in Roman society in establishing values and norms of conduct for Romans and all mankind. Nikolai Bukharin in his speech to the First Congress of the Writers Union in 1934, in this respect somewhat untypically, pointed to the enormous pedagogical impact of a great epic, which "forms people according to its precepts and canons." In ancient Rome, he added, "they memorized and recited Maron [i.e.; Virgil] in no way because this was some idle pastime." Rather, "society and its social upper echelons [thereby] reproduced themselves ideologically, in an idealized version, and inculcated their ideas, thoughts, conceptions, feelings, characters, aims, ideals, virtues."[72]

There is little evidence that other authority figures in culture thought in terms of the *Aeneid* itself, or of the classical epic, as models for socialist realism, although as scholars point out, "the story of Aeneas, along with Virgil's model of literary nation-building, held deep resonance for Russian Symbolist writers at the turn of the twentieth century" and resurfaced periodically in works by Soviet writers, most notably in Pasternak's *Doctor Zhivago*.[73]

In prerevolutionary Russia, Rome was not the only popular precedent for a great age; classical Greece and the Renaissance were as well. These three precedents were not necessarily mutually exclusive, and each was read in a variety of ways, some contradictory. For example, some prerevolutionary intellectuals saw Rome as a paradigm of empire, or of state might.[74] Others saw it as a republic with a rational legal system, or as the site of militant, dogmatic Catholicism.[75] Some of these ideas also resurfaced in the 1930s, in Mikhail Bulgakov's novel *Master and Margarita*, which was written between 1928 and 1940 and is largely regarded as the best novel of the Soviet era though actually published there first only in 1966–1967 and then in an expurgated version; in the novel a triumvirate of linked cities, Rome, Moscow, and Jerusalem, provides a conceptual frame.

In the Soviet 1930s, the aesthetic ideal underpinning claims to world cultural hegemony, hence also of the nation as a whole, shifted over time. At different times some of the cultural trends were more pronounced than others. This book opens in 1930–1931, the culminating moment of the "cultural revolution" that mandated "proletarianization" both within Soviet cultural life and in the international movement. Starting around 1931–1932, however, the Soviet Union moved progressively out of its iconoclastic phase of "class warfare," a development rationalized at the Seventeenth Party Congress in 1934, which proclaimed the "victory" of socialism in the country. And in the Comintern (though this was controversial), in the interests of fostering a strong antifascist movement, the rabidly antibourgeois stance was dropped at its Seventh Congress in 1935.

This book charts the evolution of Soviet culture beyond its "proletarian" phase, looking at the way a Janus-faced Moscow functioned as emblem of a highly centralized state and simultaneously as a center for a transnational intellectual milieu. In the cultural ecosystem of the Stalinist thirties, different trends coexisted at one time (as Schlögel has argued), but some were more pronounced than others. The book will argue that in the first half of the decade Soviet culture and its interactions with abroad were informed by what was claimed to be an appropriation of Enlightenment values, epitomized in the rebuilding of Moscow itself as a city of "light," a beacon to guide Europe out of the capitalist and fascist darkness. The second half of the 1930s, however, starting in approximately late 1935 and going through the Great Purge, the show trials, and up to the Nazi invasion in June 1941, was, as the last four chapters argue, closer to the neo-Romantic in its cultural orientation. At this time the dominant aesthetic went from an emphasis on beauty to one on the sublime, or more specifically to an imperial sublime (see Chapter 8).

To what extent, then, does Stalinist culture of the 1930s have to do specifically or explicitly with what happened in ancient Rome, and to what extent are the examples I am adducing here just analogies? Using the Roman analogy might seem to be conferring greater stature on the Stalinist regime of the 1930s than it deserved, or thrusting Stalinist culture into an arbitrary Procrustean bed, even though Soviet spokesmen periodically used the analogy themselves. Actually, after fascist Italy declared itself the "Third Rome," and especially after its national

"Augustan" spectacular of 1937, the Roman precedent for the "new Moscow" became less viable and was openly attacked.[76] Alternative lines of succession were charted, often beginning in ancient Greece. The cultural platform also appropriated other grandiose precedents, such as the French philosophes. Thus one should not overdo the analogy, but it is useful heuristically.

Soviet intellectuals wanted to lead the world, yet they also wanted to—had to—learn from it. As Michael David-Fox has shown, in the 1930s even the bureaucrats who headed Soviet cultural organizations charged with furthering its cultural influence abroad felt ambivalent about whether their cultural level was in fact superior to that of western Europe.[77] And they admitted to each other in private that Nazi Germany had some good writers, despite *Pravda*'s claims to the contrary.[78] But ancient Rome was also anxious about whether it was adequate to the Greek analogy.[79] In addition, as was true of the Soviet Union in relation to western Europe, Rome resisted adopting Greek culture in its entirety, especially since it had a different belief system.

Scholars of empire have noted in the formation of many empires a "combination of a universalistic imperial tradition with a monotheistic world religion." Examples include the Roman Empire after conversion to Christianity, the Byzantine Empire, the Islamic caliphate, the Ottoman Empire, and the Spanish and Portuguese empires.[80] Michael Doyle in *Empires* concludes that "colonization, in effect, was an entrepreneurial venture of Christendom" and religious justifications were generally used to vindicate imperial conquests.[81] But each colonizing power had a definite sense of what that religion should be. As Stephen Howe remarks, "new worlds" were won not just in the name of "Christendom" but specifically for the conqueror's particular version of it (Protestantism, Catholicism), "denying opportunities for conquest and conversion to the heretics."[82] A purity akin to the religious was also central to Russia's "Third Rome" doctrine from the very beginning, in that Filofei's pronouncement was effectively anti-Catholic. Analogously, in the 1930s among Stalinist Bolsheviks there was an obsession with schismatics within both the Communist International and the national communist movement, especially those perceived as "Trotskyites" (even France's leading communist writer, Barbusse, was not immune from censure for publishing them).[83]

Moscow under Stalin never attained the stature of a Rome, nor did it function as *the* cultural mecca for the rest of Europe. European intellectuals were still more in the thrall of Paris. But around 1935 Soviet cultural leadership was a distinct possibility throughout the transatlantic intellectual world, even for Paris-based intellectuals, a reality often ignored in cultural histories. Beckett was, for example, in correspondence with Eisenstein and eager to come from Paris, as André Malraux and André Gide did (in 1934 and 1936). And in 1935 the big names in trans-Atlantic theater (such as Brecht and Gordon Craig) made a pilgrimage to the Soviet Union, and Lee Strasberg was proselytizing for the Stanislavskian "method," which came to dominate American stage and screen acting. This attraction of the Soviet capital was enhanced by the Great Depression in the West and the rise of fascism—for the cause of Soviet cultural and ideological hegemony, total gifts. Many intellectuals, both Soviet and Western, now looked to "Moscow" as the only world power seriously committed to combating fascism (an illusion, as it transpired) and as the only power with a comprehensive counter-ideology. "Moscow" was, in turn, eager to assume that role.[84] Much of its allure, however, was lost with the purges, the show trials, and the Molotov-Ribbentrop Pact of 1939.

The culture of this time of the Great Appropriation marks a change from that of the 1920s. In my earlier book on postrevolutionary Petersburg, *Petersburg: Crucible of Cultural Revolution,* I identify the purification of space as a dominant in the symbolic system of the more iconoclastic Soviet 1920s, but in this decade the key pattern was the *enhancement* of space and the hierarchization of both space and time in a chronotope. Moscow, the metropolis, was a higher order place, one that purportedly continued the great line from Athens, Rome, and Florence. The provinces, those large swathes of profane Soviet territory, were deemed backward and at best in the process of becoming; "heroes" were to transcend, or rapidly traverse, nonsacral space, paradigmatically in flight, an obsession of Stalinist rhetoric. But flight was simultaneously a form of overcoming time. The temporal was fused with the spatial in this hierarchy. The "new Moscow" was often represented as, like Rome, essentially timeless. It was that ideal place where the contingent and the ephemeral have been transcended, an essentially aesthetic project.

As beauty incarnate, the "new Moscow" was also utopian. The title of this book hints at this. Filofei, we will recall, said there will never be a fourth. By this he had in mind an apocalyptic outcome if Moscow's religious responsibilities—that is, its commitment to Russian Orthodoxy—were not adhered to. In calling Moscow a *fourth* Rome, I am raising the possibility that the Soviet desire to make the capital a world center was unrealizable. Indeed, in actuality the ideal of Moscow as a post-Christian world center eluded those who would achieve it. Like a utopia, it was never to be. As Sheila Fitzpatrick has shown, there were loopholes, fixers, and masqueraders that undermined the perfect form of the state (and enabled it to actually function).[85] Schlögel points out that what seemed to be a utopian plan had in actuality more to do with improvisation, response to circumstances, and maneuvering.[86] As in any performance, there was always the possibility of slippage between text and interpretation, between the text and the way it is staged.[87]

Nevertheless, Moscow of the 1930s had several utopia-like features. One of them was the elevation of intellectuals to an elite existence, a position classically elaborated in the philosopher kings of Plato's *Republic*. Thanks to the new importance of culture intellectuals enjoyed an enhanced status, both materially and in power and prestige. They were, as Ivan Szelenyi said of their postwar eastern European counterparts, "intellectuals on the road to class power" (in his classic book of that title). But the intellectuals still had to negotiate a relationship with the actual "kings," heads of the "republic," Stalin, the Politburo, and the various bureaucracies such as the Central Committee's Agitprop, who passed down directives.

Stalinist intellectuals were the adepts and encoders. They were expected to divine the essence of both Marxist-Leninist ideology and the current Party platform and present it in coherent, if often allegorical form. They provided the country with idealized images of itself, often projections of the future; they, and the architects' designs for the "new Moscow" in particular, provided a model for the rest of the country. Theirs was the *Kunststadt*. The actuality of the world of politics and of the everyday was messier.

Intellectuals had their own agendas, the agendas of their caste, that often overlapped with official stipulations but did not necessarily coincide.

A case in point would be the classical direction within architecture, which had long had a powerful lobby within the field. But they were also divided among themselves.

Though the Soviet Union sought to create a national aesthetic, there were bitter debates as to what it constituted and what was its provenance. In this Soviet intellectuals were not unique. In France during this decade they argued over which tradition is truly French, the Gothic or the classical.[88] And in Hitler's Germany the Nazis never sorted out whether national socialist art approximated the ancient Greek, whose sole heir Hitler believed the German people to be,[89] or whether it was "Roman," or vernacular, which generally meant "Teutonic" or "Gothic."[90]

One senses limits to any assumption of complete *Gleichschaltung* in Stalinist culture in, for example, the fact that Russian nationalist narratives were especially evident in the Party's organ, *Pravda,* but less so in the cultural press (or even in *Izvestia*), where there was always material about western European and American achievements. In the second half of the decade, intellectuals used casuistry in continuing to plug Western models, despite the officially sponsored turn to greater nationalism (see Chapter 9).

Such disparities and gestures are indicators of a *degree* of independence on the part of intellectuals, but not necessarily of dissidence. Soviet intellectuals were not extrasystemic figures but were more implicated in the system (if to varying degrees), products of their time, than has generally been recognized. After all, and as Carl Jacob Burchardt points out, even during the Renaissance there was "a natural alliance between scholars and despots" that was a factor in the cultural flowering.[91] In the Soviet case, the fact that there was, ultimately, a single source of patronage led to intense debate as the different factions and lobbies competed for the considerable spoils. Archival sources on the intellectuals' stance vis-à-vis Soviet power that have become available recently reveal grumbling and unhappiness, hurt at being bypassed for awards, and sometimes malicious delight at the purging of a rival.[92]

Stalin was seen by many intellectuals as holding out the promise of a great culture, a culture adequate to the new society. This proved heady stuff for them. Though there was a "general line" established by the Party, there were serious intellectual debates and different positions to be found at all levels of the cultural hierarchy. Some insisted that in the modern day any great culture could only be provided by the avant-garde. Others hoped to inscribe Soviet culture into a line coming from the great culture of the past, whether a European or a purely Russian one. Not all the contributions to the various debates, inevitably, made it into print, the response of Bakhtin to Lukács being one of the most important examples of the silent participant.

Many Soviet intellectuals had been influenced by such German thinkers as Schiller, who saw the aesthetic as that which binds the individual to the state in freedom. But, again like Schiller, they also had faith in the eternal nature of true art; as Bulgakov put it in his Moscow novel *Master and Margarita,* "manuscripts don't burn." Schiller was against politicized art or overly didactic art; insofar as one can gauge such things, one can presume that a sizeable number of writers in Stalin's time felt the same, but not necessarily the majority.

The intellectuals were in an ambiguous position. Were they the bearers of the homogenized imperial message, or were they a caste with its own values and interests? Many intellectuals wanted this or that modification to socialist realism. Though far from dissident, they chafed at its epical quality and that it had been mandated de facto. This book will discuss several lobbies for loosening socialist realism's straitjacket, including the campaign for the "lyric" waged in the late 1930s (see Chapter 9). One distinctive orientation among the intellectuals, highlighted in this book, is that of those who pushed for a more cosmopolitan culture while still committed to the Soviet state, who I am calling the cosmopolitan patriots.[93]

The Cosmopolitan Patriots

This might seem a contradiction in terms, virtually an oxymoron, but "cosmopolitanism" is actually an overly vague term. Cosmopolitans are in reality not free-floating individuals who "cosmically" have an appreciation for or familiarity with each and every place or culture system. There are always limits to their conceptual horizon, always a selection (of places, people, texts) in what they will entertain. In consequence, there are in effect multiple cosmopolitanisms, multiple versions of the cosmopolitan world, often coexisting or competing in one place or even individual. Each one, rather than "free-floating," can be identified in terms of points of orientation (such as centers of sophistication), routes of exchange, or dominant languages or value system.

That anything in the Soviet 1930s could be called a "cosmopolitanism" might seem a stretch. But as this book hopes to show, one might justifiably talk in terms of a "cosmopolitanism" of a distinctive variety. A sizeable portion of the intelligentsia were enticed by the possibility of a transnational cultural space, an intellectual fraternity or a transnational confederation of leftists that I see as comparable with the "Republic of Letters" promoted during the Enlightenment by figures like Voltaire (see Chapter 8). Unlike the republic of letters, however, this confederation would not be independent of nations or borders. Earlier versions of that republic identified with Latin culture or with Paris and things French, but this new confederation was expected to identify with Moscow. But for them, as for many of their counterparts in other countries, an axiomatic value was "Europe."

The possibility of some transnational confederation hovered over European leftist and avant-gardist intellectuals throughout the 1920s (consider the Bauhaus). The situation changed in the early 1930s, when the avant-garde had less cachet, a change that shifted again after the Nazis came to power in 1933 and so many central Europeans became nomadic exiles. In exile, they had their own routes of circulation and their own mechanisms for exchange of ideas that were transgeographic and in that sense comparable with what Paul Gilroy has called the Black Atlantic, or Joseph Roach's concept of the circum-Atlantic.[94] Such spaces have to do with "the circulation of people, objects, and ideas; and to the new cultural and imaginary territories that these mobilizations effect," territories that go beyond national borders.[95]

The cultural turn of the 1930s under Stalin, ostensible patron of *this* "circum-Atlantic," was potentially transnational. Eisenstein and many of his fellow intellectuals in Moscow saw themselves as part of a pan-European intellectual space that included figures to be discussed here, such as Georgy Lukács, John Heartfield, Brecht, Walter Benjamin, Leon Feuchtwanger, Arthur Koestler, Heinrich and Thomas Mann, Ernest Hemingway, André Gide, Louis Aragon, and André Malraux. In

Eisenstein's case, "circum-Europe" extended to James Joyce and modern psychological theory. Clearly, most of these western European figures were left inclining but were not Party members. There were limits to their capacity to identify with "Moscow."

How could Soviet intellectuals interact with such Western counterparts at a time (the 1930s) when the Soviet Union became a closed society? One answer might be that though utopias are always closed communities, cut off in some way, there are always designated intermediaries who are allowed out as emissaries to negotiate with the apostate world, in this case the Stanleys and Livingstones, as it were, forging ahead in the jungles of capitalist culture.[96] Utopias are dedicated to the education of their citizens, but in the Soviet Union with its ambitions to become what I am calling the "fourth Rome," the proselytizing function beyond the borders was also important.

In this book I will be focusing on four such intermediaries. The book is not specifically about them, but as they recur in the narrative the reader will get a sense of the dynamic of Soviet cultural evolution and its European context. The intermediaries I have chosen are Sergei Eisenstein (1898–1948), the film and theater director and theorist; Ilya Erenburg (1891–1967), the poet, novelist, and journalist; Mikhail Koltsov (pseudonym of Mikhail [Moshe] Efimovich [Khaimovich] Fridliand, 1898–1940), a prominent theoretician, journalist, and publisher;[97] and Sergei Tretiakov (1892–1937), a writer of literature and journalism, photographer, and filmmaker. All four were cultural functionaries who dealt with the West, agents of Soviet power intent on converting their Western counterparts, but not one of them conforms with the image such designations might conjure up. All four were also larger-than-life characters and adventurers, Koltsov, the only Party member among them, most so. They had extensive contacts and personal connections of their own with major names among Western intellectuals, particularly of France and Germany.

The career pattern of these intermediaries generally followed one that was common for the feisty new generation that came into prominence within Soviet culture after the Bolshevik revolution. They were beneficiaries of the marginalization, silencing, or emigration of many of the old big names, and of the opportunities now offered individuals from the ethnic minorities, such as Poles or Georgians, but most particularly Jews. All four of these intermediaries came from the periphery (Riga, Bialystok, Kiev), a pattern of the 1920s, when a new generation that came into prominence with the revolution converged on Moscow from the provinces. Three of them received tertiary education in the capitals. This pattern does not apply to the older Erenburg, whose family moved from Kiev to Moscow when he was five and who attended school there, though he did not complete secondary education because in 1908 he fled to Paris to avoid trial for revolutionary agitation. There he became a minor poet; it was only after the revolution that his career took off, however, and he became a famous writer, now of prose. But Erenburg was, like Koltsov and Eisenstein, Jewish (though Eisenstein's mother was Christian and he was baptized).

My intermediaries commanded German, which many Jews learned in their childhood in anticipation of possibly having to study in Germany or Austria because most were banned from Russian universities. German became the most important second language of the first two decades of Soviet rule (1917–1941). It was the language of the Comintern, whose foreign headquarters were in Berlin. During the 1920s German had also been important, because after the Treaty of Rapallo (1922), the first to regularize relations between the Soviet Union and a major foreign power (Germany), the Soviet Union's closest foreign contacts were with German intellectuals. Then, after the Nazis took power in 1933 German remained a critical language because the antifascist cause, which all four of my intermediaries served, was adopted by the Soviet Union. Riga was a former Hanseatic port, and both Eisenstein and Tretiakov, who grew up there, had had German spoken at home. Eisenstein himself kept his intimate diary in German, the language in which he also wrote two crucial essays—"Nachahmung als Beherrschung" and "Dramaturgie der Film Form."[98] He also had both English and French governesses as a child.[99] His writings in his archive are distinctly macaronic, switching back and forth in four languages. In Tretiakov's case, his mother was a Baltic German, but his command was not native. Koltsov spoke German, French, and Spanish, all a bit imperfectly; he did not know English. Thus all four came from a polyglot world and were attuned to a greater world (Byalystok was actually the home town of Zamenhof, who invented Esperanto).

Three out of four of these intermediaries worked for newspapers. Koltsov, a prolific writer, was a leading and immensely popular journalist and member of the board of *Pravda,* the organ of the Communist Party.[100] Erenburg, though residing in Paris, was in the 1930s an established contributor to the second main Soviet newspaper, *Izvestia,* where from 1934 his school friend Bukharin served as editor. Tretiakov, also active in journalism, had in the late 1920s developed an entire theory of the way forward for culture by abandoning the old fictional forms and foregrounding the journalistic (see Chapter 1). Eisenstein contributed the odd article to newspapers, but his main work was in film, likewise a central medium of Soviet agitation; most of the films Eisenstein completed were directly commissioned by the state. Actually, Koltsov was also at an early stage in his career a pioneer in the fledgling Soviet film industry, becoming director of documentary films in the Film Committee of Narkompros in 1918, a position that enabled him to give a start in film to Dziga Vertov, an old school friend from Bialystok.

The cosmopolitan orientation of my four was not a free-floating one but was grounded in a Soviet patriotism. Three of them were active proselytizers for the cult of Moscow, as was evident from early in their Soviet careers. Koltsov made great strides as a journalist when in 1921 an article by him, "Old Mother Moscow" (Moskva-Matushka), extolling a transformed capital was published in *Pravda.* It caught the attention of Lenin's sister Maria Il'ichna, and Koltsov was propelled from stringer to staff journalist. Eisenstein also planned a film, *Moscow,* mentioned at the beginning of this introduction, celebrating Moscow and its grand progress through history.[101] As for Tretiakov, two of his plays of the 1920s, *Are You Listening, Moscow?* (Slyshish', Moskva?, 1923) and *Roar, China!* (Rychi, Kitai!, 1926), culminate in oppressed foreigners looking to Moscow for salvation. And in 1937 when Feuchtwanger arrived in Moscow, Tretiakov, in a public speech of welcome of January 5, 1937, declared: "only when our native land will become the entire world will I shake every cosmopolitan by the hand and say: yes, indeed you are now truly a citizen of the world."[102]

Erenburg, less overtly in the thrall of Moscow, was the most cosmopolitan and transnational of my four intellectual figures. A habitué of the bohemian café Rotonde in Paris, where he hobnobbed with the likes of Picasso, he was also associated with the leading French literary journal of

the time, *Nouvelle revue française.* Erenburg was at the same time patriotic, as is attested by the fact that he kept his Soviet passport while based
in Paris. His work in the 1920s matched his own habits: over the course of
the decade he penned a series of picaresque novels (his first, *The Extraordinary Adventures of Julio Jurenito . . .* of 1922 is the most infamous) and
led a distinctly picaresque life himself and was forever on the move, going
from European country to European country, sometimes because as a
radical he was expelled from one of them, sometimes traveling for professional or personal reasons. During all this frenetic movement he not
only proselytized for Soviet culture but also—as did my other three
intermediaries—introduced recent trends in European culture (primarily
the French) to Soviet intellectuals and audiences. In 1922 he lived in Berlin briefly and, together with El Lissitzky, produced *Veshch'/Gegenstand/
Objet,* an ostensibly trilingual journal, which published the Soviet avant-
garde but also reproduced a lot of material from Le Corbusier's mouthpiece journal in Paris, *L'Esprit nouveau.* In the 1930s Erenburg partially
abandoned his stance as a roué, published an attack on the Surrealists,
and even began writing production novels, albeit novels with an internationalist twist.[103]

Koltsov was most the roguish picaro yet also most the Soviet organization man. He joined the Party in 1918, the only one among this four to be
a member during the Soviet period. Earlier (1915–1918), he had studied in
Petrograd at the Psycho-Neurological Institute (as did Vertov), an intellectually broad-ranging hotbed of radicalism with many Jewish students
(it was also one of the few tertiary institutions that permitted female students).[104] March 1921 saw him working as a correspondent of *Krasnaia
gazeta* in Kronstadt, where he produced the newspaper *Krasnyi Kronstadt*
in support of the Bolsheviks, who were crushing a leftist revolt there.[105]
Thereafter he became prominent in *Pravda,* where his frequent feuilletons,
many of them attacks on western Europe or the Russian émigré press,
invariably appeared on page 1. He was extremely prolific, and selections of his journalistic writings were published in three volumes in
1928, and 1933–1934, and in six volumes in 1935–1936. Of the four, he
is also the least known in the West, although he appears as Karkov in
Hemingway's 1940 novel on the Spanish Civil War, *For Whom the Bell
Tolls* (see Chapter 7).

Koltsov was later purged, and many post-Stalin representations of him are somewhat idealized, erecting him into a dashing hero and, virtually, free spirit while ignoring, for example, articles he published endorsing the death penalty for prominent purge victims. Those who write about him seem constrained to insist that he was always traveling and seemingly "everywhere at once," a journalist who could never sit down, not even in his spacious suite of offices in *Pravda*.[106] He was one of the first Soviet writers to go abroad and roved all over Europe, visiting every capital, partly as a correspondent, partly as a representative of Commissariat of Foreign Affairs; for instance, he visited Germany ten times between 1924 and 1932. Though he was a prominent functionary, allegedly with free access to Stalin's study, accounts often present his activities as an exotic adventure tale. A man of great bravado (some of his visits to Germany were illegal), Koltsov loved risky situations.[107] He had established his bona fides in the 1920s by participating in several long-distance flights abroad that captured the popular imagination. As if in response to one of his feuilletons, "I Want to Fly" (Khochu letat') of 1929, in September 1930 he joined the crew of an epic flight of three tiny two-seaters from Moscow to Ankara, then Teheran, and finally Kabul via the Hindu Kush.[108]

Over the course of the 1920s Koltsov also became increasingly prominent as an editor of journals. In 1923 he founded the popular illustrated magazine *Ogonëk*, as well as the satirical journal *Chudak* (for which Ilya Ilf and Evgeny Petrov, Mikhail Zoshchenko, Yury Olesha, and Valentin Kataev wrote extensively); *Chudak* later melded with *Krokodil*. In the early years *Ogonëk* was a particularly cosmopolitan journal. Its editorial statement for the issue marking its first anniversary declares that it is committed to, "parallel" with coverage of the Soviet Union, "depicting the feverish tempo of the complex and interesting life of the West."[109] For this first year or so it did precisely that, giving prominent billing to technological achievements of the West, its cultural life, and its cities with their skyscrapers and neon lights; also, among the major writers who were regular contributors was Osip Mandelshtam. After Lenin died in January 1924, the journal became progressively less cosmopolitan and many of the best writers in its stable disappeared from its pages, but it was still cosmopolitan by comparison with its competitors and arguably its initial profile was indicative of Koltsov's own orientation.

In 1931 Koltsov's power in the world of Soviet letters increased exponentially when he became the head of a vast new publishing empire called Zhurgaz (Zhurnal'no-gazetnoe ob"edinenie), where he oversaw the publication of many books, periodicals, and serials (several of them, such as *The Lives of Remarkable People,* officially initiatives of Gorky).[110] A Maecenas extraordinaire in consequence, it was Koltsov who contrived to get a great deal of the translated material commissioned and published.

Eisenstein traveled, too, especially over Europe in 1926 and 1929, but also to America and Mexico. After he returned to the Soviet Union from the latter extended trip in 1932, he did not get to travel again. However, he of all the four was the most "traveled" in his intellectual pursuits. Anne Nesbet justly remarks that "the astounding heterogeneity of the materials held in Eisenstein's enormous archive serves as a constant reminder that Eisenstein's approach to art and thought was aggressively and unrepentantly omnivorous."[111] A high point for Eisenstein was his time in Christopher Isherwood's swinging Berlin of 1929 and Mexico in 1931, two meccas in these years for leftist cosmopolitans.[112] But he was also a paradoxical figure: this very heterogeneity was partly mustered in the service of his ongoing obsession, to adduce a single system from the many. A similar paradox (discussed earlier) would be that Eisenstein, who seemed consummately cosmopolitan, also produced a series of films that could be taken as distinctly antiforeign, especially *Alexander Nevsky* and *Ivan the Terrible.*

Tretiakov was born in 1892 in the Baltic town of Kul'diga into the family of a teacher, and like Eisenstein spent his childhood in Riga. He studied law at Moscow University and graduated with a first but never practiced. The Revolution found him in the Soviet Far East, where in Vladivostok he became part of a group of young avant-garde writers, called Tvorchestvo (creativity), who identified with the poet Vladimir Mayakovsky. Once Vladivostok had been taken over by Interventionists, Tretiakov escaped via China, ending up in Siberia's Chita, where the group re-formed. In 1922 he relocated to Moscow, where he began to teach in Meyerhold's theater studio. It was there that he met Eisenstein, then a student, and they did a series of collaborative projects, first in theater and then in film (Tretiakov worked on *The Battleship Potemkin,* for example). In 1924–1925 Tretiakov went to China to teach Russian literature at Peking University. Afterward he had plans to return there with Eisenstein and wrote several scripts for films they would make together, but it did not pan out, and the two embarked on separate projects.

Though Tretiakov and Eisenstein remained friends, one should not assume that these four constituted a camaraderie. In fact, though Koltsov and Erenburg collaborated in the 1930s in organizing antifascist activities in France and Spain on behalf of the Soviet government, there were recurrent tensions between them and marked differences of opinion (with Koltsov, the more authoritative, generally prevailing).[113]

I am not going to go into who sent my characters to Europe, or how they got their visas at a time when so few could travel, but clearly to some degree these figures, for all their color, were organization men, working for specific Soviet bodies. The Party, and the Soviet state generally, had its own agenda, as compared to western European intellectuals— co-optation, whether via conversion to Party membership or, more generally, by declaring some kind of allegiance to, or admiration for, the Soviet Union, and participating in activities sponsored by one or other of its international cultural arms. These bodies included organizations that came under the aegis of the Comintern, such as its various literary and theatrical bodies, which included MORP (in English, the International Union of Revolutionary Writers or IURW),[114] MORT (in English, the International Union of the Revolutionary Theatre, or IURT). Another was Mezhrabpom (International Worker Aid), a body that was originally set up in 1921 on the initiative of the Comintern to assist in famine relief[115] but came to fund, under the Berlin-based Willi Münzenberg, a number of cultural activities, notably the film company Mezhrabpomfilm, which produced some of the best Soviet films from the 1920s and early 1930s. After 1935, MORP was abolished and replaced by the Association for the Defense of Culture, centered in Paris. The international literary front was now run on the Soviet side by the Foreign Commission of the Writers Union, headed by Koltsov with Tretiakov as his deputy.

The Soviet state, as distinct from the Party, had its own body to oversee cultural interaction with the West, the All-Union Society for Cultural Relations with Abroad (VOKS), founded in 1925. It was, until its then director Aleksandr Arosev was purged in 1937, the main body organizing Soviet cultural contacts with the West: book exchanges, tours by musicians or theatrical performers, visits by scholars and professionals, art exhibitions, and visits by individuals and groups.[116] In many of these activities VOKS played a relatively neutral role (such as answering queries by foreign geologists about Soviet scholarship), but it was primarily a propaganda arm of Soviet power working in close contact with the Party hierarchy, Comintern, Commissariat Ministry of Foreign Affairs and secret police. In addition, under its aegis went the various branches of the Society of Friends of the New Russia (Obshchestvo druzei novoi Rossii), organized by country and set up in different cities around Europe, the first of which was founded in Berlin in June 1923.[117] These societies were intended to attract as members industrialists, professional people, and scholars (another body, confusingly of the same name, was for the workers); the Berlin branch could boast Einstein, Thomas Mann, and several other celebrities as foundation members.[118] In the mid-1920s, VOKS was even negotiating for links with the Institute for Social Research (i.e., the Frankfurt School of neo-Marxist critical theory).[119] But all these organizations were interrelated. For example, both the Comintern and VOKS oversaw the Societies of Friends of the New Russia, and the Commissariat for Foreign Affairs (NKID) played a supervisory role as well.[120]

As is clear from this description, the societies primarily dealt with the bourgeoisie (or at any rate the educated classes) rather than with the proletariat. Their supervising body, VOKS, periodically agonized over this orientation, asking themselves what was their mission and were they neglecting the masses, the alleged agents of future communist revolution.[121]

All four of my intermediaries enjoyed prominent careers of their own in Soviet culture, and were activists for the Soviet state in the international arena. The question as to what their intentions or self-images were must remain elusive, but insofar as such things are possible to gauge, they saw the two activities as complementary. In this, and in so many respects, they defy the usual generalizations. They were extraordinarily peripatetic in an age of greater constriction. Though in the 1920s they were to some degree allied with the avant-garde, in the 1930s they represented a state where avant-garde experimentalism was increasingly squeezed out in favor of more conventional cultural forms. These four were simultaneously actors in a transnational leftist coterie of cosmopolitans and agents of the Soviet line, of "Moscow." They were what Western historiography has often labeled "minders" and "manipulators," Soviet figures who accompanied renowned Western intellectuals during their stays in the Soviet Union. Recent Russian assessments of Koltsov range from "the most talented and most naïve eccentric in the Soviet Union" to "an experienced and cynical propagandist" and "Stalin's authorized representative"; in Western sources he is often assumed to have been a spy.[122] What is certain is that he was one of the most influential advocates of the Stalinist 1930s for a united front against fascism. In addition, clearly both he and the other three discussed here were more complex than the labels usually given them might suggest. Far from grey Stalinist bureaucrats, they were among the most colorful figures of their era.

Were they exceptions to the rule for intellectuals of Stalin's time? Did they benefit from loopholes (opportunities for the limited few to travel) that were necessary to keep the system going? Much of what they did could be written off as "manipulation," but probably they did not see it as just that. Though as lovers of modernism and even the avant-garde they were on the losing side in debates over cultural policy, they were deeply committed to the antifascist cause, dreamed of Moscow cultural hegemony, and continued to battle for a cosmopolitan version of it.

I will not pretend to be able to second-guess how these intermediaries conceived their administrative roles, but we can detect an element of self-fashioning in them as intellectuals who opted for the Soviet cause. In photos of Tretiakov from the 1920s and 1930s, for example, he appears with a shaven head (like his avant-garde friend Mayakovsky); his face gaunt, its features angular, he seems the very incarnation of fanatical revolutionary zeal. Cultural bureaucrats marveled in private at the way he kept doggedly hosting foreign intellectuals despite his meager domestic circumstances: a true believer.[123] In Koltsov's case the element of self-fashioning was more radical. In pursuit of his journalistic ends he adopted all manner of roles and disguises. For example, he went to Hungary with a false passport and reported on the fascist regime there "What Could Be" (Chto moglo byt', 1927). Then he penetrated a counterrevolutionary camp to write a sketch, "Petliurovshchina" (1927), and was able to disguise his identity sufficiently to gain access to a communist political prisoner in Germany's Sonnenberg prison. He also developed the habit of changing his profession temporarily to report on what others did, at one point, for example, working as a taxi driver.[124]

Putting on a mask, translating a self into a role, was an ineluctable gesture for an intellectual allying himself or herself with "the proletariat." This act of self-translation was fraught. Were the "translators" to link up with their intellectual counterparts in the West, to immerse themselves in current Western highbrow culture (if largely leftist or antifascist in orientation) and then purvey it to their people? Or were they to shine as emissaries and functionaries of a "fourth Rome"? In the next chapter we will see how these competing identities played out in the interactions between Tretiakov, Brecht, Benjamin, and others in pre-Nazi Berlin.

CHAPTER 1

The Author as Producer:
Cultural Revolution in Berlin
and Moscow (1930–1931)

W ALTER BENJAMIN VISITED Moscow from December 6, 1926, until February 1, 1927. Western criticism lionizes Benjamin and has tended to savor his every pronouncement on this trip as if he had been undertaking the heroic voyage of a questing intellectual. From another perspective, however, it was an unheroic, private trip by a Benjamin who went there in a futile attempt to resolve in his favor the love triangle involving himself, the Latvian theater director Asja Lacis, and Bernhard Reich, theater critic, friend, and rival. From yet another, his visit represents a marginal example of what was fast becoming a common event, the visit to the Soviet Union by the curious or left-inclining Western intellectual sponsored by VOKS (he was listed with them as preparing a scholarly work on Soviet art and theater).[1] The visit of Benjamin can, then, be seen as a minor moment in the proselytizing campaign of Soviet power whereby VOKS attempts to recruit Benjamin for the Soviet cause by providing him with subsidized accommodation and assorted privileges, the sorts of practices dismissed in standard Western accounts of cultural exchange in terms of the "manipulation" of an unsuspecting intellectual by a regime bent on expanding its power.

Benjamin's trip to Moscow was potentially, however, not an inept attempt at reclaiming Asja Lacis whereby he was the unwitting stooge of

"Moscow" but a quest for a new identity. He was, as it were, going from Berlin to the "fourth Rome." This route should have been, to use the title of a book he had just written and was reading to Asja Lacis throughout his stay, along an *Einbahnstrasse* (one-way street). Intellectuals visiting the Soviet Union (at that time generally by train) were encouraged to make declarations about their exhilaration on crossing the Soviet border.

But in Benjamin's diary we find a somewhat disgruntled record of his impressions (cleaned up when he drew on it in writing the essay "Moscow" for publication). He emerges as far from the grand flaneur, bumbling and inept. Knowing no Russian hampers his ability to "read" the city, and much of what he has to say comes from reported conversations with people who know both Russian and German (primarily Reich). When he tries to negotiate the streets himself, he keeps making wrong turns, missing trams—superficial misreadings that undermine the validity of his observations. Discouraged, he returns again and again to the familiar haunts of his hotel and a particular dining room, both privileged places to which VOKS gave him access, or he goes to the theater with VOKS-supplied tickets and translator.

Perhaps the most insightful sections of Benjamin's diary are those where he discusses how power functions in a noncapitalist society where money cannot play a decisive role. He senses an entire "civilization" of meetings and intrigues in which he cannot participate because unless he commits himself to joining the Communist Party he remains an outsider, as it were a colonial in the metropole.[2] He is marginalized not just by not knowing the language but also by a lack of commitment and agonizes over whether he should make that leap so that he could participate, but instead leaves Moscow with neither his love life nor his political direction resolved.

By 1934, when he wrote "The Author as Producer," Benjamin had seemingly resolved the question of direction and made that leap. Here he proclaims a turning point in cultural development and advocates that intellectuals retool for the new era by joining with the proletarians. Perhaps this forthrightness had something to do with his sense of his patron, in that the essay was to be delivered at the Paris Institute for the Study of Fascism (INFA), commonly assumed to have been a Communist front organization.[3] But though "Author as Producer" was ostensibly written after the Nazi takeover in Germany of 1933, its main ideas come from around 1931.

In a largely overlooked line from his later essay "Paris Capital of the Nineteenth Century" (1935) Benjamin asserts: "the *Communist Manifesto* brings [the flaneur's] existence to an end." In the same paragraph he associates the flaneur with "the intelligentsia," adding that he "sets foot in the marketplace—ostensibly to look around, but in truth to find a buyer."[4] But in "The Author as Producer" Benjamin outlines a radically different program for intellectuals, one that could be seen as elaboration of his observation in the Moscow diary that intellectual life in the new "civilization" of a postcapitalist society is totally transformed.

Many of Benjamin's most radical proposals in this essay are typical of Soviet cultural policies during the period of the First Five-Year Plan. The Plan, which extended from 1928 to 1932, was to centralize the Soviet economy for the first time, radically stepping up industrial development and collectivization. These shifts in the economic and political organization of the country were to be accompanied by a "cultural revolution" intended to propel the populace to a truly socialist consciousness and way of life. So radical was to be the break that Stalin had pronounced the year 1929 a *bol'shoi perelom,* a term generally translated as the "great breakthrough"; but since *perelom* is also used for bone fractures, it also suggests a total break in time.

The cultural revolution sought to propel the country, and by its example the greater world, to a postbourgeois culture system. A common slogan was "proletarianization," and under it militants pressed for a monopoly for "proletarian" culture and "proletarian" culture makers, though the meaning of the term "proletarian" was ambiguous; some used it to mean those who were working-class or proletarian, others to mean "of the Party" (the vanguard of the proletariat). This new emphasis spread to cultural bodies abroad that were oriented toward Moscow. At a major international writers conference held in Kharkov in November 1930, this line was promoted, and the new name, International Organization of Revolutionary Writers (Mezhdunarodnoe ob"edinenie revoliutsionnykh pisatelei, MORP; IVRS in German, AEAR in French) was given to the literary organization that answered to the Comintern.[5] The new line was soon copied in Germany, following a "signal" article in

Linkskurve, the journal of the Bund proletarisch-revolutsionärer Schriftsteller (Union of Proletarian Revolutionary Writers, BPRS, founded in
1928).[6]

Intellectuals were a problematical category in this militantly "proletarian" moment when there was a very instrumentalist sense of the role of
culture. It was considered valuable only to the extent that it could aid the
proletariat and the industrialization effort. Those who were close to the
processes of production should impart this knowledge to fellow proletarians in the hope of raising production levels. Both the highbrow intelligentsia and high culture were often found expendable. Many intellectuals
sought a kind of redemption for their original sin of being bourgeois professionals by immersing themselves in work at a factory, collective farm,
or construction project. Often, as in the case of the White Sea-Baltic Canal construction project, which used forced labor, this immersion was not
entirely voluntary. The most militantly "proletarian" writers organization
the Russian Association of Proletarian Writers (RAPP), and other cultural bodies organized writers in brigades to be sent to specific enterprises where they were to serve local needs by performing service tasks
similar to the ones Benjamin lists in "The Author as Producer," such as
supervising a factory newspaper or library, training workers to be writers,
or working on agitational projects (posters, skits). Bourgeois authors
were, by their service, to transform socialist production and its "producers," but in so doing were in turn to be transformed by their close encounter with the authentic, with labor. Millenarian expectations were
invested in prosaic material.

Benjamin in "The Author as Producer" appears to be infected with the
spirit of the cultural revolution, suggesting that "the conventional distinction between author and public [has begun] to disappear" as the worker
"gains access to authorship."[7] Here he was drawing, as he explicitly ac-
knowledges, on the ideas Tretiakov presented when he visited Berlin in
1930–1931.

Tretiakov's visit was far from a unique event. Berlin, Benjamin's hometown and headquarters of the Comintern in Europe, was at the time the
main focus of the Soviet effort at cultural hegemony. Its railway station
became what Karl Schlögel has aptly described as the "eastern station of
Europe" (Ostbahnhof Europas), the main point of transit between East

and West, with intellectuals, experts, and worker delegations shuttling back and forth with increasing frequency;[8] several of the major filmmakers (including Eisenstein) made visits. In addition, in effect, a satellite Soviet society was created within Berlin, a sort of scattering of colonialist enclaves many of whose institutions, styles, and attitudes aped those in the metropolitan center. Louis Althusser has noted the critical importance, in establishing and maintaining political hegemony, of what he calls the "Ideological State Apparatus" (schools, churches, publishers), and red Berlin was an entire world defined by its schools, libraries, and other cultural institutions, including a fleet of Moscow-centered Communist newspapers and journals, all outlets for Soviet material.[9] These duplicated the cultural practices of Soviet Russia, often adopting the same names as their Soviet counterparts.

Tretiakov was sent by VOKS to Berlin from September 1930 to April 1931 in, as it were, a reversal of Benjamin's 1926 journey. He arrived at a critical time for the Soviet cause, a time of galloping unemployment, when the Nazis, the communists' rivals in providing a panacea for it, were growing in strength; the very month he arrived they made great gains in the Reichstag elections. He commented that as he walked around lower class Berlin he saw stone walls "on which 'Red Front' and 'Heil Hitler' shouted out at each other in a voiceless contest"[10] Yet at this time of crisis, when one might have expected the left to unite, the Communists' archenemy and obsession was not the fascists but rival leftist factions such as the Trotskyites, and above all the German Social Democrats, the heirs to the Second International, who lost few opportunities to attack them in their press (such as the paper *Vorwärts*)—and vice versa.

Essentially, Tretiakov in Berlin was an emissary sent to reinforce one side of this propaganda war, if you will, an author who was to "produce" loyalty to the Soviet Union. His specific assignment was to lecture as a propagandist for the new Soviet initiative of collectivizing the countryside, which had been attacked in *Vorwärts*.[11] In this connection he was to spend time in the countryside learning about German agriculture; literary activities were to be secondary.[12] He gave the same lecture, "The Socialist Village and the Writer," in Berlin, several other major German cities, Vienna, and Denmark.[13]

Tretiakov had probably been chosen for this purpose because he could speak German (though imperfectly, and a form of Baltic German, so that a translator was also provided). But he was also an exuberant propagandist for the Soviet cause, who had a personal commitment to collectivization. In July 1928 he had responded to the call "Writers, to the Kolkhoz!" and gone to an agricultural *kombinat,* Vyzov (the challenge), that amalgamated several communes in the Stavropol region of the Northern Caucuses.[14] For the next two years, until March 1930, he worked there during extended visits, running its newspaper, *Vyzov,* and eventually joining its council. At the *kombinat,* in addition to assuming such service roles, he did his own creative work, including taking photographs of the complex, making a film about it, *Vyzov,* and also publishing a book of that name that presents his experiences in first person narrative and formed the basis of his lecture in Germany.[15]

Thus Tretiakov was in the one lecture proselytizing both for the new Soviet organization of the village and for the new conception of the writer, which he saw as linked.[16] For many of these occasions he presented visual materials about collectivized agriculture (including his own photos) and screened a film about a sovkhoz, *Giant* (Gigant), made by Lidiia Stepanova in 1929. (Tretiakov's own film *Vyzov,* which he had brought with him to screen at the lectures, having been rejected by the Soviet officials in Berlin as being, for some unknown reason, unsuitable for the purposes, *Giant* was hastily substituted.)[17] On his return Tretiakov published an account of the response to one of these lectures, given in Vienna in February 1931 "in an electrified atmosphere." Published in the resonantly titled journal *Smena* (Changeover), his article accords an evening intended to impart information about collectivization the atmosphere of a revival meeting. According to Tretiakov, the auditorium was packed to the rafters, the overflow having been chased off by the Austrian cavalry as it was. When, as he showed *Giant,* a line of tractors appeared on the screen, the audience roared. Then some of them approached him on the podium and asked him if he would stop the film because a woman had fainted in the excitement (even though, Tretiakov claims, it was not hot there); they needed to take her out but did not want to miss a moment of the film.[18] The Soviet plenipotentiary to Austria, in reporting back to VOKS about Tretiakov's success, represented it as providing lessons for "Europe" as a whole.[19]

Many of those attending Tretiakov's presentations, themselves experiencing an economic depression and the rise of militant nationalism, were particularly susceptible to the vertigo of the promise of radical change. Yet the exchange generated by Tretiakov's visit was not all one-way, not an *Einbahnstrasse* where he came to instruct, awe, and transform. The story of his visit and its fallout, a series of other cultural exchanges and joint projects between intellectuals in Moscow and Berlin to be chronicled in this chapter, is a story of translation, adaptation, and appropriation, of idealism and proselytizing, that generally never quite succeeded for either party. It is a story of projects that lured Berliners to the Soviet Union but were never implemented or never completed. But at the same time it is a story of how this exchange was implicated in major shifts in Soviet culture itself.

One of the major issues confronting the Soviet leaders, and intellectuals, at this time was developing a correct stance toward the West, about which it was in practice ambivalent, but obsessed. Paradoxically, even as the country drew farther away from capitalism in the cultural revolution, it became more dependent on the capitalist world (for machinery, know-how, and skilled workers) than it would ever be at any time except World War II.[20] Tretiakov sought to enlighten the West, but he also relished the chance to immerse himself in its vibrant culture. There is little evidence that he spent much time "on the farm," as instructed. For most of his stay, he hung out in Berlin with a number of the leading leftist creative intellectuals, such as the theater director Ervin Piscator, writers such as Ludwig Renn, Johannes Becher, and Friedrich Wolf, and the film director Hans Richter. But his closest friends there—who were also the main examples Benjamin uses in "The Author as Producer"—were leading figures of the avant-garde aligned with the Communist movement: Brecht, the photographer John Heartfield, and the composer Hanns Eisler.[21]

We do not know if Benjamin attended Tretiakov's lecture in Berlin, though the right-wing writer Gottfried Benn, who in an article characterizes Tretiakov's role in Berlin as "developing a propagandistic front for the new Russian imperialism," adds that "the entire literary world of Berlin" was in the audience.[22] Scholars generally conclude that Benjamin's conversations with Brecht in Denmark about Tretiakov were the context for "The Author as Producer," but these conversations as reported do not really deal with the points Benjamin makes in the essay. It seems unlikely that Benjamin did not come across Tretiakov's ideas earlier, during his visit, since Tretiakov was close to Brecht then. There is a newspaper record of Benjamin having made spirited contributions to the discussion at a lecture given slightly earlier, in April 1930, by Osip Brik, a former associate of Tretiakov (they had parted ways over "the literature of fact"), about which Benjamin also wrote.[23]

In his lecture Tretiakov argued that the new proletarian age required not just a sociological bouleversement but a mighty recasting of cultural forms as well, the old cry of the avant-garde. This recasting was to be tamer in terms of formal experimentation than the kinds the avant-garde had envisaged earlier, but it was to be more radical in terms of its conception of the role and character of the intellectual. Since at least 1928, when he took over from Mayakovsky as editor of the avant-garde's outlet *Novyi lef* (New Left Front), Tretiakov had sought to further radicalize and politicize the avant-garde with a new program, the Literature of Fact, whose adherents were known as *faktoviki*. This new movement, which embraced a segment of the old Constructivist camp, rejected conventional artistic forms in literature, art, and film. *Faktoviki* decried fictional invention as bourgeois falsification, calling instead for a culture based in actuality that was more publicistic and utilitarian, more journalistic. In February 1929 they published a manifesto-like collection of articles outlining the principles of the new movement, the *Literature of Fact* (Literatura fakta), edited by Nikolai Chuzhak, Tretiakov's old associate from his early post-revolutionary days in Vladivostok and Chita, and with copious contributions from Brik and Tretiakov, most of them formerly published in *Novyi lef*. Tretiakov's books of this period, examples of the new kind of writing— *Vyzov, 1001 Workdays,* and *Den Shi-Khua*—were also published in German translation, with covers by John Heartfield.[24]

The program for a "literature of fact" did not just entail an orientation toward actualities, something that was after all advocated by the German movement Neue Sachlichkeit (attacked by Benjamin in "Author as Producer"). It was presented explicitly as the cultural correlative of the Five-Year Plan. Tretiakov in outlining the *perelom* demanded by the cultural revolution argued that the most radical "revolution" should be in the role of the writer. It was time for the business of writing to be rationalized and planned, integrated with the entire modernization effort of the plan. Such an updating would liberate literature from outdated genres such as the novel and the epic; its new model would now be the newspaper, where writers allegedly work within a collective. This new arrangement would also entail a "de-individualization and de-professionalization" of the writer, who was to overcome the superficial snobbery of "high culture" and draw closer to the toilers, who should all ultimately become "authors."[25] Education should render the ability to write as automatic as the ability to read, so that the separate "caste" of writers would, as it were, wither away in a version of the death of the author.

The term Tretiakov had begun to use for the new writer, one intoned by Benjamin in "The Author as Producer," was *operativnyi* (in Benjamin *operierende*). The standard translation of this term in English versions of Benjamin's essay is "operating writer," but this is too vague and does not convey precisely the connotations of the term in Russian. *Operativnyi* means a writer who is effective, energetic, and efficient, ever at the ready to respond to the Party's commands. At the same time, *operativnyi* is used in the context of military operations. Thus he is a writer on a campaign who is an adept tactician, and works *operativno,* gets things done immediately. The writer, Benjamin says, is "not to report, but to struggle . . . not to play the spectator but to intervene actively."[26] In this context he invokes a programmatic term of Brecht, *Umfunktionierung* (functional transformation).[27]

The kinds of "functional transformation" Tretiakov and Benjamin advocate are not just in the sphere of aesthetics. A concomitant change is to be made in the function of the intellectual, with implications for the nature of subjectivity itself. This is particularly evident in the prime example Benjamin adduces of "functional transformation," the theatrical piece *Measures Taken* (Die Massnahme, 1930) by their mutual friend Brecht, one of a series of pedagogical pieces *(Lehrstücke)* he wrote after his conversion to Marxism in 1928.[28]

Brecht's Measures Taken

Generically, *Measures Taken* is very different from the kind of art generated by the cultural revolution, which was typically a saga of the factory floor or kolkhoz field laden with statistics and details about production processes. Nevertheless, it could be said to take the notion of *Umfunktio-*

nierung to an extreme. Much of the work also seems to anticipate the culture (in the extended sense) of High Stalinism (the mid- to late thirties) and not just in the way critics most often point out, that is, that the "measures taken" of the title were extreme measures—the execution of a well-intentioned Party comrade. Needless to say, this action has made the work extremely controversial in Brecht's oeuvre, but, as I shall argue, the "measures taken" extend beyond this execution to include aesthetic as well as thematic resolutions. *Measures Taken* focuses many of the issues and practices that were to become central for Stalinism, especially those having to do with subjectivity, identity, representation, and the role of the intellectual.

Measures Taken was allegedly written partly under the influence of Lenin's essay "The Infantile Disease of Leftism" (1920), published in volume 25 of a German edition of Lenin that appeared in April 1930. Some of Lenin's phrases appear in Brecht's text without acknowledgment though, since he began work on it in January of that year, this essay cannot have provided the initial impetus. "The Infantile Disease" was a volley in Lenin's ongoing campaign against assorted communists and factions in Russia and Germany whose positions at various points he found heretical. However, in delivering the volley Lenin made a strong statement about the need for Party hegemony, for "discipline," and for *besposhchadnost'*, a term that roughly means ruthlessness and mercilessness and as such is counterposed to human pity or empathy, two qualities decried in this work.

Measures Taken, however, is set in neither Germany nor Russia but in revolutionary China, at that point a popular topic of German communist culture. When a new Communist worker youth theater (Junge Volksbühne) was founded to counteract a Nazi youth theater, its first production in 1930 was *Tai Yang Awakens* (Tai Yang erwacht), by Friedrich Wolf. The play, which recounts the "awakening" to consciousness of a simple silk weaver, Tai Yang, after she moves from her village to work in a factory, was allegedly intended to "present dialectically the link between the Chinese revolution and the class war in Germany."[29] The play was directed by the experimental leftist Piscator, with sets by Heartfield, who, in the description of Tretiakov, who saw it, flooded the auditorium with placards and slogans in a veritable agitational overkill; Piscator also used, until it was banned by the censors, footage from a recent documentary film about the Shanghai uprising, in all probability the Soviet director Iakov Bliokh's *Shanghai Document* (Shangkhaiskii dokument, 1927), making this yet another example of Soviet/German cross-fertilization.[30] Tretiakov had himself recently published a documentary biography about a Chinese revolutionary, *Den Shi-Khua,* and earlier written a play about the Chinese revolution, *Roar, China!* (Rychi, Kitai!, 1925). Meyerhold had directed it for a production of 1926, which Benjamin had singled out as one of his greatest recent successes.[31] Meyerhold had brought it to Berlin in April 1930, the year of Tretiakov's arrival; police surrounded the theater, making it a cause célèbre.[32] Whenever an appearance by Tretiakov at some German town was announced, he was promoted as the author of that play.

Brecht's *Measures Taken* is not, like *Tai Yang Awakens,* about the conversion of a Chinese but about Europeans in China. In the opening scene, four "agitators" present themselves to a "Control Chorus" of the Party to account for their recent visit to Manchuria and report that they have been obliged to execute a "young comrade" whom they had recruited near the frontier to help them with their agitational work there. These were the "measures taken," and for the rest of the play the agitators proceed to justify the execution to the Control Chorus by recounting the events leading up to the killing in a narrative reenactment, each agitator assuming in turn the role of the young comrade.

In the play, the agitators tell how, when they are about to cross into China, they don masks to conceal the fact that they are not Chinese. Then, once their narrative brings them to Mukden, they describe for the Control Chorus three incidents in which the young comrade is set a task by the agitators but in their eyes fails because he has not acted as an agent of the Party's will and in accordance with the guidelines set out in the "classics" (of Marxism-Leninism) but rather is moved by pity to intervene on behalf of the oppressed. The third of these leads to a critical confrontation between the young comrade and the agitators. He argues that a general strike should be called, insisting that "the unemployed can wait no longer. Nor can I. . . . There are too many paupers," but the agitators retort: "there are not enough fighters," and the workers, though growing in political consciousness, are ignorant of how many regiments the government has. On orders from the Party, the agitators have decided to postpone armed action till the delegates of the farmers' organizations have arrived in the city. The young comrade responds in turn: "Let me ask this: is it in line with the classic writers to let misery wait?" to which the agitators reply that the classics "speak not of pity, but of the deed which does away with pity." The hotheaded young comrade expostulates: "Then the classic writers are dirt. I tear them up. For man, living man cries out . . ." The agitators urge him not to do that, but the young comrade ignores their injunctions to "silence," takes off his mask, and shouts to all who can hear: "We have come to help you! We come from Moscow!" Without his mask the young agitator appears guileless. Someone shouts "Foreigners! Throw the troublemakers out!" Locals begin to assemble for a strike but are unprotected. The agitators, sensing disaster, strike the young comrade down to silence him and then lift him up and leave the city in haste. They are pursued and have to take quick stock of the situation, concluding that they cannot get their wounded comrade over the border because they must stay in the city and direct the masses to wait so that they will not rise up prematurely and fatally. At the same time, they reason that the young comrade must not be found by the authorities, nor must they be, or the cause will be lost. And so they decide that they have no recourse but to kill him, "even if he does not agree," and destroy his body, though "IT IS A FEARSOME THING TO KILL [emphasis Brecht's]." The young comrade does agree, responding (in the 1931 version that Tretiakov saw) with a curt "Yes," himself adding that they should put him "in the lime pit." After the agitators have shot him and thrown him into the pit, they return to their work, which is "successful" in spreading "the teachings of the classics / The ABC of communism," or so the Control Chorus reports as they conclude the play with the words "In yet another country the revolution advances / In another land the ranks of the fighters are joined / We agree with what you have done."[33]

Ostensibly, then, the needs of the cause justify sacrificing the needs of the individual, and even his life. Not surprisingly, this denouement has given rise to some strong reactions. Some of the fiercest attacks on the play came from the German Communist periodicals of the time, which were uneasy about such a bald representation of brutal treatment meted out to a loyal Party member.[34] "What Was He Killed For?" one article asks in its title. Here Brecht is written off as a petty bourgeois intellectual who has fallen prey to "the right opportunist tendency," at the time a commonly cited reason why the German Communist Party lost in their revolutionary uprisings of 1923 (sometimes the play is taken as a representation of the debacle in Saxony, where the Trade Unions wanted to call for a general strike but the Communists insisted on delaying this to negotiate with the leftist government to secure broader support and, perhaps in consequence, forces of the right gained the upper hand).[35] Western commentators such as Martin Esslin have called *Measures Taken* ahead of its time because it seems to anticipate the purges and show trials of 1936–1939 where figures like the party leader Nikolai Bukharin acknowledged their guilt and acceded to their own executions.[36] The play with its rigid insistence on Party priority and its "control chorus," a term reminiscent of the Control Commission, the Party body that oversaw purging its ranks, is a contender for being more Stalinist in this respect than Stalinist literature itself where writers deftly avoided explicit mention of the brutality of a purge. Generally, if purging was featured there at all it took the form of a character's being ushered off stage by the secret police or some other agent of Soviet power. Nothing grisly was ever represented. What was explicit in *Measures Taken* was essentially encoded in Soviet literature; one of the mandatory epithets for a Stalinist positive hero was "ruthless" *(besposhchadnyi),* a term featured in Lenin's "Infantile Disease" and an encrypted way of signaling that the hero is capable of using extreme means whenever the Party or cause might demand them.

Ironically, the fate of Brecht's young comrade to be shot and have his body thrown into the lime pit recapitulates the fate of the last tsar and his family in 1918, though Brecht would not have been aware of this. Even more ironic, perhaps, is the fact that this play premiered shortly after the Industrial Party *(Prompartiia)* trial in Moscow of November 25–December 8, 1930 at which a number of prominent engineers and managers were accused of sabotage and espionage and condemned to death. The Party put a great deal of emphasis on this trial, even commissioning a feature length film on it.[37] It also circulated instructions to the effect that its members should learn from the trial and not trust the bourgeois specialist. Thus the trial was a symptomatic moment in this era of militant "proletarianization" but also in some senses a dry run for the Show Trials of 1936–1938 with the major difference that whereas in this instance prominent engineers and managers were on trial in the later Show Trials it was Party leaders.

In Europe many left-leaning intellectuals were shocked by the death penalty meted out in these earlier trials. In Germany, several public meetings were held and articles penned to denounce them. The Communist Party and Comintern had to work overtime to counteract the protests, organizing explanatory public meetings (at some of which the film of the trial was screened), while several Soviet-oriented Berlin periodicals devoted whole issues to the verdict and its rationale.[38] Koltsov, consistently an apologist for Soviet purges, contributed to the German campaign.[39]

A second assigned mission for Tretiakov in Germany was to counteract the press attacks on the trial. A VOKS progress report on his visit reveals that for most of December Tretiakov was ill and unable to do much,[40] which might lead one to speculate that this was a strategic "illness" to avoid justifying the Party's "extreme measures." But, whatever his specific reaction to the Industrial Party trial, one should not assume that Tretiakov and his fellow avant-garde intellectuals were opposed to purging. The end of his book *Vyzov* features a meeting of the kombinat at which members are tried for behavior undermining the collective effort. As some of those present waiver, Tretiakov comes forward to argue against leniency for the class-tainted accused and he successfully advocates expulsion from the *kombinat.*

Although many in the Soviet avant-garde bought into the doctrine of "ruthlessness," even for them the position of *Measures Taken* was problematical, as it continues to be for Western Brecht enthusiasts.[41] But the trial of the agitators in this work is not the same as a trial from the Great Purge, such as the famous trial of Bukharin (or even the Industrial Party trial), because the guilty party does not make a confession. In *Measures Taken,* we have merely the young comrade's perfunctory acquiescence to his sentence—"Yes"—and a reaffirmation of the revolutionary cause. Moreover, the text provides only the young comrade's response as told by the agitators in their self-justificatory reenactment. He is on trial, but not represented by himself, in his own voice. The agitators are also on trial before the Control Chorus, but they do not "confess"; they defend their actions.

This is not a superficial distinction. Confession is a self-narrative that presupposes interiority and individuality. This is precisely what is not present here. Brecht does not give his characters any inner life—or for that matter any individual features. The one seemingly individual role, that of the young comrade, is acted by the other three comrades in turn, so that he never really appears. In addition, the four agitators are not differentiated from each other, and though they are given some names and geographic origins, no class origins are indicated; their entire identity is as spokesmen-activists for the Party. Even in death the young comrade is deindividualized. In assenting to it, he accedes to his nonfit with the laws and needs of the Party and to the total erasure of his self, dramatized when his body is to be eviscerated in the lime pit and all the surface markers of individuality are to be obliterated.

This erasure of selfhood is linked with the use of masks. Both putting on and taking off the masks occurs at critical moments in the text: the group put on masks when they cross the border; and using extreme measures becomes an issue the moment the young comrade takes off his mask, thus presenting his face's actual features. Furthermore, the purpose of eviscerating his body is to erase them, a more radical version of one function of a mask, which is to simplify them. At an earlier point in Brecht's text, as the agitators and the young comrade are about to put on their masks, they are instructed: "You are not Karl Schmitt from Berlin, you are not Anna Kjersk from Kazan, and you are not Peter Sawitch from Moscow. One and all of you are nameless and motherless, blank pages on which the revolution writes its instructions."[42] In a sense, then, there is no death, only an imperfect text that has to be "edited."

Masks were extremely important in Stalinist culture, not to say the Marxist. In Marx's *German Ideology* (1845) tearing off the masks of idealist illusion is presented as the philosophical coup de théâtre of Marxism. In this period of the First Five-Year Plan, "tearing off each and every mask" (Sryvanie vsekh i vsiakikh masok) was one of the main slogans, though the doctrine of "tearing off the masks" was largely about exposing class enemies.

Masking and unmasking are not just central motifs of the Bolshevik belief system but also the stuff of melodrama, which is the stuff of the

Stalinist show trials, as scholars have pointed out.[43] But here we have a reversal—donning the mask is a positive act. In fact in Stalinist culture the meaning of the mask is itself highly ambivalent. Its use was not confined to Party rhetoric. This ambivalence can be seen for example in the theatrical theories and practice of Meyerhold, for whom masks were crucial appurtenances of "theatricality." On the one hand, the mask can potentially function as a simplifier and generalizer, something that facilitates more mechanical role-playing or more standardized "characters." On the other, because of this very cutoff between self and mask, it can play a crucial role in such orgiastic behavior as carnival.

Clearly there is nothing orgiastic about donning the mask in *Measures Taken*. The mask's ostensible purpose is functional. The group put on their masks when they cross into China so as to obliterate ethnic particularity, enabling the wearers to blend in with the Chinese. At that point the head of the Party headquarters at the border says: "from this hour on. . . . You are unknown workers, fighters, Chinese, born of Chinese mothers, with yellow skins and speaking Chinese in fever and in sleep."[44] Seemingly, the dichotomy of self and mask has been resolved, in that even in states when one might most forget oneself and reveal one's identity (in sleep or in a fever) the mask stays firmly on.

With their masks on, also, the small group expand the range of their already mixed national identity (German and Russian), suggesting the possibility of a transnational Party, hence also a transnational, or even universal, culture system, something many in the Russian and German leftist avant-gardes had long sought. The agitators acquire a transnational identity as they cross a border, but arguably that border is both actual and metaphoric. At some level this is a parable about intellectuals, Russian and German, going to "China," to a situation that is potentially revolutionary but at the same time totally other; they are crossing a border, going beyond their known world, and affecting a *perelom* of the self.

In *Measures Taken* we see an instance of the phenomenon discussed in the Introduction wherein the national and the international are not distinct but imbricated with each other. Here masking entails assuming a transnational identity, but also absolute allegiance to a particular country. At the point when the agitators put on their masks, they do not so much become Chinese as opt for *total* commitment to the Soviet model. Likewise, when Tretiakov urged *Roar, China!* (the title of his 1925 play), his

China was to roar à la Moscow, just as in his account the Vienna audience roared in 1931. Thus in a sense *Measures Taken* is about Soviet acculturation, a course confronting Tretiakov, Brecht, Benjamin, and their leftist avant-garde colleagues in this immediately pre-Nazi time. As Benjamin in his *Moscow Diary* contemplated committing himself to Moscow, he believed he could assume the role of the assimilated Communist and buy into its set of conventions—put on the mask—temporarily. But this play suggests that one must keep the mask on at all times. Tear it off, and disaster lurks.

Communist critics also attacked *Measures Taken* in terms of the interpretation of Marxist theory, arguing that "learning from the classics" is not the Marxist view of the way forward, which emphasizes praxis and associating closely with the workers.[45] In the text the young agitator tears up "the classics" at the same time he tears off his mask, implying an identification between the two. In masking, as the agitators transcend their individual selves, they also accept a simplification of the world.

While Brecht's work ostensibly poses the question as to whether the Party should use extreme measures against the well-intentioned and loyal Party member, it is also, on a more meta- level, about using extreme measures in representation. The mask in the play is both a thematic and an aesthetic strategy. The two (form and content, or aesthetics and politics) are for Brecht not distinct, as Benjamin argued in "The Author As Producer."[46] Politics and aesthetics are intertwined not just at the crude level of "repression" (of art by the state). In the Soviet Union, theories about acting were closely linked to the problem of personhood (see Chapter 6).

The mask is an artifice that facilitates a nonrealistic narrative. Realistically, the agitators would not be taken for Chinese merely because they are wearing Chinese masks. Thus at the point when they cross the border and put on their masks, the drama leaves realism behind (the agitators are suddenly able to speak Chinese, a version of speaking in tongues) and crosses into a highly stylized theatrical tradition, which Brecht was to return to again after seeing Mei Lanfang perform in Moscow, an experience leading to his essay on alienation in Chinese acting (see Chapter 5).

Yet in its use of masks *Measures Taken* anticipates socialist realism, whose positive heroes are likewise presented as mask-like with no countervailing interiority. The most positive heroes generally wear the mask of an achieved consciousness, but this is rarely sustained throughout (as it is with the agitators in Brecht). In select scenes they lay their masks aside to reveal human selves, laughing, smiling, and showing empathy for those around them. Thus *Measures Taken* presents a version of selfhood that anticipates and actually surpasses the radical degree of depersonalization in Stalinist culture.

Brecht presented *Measures Taken* as his first attempt at truly mass, proletarian culture. In this sense, it proclaims Brecht's *perelom,* his personal cultural revolution. In contemporary attacks on it by German Communists, this was the one positive aspect of it that they singled out. Writing for the masses was a shift for Brecht from his previous *Lehrstücke,* which had a more highbrow orientation. The piece was originally written for an avant-garde new music festival in Berlin in June but was rejected. It was then that Brecht made a decision to use an amateur orchestra and for the Control Chorus a massed workers' choir amalgamating three choral groups from Berlin.

In fact *Measures Taken* was not a play but an oratorio. It was to be part of the "mighty recasting" of cultural forms, yet paradoxically, as an oratorio it was a generic cousin of the medieval mystery play, and in that sense seems far from the modern, semijournalistic genres advocated by Tretiakov and Benjamin as the mainstay of the new culture. Brecht was drawn to this genre because it required no action, scenery, or costume, no illusionistic props, and anyway, he modernized it somewhat by adding to its orchestra kettledrums, brass instruments, a saxophone, and a piano. Far from setting the oratorio in a sacred space, he staged it on a special podium that suggested a boxing ring. Moreover, it was essentially a generic hybrid, combining elements of traditional Japanese theater with the European, the medieval and the modernist, the religious and the secular.

Brecht saw *Measures Taken* as a model for the theater of the future. *His* oratorio, as Benjamin put it in "The Author as Producer," turned "a concert into a political meeting."[47] Yet Brecht banned further performance of it on the grounds that no one learned from it.[48] These contradictory statements match the contradictory nature of this "oratorio." On the one hand, as we have seen, the characters' masking could be read as being about adopting a unitary belief system in a polyglot society. This seems surprising, given that while Brecht was a Marxist materialist, he was opposed to anything that whiffed of reified dogma, believing that the development of the new forms of practice would be necessitated by changed conditions. The mask of Marxism-Leninism, itself a simplification of the original Marxism, would obscure life's complexity, its eddies and flows. But there are several ways this oratorio should be seen as open-ended rather than monologic. One is that both Brecht and Eisler, the work's composer, believed that participation in this mass theatrical event was a process that would have a pedagogical impact on the workers who performed it.[49] Eisler had in the mid-1920s in large measure discarded his own creative identity as a disciple of Schoenberg in favor of what he called *Tendenzgesang*, mass choral agitational work, which he promoted in his journal *Die Kampfmusik* (1931–1933). Here he contended that the workers would learn about music and about staging as they prepared the work—so as to become, as it were, future "producers."[50] Somewhat as Brecht in his famous essay on "epic" theater decried "culinary" theater, that is, the passivity-inducing, consumerist theatrical forms that dominated the German stage, Eisler called for an active engagement or "hearing" of the music; the members of the several workers' choirs that were crammed onto the stage for the Berlin performances were to undergo their own mental transformation in the very act of collective singing.[51] He also, like Brecht, was against sympathetic identification with music, calling instead for an "intellectual-dialectic (pedagogical) moment."[52]

Brecht for his part conceived this oratorio, as he did most of his works, as more on the order of a debate than straight agitation. The Formalist theorist Osip Brik is said to have observed that most of Brecht's works are court trials, dramatizations of argument and counter-argument. Tretiakov in reporting this remark added that as a dramatist Brecht was a "wily casuist."[53] Thus, though in *Measures Taken* the summary execution of the young comrade is endorsed by the higher Party authority represented by the Control Chorus, the countervailing position remains on the table via dialogue. Tretiakov in his reminiscences on the Berlin visit dismisses *Tai Yang Awakens* as boring and ineffective because, for all its frenetic use of placards, too much of the "dialogue" consists of elaborating a particular philosophy. It is not surprising that Tretiakov made this point, given that his earlier play *I Want a Child* (Brecht was given a translation of it and tried unsuccessfully to mount a production) was meant to be a discussion piece whereby the action would be interrupted periodically so that the actors and audience might debate the issues. This provision was also written into the text of *Measures Taken.* Symptomatically, the play's songs are peppered with question marks, and "Discussion" is the title of several of the play's scenes, though for assorted reasons this did not happen in the Berlin productions. In addition, Brecht regarded the text as unfinished and looked to his worker participants to critique it at each rehearsal, so that it was always in the process of being written. Even after the oratorio premiered he refused to regard the text as final.

The intention of Brecht's "epic" theater, as outlined in "The Modern Theatre Is the Epic Theatre" (1930), was to have the audience think about the issues aired rather than become emotionally involved in the characters.[54] The mask might be seen as functional here, in that it would distance the audience from the characters, enabling them to stand back and consider the issues. In that sense, *Measures Taken* can be seen as a parable about acting and theatricality that anticipates Brecht's later theory of "alienation."[55] In another distancing effect, each of the agitators at the hearing was to take on several roles in turn, including the role of the young comrade. This oratorio, moreover, though highly agitational, was not to sustain its august tone. The music incorporated jazz and, as was typical of Eisler's musical pieces, frequently grotesque or parodic (especially of Bach) music;[56] the elevated speeches were undercut by the score, which sent up religious and kitschy music.

The oratorio might seem to be a genre of limited use as a basis for proletarian mass culture. *Measures Taken,* which took a great deal to mount as a production because for example there were three mass choirs on the stage so that it could not be staged often and was only performed twice in Berlin at that time. Effectively, it was limited as a model for the theater of the future. Thus a parable about radical *Umfunktionierung* became a semiunique event, an almost quixotic gesture toward the new age.

Tretiakov had been so impressed by the work when he saw it in Berlin that he singled out *Measures Taken* for importation to Soviet Russia, hoping to restore its discussional character. A translation he published in *Literatura mirovoi revoliutsii* in 1932 indicates places in the work earmarked for this.[57] He began negotiating to bring the work to Moscow even before he left the German capital,[58] and though he was initially unable to bring

Brecht himself, Eisler and Ernst Busch, a principal performer from the oratorio's Berlin production, came to Moscow and Leningrad in June 1931 (the first of several visits) with the aim of staging it.[59] It was to have been performed in the Communist Academy, not a workers' or mass milieu, but the closest Eisler appears to have gotten to putting it on was a lecture he delivered at that Academy in July 1932.[60]

Though this production never happened, in many other ways Tretiakov on his return to the Soviet Union functioned as an important liaison and proselytizer for his new friends' leftist avant-garde culture, something he was in a position to do as a prominent cultural journalist and filmmaker and an official of the Comintern-sponsored MORP. His authority in Soviet Russia had been enhanced by success in Berlin. His efforts clearly served the cause of attracting prominent leftist intellectuals to the Soviet side, but probably Tretiakov had a personal agenda as well. In 1930–1931 much of the Soviet avant-garde, as represented by figures like Meyerhold, Eisenstein and the photographer Aleksandr Rodchenko, were attacked in the Soviet cultural press, particularly by the militant proletarians, for allegedly fetishizing form ("formalists") and neglecting ideology and the class struggle.[61] In a sense, Tretiakov was providing reinforcements for the cause by playing the internationalist card at a time when Comintern efforts were focused on Berlin. Most of the contacts among the Berlin-centered avant-garde made by Tretiakov in 1930–1931 visited the Soviet Union over the next three years, where creative projects were set up for them. Though most of these projects did not come to much, Tretiakov was able to publish several of Brecht's plays in translation between 1932 and 1934 (including *Measures Taken*), while Brecht attempted, unsuccessfully, to mount a production of Tretiakov's *Roar, China!* (which appeared in German translation in 1929).[62]

As members of the avant-garde, several of Tretiakov's Berlin friends were particularly attracted by the possibility of representing the giant industrial and construction projects that marked the First Five-Year Plan effort. And not only they. Photographers and filmmakers from all over the transatlantic world sought to be on the cutting edge for representing the machine age. One of them was Margaret Bourke-White, the pioneering American photographer of industrial subjects, who visited the Soviet Union three times between 1930 and 1932 as a correspondent for *Fortune*, so as to wow readers with photos reproduced there and in her *Eyes on Russia* (1931).[63] Her photos were also printed in Soviet magazines and had an impact on Soviet representations of the new colossi of industry.[64]

But for the Soviet avant-garde the major creative interaction was with the Germans. A milestone in this interaction came when the Soviet documentary filmmaker Dziga Vertov visited Berlin in July 1931 and his latest film, *Enthusiasm: Symphony of the Donbass* (Entuziasm. Simfoniia Donbassa, 1931), was screened later that year. In making it, Vertov experimented with orchestrating industrial sounds in a musical score, providing live sync-sound, a technological breakthrough. The film attracted a lot of attention in Berlin, and when it was banned there in October 1931, it became a cause célèbre among leftist intellectuals; many prominent names, including our familiar cast of characters Brecht, Eisler, and Heartfield, mounted a protest.

The Dutch documentary filmmaker Joris Ivens, a frequenter of Berlin, was among those attracted by the possibility of making a film like Vertov's. He met Eisenstein, Vertov, and the Soviet director Vsevolod Pudovkin during their respective Berlin visits and with their encouragement visited Moscow in 1930 and then 1932–1934, when he went to Magnitostroi, a huge industrial complex being built ex nihilo on the windswept plains of Kirghizia, just beyond the Urals, and at the time *the* poster project of the industrialization effort. There he produced *Komsomol: Song of the Heroes* (Komsomol. Pesn' o geroiakh, 1932—premiere in Moscow, January 2, 1933). This film is not unlike Vertov's *Enthusiasm* in that it features industrial sounds coordinated as if scored; Eisler and Tretiakov collaborated on its theme song.[65] At the time, several Soviet writers and photographers had been sent to Magnitostroi and its planned city Magnitogorsk. Koltsov joined the enthusiasts, and had an issue of *Ogonëk* published there: "Ogonëk na Magnitogorske."

Another example, common at this time, of collaboration between Berlin and Moscow intellectuals would be the way Soviet officials and Mezhrabpom recruited both Soviet and German movie directors to make films about the revolutionary movement in Germany. Some of them were actually filmed there, and all were intended for screening in both countries. One such director was Tretiakov's new friend Hans Richter, an avant-garde filmmaker long associated with Soviet intellectuals and among the protestors of the banning of *Enthusiasm,* who went to Moscow in 1931.[66] Among several projects mooted while he was there was a commission from Mezhrabpom to make a film with the German writer Friedrich Wolf about a German worker uprising of 1930 and called *Metal* (Metall).[67] The same year, 1931, Pudovkin visited Hamburg to film another Mezhrabpom production, *The Deserter* (Dezertir, 1933) about a strike on the Hamburg docks, a city made famous for its attempted revolution in 1923.[68] In the later sections of *The Deserter*—the most avant-garde of all Pudovkin's films, with some impressive experimental sound and camera work—the central character, Karl Renn is sent by the German Party to visit Soviet Russia for his rehabilitation, after he has panicked and stayed home rather than supporting the strike effort in its final showdown. While working in a Soviet factory, Karl sees the light and is able to return to Germany politically conscious.

Tretiakov helped secure many of these commissions for the Germans, but in some instances, as with the film *Komsomol,* he set himself up to do collaborative work with his new friends.[69] With Ernest Ottwalt, one of Brecht's collaborators, Tretiakov began writing a book entitled, "The Director," which does not appear to have been finished. Brecht himself came for a flying visit of seven to eight days in May 1932 (invited by Koltsov's conglomerate, Zhurgaz, and accompanied throughout by Tretiakov),[70] and in its wake Tretiakov announced a collaborative project that was not to see fruition. This one was for a musical play that he had undertaken with Brecht and Eisler, one that was not on industrial themes but once again on a contemporary Chinese subject. The play was about the Shenyang incident of September 18, 1931, when the Japanese on a pretext occupied first Shenyang in Manchuria and then over the next three months all of Manchuria, where they set up the Manchukuo government. The name Shenyang in Manchu is Mukden, a city featured in *Measures Taken,* but which also has resonance in Russia as the vital link on the Russian rail network that was lost to the Japanese in the Russo-Japanese war of 1904–1905, a tremendous loss of face and the immediate spur of the revolutionary strikes and uprisings of 1905. In Tretiakov's account, this musical was to use "episodes from the colonial military blow struck in the Shenyang incident. . . . Together with this we want to show how the proletariat will avert the preparations for war and stand for the defense of the Soviet Union. That the work is being done collectively can be explained in terms of the necessity to create two variants of the piece, one for the Soviet theater and the other for abroad."[71] This acknowledgment of the two different constituencies comes up again in Tretiakov's remarks on Brecht's adaptation of Gorky's novel *Mother* (1907) for the stage (again with music by Eisler). "Brecht's *Mother* is not Russian. [The play's] characters are Germans, and moreover Germans of today. The Russian names and [details of] Russian everyday life are only a masquerade that does not prevent the German audience from hearing the words they need for the current times."[72] The play in fact included current issues of Germany in 1932 when it premiered; it was so radical that the reactionaries saw it as an incitement to revolution and the police intervened during the performance.[73] It appeared in Russian translation in *Internatsional'naia literatura,* which Tretiakov then edited.[74]

Selling German avant-garde culture to Soviet officialdom and the public was not easy. So when Tretiakov arranged the Moscow visit of Heartfield and an exhibition of his photomontages of December 1931–January 1932 he orchestrated a press campaign in which writers stressed Heartfield's long-standing Party membership and his "class-directed perspective."[75] Photomontage was at that time being attacked as "formalism"—especially the work of Heartfield's Moscow counterpart, Rodchenko. The political realities of the courtship of Berlin leftist intellectuals ensured a different reception for Heartfield, as is strikingly evident in 1932 issues of *Proletarskoe foto,* where enthusiastic articles about him follow a cluster that make pointed attacks on Rodchenko and his group Oktiabr'.[76] Despite such gestures, there was less enthusiasm for actually adopting montage techniques. Attention was then focused on mass photography.

Tretiakov in many articles of the late 1920s (his Literature of Fact phase) had recommended photographic journalism as a backbone for a new mass culture that could supersede painting. Though most Party members and cultural authorities did not agree about superseding painting, they were themselves promoting photography as the most mass-accessible of the arts and the most directly mimetic. Given the low level of literacy among the masses, not everyone could really become a *rabkor* (worker correspondent), but virtually every worker could become a photographer; it was recommended that every worker be given a camera and encouraged to record his work experiences. Factories founded photo circles where workers could be instructed in camera use, photos could be exchanged, exhibitions organized, and so forth—the "producer" was to become a photographer.[77]

Photography was also seen as a means for overcoming the language barrier that was an impediment to a mass, international proletarian movement.[78] In these Plan years, the Moscow journal *Sovetskoe foto* and its Berlin counterpart *Arbeiter Fotograf* (both founded 1926) operated virtually in tandem, a situation further regularized in 1930, when the editor of *Arbeiter fotograf* came to Moscow and visited the offices of *Sovetskoe foto* amid declarations that "we did not want our activity to be confined to national borders."[79] Willi Münzenburg also set up an International Bureau (Mezhdunarodnoe biuro) to facilitate this, while Koltsov's *Ogonëk* photography team went to America to establish a branch there.[80] In November 1930, worker photographers from America, Germany, and Soviet Russia met in Moscow and founded the Moscow-Berlin International Association of Worker Photographers (MORF).[81] This association was to reinforce the already established practice whereby worker photographers corresponded with their counterparts in America and Germany, generally through Communist-sponsored periodicals (in reality, much of this exchange occurred between professional photographers at the various Communist-sponsored photographic journals).[82]

The cultural revolution also saw the rise of the mass illustrated journal as a major focus of agitational effort. In Germany the main vehicle was *Arbeiter Illustrierte Zeitung* (Workers pictorial newspaper), henceforth to be known by its acronym, *A-I-Z*. This periodical, founded by Mezhrabpom in 1921, though it was so named only in 1924, progressively expanded its readership to become the most widely read socialist pictorial newspaper in Germany; starting in 1930, Heartfield began publishing his political photomontages there. In the Soviet Union the first such Soviet journal was the popular *Ogonëk,* founded by Koltsov in 1923, which had a stable of professional Soviet photojournalists, who began to play a prominent role in some of the new journals established during the Plan years, when his publishing empire expanded rapidly with the setting up of Zhurgaz in 1931. Particularly significant among them was *SSSR na stroike* (USSR in construction), founded in 1931 to celebrate the new industrial achievements. *SSSR na Stroike* was—symptomatic of the times—a journal intended both for proselytizing overseas (editions came out in several languages, including English, French, Spanish, and German: *UdSSR im Bau*) and for internal consumption. In fact the Russian version came out in two editions; the more extravagantly produced one was aimed at Russia's elite. The journals that circulated overseas were handsomely appointed by current Soviet standards; *SSSR na Stroike* used such leading Soviet photographers as Lissitzky and Rodchenko, and had popularly appealing, expensive features such as pop-ups.[83] Its most infamous issue, 1933 no. 12 (layout and photos by Rodchenko), glorified construction of the White Sea-Baltic Canal, which was done by convict labor.

To a large extent the propaganda battle over the allegiance of the masses in the West, and especially in Germany, was waged via these illustrated journals, which were intended to rival the Nazi and capitalist counterparts (including Bourke-White's *Fortune*). To facilitate the use of photographs in this battle, a new body, Soiuzfoto, was founded in 1931 and charged with providing photographic material to interested foreigners. Tretiakov after his return from Berlin became involved in this propaganda effort aimed at Weimar Germany, both contributing material to such journals as *A-I-Z* and *SSSR na stroike* and vetting material submitted to them.[84]

The new prominence of photography and the illustrated journal in the struggle for Soviet dominance had repercussions beyond its proselytizing intent. In the Soviet Union at this time, there were fierce debates in all branches of the arts about the kind of representation that was appropriate for a singularly Soviet culture. In photography a significant shift in the official position on this actually came as fallout from the propaganda effort in Germany.

Propaganda for External Consumption Becomes the New Model for Internal Consumption

In the history of Soviet photography an important moment, associated with Tretiakov, was the appearance in *A-I-Z* no. 38 (late September) 1931 of the photo essay "24 Hours in the Life of a Moscow Worker Family," based on an actual family, the Filippovs. Allegedly, this series was taken at the request of the "Society of Friends of the USSR" in Austria, who, inspired by Tretiakov's visit to Vienna, approached the newly formed Soiuzfoto for this kind of documentation on Soviet workers.[85] In response, in one of the first tasks undertaken by Soiuzfoto, a brigade was dispatched to the Filippovs comprising one journalist, Lev Mezhericher (somewhat of a disciple of Tretiakov), and two prominent photographers, Maks Al'pert, and Arkady Shaikhet (from Koltsov's *Ogonëk*).[86] The photographs, allegedly shot following the same principles that Tretiakov adopted for his collective farm photography, were then exhibited in Austria by the Society, and a selection printed in *A-I-Z*.[87]

The Filippovs were a poster family for the good life the Soviet Union offered its workers. Comprising husband, wife, three sons, and two daughters, the family were all workers, except one school-age son and his mother, who had left work for home duties, and they were all simultaneously furthering themselves through study. They had previously lived in a dilapidated wooden building but two years ago had been assigned an apartment in a brand-new complex of sixteen buildings that included a club, a crèche, a nursery school, a communal laundry, and a department store.[88]

The photo series published in *A-I-Z* comprises fifty-two photos, including the shot on the cover. It opens with four panoramic shots, taken at dawn, of the street in Moscow where the Filippovs live, followed by a contrasting shot of their old house. The rest of the photographs show their lives over the course of a single day, starting with the family all taking tea together in the early morning, continuing through their individual domestic and work lives, and culminating in their leisure activities in the evening at Gorky Park.[89]

The Filippov issue of *A-I-Z* was a great success and was soon sold out and given a second printing. Readers were struck by the implied contrast between the West, where so many were unemployed, and the Filippov family, in which everyone of working age except the mother had a job. The Filippovs were inundated by letters from workers in Europe and America asking about their lives and the lot of workers in the Soviet Union. Encouraged by the series' popularity, *A-I-Z* published an analogous photo series in no. 48 of 1931, this time on the German family of a Berlin concrete worker, Furnes; he sent a copy of the issue to the Filippovs. Then, for the May celebrations the following year, a meeting was arranged between the sons of the two families in the Moscow Press House, and photos of the event were published widely in the Soviet Union and Germany.[90]

German Social Democrats clearly felt threatened by this success of their rivals, the Communists, and in several broadsheets and their journal *Reichsbanner Illustrierte Zeitung* pronounced the Filippov photo series a "fake," warning that the photos could not be trusted.[91] On October 15, 1931, a delegation of Social Democrat workers arrived in Moscow determined to expose the hoax. They demanded to be taken to the Filippovs, and the next day they inspected both the factory and the apartment, where they allegedly confirmed that everything in the article was true.[92]

Thus, the Filippov issue of *A-I-Z* provided a propaganda coup for the Soviet Union. On October 24, *Pravda* published a long unsigned article that describes the series and its successes, crowing over the gaffe of the Social Democrats and quoting with relish from the many letters sent to the Filippovs to ask if the photos were genuine. The article concludes that the series shows the "right way" for Soviet photography and "the task of Soviet photography is to show and tell the entire world the concrete victories of socialism."[93] Theoreticians of Soviet photography capitalized on this authoritative endorsement and used it as their cue to declare that the Filippov series should, as Mezhericher urged, "be the starting point" for shifting Soviet photographic practice to a new "basic method" involving "documentary depiction based on serial development of the subject represented, linked to an appropriate text."[94] The authoritative account of this was Tretiakov's article "From the Photo Series to Long Term Photo Observation," published in *Proletarskoe foto* (1931 no. 4, December), where he also provides a critique of the main photographic trends to date, the individual shot and the portrait.[95] As he also insisted in his lecture "The Writer and the Socialist Village," that photography should "get rid of the old idealist fairy tale about the face being a mirror of the soul"—get rid of static portraiture.[96]

Thus a new program was established for Soviet photography, a program whose prototype was Soviet material published in a German magazine.

The Filippov series was shot in July 1931, really on the cusp of major shifts in Soviet policy that seriously affected culture and will be the subject of my next chapter. By 1931 the utopian tide of the Plan years had reached its high point and begun to retreat. The retreat was sounded from the highest quarters. In a speech of July 1931 to Soviet managers, Stalin proposed a highly differentiated system of wage payment that discriminated against the unskilled worker and a change of policy toward the old professional intelligentsia—a change from a policy of "rout" to one of "encouragement and concern."[97] Among other things, authoritative voices began to lament the fact that the age's obsession with technology, statistics, and immediate practical needs had crowded out that higher and more enduring value, ideology.

This speech did not just signal an end to industrial fetishism in favor of a focus on ideology. The gulf between "producers" and "authors" that the cultural revolution sought to bridge now widened once more. A new concern for expertise also entailed a demand for quality, and hierarchies returned in most aspects of culture, including a hierarchy in human anthropology: "Show the Country Its Heroes!" was the new demand for culture. In time, the heroes favored for representation became not just award-winning workers (like the Filippovs) but Party leaders and military commanders. Similarly, as expertise came back into fashion, the worker correspondent and worker cameraman were no longer in fashion.

But the Berlin/Moscow purview of debate had not gone out of fashion. The extent to which major policy shifts were still articulated within it can be seen in one of the most authoritative pronouncements of the year, one made by Stalin in a letter published in *Proletarskaia revoliutsiia* in December 1931.[98] This letter was occasioned by an article in the journal's sixth number in 1930 by A. G. Slutsky, arguing that Lenin did not pay enough attention before the Great War to the dangers of centrism in the German and other Social Democrat parties. Stalin in his letter expresses outrage that anyone could so much as "raise the issue of Lenin's Bolshevism as a subject for discussion." He is also extremely offended by Slutsky's suggesting that not enough official documents have as yet come to light that "bear witness to Lenin's (the Bolsheviks') decisive and uncompromising struggle against centrism." Even if more documents were found, Stalin argues, "does this mean that the presence of what are mere

paper documents could be sufficient to demonstrate the truly revolutionary quality and the truly uncompromising stance of the Bolsheviks with
regard to centrism? Who, besides hopeless bureaucrats [later he added
"archive rats"], would rely on mere paper documents" to judge "parties
and their leaders"?[99]

There were obvious repercussions for the cult of factography of this
"signal" publication by Stalin. His "letter" soon acquired the status of
writ as it was discussed and cited ad nauseam in newspapers and journals
in 1932, the very year when the Writers Union was abolished and socialist
realism introduced (in Germany it was promoted by the local Comintern
leader, Georgi Dimitrov). The letter to *Proletarian Revolution* was Stalin's manifesto. In it he effectively insisted that Lenin was not to be regarded as only a historical figure but more as a world-historical actor
fulfilling a role. Hence the function "Lenin" must be distinguished from
any actual, factually observable individual. There is a higher order truth
than what mere "facts" can grasp. In actuality, representing "the truth"
had always been problematical in trying to reconcile factography with
militant Bolshevism, even for Tretiakov. In advocating a purely fact-based
art, he had cautioned that some facts are not equal to others and that photographers and writers should be wary of presenting facts that harm the
Soviet cause.[100] Now, however, emphasis on facts was discredited. The
grand scheme was to be privileged over the historical detail, and the Party
leader over the actualities of his biography.

Stalin's article also implicitly underwrote an important attack on the
avant-garde by Georgy Lukács, delivered in Germany in its wake. During
his first Moscow period of 1929–1931, Lukács had worked in the Marx-
Engels-Lenin Institute (IMEL) on the Marx Nachlass, and particularly
on Marx's *Economic and Philosophic Manuscripts* of 1844. He had been
reassigned by the Comintern to Berlin in July 1931 after the director of
IMEL, David Riazanov, was dismissed. In Berlin, Lukács became active
in BPRS, where he was expected to counteract ultraleftist trends. This he
effected partly by teaching in the party's workers' academy and partly
with his contributions to the BPRS journal *Linkskurve* (1929–1932).[101]
Lukács's article "Reportage or Portrayal," published there in July 1932,
was a polemic against the German leftist writer Ernst Ottwalt and his recent novel *Denn sie wissen was sie tun* (For they know what they do).[102]

This novel presents actual law cases, included to highlight the contradictory nature of Weimar justice, and in his attack Lukács is effectively polemicizing with factography. In so doing, he does not reject realistic detail completely. On the contrary, he points out that it is essential to literature and that without that particularity, any literary work will be merely mechanical and abstract.[103]

Lukács's attack on Ottwalt was explicitly directed not just at him but also, and no doubt in intention principally, at a number of leading leftist experimental writers from different countries, and especially Brecht (an associate of Ottwalt), Tretiakov, and Upton Sinclair. Tretiakov was the most vehemently supportive of Ottwalt and his method, and he gave space in *Internatsional'naia literatura* to both the Lukács article and a response by Ottwalt, as well as Ottwalt's novel.[104] Here we see an early round in the developing confrontation between Lukács (and others) and the transnational leftist avant-garde, a confrontation that was to come to a head in 1936–1938 in the Expressionism debate (see Chapter 6), though in this instance Ottwalt's book had been favorably reviewed in the Soviet press until this article was published.[105] Even at a meeting of December 25, 1932, authoritative Soviet writers deemed the Lukács article too harsh, but in time his position was to prevail.[106]

In this article Lukács, in attacking Ottwalt for his "fetishization" of facts, implicitly draws authority from Stalin's recent "letter." The truly great writer, he suggests, ipso facto does not deal in paltry facts but "portrays"; he brings out the *general* in the *particular* material he deploys. Furthermore, and here Lukács has changed his position from *History and Class Consciousness* of 1923, the individual detail or fact must be subordinated to the overriding whole of any text, its defining aspect.[107] Lukács's general premise, that plot governs all and fact is to be subordinated to it, could be seen as translating Stalin's overall message into the specific context of literature (though it could also be associated with a much earlier theoretician, Aristotle).

This privileging of the general over the particular or contingent, of a character or person's role over historical detail or individual psychology, was to be defining for Stalinist culture. But the question arises: who determines what is particular, mere detail, and what is subordinated to an overriding whole, a question not just of aesthetic strategy but also of authority? Is it the "author" or some "compiler" who puts others' material together (as was the case when a group of writers, including Viktor Shklovsky, put together a book of "biographies" of convicts who were "regenerated" through their forced labor on the Belomor Canal)?[108]

Perhaps it is no accident that in Dziga Vertov's film *The Man with a Movie Camera* (Chelovek s kinoapparatom, 1929) the editing machine—that which gives the disparate shots a sequence—is the centerpiece of the film. The editing machine is also depicted in such a way that it recapitulates the actions of the main industrial machinery shown, of driving axles and all those bobbins revolving around a central pole that coordinates the revolutions of its parts, an image that could be seen as standing for the organization of the state: art, production, and the regime are in sync. Yet the editing machine does not, like the axle, run by itself as long as it is turned on. It takes an editor to "man" it (here actually a woman, his wife, Elizaveta Svilova). But in Vertov's film the editor is complemented by the cameraman, who is shown performing all sorts of stunts to get his shots, most of them parodies of clichés from the popular American action film of the silent era—such as lying on the tracks (here to shoot film) as the train approaches. But in the shift of 1931, the machine became less viable as the dominant metaphor for the state. The capital city was fast becoming the new symbolic equivalent of the nation's driving axle.

Moscow-Berlin: A Tale of Two Cities

The Filippov series and its counterpart, the Furnes series, featured worker families not from the major industrial cities but from their respective capital cities. The pointed contrast between them is brought out in the title of a book brought out by Partizdat, the Party press, *Two Families—Two Worlds* (Dve sem'—dva mira), which contains letters they received. The choice of home city for the emblematic families was a sign of a shift. Moscow, the capital city and hometown of the Filippovs, stood for Soviet Russia, a role it was to play more and more in the 1930s.

Part of the claim of Moscow (the Soviet Union) to the right to lead the world was that it had solved the problems of the modern city in the industrial age (unemployment, meaningful leisure, sexual relations, etc.). Brecht's film *Kuhle Wampe* (1932), subtitled *To Whom Does the World*

Belong, which he scripted together with Ottwalt and which is set in Berlin and Kuhle Wampe, a tent camp of the unemployed on Berlin's outskirts, shows how the failures and perils of the modern capitalist city can be overcome by everyone joining the Soviet-modeled cultural effort.[109] Brecht brought this new film with him during his visit to Moscow of 1932, and it actually premiered there before Berlin (where it was banned),[110] a chance situation but one that has its own logic, in that the plot of *Kuhle Wampe* essentially brings its central characters to "Moscow" while staying within Berlin. If in Brecht's *Measures Taken* crossing the border into China meant for the agitators and the young comrade extreme erasure of the self, in *Kuhle Wampe* we find the opposite: the workers find fulfillment and solve the problems in their private lives by joining Communist agitational work. This trajectory is, as with the Filippovs and Furneses, represented in one family.

Much of *Kuhle Wampe* depicts the hopelessness of the capitalist city, exacerbated by the rampant unemployment. In the opening scenes it tracks a large group of the jobless, who cycle frantically over Berlin from factory to factory in fruitless pursuit of work. But then the film follows one of them, previously undifferentiated from the group, as he goes home, suffers recriminations from his father for still not finding work, and commits suicide. The rest of the film chronicles the struggle of other family members, especially his sister and father, who are likewise unemployed. The situation becomes dire when the sister becomes pregnant and her lover is reluctant to marry her (raising the issue of illegal abortion, then one of the causes taken up by German Communists, especially Friedrich Wolf, the doctor activist and author of *Tai Yang Awakens*). But then the lover, too, loses his job. Still, the clouds lift late in the film as the pair join the happy, Moscow-oriented Communist cultural effort, making agitational posters, enjoying skits, and participating in Communist sports competitions. At the end, as the contented sportsmen return by train to Berlin from the sport grounds, they debate the bourgeois in their rail carriage. This would seem to be a version of a common feature from Soviet production novels of this time, the debate between representatives of the two systems, ending in either the suicide or the conversion of the Westerner.[111] But in *Kuhle Wampe* we have a broader context, not just the industrial site but the greater world: they are arguing about the practice in

Brazil of dumping coffee to raise its price, benefiting the greedy capitalists but not the little man, producer or consumer.

Kuhle Wampe, then, seems to present a Soviet formula for triumph
over the darkness of the Depression-era capitalist city in a communistic
collective but in the end steps back from its orientation around Soviet-
inspired measures, opening up the purview with a discussion. In a different way, in *Measures Taken* Brecht and Eisler also stepped back, as it
were, as they undermined its monologic character with a parodic musical
score and an insistence that it was an unfinished text, to be subject to recurrent discussion and revisions. The "mask" never quite fit: Brecht recalled that when he came to Moscow in 1932, *Kuhle Wampe* in hand, and
was introduced to Moscow's achievements by Tretiakov, he could not
share his friend's rapture. Similarly, Richter and Piscator came to Russia
full of enthusiasm for contributing theater and films to the cause (at one
point Piscator reported he was going to make a sound film there in four
languages). And though Piscator's film *The Revolt of the Fishermen* (Aufstand der Fischer von Santa Barbara), filmed between 1932 and 1934, was
one of the few Soviet-German film projects to see completion, it was
butchered by authorities and ended up dull and disappointing. In the
end both fled, leaving everything behind, afraid of the secret police.[112]
They were caught between the Bolshevik experiment, which they could
not join completely, and the rise of the Nazis in their homeland. Rather
than make that "leap," they ended up stateless, as did Benjamin.

Leftist intellectuals, however, even as they sought to perfect the modern city, were often attracted by the allure of its dark underbelly.[113] At this
time Erenburg produced *Moi Parizh* (My Paris, 1933), a book illustrated
by his photos taken with a Leica with typographic treatment by Lissitzky,
which presents itself as an exposé of the French capital, an "unmasking,"
that abjures its tourist spots and smart districts as subject matter and
shows instead its down and out, its derelict areas. Yet here the lines are
blurred between exposé of the ills of the capitalist city, voyeurism, and the
Romantic cult of the bohemian. The account of Paris's downtrodden returns again and again to the *pissoir,* the prostitute, and the inhabitants'
mating habits. Erenburg relates how for the book he would sneak a snap-
shot of lovers by ostensibly pointing his camera at something else but
taking advantage of the side aperture of the Leica.[114]

Moi Parizh was not well received by Soviet critics, hardly surprising in the land where, as Benjamin observes in the Moscow diary, sex is the human element the Soviets leave out of their purview.[115] The puritanical Tretiakov published in *Prozhektor*, just a few issues after an extract from *Moi Parizh* appeared there, a photo essay on Hamburg in which he decries the capitalist tourists as "flaneurs" drawn to the illicit delights of the "street-prostitute," the Reperbahn.[116] But at this time in the Soviet Union attention was focused on a different version of the city, on building modern, ordered cities to adorn the new colossi of industrialization. Several leading avant-garde architects from Germany made pilgrimages to view the achievements of the Soviet urbanization projects, often pitching in with their own designs (the depression had set back the new architecture in the West). Ernst May, designer of the "new Frankfurt," a famous experiment in urban planning, took his "May Brigade" of architects to Soviet Russia in 1930. They stayed until 1933, first touring such industrial cities as Magnitogorsk, whereupon May declared that there is "no comparison in history" to what the Soviets were doing with their architecture; "the new buildings transform man" and "woman is no longer a servant to her husband."[117] Then, in a whirlwind of activity, they designed twenty Soviet industrial cities, including Magnitogorsk itself. The "May Brigade" was soon followed by the "Bauhaus Brigade" under its former director, Hannes Meyer, and by Bruno Taut, who worked up a critique of the planning of Moscow and in 1932 designed large office buildings for the city administration.[118]

The most famous architect to visit Moscow was Le Corbusier (pseudonym of Charles-Édouard Jeanneret), the guru of what was later called the International style, a movement these German architects largely followed. Le Corbusier, like most Constructivists, was infatuated with the new-age machine, which was, in the words of Margaret Bourke-White in her book on Soviet Russia, "never designed to be beautiful. It has a symmetry and a force because it has no decoration. . . . Not a line is wasted. Every curve of the machine, every attribute of the worker has an element of simplicity, a vital beauty."[119] Le Corbusier's own architecture was designed to meet that sort of description: its walls absolutely bare and spare, admitting only elongated gashes of glass for windows to an otherwise unbroken surface of what he pronounced, in *Towards a New Architecture* (Vers une Architecture, 1923), "a machine for living."[120]

Le Corbusier's "engineer's aesthetic"[121] was well known in Russia. He had outlined his ideas in a series of articles he published in his journal *L'Esprit nouveau* (The new spirit, 1920–1925) and other writings, many of which were published in Russian translation. Le Corbusier himself came to Moscow in the late 1920s and between 1930 and 1933 drew up designs for the capital that would make it the antithesis of the peasant Moscow that Benjamin wrote of in his diary. All of Moscow was to be torn down, and a new city of towering buildings, organized on a grid slashed diagonally by great arterial roads, would arise phoenix-like in its place.[122] In machine-age Moscow "not a line [would be] wasted," and there would be "no decoration." To have created, as Le Corbusier stipulated, a tabula rasa in order to realize a "vital," new capital would have been the "measures taken." Just as, in Brecht's play, the features of the young comrade were to have been erased in the lime pit to ensure the Communist revolution, so the "face" of Moscow was to have been erased to purify the city. The haunts of the down and out would be obliterated.

Le Corbusier's design would eradicate all particularity, all that was singular. But in fact Le Corbusier stipulated that the Kremlin, St. Basil's, the Bolshoi, the Lenin mausoleum, and a few religious buildings were to be kept, concessions to Russian specificity.[123] Keeping these Moscow landmarks, a lapse on Le Corbusier's part, was ironically to anticipate the cultural turn of the 1930s, when the Kremlin had a special relationship to culture.

As recently as 1929 in Vertov's *Man with a Movie Camera*, a composite version of the Soviet city had sufficed. Now Moscow, one of the several cities used in that composite, was not to be alloyed, because it had assumed a central role in the national narrative. In 1931, just after Tretiakov returned from Berlin, plans were announced to rebuild the capital. As we shall see in the next chapter, the "new" capital city would be neither Benjamin's village nor a "machine for living" but the centerpiece of an aesthetic state.

CHAPTER 2

Moscow, the Lettered City

STREET NAMES ARE OFTEN arbitrary, banal, or even ridiculous, but the way streets in the center of a city are named can be indicators of what the city fathers had been trying to claim as its identity. In the Soviet Union, where everything was closely coded, this was particularly so. Under Stalin, the center of Moscow for ordinary citizens became the point at which the main street, which had been *re*named Gorky Street, intersected with another central artery that had been *re*named Marx Prospect. The very geography of the streets as it were, proclaimed a marriage between literature and ideology, between art and politics. Several adjoining and neighboring streets and squares in central Moscow were also renamed for writers, to become as it were, attendants at this union; the (renamed) Belinsky, Ogarev, and Stankevich Streets ran into Gorky Street as it progressed away from Marx Prospect; Gorky Street was flanked on either side by the parallel Herzen and Pushkin streets; and two of the main squares that punctuate Gorky street at the city's center were renamed Mayakovsky Square and Pushkin Square (the only other square had been renamed Soviet Square already in 1918). This configuration did not emerge in a single flurry of renaming. Initially, during the Civil War (around 1920 or possibly before), some of the central streets had been renamed after writers in the radical tradition, such as Herzen and Belinsky.[1]

But in the 1930s when authorities started to rename points on the central artery, Tverskaia, they called them after literary figures, as distinct from, as before, social activists who were also writers: the two squares that together with Soviet Square punctuated Tverskaia at Moscow's center, Pushkin Square and Mayakovsky Square, were so named in 1931 and 1935, respectively, and Tverskaia became Gorky Street in 1933 (in the post-Soviet period, it reverted to Tverskaia).[2]

What I have read into these street patterns might seem a banality. Of course literature was tied to politics in the Stalin period. We have always known that. Here, however, I am suggesting a marriage rather than a subjugation (though, as we know, marriages are not always between equal partners). During the 1930s, a close symbiotic relationship between literature and politics was at the heart of official culture.

A flurry of erecting new statues to literary figures and countless other such details from the capital's history in the thirties bespeak the closeness of literature and politics.[3] For example, the year 1937 was dominated in terms of public celebration by two anniversaries, the centennial of Pushkin's death and the twentieth anniversary of the Bolshevik Revolution. The interconnectedness of the two can be seen in the fact that the leaders of the city government, as they looked for appropriate ways to celebrate twenty years of revolution, resolved that by the November anniversary they would demolish Strastnoi Monastery, which stood on Pushkin Square and after which the square had previously been named. Now the monastery was to go, "leaving not a trace." They also resolved to move the statue of Pushkin to a more central position on the square.[4]

This relatively minor detail from the year 1937 throws into relief the close relationship not just between literature and politics but also between literature and architecture, both of which were privileged occupations at this time. In each of these two fields, there was a particular project that dominated activity during the thirties. These two projects ran virtually in tandem, hitched together by the national master narrative.

In literature, the project was the creation of socialist realism as a tradition centered around a biographical narrative. In April 1932 the Writers Union was formed, and in May of that year the term "socialist realism" was introduced as the name of a new Soviet literature. A year earlier, Gorky had been essentially imported back from the West and would serve as titular head of the Writers Union and godfather of socialist realism (the term was allegedly conceived at a meeting in his apartment, and he gave one of the two canonical speeches on socialist realism at the First Writers Congress in 1934).[5] Hence when Moscow's main street was renamed in his honor, this gesture proclaimed the centrality of socialist realism in Soviet political culture.

In architecture, *the* project of this time was the creation of a new "socialist city" centered around the remodeling of the capital city, Moscow. In June 1931, at a plenum of the Communist Party's Central Committee, a resolution was passed providing guidelines for a new project for rebuilding Moscow. Work on it began soon, though it was not until 1935 that a systematic plan for a "new Moscow" was completed and, on July 10, was promulgated in a joint decree of the Party's Central Committee and the government's Council of Ministers (Sovnarkom), "On the General Plan for the Reconstruction of the City of Moscow." This decree largely reiterated the same guiding principles and endorsed the same major projects as had the 1931 resolution but added more specifics, such as target dates for completing particular projects. The Union of Soviet Architects was formed in 1932, in the wake of the formation of the Writers Union, but it did not hold its first congress until 1937. In the interim, in effect, the plans for a reconstructed new Moscow functioned as the best practical guide to what socialist realism might mean in architecture. Plans for reconstructing other major Soviet cities were announced as well, the most prominent of these being the plan to reconstruct Leningrad, which also got its General Plan in 1935. However, Moscow was given the lion's share of the funding. It was the nation's capital.

Thus Gorky Street was so named at a particular historical moment (1933) when those in authority in politics and literature not only were in the process of formulating what socialist realism was—that is, providing guidelines that would be announced with great fanfare at the First Congress of the Writers Union the following year—but also, as part of the project launched in 1931 for reconstructing Moscow, were planning to straighten and broaden Gorky Street itself and erect grand buildings to flank it. Another banner project for the "new Moscow" was a metro, which would use the intersection of Gorky Street and Marx Prospect as the hub of its radial network. Gorky Street itself provided the western

axis of the "new Moscow," running almost to the Kremlin. At its down-
town end it was, according to the plans, to be intersected by "Alleia Il'icha
[Lenin]," a new arterial north-south axis. In other words, ideology, architecture (or urban design), and literature all came together in the one
place. Actually, the intention of the designers had been to recenter Moscow: to place as the centerpoint of Alleia Il'icha a massive structure, the
Palace of Soviets (see Figure 3, page 216), which was to be a meeting place
for national assemblies, the headquarters for various bureaucratic bodies,
and a place of assembly for the masses, who would attend ritual and agitational events in its great hall.

When the Palace of Soviets was being designed as the center of Moscow and the arts corralled into a single creative union for each field, Moscow herself was becoming the primus inter pares of Soviet cities. Soviet
culture and geography were being centralized to accord with the centralized state. The Party leadership began to play a much more active role in
cultural matters, particularly the Politburo (Political Bureau) a select
body comprising the top leaders that occupied the highest level of the
hierarchy of power in the nation, other than that occupied by Stalin personally. Bodies of the Party's Central Committee were also involved in
legislating on cultural matters: its Secretariat, its Orgburo (Organizational Bureau), and the apparatus of its various departments, such as Culture and Propaganda (Kul'tprop). Of these various bodies, however, the
Politburo was the preeminent decision maker in the cultural sphere.[6]

What is truly extraordinary is that the heads of state of a country that
boasted of being the largest in area and was for much of this period undergoing rapid modernization and a buildup of its military coupled with
a protracted socio-politico-economic revolution, spent so much of their
time on cultural matters. In the thirties, culture was *always* in the purview
of the Soviet leadership, and *especially* of Stalin. When the Politburo divided up oversight of the various branches of government, that busy head
of state took the area of culture for himself. Even in the most critical moments of inner Party struggle or of the terror or of war, not only did the
routine apparatus of control over cultural matters function, but decisions
were taken at the highest levels on cultural issues of a fairly minor order.

Why so much attention to culture? Arguably, this was not just a matter
of gratuitous repression or of imposing the leadership's own tastes on an

entire nation's culture (though both were true). It was a larger phenomenon than that. Culture was important to the political hierarchy because it
played a central role in articulating the new belief system. The Soviet
state claimed to have dispensed with religion, hence culture replaced
many of religion's former functions, as is illustrated in the tearing down of
a monastery to create a purified Pushkin Square, giving prominence to
Pushkin's statue.

In fulfilling culture's sacral function, literature played the central role.
Pierre Bourdieu and others have written of literature as a form of "cultural capital." In the postcapitalist world of the Soviet 1930s, this capital
was valuable as a legitimizing asset, a reason in itself for the ubiquitous,
ritual incantations that one finds in Stalinist sources of lists of great writers or great books.

Literature was elevated to enjoy a special status in the thirties because
it represented the most eloquent and elaborated version of the written
word. There is an ancient prejudice that writing is true in a way that
speaking is not. Although Plato (and many subsequent philosophers) was
himself opposed to writing and preferred oral forms, deeming them more
direct forms of expression and hence closer to the truth, writing has many
attributes of the Platonic Idea. It lasts in time as spoken speech does not,
claiming a permanence, a kind of autonomy from the material world, that
imitates eternity and appears free from the vicissitudes and metamorphoses of history. The emphasis on letters also has to do with permanence,
rationalization, and consolidation. Writing is a way to give governance to
speech. Behind this prejudice is the view that there is a hidden order in
speech that becomes manifest in writing. And in Stalinist Russia writing
emerged as the highest occupation because it was felt that it would reveal
the truth of the order to be found in Bolshevik experience, the reason
behind it.

An especially exalted role in the Soviet political hierarchy was given to
Gorky, who was made the first secretary of the Writers Union after it was
formed in 1932, in other words, titular head of Soviet literature. When
Gorky died in 1936 Molotov, the spokesman for the Politburo, declared at
the memorial meeting: "after Lenin, the loss of Gorky is the greatest loss
for our country, and for mankind."[7] Since other Bolshevik leaders had
died earlier in the Soviet period, most notably Sergei Kirov, this suggests

that Gorky enjoyed an elevated status, above that of the members of the Politburo and just below Lenin (and Stalin). They, like him, were writers; the others were largely only implementers.

As literature emerged as primus inter pares in every sphere of the arts, there was a campaign for "literaturization." In film, for example, it was announced that no longer were scripts to be written by the director or some minor writer. Instead, leading writers were assigned to the major film directors for particular film scripts.[8] In this way, such famous Moscow writers of the 1920s as Isaak Babel and Yury Olesha spent much of the 1930s writing commissioned film scripts. Eisenstein, for his major film projects of the decade, was assigned successively the former RAPP leader Aleksandr Fadeev (for *Moscow in Time*), Babel (for *Bezhin Meadow*), and Petr Pavlenko (for *Alexander Nevsky*).[9]

Even such unlikely genres as press photos were now discussed in terms of the imperative to get closer to literature. Critics announced that "the catalogue character" of photographic practice had to go and no longer should newspapers simply publish photos with brief identifying descriptions below. Magazines such as *SSSR na stroike,* which had initially used only the curtest of captions, now often provided extended narratives for their photos. In addition, the one-day photo series promoted by Tretiakov in his 1931 essay "From the Photo Series to Long Term Photo Observation" (see Chapter 1) was modified so as to take its subject over a long stretch of time, to show the process of transformation in a human subject.[10] Critics, meanwhile, scrambled to find literary equivalents to the photo series, insisting that it should present an organically unified story *(rasskaz);* have a plot, which would enable it to present causes, establish links and illustrate the dialectic at work—or that "each photo should be set up like a line in a poem."[11] In addition, as a consequence of this new policy, writers began to assume priority over the photographers, and actual writers began to head the shooting teams. An analogous change took place in literature, where the short journalistic genres that Tretiakov and the *faktoviki* had advocated recently were sidelined in favor of the novel, a shift effectively endorsed by Tretiakov himself.[12]

The cult of literature was far from exclusive to the Bolsheviks. If anything, dissident intellectuals were more messianic. Particularly striking is the semireligious awe for literature in the first volume of Evgenia

Ginzburg's memoir, *Journey into the Whirlwind* (Krutoi marshrut), about her arrest in 1937, the height of the purges, and her consignment to the camps. Ginzburg and her fellow inmates, like Christians in the catacombs, sustain themselves throughout the harrowing ordeal by recalling lines from Pushkin and recording them on anything they can (scraps of paper, walls). In a bleak moment she contemplates suicide but is brought to her senses by the thought that "tomorrow Tolstoy and Blok, Stendhal and Balzac will come to me [from the prison library]. And you thought of death, you idiot."[13]

Architecture, though it enjoyed less of this aura, also played a central role in Stalinist political culture. While the practical advantages of reordering and modernizing the capital city were no doubt a factor in launching the new project for rebuilding Moscow, the symbolic function of its "transformation" was paramount. In 1931, even before plans were announced for reconstructing Moscow, architecture provided the dominant tropes in official speeches and *Pravda* editorials for representing the stage reached in the progress toward Communism. As such texts characteristically went, with the revolution in 1917 the leadership had cleared away the old; during the 1920s, and particularly with industrialization and collectivization during the First Five-Year Plan, the state had built the "foundation" of the new society; and now it was time to erect the socialist "building" *(zdanie)*.[14] Here official spokesmen were drawing on the metaphoric use of architecture in *The German Ideology* (1845–1846), where Marx and Engels used a figure from building, the relationship between the base and the superstructure, as a model for conceiving the relationship between all elements of society. In addition, the new emphasis in Party rhetoric on "building" signaled that the country had gone beyond the iconoclastic phase of the cultural revolution.

Party leaders, in expanding on the Marxist trope, declared that it was time to rebuild Moscow as the "model" for proletarians and Communists throughout the world, who would be inspired to follow it. The redesigned Moscow was to be a dazzling capital whose glory reflected on the regime that erected it, and was to provide the core of its symbolic system, an exemplum for the new (Stalinist) sociopolitical and cultural order. Symptomatically, starting in 1933, on the eve of the great revolutionary holidays, May Day and November 7, designs for the "new Moscow" were showcased in the windows of lower Gorky Street, and citizens were expected to pay obeisance by filing past to view them.[15] When, in 1934, a new building by the leading architect Ivan Zholtovsky, modeled on a Palladian palazzo, was promoted as a paradigm for the new architecture, crowds marching to the Red Square for the revolutionary anniversary paused in their procession to hail it before moving on.[16]

At the center of Stalinist culture, then, was a close nexus of power involving architecture, literature, and the leadership. Of the two branches of the arts, literature was the dominant one, but it was closely tied to architecture. Given this nexus, a particularly appropriate, if unexpected, paradigm for the rebuilding of Moscow could be the account given by Angel Rama in his book *The Lettered City* of the new cities of the Americas built by the colonizing Spanish and Portuguese in the sixteenth and seventeenth centuries. In designing these new cities of the Americas, the Renaissance ideal city was templated onto the American terrain without regard to local specificity, ensuring that the Renaissance city was, ironically, realized in a more perfect version on the other side of the Atlantic than was ever obtained in Europe itself.

What is most pertinent for the case of Stalinist Moscow in Rama's interpretation of this new city of the Americas, an aspect foregrounded in his title, is the crucial role played in its foundation and maintenance by a nexus of lettered culture, state power, and urban designers. Rama means by lettered culture a culture of the *letrados,* or lettered classes, in other words, not just that of the literati but also that of the planners and the professionals who deal in edicts, memoranda, reports, and notarial work, all the official correspondence that held the empire together. In Rama's account, in seeking to impose order on their vast empires, they created urban networks as their political and ideological centers, and standardized their cities' geometrical layout by detailed *written* instructions. Writing consolidated the political order by giving it cultural expression, but even antiestablishment intellectual movements that emerged later in Latin America articulated their positions within the established framework of this "lettered culture."[17]

Clearly, the analogy with the Latin American colonial city is not watertight. The rebuilt Moscow was not to be a purely Renaissance city; although the styles and models of the Renaissance were a major referent, the architecture was somewhat eclectic, as will be discussed below. In addition, the "new Moscow" was not to be created ex nihilo in a far-flung colonial outpost or "virgin" periphery but from a city that had evolved over the centuries from a medieval settlement founded in 1147. Moreover, even in the most ambitious plans of the thirties, the capital was to be only partially reconstructed.

The parallel I am drawing with colonial Latin America is useful, however, in that it draws attention to the element of internal colonization in the Soviet regime's imposition of its own "civilization" on what it saw as a kingdom of darkness. The rebuilding of Moscow became the poster act for this process. The fact that thereby the regime was supplanting a culture of no small achievement became a source of ambiguity surrounding the reconstruction of the ancient capital, and of anxiety. In the rebuilding of Moscow, the aim of establishing the regime's legitimacy was a stronger motive than was the case when the Spanish colonizers designed their Latin American cities.

In a decade when the Soviet leadership sought to legitimize and codify its regime, written texts assumed enormous significance. Belles letters were far from the only written form given a special status in the culture of the 1930s. That decade began with a flurry of publication of texts by Marx and Engels, many of them for the first time, in authoritative translations and with commentaries by scholars from the Marx-Engels-Lenin Institute (*The German Ideology,* which appeared in 1932, among the first). *Pravda* gave prominence to these new publications and under the rubric "In IMEL" (i.e., the Institute) recurrently reported on the latest titles; 1933, the year Gorky Street was renamed, was also the fiftieth anniversary of Marx's death and a high point for these publications.[18] In the early thirties, the Soviet Union was appropriating Marx for itself (having spent a great deal of foreign currency on obtaining photocopies of the original manuscripts in the 1920s) and claiming for Moscow the role of center of Marxist scholarship. Thus, while these publications were in part acts of genuine scholarship—the fruit of the efforts of IMEL, whose mandate it was to do such work—they were also used to provide weapons from the canonical texts against opponents in the Communist movement, both within the country (such as Trotskyites) and abroad (such as the German Social Democrats and the Second International). In the Party purge of

1933 and especially in the next purge of 1936, in contrast to the earlier one of 1929, a poor knowledge of Marxist texts became a criterion for expulsion, and many were expelled on those grounds.[19]

Written texts were also the greatest preoccupation of the Politburo and of Central Committee bodies with oversight on cultural matters such as the Orgburo and Kul'tprop. In the early years (1932–1934) in their deliberations on culture, all the energy in went into literature. After the Writers Union Congress (1934), when socialist realism was defined officially, and as the decade progressed, Stalin and the Politburo became more and more involved as arbiters of the content of works in other media—plays, operas, films, and paintings—as well as books. Almost invariably, it was the script—the text—of these works that was subject to the authorities' regulation.[20]

In general, the written word *(pismennost')*, as distinct from the oral or especially the vernacular, was held in particular awe. Among the many kinds of writing that played a major symbolic role, newsprint was prominent, especially *Pravda,* where Stalin's speeches and other such authoritative texts were published. In fact in a Party decree of 1938 about the new primer, the *Short Course of Party History,* members were instructed to put less reliance on oral forms for disseminating ideology—they should only be "supplementary"—and more on the press.[21] Benedict Anderson and others have written about the central role of the newspaper in fostering a sense of national identity and in facilitating distinctly new, and profoundly secular, modes of apprehending time. *Pravda,* with its single edition circulating throughout the country, was critical in facilitating the process in the Soviet Union.[22] As if to confirm this, successive portraits of Stalin (1928, 1931, 1937) by Isaak Brodskii, who was virtually a court painter of the 1920s and 1930s, were apparently not complete without a copy of *Pravda* laid out on the desk before the gigantic torso and head that otherwise filled the canvas,[23] and in the thirties, political posters frequently included a cutting from an article clearly identified as from *Pravda.*

Stalin was himself particularly associated with texts. In the visual iconography he was rarely represented as speaking, perhaps because Stalin's word was so sacral that for the masses it was not to be relegated to mere oral form, which is always in danger of vernacularizing and particularizing (and as a Georgian, he spoke Russian with an accent). The decade was punctuated with the issuance of authoritative texts of which Stalin was either the alleged, or the rumored, author. The list includes his letter to *Proletarskaia revoliutsiia* of 1931 (discussed in chapter 1), several decrees about the writing of history, and the aforementioned *Short Course,* published in 1938, that served as the Soviet Union's "little red book" until after Stalin died in 1953.[24] Stalin was also credited with authoring the term "socialist realism" (hence, by implication, he was the author of its overall theory, regardless of actuality), and when in December 1936 a new constitution for the country was promulgated with much fanfare, Stalin was named its "author" (actually *tvorets,* or creator). Stalin, then, was a version of Moses, who commits the divine law to sacred tablets. Like Moses, he did not speak, as a rule, but dealt in written texts. Unlike Moses, he did not receive "the law" from a god. Rather, he uniquely had the ability to divine the essences, a reason in itself why he "authored" so many of the key texts of the decade; whether he actually authored them or not is in a sense irrelevant, because he was the ultimate "author" of anything deemed authoritative. Hence writing, which was prior to reading, was also higher in the hierarchy of value.

The biblical story of Moses articulates a hierarchical cosmology. Moses received the law (from God) on a mountain (Zion), then he descended and gave it to the people. Stalin's authority derived from more secular sources. Stalin's study in the Kremlin effectively functioned in the hagiography as the sacral space where he had access to higher forms. His writing officially (though often not actually) took place within the Kremlin, enclosed by walls, cut off. This separation facilitated its status as an ontologically different, autonomous space "not subject to flux," in itself a marker of the extent to which he did not operate within the tradition of the democratic leader.[25] This implicit cosmology of place corresponded to a temporal hierarchy: in film and painting, Stalin was represented as monument-like, either immobile or with a lumbering gait à la the commendatore of *Don Giovanni,* and this was implicitly contrasted with the quicker movements of those around him, a contrast that effectively represented the opposition between being and becoming.

In most official portraits of Stalin painted in this period, and in many of the political posters featuring him, he is shown with some form of writing, such as a shelf of books, or, ideally, is actually writing himself. Lenin, by contrast, a figure from the revolutionary-democratic phase, is generally depicted striding forward or delivering a speech. Even when Stalin was depicted on a podium, that is, outside the Kremlin, in profane space, he was usually not represented as speaking and is often shown handing a text to someone else who will deliver it (for example, in G. M. Shegal's frequently anthologized painting *Leader, Teacher and Friend* (Vozhd', uchitel', drug of 1937); alternatively, citizens are shown composing a text for him. Such a text effectively functioned as the link between the leader and the common man, who otherwise participated in a different temporality.[26] But both the temporal hierarchy and the spatial were affects of the basal hierarchy, a hierarchy in epistemology.

The hierarchical cosmology of the 1930s is generally seen as articulated vertically, but it was also articulated horizontally (actually, a superficial distinction). The horizontal hierarchy was organized in a series of concentric circles, somewhat like a national *matryoshka* doll: the outer rim was the country at large (the periphery), the first inner circle was Moscow, and then came the Kremlin. There was also an innermost inner, Stalin's study in the Kremlin. This pattern is not unlike the one Benedict Anderson describes in *Imagined Communities* for "kingship," which "organizes everything around a high center." As Anderson puts it, "its legitimacy derives from divinity, not from populations who, after all, are subjects, not citizens."[27]

Stalin is typically depicted in connection with texts rather than oratory because he is the *origin* of the *word*, the author of authors.[28] Were he to be at the podium addressing others in a fiery oration, he would take the form of the democratic leader who gains authority and legitimacy from the people. Stalin was not necessarily the origin of *all* words. He was the origin of the sacral word, of that word which is nonvernacular and nonephemeral. In the Bolshevik literature of the 1920s (especially in "proletarian" novels) one recurrently finds passages where a worker's unlettered utterances are proclaimed more authentic than the superficial, bookish polish of the educated, but this trend was largely reversed in the 1930s, with its mania for the written word.

In the iconography of Stalin, rather than the podium one finds more often a very spare setting comprising all or some of the following: a desk,

О каждом из нас заботится Сталин в Кремле

Figure 1. Viktor Ivanovich Govorkov, "Stalin in the Kremlin Cares for Every One of Us (O kazhdom iz nas zabotitsia Stalin v Kremle)," 1940. From the Russian State Library.

a map or other text (handwritten or printed), and the Kremlin. Consequently, I see as paradigmatic Viktor Govorkov's poster "Stalin in the Kremlin Cares for Every One of Us" (O kazhdom iz nas zabotitsia Stalin v Kremle) of 1940.[29]

In this simple, austere poster, Stalin is writing at a desk in the Kremlin with pen and inkwell. Next to him is a desk lamp, which suggests both the "lamp of Ilyich [Lenin]," a slogan of the electrification campaign in the 1920s, which rendered lamps both symbols and means of enlightenment and agitation, and the "green lamp," a common symbol of the intelligentsia. Thus this scene implicitly links politics and literature as writing. Through the window, a single tower of the Kremlin is seen, topped by a red star that shines in the Soviet night. This poster, then, provides a version of that cliché about Stalin as someone so devoted to the cares of the nation that he writes well into the night, often encapsulated as "the light in the window" (of the Kremlin). The poster purports to give the public a look into the other side of his window; showing how Stalin cares for "us" while "we" sleep, how he alone bears all "our" cares, as he "writes the nation."

The Kremlin was to have been supplanted by the Palace of Soviets as the center of Moscow, but it never got far beyond its foundations. Generally this failure to complete it is attributed to its being unfeasible from an engineering point of view and to progress being delayed by World War II, but one wonders whether it would ever have supplanted the Kremlin in the national spatial hierarchy.

In representations of Stalin one generally does not see the entire Kremlin, just a single tower, which virtually functions as his totem or some sort of symbolic double. This is particularly apparent in one of the most canonical paintings of Stalin of the thirties, Aleksandr Gerasimov's *V. I. Stalin and K. E. Voroshilov in the Kremlin. After the Rain* (1938), a painting that is a candidate for *the* exemplum of socialist realist art in that it won one of the first Stalin Prizes (in 1941) and thereafter few civilian institutions would fail to have a copy.[30] Here a Kremlin tower is placed diagonally opposite Stalin in the composition of the picture to suggest isomorphic duplication.

The Kremlin tower potentially encompasses several meanings. In the Govorkov poster it functions as a sentinel with an almost mystical quality about it. As a single tower it is also clearly a pars pro toto, symbolizing unity. It stands as a sentinel because it resists multiplicity, hence could be seen as resisting the fate of that other highly resonant tower, the Tower of Babel in the biblical parable that stands for humanity's fall into linguistic and cultural chaos.[31] Writing has been seen as particularly important in avoiding this devolution, which could be read as a reason in itself why in the Govorkov poster the tower stands on guard while Stalin writes. In this iconography the tower could be seen as a Tower of Babel that succeeded where the biblical tower failed: it *did* reach god (some sort of

Figure 2. "I. V. Stalin and K. E. Voroshilov in the Kremlin (I. V. Stalin i K. E. Voroshilov v Kremle)," 1938. Painting reproduced with permission from the Tretiakov Gallery, Moscow.

sacral god). Indeed, had the Palace of Soviets ever been built, the gigantic statue of Lenin that topped it would have reached beyond the clouds, as if in challenge to the biblical Babel. Another benefit of a tower, traditionally, has been its epistemological advantage: the tower rises above the flat plain of everyday reality, transcends it, so that from it you can see all around, much farther than from ground level. Conversely, those approaching a place from afar can orient by a tower because it can be seen from a great distance. Stalin in the iconography of this decade was identified with a tower in all these senses. He was guardian and guarantor of the sacred law; he saw "farther" than any of the people, in all directions; he commanded orientation in space and pronounced on where everything in the material world will be placed; *zodchii*, (architect) was a favorite epithet for him.

The Govorkov poster is grateful for my analysis because it suggests the close links in Stalinist culture between writing, the military (Stalin is wearing a military uniform), and the secret police. Here the Kremlin tower in its sentinel likeness symbolizes the need for that characteristic value of this purge era, "vigilance" *(bditel'nost')*, to ensure the purity of the Party and its doctrine. In the 1930s there was a close connection between writing and purging, both central features of political life. Several leading writers, including Babel, were friends of higher-ups in the secret police.

The show trials demonstrate the centrality of the textual. While there was a definite oral element in the *performance* of them,[32] they not only were somewhat scripted but also were based on the reams of written documents deposited behind closed doors to which the accused had no access but to which the prosecutor general, Andrei Vyshinsky, kept referring by volume and paragraph. At the trial of Bukharin, key moments in his exchange with Vyshinsky were essentially about who has the right to be an interpreter of texts, an exchange that Bukharin, as an "enemy of the people," Vyshinsky implied, had lost. But what had Bukharin been doing in prison while awaiting trial? Writing a philosophical treatise, a diary, and a novel![33]

Western historiography has tended to foreground the arbitrariness of the purges and the insubstantiality, not to say fantastic nature, of the charges leveled, yet generally for each purge victim care was taken to provide a written record of the interrogation justifying the verdict. The "confessor" was expected to sign the document; in some instances he had to sign every sentence![34] In Western biographies of purge victims, when the text comes to the moment when the victim's initial sentence had been served but, as was often the case, he or she is given a second sentence, the narrative generally runs "and then they clapped on another" eight or ten years, suggesting a quick, unsubstantiated sentence. Yet, as the files of purge victims have become available to their relatives since glasnost', it has emerged that even when these sentences were passed in the remotest camps, as many as five hundred pages of written reports (of interrogations, trials, etc.) were often generated to support the verdict. The case of the executions is even more striking. When, in one famous case, Meyerhold was arrested in June 1939, the original order was signed by Lavrenty

Beria (head of the secret police) in blue pencil, indicating that he was destined for execution. Yet the secret police, rather than carry this out summarily, subjected him to seven months of torture (some of which Meyerhold himself described in a petition to Vyacheslav Molotov) to extract a documented confession before he was shot on February 2, 1940.[35] Why so prolong the execution, a prolongation that for major figures could last one or two years? Arguably this was because the regime needed not just an execution but a written narrative to underwrite it.

In the thirties, there was in effect a hierarchy articulated in terms both of who has, and who has not, *access* to written documents, and in terms of the ability or *right* to control their content, ranging from mere scribes at the lowest levels through ever higher degrees of authorship, and editorship—including censorship, in this system a version of authorship.[36] Clearly, literary professionals occupied one of the highest levels, one of the reasons why they were so privileged. There was also a hierarchy in terms of reading: a Party decree of 1938 about the *Short Course of Party History* stipulated that only the top echelon in the Party should actually read Marx and Engels; the rank and file could confine themselves to the *Short Course*.[37] As it were, Stalin in his letter to *Proletarskaia revoliutsiia* dismissed the archival sources on Lenin as "mere paper documents" because they lacked an authoritative "author."

The symbolic geography of the country was tied to a hierarchy in lettered culture—one reason why I am drawing an analogy with the Ramos "lettered city," even though Moscow of the 1930s was not *literally* like a Latin American city. In this geography, the "new" Moscow occupied a place that was homologous with Stalin's (or, more broadly, the leadership's) place vis-à-vis the populace at large, and, looking more broadly, in relation to the entire world (a "Rome"). Moscow was to be both an exemplary text in its own right and the site where all authoritative texts would be generated.

The "New" Moscow

At the June 1931 plenum of the Communist Party's Central Committee, when a resolution was passed providing guidelines for a new project for rebuilding Moscow, the project was given high priority. Construction began quickly. By 1932 workers were already tunneling for the metro (the first section opened in May 1935) and working on some grand apartment complexes and major buildings. As the project progressed, streets were straightened out and widened, and many structures were pulled down to ensure easier movement of traffic, enlarge the city's squares, and enhance the overall panoramic effect of the cityscape. A great deal of attention was also paid to modernizing the city's waterways and constructing granite embankments, bridges, and the Moscow-Volga Canal.

One of the aims was to modernize the capital. Several other major cities of Europe were also redesigned at this time.[38] In the post–World War I age of the motorcar, the burghers of Europe needed to update their cities so that traffic could move through them efficiently, a preoccupation, too, in redesigning Moscow. Indeed, several features of the plan for the "new Moscow" were typical of those of the time for redesigning other European cities: zoning, widening streets, green belts, paying attention to pollution, light, air, and cleaning up the river system and giving priority to housing.[39] In addition, many sections of Moscow's old city walls were pulled down, something generally regarded in Europe as a sign of modernization. It could even be said, though this "bourgeois" precedent was hotly denied at the time, that the project for the "socialist capital" represents an updated version of what Haussman did in remaking Paris between 1858 and 1870 (updated with elements of the Garden City, plus a metro).[40]

Moscow was remodeled less in the interests of modernization, efficiency, and public health than in order to realize a new conception of the capital as a template for the Soviet cultural order. The "new" city was to be both facilitator and emblem of this change, a significant shift in its function within the country. In the 1920s, even though Moscow had become the capital of the Bolshevik state in 1918, really no significant cult of Moscow had emerged (except among the avant-garde). And during the First Five-Year Plan and the cultural revolution, though the country had become more centralized with economic planning, there was a marked tendency in literature, film, and architectural practice to privilege the periphery *(okraina)* over the "center."[41]

A cult of Moscow emerged around 1933. That year a recurring lament in the press was that there were few books, albums, or films on contemporary Moscow. In July a campaign was launched in *Literaturnaia gazeta* as cultural workers were urged to undergo a "creative perestroika," reorienting their texts from production topics to the transformation from the "old Moscow" to the "new Moscow," essentially fleshing out the extravagant claims of radical change made in speeches and in the press. Prominent Western and Soviet writers, such as Theodore Dreiser, were given space to extol the glories of Moscow as a world center.[42] Some of the finest creative people of the day, such as Eisenstein and the writer Andrei Platonov, responded to this call, if in their cases somewhat eccentrically; their respective Moscow projects—the film *Moscow* (also known as *Moscow in Time,* [*Moskva vo vremeni*])[43] and the novel *Happy Moscow* (Schastlivaia Moskva)—were never finished.

In the Stalinist thirties, the transformation of Moscow functioned both in official rhetoric and in many of the novels, paintings and films as a source of the master metaphors legitimizing and explicating the Stalinist political program: the building of a new capital city stood for transforming the society, *the* practical example of what achieved socialism might look like. Particular buildings in the "new Moscow" were successively cited in speeches and articles as *the* model for architectural practice. This was similar to the standard practice in Soviet literature whereby particular novels or their positive heroes were singled out as exemplars for writers to follow.

Clearly, given that so much was invested in the "new Moscow," the kind of architecture built there was not a matter of indifference. In the 1930s, those in authority rejected modernist architecture as inadequate to the great age and recommended that attention be turned to schools of architecture that favored more appropriate, grander styles. During the 1920s, Russian avant-garde architects (such as the Constructivists) who had close ties to their counterparts in Europe and America had dominated Soviet architectural practice. But around the time the plans for reconstructing Moscow were announced in 1931, these architects fell ever more out of official favor.

In terms of styles, during the first half of the 1930s, the general prescription for Moscow's new buildings was that they draw on the architecture of ancient Greece, on that of Rome as its direct heir, and on that of the Renaissance as the next high point in a great tradition that might see its realization in the "new" Moscow. The general formula for Moscow's architecture, which had emerged even before the 1932 Central Committee resolution on the Writers Union (in this case formulated in a resolution of the Construction Council of February 28, 1932) and was later reiterated in authoritative variants, was to use "the best of the classical heritage . . . [plus] the achievements of contemporary architectural construction technology,"[44] a stricture that guided architectural practice until a more nationalistically oriented culture emerged later in the decade.[45] For the time being, both the Russian national tradition in architecture and the Gothic were largely ignored, or even in some instances explicitly rejected.[46] Within the overall "classical" orientation, individual architects and officials emphasized different moments in its development; some, especially initially, emphasized ancient Greece (for which they found gratifying quotations in Marx), others Rome, or the French revolutionary era.

The dominant assumption was that the "new Moscow" would rework and perfect some great antecedent, which would in turn confer greatness on the state and its citizens. But in practice, socialist realist architecture was rather eclectic in its precedents. There was, in effect, a battle over the styles, a battle in which most of the leading architects participating took positions similar to those they had espoused in the twenties, or, among the more senior, in the prerevolutionary years as well. This is most apparent at the 1933 meeting in the Union of Architects, which essentially celebrated the shift in received styles from the modernist to the "academic"; most strikingly, Mosei Ginzburg, as a strategy to support his lingering Constructivism, claimed in his speech that that movement captured the spirit in which Renaissance architects operated.[47]

In the statements of newly authoritative architects and critics (notably Ivan Zholtovsky, Aleksei Shchusev, Ivan Fomin, and Vladimir Shchuko), rather than those of the Party or government leaders, a "Roman" precedent for the new architecture was particularly promoted. Such figures not only drew the analogy of "the new Moscow as heir to the architectural greatness of ancient Rome" but also liked to cite specific Roman buildings as the precedent for the projects of contemporary Moscow that had the greatest political resonance; for example, the plans for transforming Red Square or building the gigantic Palace of Soviets were for a "socialist forum" or "Roman forum."[48] Boris Iofan, architect of the winning design, recounted how in order to design it he went to Rome, where he "took without copying features linked to its great epoch."[49] Rome's Colosseum, its Parthenon, the axial roads of the city, and its overall city plan were also often explicitly identified with specific new projects for Moscow.[50]

The historical precedent most emphasized in architectural journals of the 1930s was the Renaissance, in particular the work of Filippo Brunelleschi (1337–1446) and Andrea Palladio (1518–1580). Ivan Zholtovsky, the most ardent proselytizer for the Renaissance, was a dominant figure within architecture and guru for the new generation.[51] His "Palladian palazzo" (the future American Embassy and later headquarters of Intourist) was the first achieved model for the architecture of the future. Placed on Marx Prospect itself, but one building away from the point where it met Gorky Street, the project had such priority that a special factory had to be established to produce components not otherwise available. Thereafter, many of the apartment and public buildings of the "new Moscow" were fitted with loggias and other such Renaissance affectations.

But when architectural experts advanced buildings from the Renaissance as models for the new Moscow, they stressed that their architect's greatness was in no small measure due to the fact that he continued the Roman tradition; Brunelleschi, it was said, first studied the classical tradition in Rome before moving to Florence to do his great work,[52] while Palladio was guided in his writings and practice by the great Roman treatise on architecture, Vitruvius's *De Architectura* (written before AD 27). Contemporary Soviet architects who won favor were sent to Italy to study the architecture of such masters; commentators stressed that Boris Iofan had based his design for the Palace of Soviets on the classical traditions, and on Vitruvius in particular.[53]

These architects' writings and buildings also assumed a central place in the curriculum at Soviet schools of architecture, which institutionalized the new canon. In October 1933, the Central Committee passed a decree that founded a new Academy of Architecture and set up a publishing house attached to the Academy for the sole purpose of publishing new textbooks and monographs on architectural practice and history.[54] In response, many of the architectural treatises from the classical and Renaissance eras, but particularly two texts almost invariably cited as sources to guide the new architecture, Vitruvius's *De architectura* and Palladio's *Quatro libri dell'architettura,* were published in Russian translation in the 1930s. Zholtovsky, a fervent Palladian, translated the master's

monumental treatise himself, commenting in his introduction: "I have always been of the opinion that in the building arts, as in many other matters, the ancient Romans surpassed all those that came after them [and
so] I chose Vitruvius as my teacher and guide."[55]

As we have seen, then, translations from Western sources played a significant role in the development of "socialist realist" architecture. Furthermore, the actual selection of authoritative sources to guide the new
architectural aesthetic came from within the intelligentsia, if only from
one faction within it.[56] Besides the classical tradition another, largely un-
acknowledged, source was the architecture of contemporary Manhattan.
Soviet architecture had an entire journal devoted to reporting the latest
developments in the West, *Arkhitektura za rubezhom* (Architecture
abroad), founded in 1934. The principal architectural journals, *Arkhitektura SSSR* and *Stroitel'stvo Moskvy,* also covered Western trends. At the
same time, several works on Renaissance art were published, including a
new translation of Leonardo da Vinci's works on art (1935) and a version
of Heinrich Wölfflin's *Die Kunst der Renaissance; Italien und das deutsche
Formgefühl* (Iskusstvo Italii i Germanii epokhi Renessansa, 1934).

Why did those in power prefer classical and Renaissance models for
the "socialist city" of the twentieth century? Obviously, throughout Europe and the Americas the classical tradition has generally been used for
public buildings, particularly when regimes seek self-aggrandizement, as
did the Stalinist one. In this instance, the choice was particularly dictated
by the reaction against all the varieties of modernism that characterized
the decade.

How, then, was the new Moscow to be deemed specifically a model of
the "socialist city" or seen as on the architectural cutting edge? How
could a building or a city exemplify Marxism-Leninism if a similar design
could be, or most likely had been, used elsewhere in a capitalist or pre-
capitalist state? This was especially problematical given that the General
Plan for Moscow envisaged a fairly nonindustrial landscape: industrial
plants were to be banned in the central area and mass housing substantially reduced.[57]

The rhetoric occasioned by the plans to remodel Moscow implicitly
met such charges in several ways. First, the claim was made that *Soviet
Russia really cares about man as compared with the capitalist West where*

a dog-eat-dog mentality reigns. A favorite rhetorical strategy was to compare the working-class slums of the Western, bourgeois city, largely as
presented in Engels's *Condition of the Working Class in England* or *On
the Housing Question*, with the living conditions of the new Moscow.[58]
Stalin joined this trend when, in his speech to the Seventeenth Party
Congress in 1934 (the so-called Congress of Victors), citing Engels, he
declared slums a hallmark of the big cities of bourgeois countries and described them as "a heap of dark, dank and dilapidated buildings" where
the working classes were forced to "wallow in filth." In Soviet Russia, by
contrast, with the Revolution such hovels had "disappeared" and been
replaced by "bright [svetlymi] workers' neighborhoods."[59]

As this example suggests, the rebuilding of Moscow was generally represented in a Manichaean scenario of instantaneous transformation from
dark to light, from filth to purity. In 1931, 1935, and beyond, as Stalinist
authorities blazoned forth a new national identity articulated in terms of
the new model city of Moscow, they did so by marking their plans off
from old Moscow—described typically (in this instance, in one of the albums of the time, *Moscow under Construction* [Moskva konstruiruetsia,
1938]) as a city of "dirty, crooked, dark lanes, dead-end streets and forty
forties of churches."[60] Physical attributes of the old city became negatively
charged qualities of ideological significance. The streets are "dirty" and
"dark," but the "new Moscow" will give them light. They are "dead-
ends," but the new regime will give its people major thoroughfares.

The straightening out of Moscow's streets, subsuming their very outline to an overall plan (allegedly "for the first time"), was an act of political
resonance that stood for the "straightening out," planning, and "stream-
lining" of the nation as a whole. The "haphazard," "poorly planned," "illogical," and inefficient configuration of old Moscow was to be eliminated
in a *consciously* ordered new city. Such "straightening out" did not just
mean modernization, for the reconstruction of the city was, as we shall
see in the next chapter, inscribed into the main model of the day for the
progress toward Communism.

It was not actually the case that this project was a new initiative, that
modernizing the capital was a strictly Stalinist venture. Even before the
Bolsheviks came to power in 1917, there had been periodic bursts of planning activity (including plans for a metro); several overall plans, similar to

that of 1931, had been generated in the 1920s as well. The major difference was the emphasis and rhetoric given the 1931 plan, and the fact that it was actually implemented.

The way Moscow was to be remade was to provide a blueprint for the postbourgeois, "socialist city." It was to stand ahead of any rival world capital because—and this was the argument that was most foregrounded—it would be a planned city, not one that had grown up chaotically like any capitalist city where the dread stock market held sway. The General Plan resolution of 1935 identifies Moscow's "narrow and winding streets" as markers of "the barbaric character of Russian capitalism."[61] In official Soviet writings about the General Plan, institutions of the capitalist market economy (such as the stock exchange) were represented as the root cause of much of the "haphazard quality" *(stikhiinost')* of old Moscow. The resolution on reconstructing Moscow maintained (a point that was picked up ad nauseam in subsequent literature) that during the capitalist era competing enterprises each erected their own structures in Moscow and that it was impossible for a municipal body or any planning agency to implement any overall plan or design. A favorite epithet for Moscow from the prerevolutionary years, "calico Moscow" (actually *sitsevaia Moskva*), suggesting a Moscow of small (largely textile) manufacture, merchants, and petty traders, was now used as a dismissive way to characterize the old Moscow, which would now be upgraded to the age of large-scale, heavy industry.

In rebuilding Moscow, many of the structures of capitalism, such as the stock exchange and bank buildings, were destroyed or converted to other uses. Official accounts also stressed how planners were ridding the city of the clutter of "minor structures" *(melkie stroeniia),* by which was meant not so much structures that were small literally as the structures of the capitalist, and particularly petty bourgeois, world, such as booths, market stalls, and small shops and enterprises.[62] These were slated for destruction, together with many old churches and several other historic structures (towers, walls, city gates) that official spokesmen saw as standing for an obscurantist and limited mindset and that often, as if to confirm this, obstructed traffic or marred the ensemble of the street or square on which they were located. They were replaced by broad, straight streets, granite buildings, and vast (often expanded) squares. Members of organizations dedicated to the preservation of "old Moscow" were persecuted.[63]

A reconstructed Moscow was to be the emblem of a *militantly* postre-
ligious order. One of the principal activities occasioned by the call for a
"new Moscow" was the pulling down of scores of those "forty forties" of
churches ("forty forties" had been a capsule way of referring to Moscow
in prerevolutionary times, intended to evoke a city suffused with religious
sites). Starting from 1931, a year particularly infamous today as the time
when Moscow's largest church, the Cathedral of Christ the Redeemer,
was blown up to make way for the new Palace of Soviets, the 1930s were
punctuated by demolitions of Moscow's churches.

A major difference between the new plans for Moscow and those for
most other European cities was the controlling interest of the Party in the
design process and the highly authoritarian structure that supported it.
The official authority was not the architects themselves but Lazar Kaganovich, the first secretary of the Moscow Party Committee and, allegedly,
de facto second secretary, after Stalin, of the Party itself, high priest of
Stalin's personality cult, and generally considered Stalin's right-hand
man on the Politburo. Stalin himself exercised ultimate authority in this
area on occasion, especially for the waterways. In addition, both the planning of Moscow and the actual process of designing its new buildings
were centralized. In 1932 several planning authorities in Moscow, from
the Moscow Party Committee and city Soviet, were merged to form
the single Architectural Planning Committee (Arkhitekturno-Planovoi
Komitet—Arkhplan), a joint body headed by Kaganovich. At that time,
the principle of the "single" *(edinyi)* plan was announced, whereby only
the Moscow Soviet could approve the construction of any building within
Moscow.[64] Arkhplan was responsible for drawing up a General Plan
(Genplan), with whose stipulations all construction was to accord.[65]
Then, in 1933, the design process itself was also centralized. Architects
were herded into huge "studios," each headed by a leading name, where
hundreds of architects would work on the buildings and overall layout of
a particular complex in Moscow (generally a major street, a square, or an
individual public building).[66]

Since at least the late 1920s, architecture and town planning had been
discussed in terms of their pedagogical potential, but the conception of
how they were to fulfill this role underwent successive metamorphoses.
During the 1920s and the cultural revolution, the aim in designing cities

had been to create spaces for living, work, and cultural activity that would foster in citizens a proletarian, collectivist consciousness and rational habits of mind. Special attention was paid to housing and particularly to the individual apartment unit, which was to be designed to maximize efficiency of movement within. Many of the activities citizens might have performed in their homes (such as eating and reading) were no longer to take place within their apartments but were transferred to communal spaces.

In conceiving the "new Moscow" of the 1930s, planners also sought to create a space that would conduce to a "new Soviet man" by organizing efficient patterns of motion within the capital. But the emphasis was now on the circulation of traffic and pedestrians on the streets rather than on how individuals moved around their domestic spaces. There was also a shift in scale and focus to *public* architecture—or, more accurately, to a different kind of public architecture. Whereas architectural commissions had been given out for workers' housing, factories, and clubs during the cultural revolution, now the main commissions were for public buildings for the center of Moscow (both cultural and administrative), facilities for the new elite (apartment complexes, theaters, hotels), and transportation (by road, metro, and waterway).

The aim in rebuilding Moscow was of course to improve the citizen's well-being, but a greater aim than his *physical* benefit was his *specular* benefit. Architects attempted to create an incredible space of grandeur that would inspire citizens, impressing on them the greatness of their state and inspiring them to become "grander" human beings. In a sense, the Soviet citizen of the 1930s was to be a (somewhat unexpected) twentieth-century version of the flaneur, in the sense of a person whose very raison d'être was to stroll the streets and sample its visual impressions (though, unlike Benjamin's paradigmatic flaneur of mid-nineteenth-century Paris, he was also expected to work).

Architecture had its limits as a model for the new society. The architecture of the new Moscow could make the city more efficient and grand and, by osmosis, its citizens as well. But it was ultimately no more than a static organization of material space. Literature was to flesh out the abstractions and rationalize Party decrees in some narrative form that would provide coherence and legitimize the status quo. Like the great religious systems, it centered around a biographical narrative.

The Bolshevik regime needed a new narrative of identity to supersede the tsarist one. Those in power had to rationalize the Revolution, the change from one world order to another. All states have to manufacture subjects, but what is peculiar about the Soviet example is the need to create *new* subjects. They needed to put new software into the machine, as it were. The leadership had recurrently sought an exemplary representation of the nation, whether in literature, film, or art. But in this era they focused with redoubled interest on establishing a standard biographical narrative in literature, one of several reasons why literature was to provide the model for all the other arts. The fictionalized biography was a synecdoche for the national biography, for the movement of man and nation over time; the "new Moscow" was a synecdoche for the nation in a different sense: marking the progress of the material world over time.

Thus, the early 1930s were a moment when literature, architecture, and ideology came together in the one "city," a moment when, as Gorky and Marx "met" at that city's center, disparate biographies, disparate subjectivities, came together in one narrative. Gorky Street ran into Marx Prospect cum Alleia Il'icha at the center of secular Moscow as if in celebration of the marriage of literature and politics that was so crucial to this lettered city as the model of the new society. Ordinary citizens had been corralled into massive projects for inscribing themselves into the new society by writing their "own" (templated) autobiographies, while nearby, though hidden from view, Stalin as original author was planning and writing in his study. This was a total system (a "civilization") supported by a cult of writing. There were of course exceptions, and gradations of compliance. But the model, though far from perfect in execution, was clear.

Architecture, literature (lettered culture), and politics came together in a new city, a city that had been written to be read. Writing the city, writing the nation, and writing the self were all to be coordinated in one system, as will be shown in the next chapter.

CHAPTER 3

The Return of the Aesthetic

IN THE 1930s, as Moscow was being rebuilt, a cliché of press accounts was "all of Moscow is under scaffolding" (Vsia Moskva v lesakh). The city was a chrysalis, as it were, waiting for an entirely new self—a butterfly—to emerge. And emerge it did (or was said to have done). A number of glossy albums of photographs were produced by figures like the erstwhile Constructivists Aleksandr Rodchenko and Varvara Stepanova in which contrasting shots of the same spot in "old" Moscow and as it is/would be in the "new" city faced each other across adjacent pages, celebrating Moscow's conversion experience.[1] And in 1938 Aleksandr Medvedkin's 1938 film *New Moscow* (Novaia Moskva) the hero screens a film that shifts, through dissolves, from "backward" Moscow to a futuristic "new" Moscow (as in the albums, the latter shots were largely of mock-ups of the future city).

When the butterfly-Moscow emerged from its chrysalis it was to be "beautiful," a new self-evident value. As Kaganovich put it in his speech to a Jubilee plenum of the Komsomol in 1933 in a veiled attack on Constructivism, "many consider that a simplified and crude design [oformlenie] is the style of proletarian architecture. No, excuse me, but the proletariat does not only want to have housing, not only have places where they can live comfortably, but have beautiful houses. And they will make sure that their cities, their buildings and their architecture are more beautiful than in other towns of Europe and America."[2] Avant-garde architecture, which had proclaimed itself the "new architecture," was attacked as "formalist," "arid," and "soulless," for its "aestheticization of technology" and cult of the machine, which had allegedly crowded out "art itself."[3]

The turn to "beauty" entailed a return to conventional tastes, but the foregrounding of the beautiful was also tied to a system that cut across discursive boundaries. This meant the aestheticization of politics, or more accurately, since political life then was palpably messy and even bloody, the aestheticization of metapolitics, of the model that subtended and justified practices in the political arena.

In this historical moment of state aggrandizement and consolidation of power, the beautiful was in. This was not a unique phenomenon. As James C. Scott points out in *Seeing Like a State*, in a variety of historical examples involving urban planning under powerful leaders, "aesthetic considerations frequently won out over the existing social structure and mundane functioning of the city"; examples he adduces include the impact of Leon Battista Alberti and Palladio, both influential in the designs for the "new Moscow."[4] But one is reminded in this instance of Benjamin's oft-cited pronouncement in the epilogue to "The Work of Art in an Age of Mechanical Reproduction" (1936): "the logical result of fascism is the introduction of aesthetics into political life." But, he suggests, "Communism responds by politicizing art," thus suggesting that the politicization of culture was a necessary counteractive.[5] I would argue, however, that "Communism" as represented in the Stalinist 1930s also featured the "introduction of aesthetics into political life," but not just at the crude level of what Siegfried Cracauer called the "mass ornament," such as the parades on Red Square. "Politics" were "aestheticized" at a more profound level.

In the early 1930s, the aesthetic returned as a value.[6] This occurred around 1931, the same year that architecture became a major source of metaphors for society and the plans to rebuild Moscow were announced. These developments can be seen as part of a general shift in political culture that occurred that year, when defining values of the First Five-Year Plan and cultural revolution were reversed (see Chapter 1). Of relevance here is the drawing away from the radical democratism of the Plan with its emphasis on the proletariat and the movement toward foregrounding the more inclusive term "socialism," with the society becoming ever more hierarchical. In culture, there was a concomitant shift from promoting proletarian culture to a call for socialist realism, and a call for "quality" that facilitated a return to aesthetic considerations.

Marxist theoreticians of the 1920s had not generally used the word "aesthetics" *(estetika)*—except in commenting on Georgi Plekhanov's theories, which were by now largely discredited. Their theoretical investigations, such as there were, were more tied to a particular branch of the arts,[7] while the avant-garde and their Formalist associates had decried all mention of "art" and "beauty" as vapid and unscientific fetish. Starting around 1931, however, one sees a more concerted effort to elucidate a comprehensive Marxist aesthetic theory, one that would cover not just literature, let alone just proletarian or avant-garde literature, but also general principles governing all the arts, though literature was the main focus. Marx, Engels, and for that matter Lenin never produced a systematic aesthetics.[8] Hence their scattered remarks had to be stitched together to form a whole. The new scholarly serial *Literaturnoe nasledstvo* (Literary heritage), starting with its first number in 1931, presented previously unpublished letters by Marx and Engels on literary matters, accompanied by scholarly introductions and interpretive commentaries.[9]

Interest in aesthetics was not confined to the Marxist classics. One anthology of 1937, *Antichnye mysliteli ob iskusstve* (Classical thinkers on art), includes Plato's dialogs on the beautiful and a selection from Aristotle's *Poetics.*[10] Eisenstein also turned to aesthetics at this time, especially in his book *Metod,* which he worked on from 1932 to 1948, and where he especially shows the influence of Hegel's *Aesthetics,* Ernst Cassirer's *Philosophy of Symbolic Form,* and Joyce's *Ulysses.*[11]

In addition, leading Marxist literary theoreticians associated with Lukács launched a somewhat catholic new book series, "Classics of Aesthetic Thought," to come out of the Institute for Literature and Art of the Communist Academy; writings by Schiller, Gotthold Lessing, and others appeared in this series with introductions by members of Lukács's coterie.[12] Lukács himself, in an extensive introduction to Schiller's aesthetic thought, asserted that Schiller—the first German thinker to embark on an "objective idealism," he proclaimed—"consid[ered] aesthetics the most important means for resolving the social problems of his time." The assessment of Schiller "should not be limited to facile criticism," he argued with some casuistry, for, as Engels said of Hegel, "it is much more important to tease out, beneath the incorrect form and artificial formulation, what is correct and genial."[13] Though Marx and Engels fought against Kant's aesthetic idealism, still Engels identified Kant, Fichte, and Hegel as "those thinkers from whom the German socialists proudly trace their origins."[14]

As we can detect in Kaganovich's remarks about the proletariat wanting not just comfortable houses but beautiful ones, these years saw a reaction against the largely pragmatic, utilitarian, and materialist approach to most fields of culture that had characterized the cultural revolution. Now "beauty" trumped "comfort." Authoritative voices began to lament the fact that the cultural revolution's obsession with technology, statistics, and immediate practical needs had crowded out those higher and more enduring values, ideology and beauty. Culture itself became a value, and not only for its instrumentalist potential but also *in its own right.* Intellectuals, workers, but also the leadership, aspired to attain a higher cultural level.[15] Symptomatic of this is Stalin's arrogating to himself Politburo stewardship over culture, his presentation of himself as a man of culture, and the way the leadership began to frequent the Bolshoi, the Moscow Art Theater, and the Maly Theater.

In Soviet architecture, there was a general reining in of the "international style," seen as an enemy of "beauty." This particularly delighted some Soviet architects who had long favored the more classical or "academic" schools and had been seen as passé in the twenties. Those now in power rejected Western modernist trends in general and especially Le Corbusier's architectural theories. Indeed, Le Corbusier, nominated "the leading ideologist and practitioner of contemporary Western architecture,"[16] functioned in the Soviet press and speeches of the first half of the thirties as a sort of titular worthy antagonist of Soviet architectural principles. Critics pounced on his work as epitomizing a trend to which all too many Soviet Constructivists had succumbed, though it should be pointed out that some in the Soviet avant-garde were themselves gravitating back toward Renaissance models (consider Malevich's self-portrait of

1933, indebted to Holbein, or Vladimir Tatlin's *Letatlin* of 1932, indebted to Leonardo).

The rejection of the international style and return to more traditional architecture does not have to be written off as a function of the gross interference of the Party in culture. The pattern was not unique to the Soviet Union. For example, there was a broad-based reaction against Le Corbusier in the architectural community of France at this time, too; there, attackers called his work "antipatriotic" because he did not use the classical tradition of the country's past.[17] The distinctiveness of the shift in the Soviet Union as compared with elsewhere would consist in the rigid central control that progressively narrowed the range of competing trends.[18]

In the Soviet press Le Corbusier, with his insistence that form must be subordinated to function and his "reinforced concrete dogma," epitomized all that was wrong with "Western" trends: his exteriors were all flat, unmodulated surface with no decoration other than the pilotis on the ground floor and the elongated gashes of windows. A second bête noire was the kind of building designed by Ernst May or the Bauhaus architects who had worked in Soviet Russia in the early thirties, and their colleagues the Constructivists.[19] Critic after critic at this time dismissed their buildings as "box-like" ("doma-iashchiki" or "doma-korobki") or as "barracks" *(kazarmy)*. The new socialist housing built in the Soviet Union in recent years under these influences was dismissed as a blind imitation of trends in the West developed to serve the "bourgeois" or "petty-bourgeois" client of the capitalist world and hence totally alien to the needs of a socialist society.[20] Though this attack might seem anticosmopolitan, we should remember that there are different cosmopolitanisms and the preferred styles of the 1930s also came from the West.

The greatest sin of the "barracks," however, was the totally blank faces of their façades.

Inasmuch as it was hardly self-evident how architecture might meet the new demand (from 1932) that all Soviet culture be socialist realist and have "socialist," "Marxist-Leninist," or "Party-oriented" "content," ornamentation on a building became in effect one of the main ways architecture met this demand. As authorities sought to provide an architecture that was more "beautiful," a new slogan, "dekorativnost'" (literally "dec-

oratedness"), entered programmatic accounts of architecture. The demand for *dekorativnost'* was aimed explicitly at counteracting the
extremes of the "international style" and in particular Le Corbusier's
purist campaign against all nonfunctional detail in buildings, a campaign
so fanatical that he even banned cornices. At the end of April 1932, in
other words just after the Writers Union resolution of April 23, the Presidium of the Moscow Soviet called a large meeting of Moscow architects
and planners at which it was resolved to form a "single society of Soviet
architects."[21] The main address, titled "Architecture Will Have the Decisive Role," was given by an engineer, Cherkassky, and though the term
"socialist realism" would not be promulgated until the next month, his
speech with its emphasis on the decorations and façades of buildings
provided a framework for what, once the term was coined, was to be so
labeled. In his predictable attack on modernist architecture as "barracks,"
Cherkassky foregrounded the sin that they had ornamentation, not even
"balconies or stucco." In his zeal to correct this bareness, he even suggested "plastering over the exteriors of buildings erected last year." From
now on, he instructed, "put stucco on all the façades" and "introduce the
practice of decorating the main façades with [his repeated formula]
sculptures, bas-reliefs, with new socialist thematics characterizing the epoch of the construction of socialism"; he also advocated frescoes and
mosaics.[22]

This new line giving central importance to decoration and the façade
was reiterated next year at an important meeting (July 9–11, 1933) of the
newly formed Union of Architects where this program was debated.[23]
David Arkin in his keynote address, when he came to that now standard
moment of attacking the "boxes" *(korobochki)* of Constructivist architecture, singled out as their most besetting sin the fact that they had no
"face" *(litso)*.[24] To have no "face," Arkin insisted, is a "denial of art," and
he went on to contend that the official demands that new buildings be
"cheap and simple" had been falsely understood.[25]

This general shift was encapsulated in a cluster of slogans to be found
in Cherkassky and Arkin's speeches, slogans that for the next few years
were invoked recurrently in countless other speeches and articles about
architecture: "dekorativnost'," "vyrazitel'nost'" (expressiveness), "litso"
(façade), sometimes "edinoe arkhitekturno-khudozhestvennoe litso" (a

unified architectural cum artistic profile) or "oblik" (image), "façade," and "vozdeistvie."[26] "Vozdeistvie" (impact) had been a banner term of the Constructivists, too. But *their* austere designs were now considered politically dangerous.

During the heyday of Constructivism, the ideal had seemed to be the marriage of the architect and the engineer. Now socialist realism in architecture was sometimes defined as a work in tandem by the architect, artist, and sculptor.[27] New studios and other institutional bodies were set up to foster this.[28] The purpose, made explicit at the time, was that the desired "synthesis" in architecture "provide in monumental and simple images a powerful expression of the epoch's ideological content."[29] This stricture could be viewed as calling for a return to the kind of art and architecture to be found in a period of low general literacy when frescoes, mosaics, bas-reliefs, and sculptures were used to tell a story to the unlettered masses (as on the doors and glass windows of the great medieval cathedrals). In Stalinist buildings this ornamentation tended to be classical in inspiration. Far from all the decoration on them from this period could be classified as "socialist thematics." Often it featured plant motifs (flowers, leaves, vines), curlicues or other ornamental flourishes, and endless pillars, loggias, and so forth stuck onto the exteriors to give them a Renaissance look.[30]

In writing about architecture and in the designs themselves a distinction was also made between the inside and the outside of a building. The outside, designed to impress, was to present an elaborate façade, be ornate, and probably present some appropriation of the classical style. In order for them to be visible at all times, Cherkassky in his speech (and others) stipulated that the grand façades of the new buildings be lit up at night.[31] But the interiors were to be constructed according to different principles. Though the reinforced concrete so beloved by Le Corbusier was explicitly banned from the façades as too "drab" *(unylo),* in the same breath it would be recommended for every building's "skeleton."[32] Similarly, in the case of the Palace of Soviets, the profusion of pillars and gigantic statue of Lenin on its exterior essentially masked the reality that the latest American techniques were used for its foundations, its walls, its cavernous main hall with its cupola roof, and the steel frame supporting the gigantic statue in the hall's interior.[33]

This dichotomy in the typical monumental building should not be seen as specifically Stalinist, since it was a trend in America and Europe at this time. Arkin, a leading spokesman in architecture, in an article describing his impressions of American architecture after a trip there, pointed to a contradiction in the design of American skyscrapers between their exteriors, presented in "cathedral-Gothic" style, and their eminently "practical and business" functions. These exteriors, he concluded, remind one of "hastily put on make up, or of some kind of random [sluchainuiu] mask."[34] Nevertheless, American architecture was a major source of ideas for "dekorativnost." When American skyscrapers were discussed in the Soviet architectural press, as they often were, in some articles photographs of their ornamented façades were provided,[35] and others described their thematic murals (especially Diego Rivera's ill-fated mural for Rockefeller Center in New York).[36] European attention to decoration was also stressed. Critics noted with chagrin that architects there paid more attention to the finishing or trim *(otdelka)* than did Soviet architects and made extensive use of "monumental art."[37]

The appropriation of such trends did not amount to mere imitation. The ornamentation or "mask" Stalinist that architects put on their buildings was not to be individual or "arbitrary," as Arkin complained it was in America, but integrated into a coherent system. No decorative detail, not even the slightest curlicue, could be considered random or politically neutral. The function of the new buildings was both aesthetic and "discursive."[38] As was said at the time, "the walls must speak."[39] They were encoded in a semiotic system.

The main criterion for "socialist realist" architecture was that it be "simple" *(prost)* and "comprehensible" *(poniaten)*. It was to be "simple" in the sense that it was to be maximally *readable* and was to have the maximal *effect* on its citizens. Thus the exterior of a building had become a text, a "face" (the word *litso,* face, can also be translated as "façade" or "profile"). In a society that was drunk on codified representation, the outsides or façades of its buildings—their face to the outside world, that which is maximally read—was critical, a reason why authoritative spokesmen did not want those blank "faces" that were so typical of the international style architecture.

Most of the new buildings, obviously, also had an eminently practical function. Thus in socialist realist architecture, buildings functioned both as practical spaces—office blocks or apartment buildings with modern conveniences—*and* as proleptic rhetorical devices. Here you see the reverse of the general pattern of inside/outside. Rather than have the inside be the sacral space and the outside its shell (as with a temple), in the new architecture the inside typically had banal functions while the outside was to inspire awe (though in the case of spaces associated with the secret police, or Stalin's study, this is reversed). A virtual corollary of the new emphasis on the façade was the rejection of all that smacked of interiority. "Intimacy" *(intimnost')* became a negative term in the architectural press, one often contrasted with a "civic sense" *(grazhdanstvennost')*.[40]

The turn to aesthetics was at the heart of a new moment in cultural evolution. As creative intellectuals produced work in the various branches of the arts that drew on existing models, a single aesthetic system evolved, one that crossed all these branches' discursive boundaries. Socialist realism was not just about heroes building power stations or even about the wisdom of Party decrees. Aesthetic value and political value were closely linked. Specialists in the two leading fields, literature and architecture, began to use the same critical vocabulary, the same discursive repertoire. In architecture, this repertoire defined "the beautiful"; in literature it identified the "hero" as an example of anthropological ideality.

In architecture, those in authority, in seeking to define what socialist realism might mean for that field, generally invoked classical precedents. They championed the art of the Renaissance, but they also looked beyond it to the great codifiers of the beautiful in Greece and especially Rome as having distilled the essence of the beautiful. Fomin, a leading architect of the 1930s, insists, in his contribution to a major debate of 1933 about the styles appropriate for socialist realist architecture, that architecture must have its own "language" and that language be the classical, arguing (somewhat Eurocentrically) that that language has been "understood by all peoples in all cultural eras of mankind," grounded as it is in "the only architecture which has captured an international status for itself." "It is essential," he continues, "that this language be simple, laconic, and [disciplined] because [architects] must be able, using few means, to say a great deal both powerfully and convincingly."[41]

Buildings were to "say a great deal both powerfully and convincingly." They were to be read as texts. When in the 1930s prominent Soviet architects declared recognized principles of classical architecture central to a "socialist realist" architecture, they did not merely mean that a particular inventory of stylistic features was to be adopted. As they called for such alleged qualities of their preferred architectural styles as "simplicity," a "serene" *(spokoinyi)* exterior, and "a unified whole," these "qualities" were themselves markers of an ideological and epistemological stance. Similar qualities were required for literature.

The regime needed not just "beautiful" buildings, mere shells, or even model cities as structures of streets and amenities. It needed a narrative about that shell to give them order, cogency, and above all *meaning*. Although the branches of the arts were all linked in the thirties, and especially literature and architecture, literature was dominant because it relates part to whole not just in an abstract way, as in architecture, but in a human narrative. Though, chronologically, the founding of the Writers Union and the institution of socialist realism postdate launching the project for the reconstruction of Moscow by almost a year, literature was in the Stalinist system prior to architecture. Tellingly, though two prominent writers, Aleksandr Fadeev and Aleksei Tolstoy, were put on Arkhplan, no architects were put on the leading bodies of the Writers Union.[42]

Socialist realist literature became the cornerstone of the Stalinist culture system. Its overall formula was presented in capsule to the First Writers Congress in the canonical source, the keynote address of the Central Committee delegate, Andrei Zhdanov, to the First Writers Congress of 1934: "A combination of the most austere, sober, and practical work with supreme heroism and the most grandiose prospects."[43] Literature was *both* to depict life in its messy particularity, in its mundane, practical detail, *and* to idealize. The glue that put them together was an exemplary biography. The "grandiose prospects" underwrote the way the socialist realist novel stitches a biographical narrative to the overall theory of Marxism-Leninism.[44]

An exemplary biography defined socialist realism and became the core of Stalinist culture. Citizens were to be transformed—assimilated—by inscribing themselves into the master narrative of history. This was to be effected by writing a diary or a memoir or by writing the history of one's place of work, the latter one of Gorky's pet projects.[45] This kind of writing served to collectivize individual memory.

The biographical master narrative implicitly informed architecture, a result of the convergence of all the arts in this period under the sign of literature. The novel acquired over time its own morphology of symbolic forms, and became more systematically articulated in order to encode the master narrative of Marxism-Leninism in allegorical form. Just as a building was not to have a "random mask" (façade), novels were not to be put together "randomly." The insistence in directives to architects on privileging the "façade" had its analogue in the socialist realist novel, where the representation of the facial expressions of exemplary characters became so standardized and encrypted that the face became, in effect, a verbal icon, in the sense of an icon formed from words rather than brush strokes.[46]

In the thirties, the standard account of how society would progress toward Communism (one that informed most literary works and films, and much journalism and Party rhetoric) was in terms of the working through of the dialectic not of class but of "consciousness" *(soznatel'nost')* and "spontaneity" *(stikhiinost')*. These terms play a central role in the Leninist appropriation of Marxism, starting from his programmatic "What Is To be Done?" (Chto delat'?) of 1902 (they are to be found also in Marx's texts, but there this dialectic plays a much more minor role). "Consciousness" stands for acts, bodies, or individuals that are undisciplined and not subordinated to the principles of Marxism-Leninism and Party guidance. According to the master model of history, society in general and individuals within it are progressing from a stage in which all their actions are primarily "spontaneous" in nature, through stages of ever greater "consciousness," and to that ultimate point, the state of communism, where all actions will be guided by "consciousness," but by a form of "consciousness" that will not be in conflict with the higher form of "spontaneity" that both society and its citizens will by then have achieved.

The plans for transforming Moscow were inflected by this master narrative of historical progress. Authoritative sources represented this project's principal function, not only in terms of ameliorating the material conditions of its citizens but also in terms of bringing them to a higher degree of consciousness. The 1935 resolution "On the General Plan for the Reconstruction of Moscow" *begins* with the word "spontaneity" *(stikhiinost'),* used as an iconic characterization of the old city. In this source, as in the 1931 resolution and in many of the official speeches and articles generated by this project, the building of the "new Moscow" to replace the "old" is explicitly represented as rectifying the "spontaneous"— that is, arbitrary ("proizvol" is sometimes used)[47]—haphazard, poorly planned, illogical, and inefficient configuration of Moscow in a *consciously* ordered new city.

As I have argued elsewhere, this dialectic of "spontaneity" and "consciousness" underwrote a masterplot that informed the socialist realist novel.[48] As the masterplot evolved a repertoire of clichés were developed for use by all novelists in tying their novels, whatever the subject matter, to this masterplot. The epithets—"simple" *(prostoi),* "severe" *(strogii),* "austere" *(surovyi),* "restrained" *(vyderzhannyi),* "lucid" *(svetlyi),* and "calm" *(spokoinyi)*—are used for identifying the positive hero and his mentor figure. He or she presents, as it were, successive establishing mug shots, each of which serves to triangulate the point that the hero has reached on the ascent toward pure consciousness. Essentially, then, the portrait given is no longer descriptive of an actual appearance, as in a novel of the realist tradition, but is discursive.

Virtually the same epithets that were used in Stalinist novels for identifying the positive hero as an emblem of "consciousness" were also used to characterize the new architecture of Moscow. With the extreme emphasis on the "face" of a building or of a positive hero, the distinction between exemplary human and exemplary building began to break down. The hero had become all surface appearance, text-like. Particularity and interiority had been eliminated, just as architecture was not to have any "intimacy" *(intimnost').* Both the buildings and the literary heroes were "masked."

This single repertoire of symbolic attributes, which was used in architectural discourse, fiction, and political rhetoric, formed the core of a general aesthetic. Of course the new buildings were not conspicuously "calm" (Nazi buildings were much "calmer," in the sense that they were often extremely austere). If anything, the overly busy façades of the typical Stalinist buildings from the thirties are less calm than their maligned Constructivist predecessors, whose architects placed a taboo on decoration. Rather, writings about these buildings used the encoded epithets such as "calm" that confer ideologically charged attributes on them. Thus some sort of narrative, and in this decade generally a written narrative, was prior to visual representation or material instantiation in architectural form. "Calm" as applied to a positive hero stood for "consciousness." In effect, when a person or building was said to be "calm," this ascription signaled that he/she/it had transcended ordinary time and crossed into timelessness.[49] Ostensibly, spatial qualities had a predominantly temporal meaning.

In architectural literature these epithets such as "calm" were not new.[50] They were fairly standard in writing about neoclassicism and are implied in its classic formulation by Johann Joachim Winckelmann (whose writings were also published in translation at this time): "noble simplicity and calm grandeur" (eine edle Einfalt und eine stille Grösse).[51] In the two decades prior to the Revolution, the same adjectives had been conventions for characterizing the architecture of Moscow's rival as capital city, Petersburg. This rhetoric essentially appropriated the clichéd prerevolutionary opposition that was a focus of narratives about Russian national identity, at whose center was the contrast between Moscow as a city of narrow, winding lanes and onion domes and Petersburg, which had supplanted Moscow as the national capital, as a city of broad and straight thoroughfares laid out in an "intentional" (Dostoevsky) and regular pattern. In this instance, however, the opposition has been internalized and temporalized in an "old"/"new" pattern applied to Moscow only.

Not coincidentally, perhaps, the "new Moscow" was in many respects a transplanted "old Petersburg," a city of grand façades, vast squares, granite embankments, statues, and imposing vistas. The architectural establishment, and especially the gigantic design studios that drew up the plans for the new, monumental buildings, streets, embankments, and squares of Moscow, gave prominence to several architects, such as Ivan Fomin and Vladimir Shchuko, from the movement for "old Petersburg" of the 1910s.[52] They promoted as precedents the work of earlier architects known for their work in Petersburg such as Carlo Rossi and Vasily Bazhenov, as well as that of leading prerevolutionary architects from Moscow who favored classical and Renaissance styles (such as Zholtovsky, and Aleksei Shchusev, who designed another model building, the Hotel Moscow, which was placed opposite the point where Gorky Street ran into

Marx Prospect).[53] The German avant-garde architects, such as Hannes Meier and Bruno Taut, who had come to Moscow in the belief that they would be designing a new world and even represented themselves as "we Soviet architects" (Meier) were kept busy with commissions and financed with millions of rubles in their separate studios but essentially sidelined in terms of actually being able to realize their projects. In consequence, they did not remain in the Soviet Union long (Taut left before the Nazi takeover in Germany).[54]

The avant-garde were redundant, for in effect Moscow was to assume the form of the capital city as it figured in the imagination of many Russians with Petersburg as the model. But as many have pointed out, "Petersburg" has never been just a paradigm of the modern city; it has always also been the symbolic site, the embodiment of an ideological system. More often than not, those who wrote about the alleged features of Petersburg architecture were not just providing descriptions but also deploying well-codified symbols for their own ends.[55]

In the early twentieth century, Russian architects promoted these very (alleged) qualities of Petersburg architecture as an "empire style" in the service of very different political positions, primarily the liberal democratic, but in some cases monarchical. A decade or so later, in the Stalinist project for a "new Moscow," when the same principles and repertoire of encoded vocabulary were invoked once again, they were reinflected by a new ideological narrative. In this sense, the appropriation of styles from the late imperial epoch did not just represent a return to czarist culture.

The Great Appropriation necessitated a great reworking of the significations.

In aesthetic practice, there was in effect a division of labor between the various branches of the arts that were linked by this standardized system of clichés. While in architecture it established what might be called "transcendent being," in literature it functioned as a marker of the degree of progress. It is the literary hero's function to link static ideality (being) with progress (becoming), space and time. In fact architectural discourse used several clichés not found in literature, such as "harmony" and "ensemble," which reinforced the architecture's static ideality but at the same time helped its products function as emblems of a unified social order. In the case of architecture, the image of the ideal to be realized in the "new

Moscow" was to a large extent linked to Rome. But what "Rome," or more generally "the classical," represented for many in the Soviet architectural establishment of the thirties was less the actual city, or actual buildings erected there in the classical era (though, to varying degrees, they were important models for those guiding architectural practice) than a set of underlying aesthetic principles. When the new "socialist realist" architects sought to recapture Rome and the classical past and studied the old Roman monuments, they took Vitruvius as their point of departure as they sought to divine the essence of the classical order, to evince a repertory of forms organized in a morphology, what was sometimes called a "grammar" of building.[56]

It was an ideologically inflected "grammar," conferring on "Moscow," where, allegedly, this new architecture had transformed the city, the status of an ontological ultimate. In Stalinist novels, and to some extent in films, the protagonists go to Moscow as a way of completing the symbolic journey of the country from a peasant to a modern, urbanized, and industrialized society, a journey that stands for the general movement of the society from spontaneity to consciousness, from "primitive" nature to culture and civilization.

Moscow, City of Enlightenment

The "new," postcapitalist Moscow was to be, as Soviet rhetoric suggested, a city of light. Thus, in its own way the scheme to transform Moscow was inspired by a vision of the Enlightenment, another time that sought precedents in the classical. In a sense, the Marxist-Leninist historical model (encapsulated as a road to consciousness) is the way the Bolsheviks read off the Enlightenment. It provides a version of the triumph of culture over nature. Kant, for example in his essay "Conjectural Beginning of Human History" (1786), outlines the general progress of humanity in terms of the transition from an uncultured, merely animal condition, to rational control. And in the opening sections of his essay "What Is Enlightenment" (1784) he specifically uses coming of age as a figure for attaining enlightenment: as man threw off the shackles of superstition, he could make a claim to be recognized as an adult, responsible human, and construct an environment for himself that both exemplified and conduced to this more advanced state. Engels, it is to be noted, in his *Condition of the Working Class in England* where he delivers a blistering critique of the slums of English industrial cities, also recommends that the working classes be familiarized with the classic texts of the Enlightenment as aids in their growth toward consciousness.

Stalinist Russia might seem to have appropriated a *version* of the Enlightenment vision, one that had been inscribed into the historical models of Marxism-Leninism. But the Stalinist "enlightenment" was of course a very restricted kind of enlightenment whose parameters were circumscribed by Marxism-Leninism. No doubt a Kaganovich's sense of what "Enlightenment" meant was pretty simplistic, but this does not prevent us from getting beyond the "mass ornament" and analyzing the culture system in more general terms as an Enlightenment project.

What exactly might that mean? To make any generalization about the Enlightenment is, as Peter Gay points out ruefully in his classic account of it, to have to acknowledge a countervailing example. Nevertheless, he proceeds to make a general characterization of that intellectual movement, and here I do so, too, largely drawing on his study as my source.[57] The Enlightenment might, in thumbnail sketch, be defined as a movement that, without necessarily rejecting religion, emphasized a more secular version of progress and redemption. This entailed a privileging of science and reason, and an optimistic sense of man's powers were he but to be liberated from "superstition," "stupidity," "Christianity," and "ignorance."

The Stalinist authorities who sought a "new Moscow" had a blithe confidence that their "scientific" principles, including their account of human nature, were universally applicable. Most thinkers of the Enlightenment also saw themselves as universalist in the reach of their ideas; indeed the very French word *philosophe* denotes an international type.

Characteristic of much Enlightenment thought was a centralizing aesthetic, one that favored straight lines and visible order. As Scott has remarked in *Seeing Like a State,* to many thinkers an "elective affinity between a strong state and a uniformly laid out city is obvious," but "no one expressed the prejudice more clearly than [the encyclopedist] Descartes," who commented on the "poorly laid out" towns with their "streets crooked and uneven" that *"it is chance more than the will of some*

men using their reason that has arranged them thus."⁵⁸ The writings of
Descartes, a favorite of Marx, were extensively promoted in the Soviet
culture of the mid-1930s, not surprisingly in that they exude faith in the
sacerdotal nature of literature; the anthropological hierarchy that informs
Descartes's *Discourse on Method* (1637) privileges the "gens de lettres."

A useful general model for the particular way I see some affinity between the thought of the Enlightenment and the way the rebuilding of
Moscow assumed a central role in Stalinist political culture is, in effect,
explored in Terry Eagleton's *Ideology of the Aesthetic.* Here Eagleton foregrounds the fact that during the Enlightenment there was a palpable shift
to foregrounding the aesthetic. He sees this preeminently in the work of
Kant, but also in a number of other philosophers, mostly Germans, whom
he discusses in his initial chapters, ranging from Baumgarten and his
treatise *Aesthetica* of 1750 through Schiller to Hegel, allowing also that
many of "the aesthetic motifs I trace can be pursued back to the Renaissance or even to classical antiquity."⁵⁹ In Soviet Russia, Kant was considered the archenemy of the "materialist point of view" as an "idealist," yet
arguably, though this could not have been recognized, in some defining
aspects the first half of the thirties went under the sign of Kant, and of
others in his approximate cohort.

In this book Eagleton is not really talking about the aesthetic per se,
not really exclusively about the category of beauty, but is using the term
"aesthetic" in a broader sense that encompasses the ethical and the political as well. He insists that philosophers were drawn at the time of the
Enlightenment to work on aesthetic issues because the aesthetic, more
than the purely ethical, which was more abstract, offered a model for relating particular to general (or universal), for integrating what Kant calls
the "egoism of taste," of the individual subject's impulses, into a higher
system:

> Within the dense welter of our material life, with all its amorphous
> flux, certain objects stand out in a sort of perfection dimly akin to
> reason, and these are known as the beautiful. . . . Because these are
> objects which we can agree to be beautiful, not by arguing or analys-
> ing but just by looking and seeing, a spontaneous consensus is
> brought to birth within our creaturely life, bringing with it the prom-

ise that such a life, for all its apparent arbitrariness and obscurity, might indeed work in some sense very like a rational law.[60]

This is what the Soviet theoreticians of the thirties effectively believed, too. The Stalinist "aesthetic" or "beautiful" was not self-valuable or "autonomous" but was incorporated into an ideological system *as its nodal point.* The beautiful was also represented as being the "harmonious," in effect that which marries the subjective to the objective in concrete actuality.

Eagleton further argues that these philosophers of the late eighteenth and early nineteenth centuries, though their ostensible concern is the aesthetic, address, explicitly or implicitly, such questions as "how can one get around that old problem that if one, or an entire society, is guided by pure reason, by purely abstract principles," then actuality and particularity, the "sensible" life,[61] and even history itself "will slip through the net of conceptual discourse to leave one grasping an empty space."[62] Kant, Eagleton contends, held that "the ultimate binding force of the bourgeois social order, in contrast to the coercive apparatus of absolutism, will be habits, pieties, sentiments and affections. And this is equivalent to saying that power in such an order has been *aestheticized.*" "Power," he continues, "is now inscribed in the minutiae of subjective experience, and the fissure between abstract duty and pleasurable inclination is accordingly healed. . . . The new subject, finding its freedom in its necessity, is modeled on the aesthetic artifact."[63]

In its Soviet variant, however, "enlightenment" was not only an ideal but also an authorization, a virtual mandate, and was used to justify extreme measures. As in the Enlightenment itself, there was a marked Manichaean proclivity in the Stalinist view of the world. After all, light always presupposes the dark that is to be banished. The infamous purges of the thirties could be read in these terms. But the Enlightenment was no innocent time in this respect either, though less "terrible." For example, Bacon as England's attorney general personally oversaw interrogations involving physical torture (such as that of Edmund Peacham).

There is, however, a less sinister aspect of this Manichaean proclivity. Many thinkers of the Enlightenment believed that in order to keep "ignorance" and the dark forces at bay, one had to *know exactly,* scientifically, and by rational investigation. Some of them (Diderot, Linnaeus) had a passion for classification, and for setting up institutions that might collect, categorize, and disseminate culture and knowledge such as encyclopedias, museums, and libraries, a passion that devolved in the Soviet case to what Regis Debray has dismissed as "academism, museomania and the general smell of mothballs impregnating Soviet society."[64]

An important distinction, however, between the ideology of the Stalinist thirties that sought to erect a "new Moscow" and that of the Enlightenment is the Enlightenment's stress on individual judgment, which the Stalin era, in effect, claimed to have superseded with its "scientific socialism" that was more "collectivist"—and doctrinaire. What several philosophes and other representatives of the Enlightenment valued most highly—a "critical mentality" and the development of a cultivated sensibility—might be seen as the very opposite of the kind of mentality to be fostered in the "new Moscow." Kant in his conception of Enlightenment stresses that individuals should throw off the tutelage of their "guardian(s)" and exercise their reason in *freedom*. Stalinist political culture, with its rejection of that "courageous skepticism" so valued in the Enlightenment, represents a virtual reversal of such key Enlightenment values.

But in the Stalinist discourse of the 1930s, "Enlightenment" was inexorably linked to the values of the political establishment, symbolized in Moscow as the space of ideality. Consequentially, in the socialist realist novels generated in this decade (and even more blatantly in some films), the hero's progress in political consciousness is correlated with his spatial progress, as a necessary step in the ritual of self-mastery. Toward the end of the novel he makes a trip from the provincial backwater where he lives to the new Moscow.

Moscow represents achieved socialism, an ideal city, and the hero of a novel functions as an emissary, binding Moscow and the provinces, imperfect space. His reaching Moscow intimates that the Soviet Union is on track to its destination in communism. Consequently, only the hero and his mentors, that is, those who are advanced in consciousness, can advance in spatial terms, go and see Moscow (or Stalin). The hero is dazzled by Moscow, which is often represented as gleaming white, but he cannot remain there. He must return to his provincial reality (the periphery). Like the rest of Soviet citizenry, he is still in a state of becoming, though he represents them in a more idealized form. He is not destined to achieve the level of "Moscow" itself. Time and space are intertwined in a chronotope of progress. Moscow remains a closed, utopian space, and as with classic utopias only designated intermediaries and emissaries can breach its fortified border.

The Fourth Rome as Utopia

This very boundedness and internal segmentation of Stalinist political culture renders Moscow less the center of a new-age enlightenment than the site of a utopia. Significantly, perhaps, Rama's "lettered cities" of sixteenth- and seventeenth-century Latin America arose in the period just after several of the classic utopias were written: Tommaso Campanella's *City of the Sun* (Citta del sole) of 1602/1623, Thomas More's *Utopia* of 1515, and Francis Bacon's *New Atlantis* of 1627. Indeed Auerbach links the appearance of these utopias with the exploration of the New World of the Americas.[65] As Gulio C. Argan has noted also in his study of the Renaissance, "treatises on architecture in the fifteenth and sixteenth centuries were full of ideal cities, that is, of cities planned *ex novo,* based on purely rational and geometric planning. The ideal city was, in fact, an artistic and political invention of its time since it was founded on the principle that the perfect architectural and urban form of the city corresponded to the perfection of its political and social arrangements."[66]

The possibility of the perfect city, the perfect articulation of space, attracted many Soviet planners. They sought to match the "beauty" or "harmony" of social organization and practices to the "beauty" or ideality of their physical layout and buildings. But the utopian possibility for Soviet Russia had been on the cultural horizon from the very beginning. In the initial postrevolutionary years, Soviet publishing houses brought out many of these classic utopias. Lunacharsky, then Commissar of Enlightenment, was particularly taken by Campanella and wrote a play about him that was staged in the 1920s. That classic utopia was also republished, along with several others, in 1934–1935, a time when, somewhat as in Campanella, murals were painted on the new architecture to edify the citizens.[67] But parallels between the "new Moscow" and the classic utopia went far beyond this relatively surface feature.

Richard Stites in his *Revolutionary Dreams* provides an almost breathless catalogue of all the manifold utopian experiments undertaken in the 1920s and laments the 1930s as bringing an end to utopian striving in the Soviet Union. Yet in some senses the thirties were more utopian than the twenties, and particularly in regard to Moscow. A distinction has to be made here between "utopian" and "utopia." "Utopian" may refer to an actual utopia but also means something that is idealistic, impractical, and quite probably communalistic but not necessarily involving a utopia, which is a distinct, separate, and defined place—generally a city-state, or possibly a separate building, as in the phalanstery. Though some utopias, such as *The Land of Cockaigne,* are freewheeling and hedonistic, the classic utopia is bounded and restrictive (essentially puritanical). Almost all of them are set on some remote island or at least a space cut off from all contiguous habitation (you must cross an ocean or a wilderness to get there).

Most accounts of utopias are obsessed with borders both physical and metaphorical (bounds of the permitted). Classic utopias organize an entire city or cluster of cities as a hermetic nation, paying a great deal of attention to policing and fortification to ensure the purity of the utopia. Crucial to Campanella are the multiple fortifications organized in a geometric pattern of concentric circles. And in More's *Utopia,* though there are separate cities, each is encompassed by a high and thick wall supported by a series of towers and forts. In fact though his utopia was not originally an island, a wise founder's foresight had ordered construction of massive earthworks, making it possible for the sea to engulf the resulting huge cavity, cutting the utopia off from the mainland.

Policing and fortification are also important *within* the utopia. In More, citizens cannot visit another city or stroll outside their own without an internal passport and permission from local officials; the punishment for a repeat violation is being reduced to slavery. And in most utopias exclusions of various kinds (ranging from being denied a seat in the communal dining facility to expulsion from the utopia) are critical to the maintenance of conformity; one need hardly add that an elaborate system of practices of exclusion (from the Komsomol or Party, from a city, banishment to a labor camp, or physical annihilation) was a central feature of the Soviet 1930s.

Utopias are not only impossibly ideal, unrealistically hyperorganized city-states but generally also places where the intellect and the arts are privileged. But the privileging of professionals within the arts is something that was occurring at about the time the classic utopias were being written. A similar division can be seen in Soviet society as it drew away from the cultural revolution, where the "proletarian" had been privileged and the intellectual required to subordinate his activity to the needs and concerns of the workers. Now the intellectual was favored, de facto (unofficially), enjoying a privileged status vis-à-vis the non-professionals, the masses. Symptomatically, in the "new" Moscow as a "city of light," there was a reordering of space. Factories were to be relegated to the periphery, and buildings for culture were to be given greater prominence.[68] Admittedly, the factories were dirty and polluting, hence their removal can be seen as part of progress and modernization, but "dirty" had now become a negative attribute: filth, vermin, disease, and so on were prominent terms for "class enemies" in discourse about the purges but were also, as "unhygienic," markers of primitivism and ignorance.

In literature and the press of the 1920s, "bourgeois professionals" had been dismissed as "beloruchki," literally "white-handers," a class who wore white gloves so as not to be besmirched by the soot and grease of the factories, the mud and concrete of construction; the proletariat, by contrast, were represented as being full-blooded, not squeamish about getting right into the belly of production or going right up to the hellish heat of the blast furnace. In the thirties, however, this pattern was somewhat reversed. In art and especially films, there was a hyperbolic use of white for things associated with positive characters—their clothing, furnishings, and surrounding architecture—as if to emphasize the "cultured" nature of their existence.

Although ostensibly communalistic, most literary utopias are in fact organized in a hierarchy in anthropology, dividing up their citizenry into fixed categories. One of the most privileged of these categories is generally the intellectuals. In Bacon's *New Atlantis,* for example, citizens enjoy all sorts of technological marvels made possible because of thirty-six "fathers" who form the core of the scientific institute cum monastic colony known as Solomon's House.

As in Plato's utopia, in Stalinist Moscow of the 1930s the most privileged categories were the philosopher kings (writers and legislators) and the guardians (military and secret police). Indeed, the links between the two were closer than many who idealize the intelligentsia admit, though the hierarchy of intellectual elite and political elite was reversed, so that in general the "guardians" were more powerful than the intellectuals (but Stalin combined both functions). After the Writers Union was founded in April 1932, writers became one of the most privileged categories of the population in the Stalinist thirties. A new system of (greatly enhanced) royalty payments was introduced, a differentiated system largely based on ideological criteria. The Writers Union now treated its members to dachas, a high-class restaurant in their headquarters, new apartment blocks, and subsidized vacations in choice locations.

In literary utopias, as Northrop Frye has observed, intellectuals are privileged because a utopia is a social order whose entire raison d'être is the education of its subjects.[69] In More's *Utopia* this is taken to such an extreme that lectures are delivered before dawn so that citizens can go off to work properly edified. Much of the sense of education and learning in these early utopias is of an earnest, improving variety, but also humanistic, in the specific sense that emphasis is put on texts from the classical era. The utopia's intellectual elite are often guided by philosophical, architectural, or moral treatises in ancient Greek and Hebrew (some casuistry has to be used to account for how the utopians, in some remote location, managed to acquire and be able to read these texts— a fortuitous shipwreck, a chance traveler instructs them or leaves his library).

In Stalinist Moscow the *letrados* were privileged, white-collar workers, a category broader than the writers or architects. In the same issue of *Stroitel'stvo Moskvy* where the Central Committee resolution announcing the formation of the Writers Union was published, there appeared a resolution of Sovnarkom and the Central Committee calling for an immediate start on the construction of 102 new apartment buildings, to be erected over the next two years, for "specialists and scholars."[70] In reality, most were allocated to particular bureaucratic bodies (a category that includes the Writers Union).

One is compelled to ask: was the "new Moscow" an aesthetic utopia or a civil service town? Were writers realizing, if only partially, that old dream of a literatocracy or were they confronting the reality that they, too, were just civil servants, if privileged ones, scribes copying texts who were em-

powered only to make individual embellishments but could not otherwise deviate from them, a grander version of the lowly Petersburg copying
clerk Akaky Akakievich in Nikolai Gogol's story "The Overcoat" (Shi-
nel', 1841), who took pride in his penmanship?

Moscow as a "lettered city" was at one and the same time a civil service
town where, to an inordinate degree, everything was controlled by paper-
work, and a visionary space, a space of beauty, a fantastic narrative. But
the "new Moscow" turned out to be somewhat utopian, in that only a
small fraction of the grandiose plans for it were ever executed. In a sense,
the utopia was best realized in the metro, which was an ideal city, except
that no one actually lived there.[71] In one of the illustrations in Rodchenko
and Stepanova's glossy album *Moscow Reconstructs* (Moskva rekonstruiruetsia, 1937), Stalin and Kaganovich stand above a city laid out in a ra-
dial/concentric pattern, the shape of Moscow's metro.[72] To reach the
metro, Soviet citizens had to go underground, to a netherworld of reversed symbolism in the sense that its stations with their lavish appoint-
ments (marble, candelabra) were to suggest to the popular imagination a
higher order of existence. But their magnificence was not gratuitous; the
murals, frescoes, and statuary were intended, à la Campanella, for their
edification. Bruno Taut, the German modernist architect who had waxed
so lyrical about the new Soviet construction when he visited in the early
1930s (see Chapter 1) expressed disgust at the vulgarity and waste in the
metro when he was shown it during a visit of November 1936. "What a
mania for the grandiose!" he exclaimed, adding that the metro stations
were like "nobles' estates" or Roman baths with their unnecessary and
magnificent marble. "Just think how many Moscow apartments for workers could have been built with the money spent on this excess," he expos-
tulated.[73] But of course Moscow's planners were operating with a different
sense of what would be most for the workers' benefit.

Intellectuals as Ideologists

What was the role of intellectuals in this utopia manqué? Here, once
again, a good model is to be found in Eagleton's account in *The Ideology
of the Aesthetic,* in this case of the ambiguities and ambivalences surrounding the stances of leading intellectuals of the German "bourgeois enlight-

enment." Kant, to Eagleton the paradigmatic example, he characterizes as a "courageous Aufklärer and docile subject of the king of Prussia."[74]

Though Eagleton may have exaggerated the extent to which Kant was a "docile subject" of the king of Prussia, an analogous contradiction was inherent in the situation of the aesthetic theoreticians and practitioners of the early 1930s. The Marxist intelligentsia as a group had been sparsely represented before the 1930s. Now, as spokesmen at the "Congress of Victors" (the Seventeenth Party Congress of 1934) contended, the majority of Soviet intellectuals were working within the parameters of Marxism. To some extent this intelligentsia had been created by political pressures and the great upheavals of the 1920s. To some extent they had just adjusted to a new patronage system. The point is, however, that many members of this "Marxist" intelligentsia both believed in the relative autonomy of their own inquiries yet were also Stalinism's "docile subjects" and apologists.

In Stalinist culture the men of letters, the *letrados,* were essentially the translators. Some, like those who wrote about architecture, were charged with inscribing ideological meaning into essentially banal architectural styles, while others, such as the socialist realist authors, were to translate the sacred, eternal texts (of Lenin and Stalin) into profane (more particularized and evolving) stories and novels. Their role was in some senses comparable to the one Anderson has described for the literati in the medieval European world dominated by the Catholic Church: "adepts, strategic strata in a cosmological hierarchy of which the apex was the divine." This "bilingual intelligentsia," Anderson continues, "by mediating between vernacular and Latin, mediated between earth and heaven. (The awesomeness of excommunication reflects this cosmology.")[75]

At the same time many of the leading Stalinist intellectuals were prosecuting their own vision. They were inevitably obedient servants and implementers of Stalinist plans ("engineers of human souls"), but they also saw themselves as *Aufklärer.* Many believed that, after all, they were more enlightened than their predecessors in tsarist Russia because they were armed with Marx ("scientific socialism"). Often their main mission was to recover Soviet Russia for great culture (which Marx had always believed in, anyway). Kaganovich had said in his speech to the Komsomol of 1933, cited earlier, "they [the proletariat] will make sure that their cities, their buildings and their architecture are more beautiful than in other towns of Europe and America."[76] "They" here was explicitly "the proletariat," but intellectuals were particularly enticed by that prospect. In the name of establishing Soviet cultural preeminence and claiming custodianship of the Great Tradition, they fought against the primitivism and narrowness of "proletarian culture," which was in practice very Russo-centric, and against what they saw as the self-indulgence of modernism.

In the campaign to return "culture" to Soviet Russia, initiative was often taken by prominent intellectuals themselves. For example, as we saw in the previous chapter, Zholtovsky, who in the early thirties was the premier architect, translated Palladio on his own initiative,[77] but Palladio's theories became very influential and, as mentioned, Zholtovsky's "Palladian villa" erected on Marx Prospect functioned initially as the official model for (socialist realist!) architecture. Thus Zholtovsky to a considerable degree established the form of the "beautiful" in his field while yet responding to the whims of a Kaganovich or a Stalin.

In the case of the literary intelligentsia and the leading exponents of a "Marxist-Leninist aesthetics" there was a distinct drive for greater independence. Symptomatically, many sought, and the privileged attained, some physical separateness that facilitated this. The writer Marietta Shaginian proposed building a little town *(gorodok)* for literature outside Moscow, one where both writers and their publishing houses would be located. This was never realized, though Peredelkino, a writers' settlement outside Moscow, was built as an idyllic retreat for the most favored. There they lived as virtual gentry on estates. Both Stalin and Gorky were against establishing a separate settlement, yet it was built.[78] As security agents frequently complained to the Soviet leaders, writers met and prosecuted their literary interests there in all too independent a fashion.[79] And—a mark of the status of literature—in 1936 plans were announced to erect a grand new building to house the Institute of World Literature (IMLI) to form one point in a prestigious triangle of buildings, the other two to be the Palace of Soviets and the Commissariat of Heavy Industry.[80]

At this time also, the humanities were reinstated, as Stalinist cultural policies drew away from total emphasis on pragmatic and doggedly "materialist" approaches. In the 1920s, as part of the constant reorganizations of the universities, they had done away with their humanities programs or given them a sociological, political, and economic orientation. But now that, in effect, culture was "married," rather than subjugated, to Marxism, the humanities were revived and even given a special status. Symptomatically, the Communist Academy was abolished in 1934 and melded with the Academy of Sciences.

The Institute for Philosophy, Literature, and History, known by its acronym (IFLI), was an institution that typified this moment. Founded in the critical year 1931, when it was separated off from Moscow University it offered the very nexus of subjects that was to be so crucial in "writing the city" (history of art was included among its subjects as a branch of the History Department). The institute was semiautonomous—in fact, starting in 1934 it was located on the then periphery of the capital, in Sokoloniki, which gave it greater independence. It was a trendy institution for the times; consequently, it was hard to get into and largely served the elite.[81] It was also distinctly Marxist. By contrast, in such comparable semiautonomous institutions of serious intellectual endeavor from the twenties, as the State Academy of the Artistic Sciences (GAKhN) in Moscow or the State Institute for the History of the Arts (GIII) in Leningrad, scholars had studied literature, philosophy, and art history but largely in a non-Marxist framework (both institutions had been purged during the cultural revolution, when GAKhN was closed and GIII bolshevized).[82]

The Institute for Philosophy, Literature, and History provided its students with a blend of Marxist education (especially of *Capital*), with a rigorous grounding in culture that emphasized the classical era, the Renaissance, and modern European literature and thought, as well as Russian traditions (its graduates range from Alexander Solzhenitsyn, who studied as a correspondence student, to Vladimir Semichastnyi, the future head of the KGB). In their lectures the professors emphasized "the self-determining nature of human powers and capacities which becomes, in the work of Karl Marx and others, the anthropological foundation of a revolutionary opposition to bourgeois utility."[83] In other words, and as is commonly to be found among those Marxists who draw on the *Economic and Philosophic Manuscripts,* "utility" was rejected as a value in favor of more humanistic approaches to Marxism. And as the lecturers there weighed in against mere "utility," they particularly advanced the Renais-

sance as a historical precedent for the new age, picturing it as a time of
"beauty" and "humanism," values for which they could find ample endorsement in the early Marx. Their students were responsive; the lectures there on the Renaissance were always packed.[84]

Several of the prominent literary theorists at IFLI, and notably Lukács
and his close associate Mikhail Lifshits,[85] were also key players in the one
central journal from the 1930s that was devoted to literary theory and
criticism, *Literaturnyi kritik.* (Literary critic; founded 1933). Elena
Usievich, a leading editor, was the daughter of Feliks Kron and had traveled with him in the armored train that brought Lenin back from Zurich
in April 1917 and was hence to some extent the journal's protector. The
theoretical positions in the thirties of this clique are generally labeled
"Stalinist," and indeed their being in favor is alleged to account for the
very founding of the journal. *Literaturnyi kritik* played an active role in
the theoretical campaign against "vulgar sociology," which was being
promoted on high as well (by "vulgar sociology" was meant analyzing
literary works or literary history entirely in terms of material relations and
the class struggle). Lukács and Lifshits had formulated their respective
understandings of "Marxist aesthetics" in the twenties (Lifshits in 1927,
Lukács around 1923), when they were out of step with the dominant Soviet trends of that time (proletarian culture and Constructivism), and they
maintained much the same views even after they were attacked in the late
1930s (see Chapter 9) until their deaths well after Stalin died (Lukács in
1971, Lifshits in 1983). In other words, sometimes their positions coincided with "the line," and sometimes not. At any rate the thirties were a
high time for the Lifshits coterie, and he characterized them later in his
memoirs as a time of exhilarating polemics (perhaps exhilarating for him
because for most of the decade power was on his side).[86]

The theoretical work presented in the journal was preceded by the
aforementioned appearance of previously unpublished letters by Marx
and Engels on literary matters. Both the publication of the relevant writings from Marx and Engels in 1931–1933 and the subsequent publication
of comprehensive, interpretive accounts of "Marxist-Leninist aesthetics"
were almost entirely undertaken by the same small group of scholars,
most with links to *Literaturnyi kritik* and IFLI: Lukács and Lifshits, together with Mikhail Ernst Fischer, Frants Shiller, and their erstwhile patron,

the former minister for Culture and Education, Anatoly Lunacharsky (until his death in late 1933).[87]

Lukács had returned to Moscow from Berlin in March 1933 and was installed first in the Literary Institute of the Academy of Sciences and then in the Philosophical Institute, where he remained until 1938. At that time socialist realist theory was being formulated most intensely, and he became an authoritative figure in the debates. Though he was not an official formulator of the theory, his publications in the mid-thirties effectively provided the most cogent, economical, and intellectually respectable account of the implications of the basal dynamic underpinning this "method." In it he advanced a vision of a totality to be found in aesthetics, but not aesthetics as an academic "science of the beautiful" so much as an entire philosophical cum historical worldview.

At the heart of Lukács's writings in these years is the binary of particularity and universality, a problematic one that, as indicated earlier, Eagleton alleges aesthetics redresses. Of the many articles Lukács published in *Literaturnyi kritik,* the key one in this regard was his essay "Narration or Description?" (Rasskaz ili opisanie), published in 1936.[88] In this essay, which in many respects represents a reformulation of a position he had presented several times before, particularly in his Berlin essay "Reportage or Portrayal" of 1932 (see Chapter 1), Lukács is ostensibly *de*scribing what happens in the European novel of the nineteenth century, but in effect he is *pre*scribing what should happen in the socialist realist novel of the twentieth. Lukács counterposes "narration" and "description" as two strategies for representation but valorizes them (narration as positive, description as negative), using as paradigms for the two approaches the different ways Tolstoy and Zola describe a horse race (in *Anna Karenina* and *Nana,* respectively). Lukács's particular focus is the use of detail in these two scenes: he insists that while in Zola the specifica of the horse race have, virtually, the status of self-valuable material, in *Anna Karenina,* his positive example, Tolstoy introduces ample detail but in deploying it subordinates the detail to his overall plot scheme. Lukács does not actually use the word "detail" in this essay so much as "the contingent" (or random; *sluchainost'* in the Russian version, *das Zufällige* in the German). In other words, he condemns the use of gratuitous facts and particularity and calls instead for the hegemony in composition of some overarching narrative ("fabula," "rasskaz"), insisting that all detail have a discursive function.[89] Characters in a novel are not to be depicted with a lot of detail about the inner psyche but must be connected to the details in a narrative of action and praxis.

To Lukács, the problem with overemphasis on detail, and doubtless the reason he chose to use the word "contingency" for it, is that it is precisely *contingent* and needs to be raised to the level of the essential, of "necessity" (*neobkhodimost'* in Russian, *Notwendigkeit* in German). Moreover, "necessity" to him, as a Marxist, meant in effect the Marxist-Leninist account of history. As he put it: "A chance [sluchainaia] feature, a chance similarity, a chance meeting should become an *unmediated* expression of important social interrelations [sootnoshenii]."[90]

Zola, arguably, was in this essay condemned by Lukács not just for the way he used "random," unsystematized detail (far from a watertight argument—after all, what is system and what not?) but also for the precise *detail* he used in a novel about a courtesan who ends up with a face grotesquely disfigured from smallpox. In the official formulation of socialist realism presented to the First Writers Congress of 1934, all "physiologism" (read sex and lower bodily functions) was proscribed.[91] But an obsession with the bodily characterized quite a bit of the literature and public culture of the 1930s. Dwelling on lower bodily functions can be found in such works as Shostakovich's opera *Lady Macbeth of Mtsensk,* completed in 1933 and premiered in 1934. Another good example would be Andrei Platonov's ironically titled novel *Happy Moscow* (Schastlivaia Moskva; 1933–1936). Never finished and never published under Stalin, this novel was actually begun in response to the call from on high to generate more cultural products about the nation's capital. It presents emblematic features of 1930s "Soviet civilization" such as komsomols, building the metro, and parachute divers. But it also treats obsessively lower bodily functions, and systems for carrying human waste invisibly, both the system of canals in the body for ingestion and e-gestion with their rotted contents (intestines, colon, and anus) and the system for transporting effluent within the city's buildings (sewerage pipes).[92]

Part of the reason the bodily functions were so problematical in Soviet culture of the 1930s was because, as Eagleton points out, "how can reason, that most immaterial of faculties, grasp the grossly sensuous."[93] In addition, as the body is so closely associated with the "body politic," it was a particularly sensitive subject in this decade of "purging." In seeking to aestheticize the body, in large measure Stalinist cultural policies dematerialized it. But a further reason why Stalinist culture downplayed the sensuous is that all reminders of rot and decay, of bodily perversion and decline, are threats to any claim for the eternal. There was a long Russian tradition of rejecting the bodily and procreative (often called "pathological" or "perverse").[94] Bodily functions and their consequences (death, waste, sexual encounters resulting in births or divorces) are also problematical in any utopia because they undermine the perfect, timeless order. One is struck in looking at *Pravda* and other Moscow newspapers of the 1930s, especially the lower brow *Vecherniaia Moskva* (Evening Moscow), by the recurrent appearance of articles claiming that some miracle cure, some elixir, mental or chemical (one might almost say alchemical), has been invented for overcoming mortality, reversing time's arrow and prolonging or restoring youth, a task particularly charged to an institution with the curious title Institute of the Second Life.[95]

In texts of the 1930s, ordinary time is often overcome in epiphanic moments, not in chronological time. Soviet novels took their heroes from the prosaic and inadequate to the heroic in great leaps, or in highly ritualized scenes. Lukács also provided a theoretical model for this tendency. In "Narration or Description?" he argues that novels should feature culmination points, moments in the narrative that result in a shift from the old to the new. In this way, details of the setting and characters would be connected in a narrative of action and praxis, would take place in what he called an "epic" world of action and movement.[96]

Discourse about architecture was aligned with this temporal model. The butterfly—"new"—Moscow would emerge from its chrysalis of scaffolding in an abrupt transition. In Aleksandr Medvedkin's film *The New Moscow* (Novaia Moskva; 1938) an artist is attempting to paint city scenes, but every time he tries to do so, its buildings are moved or replaced before his very eyes. The space of the city (Moscow) was turned into a theater of progress where one could witness chaos being turned in an instant into mind.

CHAPTER 4

The Traveling Mode and the
Horizon of Identity

O N JUNE 19, 1933, in response to an injunction that film directors use professional writers for their scripts, Eisenstein published an article in *Literaturnoia gazeta,* "The Discriminating Bride" (Razborchivaia nevesta). After a preamble the article opens with a startling sally (startling for the puritanical Soviet 1930s): "May I make her take supper with her lover in bed after the love-making." It emerges that here Eisenstein is citing a question that Zola, in researching his novel *Nana,* asked his informant Henri Céard about the lives of courtesans; Zola envisions the possibility whereby, if the courtesan and her lover eat together in bed, this could mean crumbs on the sheets leading to a spat, and this spat would be a way of inserting into the plot an extended quarrel he wants the lovers to have. Céard explains that this would be impossible for a high-class courtesan of the Paris demimonde during the Second Empire. In Eisenstein's article we next see Zola, "short-sighted," "flustered" *(poteriannyi),* and in evening dress with a pince-nez researching in a leading courtesan's boudoir. She, semi-déshabillée, is reclining on a couch with her leg resting on his knee, while he, notebook in hand, is furiously jotting down her account of the routine and strategy used when a courtesan puts on her makeup.[1]

Such a scene might seem totally unexpected in an article from the Stalin era, but Zola was one of Eisenstein's favorite authors, and he especially valued him for the sensuality of his writing. Of course Zola was also politically acceptable (though as Eisenstein ruefully remarked, as ill luck would have it, Engels praised Balzac, and spoke less warmly of Zola).[2] In 1930 Eisenstein had planned a film on Zola and the Dreyfus Trial, but here the reader is not getting the politically correct Zola.[3]

The jolt for a Stalinist reader of Eisenstein's opening sally in this article about courtesans and lovemaking is also the jolt of a horizon opened up. The blunt sexuality should not blind us to the fact that he is situating the writing of literature not in the steel mill or state farm milking shed (the latter features in his last finished film, *The Old and the New* (Staroe i novoe; 1929)[4] but in the Paris boudoir. This is an extreme case of a general shift that we see in the 1930s to a broader, less parochial purview. Here we have a discussion of Zola, Flaubert, Balzac, and at one point Dreiser (in one of his many abortive filmmaking attempts during the 1930s, he had tried to film Dreiser's *American Tragedy*). In this article he makes passing mention of Pushkin and Modest Mussorgsky but otherwise operates in a totally western European cultural sphere (though not a modernist one).

Eisenstein published this article in 1933, while the debate was on as to what might be the meaning of "socialist realism," a term for the mandatory "method" of Soviet literature minted only a year earlier (May 1932, actually the month Eisenstein returned from Mexico). Before the announcement of that method, on April 23, 1932, by Central Committee decree, all independent writers' organizations had been abolished and a single Writers Union formed. These two events are in Western historiography normally associated with regimentation, homogenization, and control by a rigid, dogmatic Party. Eisenstein's moral in this article is that in order to be a good writer one must know life, have "experience," but the experience he describes is hardly that of the factory bench, which so recently during the Plan years (1928–1931) had been considered crucial for a writer's education. Yet he is writing about a form of "realism," as attested by the notebook in Zola's hand.

But, after all, a courtesan cannot be a "bride" *(nevesta)*. She belongs to the demimonde, a world that is "demi-" in the sense that it largely exists outside official moral and legal provisions. All its highly "physiological" reality belonged to a demimonde that was not to exist in comme il faut socialist realism. But we may read Eisenstein's article in terms of a different demimonde, which was not to be proscribed but rather to be, as it were, accepted by societal norms in the wake of the April 1932 decree, and that is the demimonde of Western culture. Like the Parisians of the nineteenth century with their demimonde, much of the Soviet cultural world did not really know what to do with it. They were "flustered," like poor, short-sighted Zola in the courtesan's boudoir, but also attracted.

Eisenstein was operating in a cultural and existential horizon that had been increasingly proscribed over the course of the 1920s, the horizon of European culture (other than proletarian or communist European culture). As recently as 1930–1931, there had been a major campaign against "Formalists" (including Eisenstein himself), this term being effectively a cipher for modernists and Western trends.[5] Now the horizon of what could be entertained both suddenly expanded and simultaneously contracted. Most of Eisenstein's film projects of the 1930s (especially those he came at all close to realizing) were on Russian topics, but his lectures at the State Film Institute (VGIK) were saturated with discussions of western European literature and art, like the column titled "The Discriminating Bride."[6]

The abolition of all independent writers' organizations in 1932 may have "herded" Soviet writers into a single union under Party supervision, but in many respects it also represented a liberalization. The possibilities were greater literally thanks to a dramatic improvement in their material situation (higher royalty payments, etc.), which propelled writers into the New Class. But the cultural horizons also became broader. The April decree explicitly disbanded the powerful RAPP, which was not just militantly "proletarian" (Communist) but essentially also an entity of narrow, Russo-centric horizons.

The demise of RAPP was for most writers liberating. The change was almost immediately reflected in *Literaturnaia gazeta,* where in recent years RAPP had been the driving force. Its editorial board was revamped—now to include Koltsov—and the amount of material it published about Western writers and intellectuals increased exponentially, with regular columns such as "Literary New York"[7] and items on current developments in English culture by Prince Dmitri Sviatopolk-Mirsky, who had recently returned from London after twelve years in emigration.[8] Most striking were the intermittent articles extolling such members of the Western avant-garde as Joyce,[9] Dos Passos,[10] Picasso,[11] and the French Surrealists.[12] By 1935 a *Pravda* editorial, "The Style of *Soviet* Culture," was citing Balzac, Goethe, Shakespeare, and Tolstoy as its models.[13] And in 1932 Koltsov founded and edited a new journal, *Za rubezhom* (Abroad).

"Boy" was not just meeting "tractor," he was also encountering Western culture.

There had been a time before when a lot of Western material was published. Between 1922 and 1924, the previous high point for this, journals such as *The Contemporary West* (Sovremennyi zapad) had regaled readers with information on the latest developments there, while the Gorky-sponsored publishing house Vsemirnaia literature (World Literature) had been at the heart of an ambitious translation project. At that time, with four-fifths of the population illiterate, such enterprises essentially served intellectuals and professionals. By the 1930s, however, the Soviet people were largely literate and were avid readers. Massive enterprises were established to publish the work of European writers, a gesture that expanded the purview of the reading public. In March 1931, in the wake of the international conference on proletarian literature held in Kharkov the year before, a new publishing house, Verlagsgenossenschaft ausländischer Arbeiter in der UdSSR (VEGAAR), was established to publish works in translation. This press had initially put out a lot of the Marx-Engels Archive and—since the Kharkov conference had been conducted under the aegis of RAPP—proletarian literature, but in this new climate VEGAAR began publishing more and more nonproletarian Western literature. *Inostrannaia kniga* (Foreign book), which reviewed Western literature and Soviet translations of Western texts, started to appear in 1932 as a by-product of Kharkov, but it took off and became remarkably catholic in its fare.[14]

Clearly the reentry of Gorky (no lover of the avant-garde, but a veteran *Kulturträger*) into a leadership position in Soviet literature after he returned in 1931 was crucial in this development. Both Mirsky and Koltsov were among his protégés. But this cosmopolitan trend not only affected literature; it was to be found in all branches of the arts, as the parameters of the models cited for Soviet culture were expanded. Art journals began to feature as "realists" such western European painters as Gustave Courbet, Rembrandt van Rijn, Pierre-Auguste Renoir, Paul Cézanne, and Jacques-Louis David—even Leonardo,[15] while articles on theater fore-grounded Molière (Jean-Baptiste Poquelin) and Shakespeare.

One clear aim in the shift was national aggrandizement and legitimization in the eyes of the world (Moscow as center of "world culture"). Hence literary officials sought and publicized foreign intellectuals swearing allegiance to Moscow, something they had been doing for some time but now pursued more aggressively. The Soviet Union had always featured invited visits by prominent foreign intellectuals, but the early to mid-1930s were a peak time for this. Intellectuals came not just for revolutionary anniversaries, as in the past, but for longer stays.

The main public attention was paid to French visitors (one will note that most of the Western artists promoted at this time were French). Prominent among the invitees was Malraux, who was escorted to the Soviet Union in 1934 by Erenburg to attend the Writers Union Congress. Eisenstein was to have made a film based on *Man's Fate* (La condition humaine, 1933), which had been translated by Erenburg.[16] Malraux wrote some of the script, and Brik worked on it a little, too, but the project was stopped because of problems with the Chinese subject matter.[17] Romain Rolland was enticed to visit in 1935 and was likewise published in translation; by November 1937, 1.3 million copies of his works had been published in the Soviet Union.[18]

Literary leaders were constantly courting Gide, who was the big fish of French letters, more so than Malraux or Rolland, then in any case largely hooked, let alone Barbusse, the most reliable catch. The Soviet Union and Gide started a love dance as a prelude to the actual visit of this "discriminating bride." Gide obliged his suitor with extravagant public statements and diary entries about how the Soviet Union was the country of the future and how he would soon visit, all proudly reported in the Soviet press.[19]

Gide was important because he was the leading intellectual of Paris, which has been recurrently claimed as *the* capital of world culture. But he was also a risk, because—as Mikhail Apletin, a head of VOKS, warned regarding his impending visit—"He's not a simple writer like Rolland."[20]

Paris was the capital not just in the sense that French literature, or art, was the best in the world. It was the mecca to which disaffected or exiled intellectuals from all over the world flocked, or where they sought to have their work published or recognized, a key to their elevation from the category "national writer" to an international or cosmopolitan author with "world" recognition and sales. The Soviet Union coveted a similar status, and in consequence the proletariat became less viable as the standard-bearers of Soviet culture.

Pascale Casanova has argued in *The Republic of Letters* that Paris has endured as *the* world center of literature not because of economic or political might, which it could not always claim, but because of its "symbolic capital" as the site of a revolution.[21] In the 1930s, intellectuals from "revolutionary" Moscow aspired to be, somewhat analogously, at the center of a transnational group of the like-minded. There are some earlier precedents for proposing the sort of transnational cosmopolitan association, which they hoped to lead, especially among thinkers of the Enlightenment, such as Kant.[22] Another Enlightenment version of a pan-European formation was not based in geopolitical formations but, on the contrary, defined itself as alternative to them. That was the Republic of Letters, a project particularly promoted by Voltaire, though with precedents in the Renaissance.[23] As Robert Darnton has defined this Republic in an article in *The New York Review of Books* titled "A Euro State of Mind" (2002), it "depended on a distinction between the national potentates who wage war, and a trans-national gentry of the cultivated elite." This Republic "developed a pan-European mode of existence known at the time as cosmopolitanism," which "set off persons of quality from the unwashed masses, whose mental horizon did not extend beyond the territory that could be viewed from the tower of their church, hence *l'esprit de clocher* and *campanilismo* to denote the narrow-minded *(l'infame)*. The cosmopolitan view of the world took in all of Europe, sometimes even all humanity."[24]

Koltsov had expressed a similar sentiment in *Pravda* in his article "Soviet Patriotism" (1925), where he defined it as counterposed to "the patriotism of one's own bell tower" *(kolokol'ni)*.[25] By the Soviet early to mid-1930s, this sentiment was widespread, and "provincial" had become a negative label. Bukharin in his address to the First Congress of the Writers Union in 1934 drew a contrast between "the provincial" and breadth of intellectual horizons," between the "brutal [zhestokaia] and uncultured provinces" and "the dimensions of the world-wide [mirovye masshtaby]."[26]

In the language of the Republic of Letters, "esprit de clocher" refers not just to narrow localism but also to the narrowness of the Church itself. The republic's cosmopolitanism was grounded in the secular ideals of the Enlightenment: "it promoted the critical use of reason" and "engaged in a crusade against *l'infame*—that is, against intolerance and injustice in general and the abuses of the Roman Catholic Church in particular."[27]

In the 1930s the anticlerical stance of the Soviet Union attracted a lot of Western intellectuals, though there were different conceptions of *l'infame.* Some who declared for Moscow misread their suitor (*razborchivii,* incidentally, also has the meaning of legible). For example, Gide, like several other intellectuals, was attracted to Moscow as a place where, he mistakenly believed, the more secular society of the Soviet Union could accommodate their cosmopolitan, gay fraternity against "l'infame" of Catholicism and bourgeois society. In 1932 he joined AEAR, the French branch of MORP, and planned to visit the Soviet Union, bringing with him as his dowry the manuscript of his prewar, satirical anticlerical novel *The Cellars of the Vatican.*[28] Homosexuality became illegal in 1934, and though Gide was disappointed to learn that, he nevertheless, if less enthusiastically, continued to be interested in Soviet Russia as a bastion of anticlericalism. In fact he told Erenburg he wanted to discuss with Stalin giving rights to homosexuals and would not be dissuaded.[29]

Intellectuals subject to other forms of discrimination in their own countries were also attracted to the Soviet Union. Langston Hughes, not only gay but also black, arrived in June 1932 with the Louise Thompson group of African Americans. Frequently published in Russian translation, Hughes came to perform in a Mezhrabpom film about race in America that was intended for U.S. distribution but directed, symptomatic of this cosmopolitan moment, by a German, Karl Junghans.[30] When the group's film project *(Black and White)* fizzled, several of the group's twenty-two members, including Hughes, opted to visit Central Asia as the closest Soviet approximation to the American South with its people of color.[31] Then there was Friedrich Wolf, doctor and dramatist, who came to the Soviet Union as the one place that would support his crusade to legalize abortion (again to be rendered illegal there—in 1936, the year he and his family took Soviet citizenship).

Clearly, there are important limitations to drawing a parallel with Darnton's Republic of Letters. A crucial distinction was that in the Soviet Union writers and the cultivated in general could enjoy no autonomy from the powers who ran the state and waged the wars. In reality this movement, rather than taking the form of a "Republic," might be seen as choreographed by such organizations as MORP.[32] Based in Moscow, along with parallel organizations in other cultural fields such as MORT in theater, it was potentially the core of this international fraternity—but it was never funded to the extent its enthusiast-leaders required.[33] In addition, intellectuals in this transnational orbit could not define themselves in contradistinction to the great unwashed, who were meant to be their cause and perhaps even their anthropological superiors. Furthermore, though Soviet intellectual life became markedly less parochial, many intellectuals remained doggedly defined by the limited horizon of *Pravda,* where, though it printed more and more material about Western culture, so often the editorials and leading articles were about sowing crops or producing pig iron.

This dual orientation (cosmopolitan/local) is evident in the careers of the four writers we are following here. Erenburg at about this time produced two books, *Moi Parizh* and *Ispaniia,* both assuming a cosmopolitan European perspective and with risqué material. But, perhaps because of the depression, perhaps because of the rise of fascism, he was drawn back to more orthodox Soviet writing. In August 1932 he spent a month and a half in the Soviet Union and produced a celebration of Soviet industrialization, *The Second Day* (Den' vtoroi; 1934); the Russian title, sometimes translated as *Out of Chaos,* is an allusion to the biblical "second day" of creation),[34] followed by another production novel, *Without Pausing to Take Breath* (Ne perevodia dykhanie; 1935). Both novels were widely promoted by the state (set for discussion groups, given large circulations, etc.) and both were obsessed with the contrast between the Soviet Union and the bourgeois West, though Erenburg contrived to introduce, sometimes somewhat incongruously, workers well versed in Western literature.

Thus the factory was still in as a topic, but no longer so narrowly depicted. Also lingering as a genre was the short journalistic sketch such as had been promoted when the "author as producer" was in its heyday. Writer-journalists traveled all over the country producing sketches and feuilletons for *Pravda* and assorted Moscow journals. Koltsov and Tretiakov were leading practitioners. Some of their sketches were about the industrial effort; most of them focused on bureaucratic corruption and inefficiency, generally naming specific errant individuals. But at the same time, as we shall see, Koltsov was going back and forth to Berlin to link with German leftist intellectuals there.

Tretiakov had, since at least his Berlin trip, enjoyed a similar role, producing sketches on Soviet economic efforts and (as we saw in Chapter 1) at the same time promoting his German friends and overseeing assorted Soviet journalistic ventures in periodicals that appeared within Germany but were overseen by MORP or other Comintern bodies. But just as Koltsov had been elevated to the editorial board of *Literaturnaia gazeta* in 1932, after RAPP was cleaned out there, so Tretiakov began to enjoy an enhanced status within MORP. Prior to the April decree that abolished RAPP, its leader, Leopold Averbakh, had been active in the MORP leadership.[35] But on August 5, 1932, *Literaturnaia gazeta* announced MORP's "perestroika" to get closer to "fellow traveler" *(poputchik)* writers:[36] the Secretariat was revamped, and Tretiakov became a prominent member.[37] Later that month, in addition, he was sent as the MORP representative to the Organizing Committee of the Writers Union and to VOKS, yet another example of how all the bodies involved in the international cultural effort were linked.[38]

Tretiakov was also assigned to make the big speech to the MORP Secretariat about MORP's transformation. In it he declared—before the Nazi takeover in 1933—that their main task should now be to oppose fascism in a united front. He also recommended that instead of just organizational contacts with Western writers and "cultural workers," there should be individual, writer-to-writer contacts (shades of his own work with Brecht and company from his Berlin visit), this at a time when the Soviet and German Communist parties were still locked in their old battles with the Second International and the Social Democrats.[39] In late 1932, the Secretariat of the Writers Union founded a commission, headed by Tretiakov, which was to liaise with MORP and its *Lenderkomissii* to facilitate more translations of Soviet authors into foreign languages, and translations of foreigners, as well as promote contacts with those writers.[40] And Koltsov and Tretiakov were prominent among those present on August 20 at a combined meeting of Soviet and German writers under the auspices of the German commission of MORP where the need for more international cooperation in combating fascism was declared and speakers called for a "union" *(smychka)* of German and Soviet writers (participants included Eisler and Karl Wittfogel, who gave the main address).[41]

A New Horizon of Identity?

A great paradox defines the Soviet 1930s. During this decade the country sought to define itself within the great cultural tradition of Europe, yet it was also then that an iron curtain fell more resoundingly than before, and the country became an ever more hermetic place of cultural autarchy. The Soviet Union became a relatively closed society, closed not just in the sense that generally only the elite could cross its borders but also in the sense that citizens were fairly confined to their immediate locales. In 1932–1933 a new system of internal passports was introduced, and residents now had to be registered in a particular city in order to have the right to live there. At the same time, there was increasing emphasis on securing the Soviet borders. Sanatoria were built for vacations and group excursions organized within the country (hikes, mountain climbing), but for most, "travel" was more likely via a subscription to a journal or a book purchase.[42]

As if in compensation for the citizens' reduced mobility and more circumscribed world, dramatic and exotic travel became a particular feature of Soviet culture. Especially popular among readers were accounts of dangerous trips to the frozen North, notably the heroic rescue of the Chelyuskin mission (1934) when a ship of that name sent to the Arctic to conduct scientific experiments became stuck in the ice and the entire populace followed its rescue with bated breath (Koltsov and Tretiakov contributed to a glossy book on it).[43]

Actually, the vogue for travel and adventure romance was widespread in Europe at this time. Paul Fussell in his book on travel literature sug-

gests more or less an inverse relationship between the increasingly seden-
tary and domiciled nature of modern life and the vogue for literature of
exotic travel. As he elaborates: "the illusion of freedom is a precious thing
in the twenties and thirties, when the shades of the modern prison house
are closing in, when the passports and queues and guided tours and social security numbers and customs regulations and currency controls are
beginning gradually to constrict life."[44]

While in the Soviet 1930s travel across the borders was a privilege reserved for the very few, in the Republic of Letters (according to Darnton),
by contrast, "the most civilized people thought of themselves as European and did not worry about national boundaries or even carry passports." They "took grand tours" and "received hospitality from other
'persons of quality'" who "shared the same code of conduct."[45] Though
the comparison must remain limited, a select group of Soviet cultural emissaries and their Western colleagues who shared similar values could be
seen as forming some sort of functional equivalent of Darnton's republicans; they saw themselves as more cultivated and, in their own terms,
more aristocratic than the majority of the population in their countries.
Koltsov, a member of the Soviet elite, was a leader among them.

In the 1930s Koltsov seems to have been permitted quite a bit of lati-
tude in his personal behavior. In 1932 on one of his trips to Germany he
fell in love with his translator, the journalist Maria Gresshöner. It is a mark
of Koltsov's stature in the Soviet Union that he was able in a matter of a
few days to obtain a visa for her to return to Moscow with him in September as his mistress (he was married) and arranged a position for her as a
journalist on Moscow's German-language newspaper *Deutsche Zentral-
Zeitung*, enabling her to accompany him on most of his assignments as a
roving correspondent. She in turn assumed the pseudonym Maria Osten,
as it were the Maria who has opted for the eastern (Moscow) variant of a
world order.

Koltsov and Maria became a sort of royal couple on the horizon of Soviet intellectual life, she the glamorous and elegant blond, he the powerful
publishing baron heading Zhurgaz, a conglomerate whose network extended to a quarter of a million employees, and a highly popular journalist in his own right.[46] By the time he met her he had published twelve
hundred feuilletons in *Pravda*, a selection of which had appeared in

twenty-four books of his collected journalistic writings. A second multi-volume edition of his collected writings was in the works, as were book publications in Germany.⁴⁷ In 1932 his stature was recognized when he was awarded an apartment in the recently constructed residential complex known as "the house on the embankment," diagonally opposite the Kremlin and the new prestige address in town. After 1933 Koltsov and Maria flitted over Europe; she brought back from each trip suitcases of the latest fashions from Paris.

This couple problematizes the issue of identity. Was Koltsov a member of the Soviet new class who benefited from his loyalty (such as his recurrent articles endorsing the harsh sentences for those condemned in the successive purges)?⁴⁸ Was he a *Wandervogel* or an operative and intelligence gatherer? Or does he represent an exception to the new standard pattern for the Soviet intellectual; do such cases function as limited loopholes that enable the "totalitarian" state? I would say that the Soviet Union was not seamlessly "totalitarian," though mobility was limited. As Sheila Fitzpatrick has investigated in *Tear Off the Masks,* identity was constantly being negotiated, even at the most primitive level of the curriculum vitae *(avtobiografiia);* imposters and assorted variants of the trickster abounded, especially in the provinces, further undermining fixed identity and fixed residence. But for the ultramobile Koltsov, questions of identity were arguably particularly fraught and complex.

In 1930s Moscow, a feature of the elite—and an exception to the strict Soviet moral social codes—was, as Zola would have been interested to learn, the mistress, a fact never acknowledged in published sources. Foreign mistresses or wives were especially prized as status symbols, this even though so much of the official political culture was structured by a myth of the Great Family (of Stalin's state) to which the nuclear family was to be subordinated.⁴⁹ But Maria also had maternal proclivities. In late 1934 Maria, while traveling in the Saar with Koltsov, took custody of a local working-class boy of ten, Hubert L'Hoste. Later, in 1937, she adopted an orphan, a Spanish baby plucked from the smoldering ruins of a train and hence called Chemino, though she changed the name to José, in Russian Iuzik, after Stalin. Thus she was not only the mistress of a member of the elite but also the matriarch of an alternative, transnational (nonbiological) family, as it were a synecdochal instance of that Great Family of transnational leftists that was in tandem with, and partially overlapped with, the Great Family of the Soviet state.

In 1935 Maria published as a special issue of Koltsov's journal *Ogonëk*, *Hubert in Wonderland* (Gubert v strane chudes) an account of Hubert's experiences starting from the moment Koltsov and Maria visited his family in the Saar. The first person narrator ("Hubert") marvels at such Soviet "wonders" he encounters as the radically rebuilt Moscow with its metro, the Chelyuskin expedition, flights to the stratosphere, a pioneer camp—and the *Pravda* caricaturist Boris Efimov, who happened to be Koltsov's brother. At the end of the book, it addresses its young readers with a question and provides an envelope for them to send in their response: should Hubert return to his family in the Saar or remain in "wonderland"?[50] Essentially, this is a rhetorical question as to which world system Hubert should opt for. It is particularly rhetorical given that the Nazis, to the great disappointment of Soviet officials, won a plebiscite conducted in the Saar during November-December 1934 and the area was returned to Germany. The Soviet Union had invested heavily in the plebiscite; Joris Ivens had made a film for the Soviet Union about it.[51] But in that Hubert would be assimilated in the Soviet Union, his story became a sort of parable prefiguring a day when the entire world would be assimilated into the Soviet system.

Koltsov's most dramatic gesture in these years came in September 1932 when, as a preparation for commemorating the fortieth anniversary of Gorky's career, he launched a campaign to collect money for a "squadron" of planes. The planes were to fly to different parts of the country with writers, experts, and officials on board, swooping down from the skies to illuminate the locals, overcome "provincialism," as Tretiakov put it, and expand their horizon of identity.[52] To this end Koltsov prevailed on the thirty-nine periodicals in his Zhurgaz empire, and other cultural institutions such as theaters, to collect money (virtually a tithe) to finance the squadron.[53]

The squadron's planes were to be of various sizes, the smallest capable of landing on a collective farm field in a remote region inaccessible even by road, a version of overcoming the *esprit de clocher*.[54] The largest, to be named the *Maxim Gorky* (one of the Soviet "wonders" presented to

Hubert), was by far the most gigantic and technically advanced Soviet plane as yet, a "goliath" that "provided material evidence that the Soviet Union was overtaking its capitalist rivals."[55] It was designated for service in the mass agitational effort, and on board were to be a salon for press conferences, an editorial office for a newspaper, a printing press, photographic and film laboratories, a radio station with broad wave, and a state-of-the-art apparatus for light projection of slogans onto the clouds.[56] This project must have been approved on high, but Koltsov was also acting as if on his own initiative, an example of how everything both is, and is not, locked into a "totalitarian" model.

During the Civil War, the agitational train had been a central feature of the Soviet effort (Eisenstein worked on one), and it was cited as a precedent for the squadron.[57] In a more recent version, starting in March 1932 the zealous Alexander Medvedkin had toured the country for three months with his "cinema train" equipped with a mobile film factory, filming locally and exposing bureaucratic ills.[58] Koltsov with his squadron was essentially one-upping Medvedkin, updating Medvedkin's train initiative for the new age of the airplane (though there was an earlier precedent of 1925 that had involved Shklovsky); it was a mark of Koltsov's stature that his squadron was much more prominent in the Soviet press than Medvedkin's train had been.[59]

The squadron began its work as part of the Civil Aviation Fleet on 17 March 1933, even before construction of the *Maksim Gorky* was begun. The fleet's initial sallies were led by Koltsov himself. Then in April 1934 the *Maksim Gorky* was finally finished. On May Day 1935 the *Maksim Gorky* flew over the Red Square, with Barbusse on the platform and the science fiction visionary Konstantin Tsiolkovsky delivering a speech. But during a later flight over Moscow on May 18, 1935 the *Maksim Gorky* it crashed, after a smaller airplane carrying a crew making a documentary alongside collided with its wing (to Stalin's considerable displeasure).[60] The prestige value of such a behemoth meant that, despite this setback, plans were soon made and "within days," money was collected for creating an entire squadron of "airplane-giants" to be dominated by the *Vladimir Lenin, Joseph Stalin,* and *Maksim Gorky.*[61] Nevertheless, this tragedy somewhat took the wind out of the squadron's sails, though it continued to make its sallies for a while, if on a reduced scale. Koltsov was in any case by then preoccupied in the international arena.

Actually, the international arena had been in Koltsov's sights even in the squadron project. He had borrowed the idea for it from Hitler's 1932 electoral campaign for the Reichstag, some of the success of which was attributed to Hitler's being equipped with a Lufthansa Junker that enabled him to make appearances all over the country.[62] In other words, as we have seen with Tretiakov, Koltsov's work within the country and abroad were not separate occupations but interrelated as part of the one national effort.

But the careers of Koltsov, Tretiakov, and Erenburg were already becoming radically altered by dramatic developments in the international sphere that impacted the "closed" Soviet culture system and further accelerated the opening up of the country to Western influences.

The Nazi Takeover in 1933

Eisenstein published "The Discriminating Bride" in June 1933, after not only the April 1932 decree forming the Writers Union but also another fateful date, the Nazi takeover in Germany of January 1933—an event that defined much more cultural activity in the Soviet Union during the 1930s than is generally recognized.

After the Nazis came to power, Koltsov and Tretiakov more or less abandoned running around the provinces and churning out all those feuilletons about recalcitrant officials or economic projects, leaving second-string figures to such tasks while they became major players in the international antifascist movement. Erenburg, that recent convert to singing the praises of industrialization, soon made this shift, too.

It was the Reichstag Fire trial that propelled Koltsov to the role of leading Soviet figure in the antifascist movement. The Reichstag burned on February 27, 1933, not long after the Nazis came to power, and they seized the opportunity to blame the Communists for it and crack down even further on the movement. Four communists (together with von Lubbe) were arrested and accused of the arson, the leading figure being Georgi Dimitrov, a Bulgarian communist and Comintern leader in Berlin.

The Soviet Union was heavily invested in this trial. In consequence, they yanked Koltsov out of his *Pravda* Russia beat and assigned him to be that paper's main correspondent for the trial. The Germans denied him permission to go to Leipzig, where it was held, so instead he covered it first from Prague (briefly) and then Paris (together with Maria). *Pravda* gave his reports prominence, generally putting them on page 1. In Paris his mission expanded from that of correspondent, and he became the principal Soviet representative involved in the antifascist cultural effort then centered there, especially as concerned the trial. The accused did not come to trial until late in September 1933. By then, many international intellectuals had taken up their cause, issuing the *Brown Book* (from Paris and London), which exposed the weaknesses in the case for the prosecution, and staged a counter-trial in London. The *Brown Book,* released the day before the Leipzig trial, undermined its credibility.[63] Dimitrov was found not guilty and flew to the Soviet Union a few months later, on February 26, 1934, after he became a citizen.

In narratives published in the Soviet press, many extravagant claims were made for the significance of the victory in the trial, which was often called a turning point for the Nazis, a "fiasco" that was the impetus for their (alleged) decline in power.[64] Certainly it was a propaganda coup for the Soviet Union. A film about resistance in Germany, Gustav von Wangenheim's *Fighters* (Kämpfer, Russian Bor'tsy; 1935), on which Ivens also worked, and which features Dimitrov's defense at the trial, was shown all over the world to alleged great success, especially in New York.[65]

Koltsov's close identification with the trial (he was involved in preparing the second *Brown Book*) enhanced an already brilliant career. When Dimitrov was released to the Soviet Union in 1934, it was Koltsov who greeted him at the airport. Dimitrov after his return was first promoted to the Presidium of the Comintern and then at the Seventh Congress made its general secretary, and thereafter Koltsov's power grew even further. For the next couple of years his main sphere of operations was not the Soviet Union but Europe.

The Leipzig trial was but one incident in an ongoing rivalry between Nazi Germany and the Soviet Union. But much of this competition between the two powers was played out via the soft underbelly of culture. In the 1930s both Germany and the Soviet Union laid claim to representing a higher order civilization as a mandate for their respective bids for world domination. Moscow was increasingly claimed to be *the* city of "world culture,"[66] while in Nazi Germany, Soviet spokesmen claimed, it was withering away.[67] Commentators belittled the way the Nazi regime, for all its technological and military achievements, ruled a land of "medieval barbarism and terror."[68] It had failed to use an advanced science of society (read Marxism-Leninism) and hence, as Bukharin put it, failed to read "the book of history" and was hurtling Germany backward into the dark ages.[69]

In Soviet rhetoric, and in that of the antifascists, "culture," or "humanism," an ism particularly associated with a textual culture, provided one side of an overarching binary that structured their contrast between Nazi Germany and, variously, the Soviet Union, true Europe, or a true representative of humankind. The other (Nazi) side of the binary was "barbarism." In the international antifascist movement, literature played a central role in cementing a sense of common cause bringing together politicians and intellectuals of widely differing political and class backgrounds. Somewhat similarly, Darnton has noted of the Republic of Letters that "writers were at nodal points in its system" and networks of them were "important institutions in its running."[70] During the 1930s, those active in the antifascist networks were also forever traveling, in many instances literally, in others figuratively. They made connections with fellow exiles and activists at the interminable congresses and thus participated in transnational networks, many of them conducted by correspondence with far-flung colleagues.

Theirs was the traveling mode.

With love of literature their bonding glue, these antifascists dismissed the Nazis as "destroyers" of Europe's great spiritual treasure, representing themselves as its protectors. Thus, for example, Dimitrov, and this was typical, represented himself in the German prison as a man of letters, a devourer of books, writing against the Nazis and other retrograde forces.[71]

The Nazis in a sense obliged the antifascists, confirming their barbarism by burning books. The books were burnt during the infamous night of May 10, 1933, in a bonfire in Berlin on a square opposite the main building of Humboldt University (many of its students participated), a fact that was particularly poignant, given the role of von Humboldt in fostering a humanist education in the German universities (something Karl Radek was quick to point out in his commentary, where he also alluded to Fichte's addresses from Berlin University to the German nation).[72] This event was just the most dramatic in a systematic campaign by the Nazis to eradicate the kinds of literature and culture they found threatening, whether by actual physical destruction, as in this case, or by banning or bowdlerizing texts. Many of the big names in literature and culture had already emigrated from Germany, but this gesture alienated them further.

The Soviet Union took up their cause and acted as patron of a transnational fellowship of what Tretiakov called, in the title of his book that contains chapters on several of them, *Liudi odnogo kostra* (People of the one bonfire; 1936). Tretiakov's title is ambiguous. The "bonfire" could be taken as a metaphor for the fire and light emanating from "true" literature that guides and warms, sustaining the faithful and ignoring all borders as it draws them to its flames in a transnational fraternity. The "bonfire" here also has a more specific referent. Tretiakov's fraternity is of those whose literary works were burnt by the Nazis in May 1933, a date that for the anti-fascist movement was more of an originary moment than the Nazi ascent to power a few months earlier. The antifascist writers, like those who had been burned at the stake for their faith, were martyrs, but their martyrdom was not of bodies but of books. Among them it became a point of pride to have had one's books burnt. The writer Oskar Maria Graf was distressed to find that only some of his had been burnt, and in an open letter titled "Burn Me" he begged the Nazis to consign the rest to the flames.[73] Tretiakov's title, then, suggests the willful destruction wreaked by the Nazis, versions of the two poles of possibility that structured the main Soviet narrative on the Nazis: culture/barbarism.

Soviet rhetoric used this binary, but it was not original to their Communist Party or their intellectuals. It has a long prehistory, and was popular during the Enlightenment. In Germany it had been used against the Nazis since at least the late 1920s when they began to emerge as a threat.[74] One of its most explicit and pointed formulations is to be found in Lion Feuchtwanger's novel *The Oppermann Family* (Die Geschwister Oppermann),[75] which was first published in 1933 and was thus a trendsetter in representing the Nazi regime (a similar representation can be found in

Friedrich Wolf's play *Professor Mamlock* of 1933, which was produced on the Soviet stage and also made into a film in 1938).[76] As Feuchtwanger makes clear in his preface, the novel is essentially a fictional rejoinder to Nazi theory and practice and especially draws, in representing them, on Hitler's *Mein Kampf.*

Though somewhat Moscow-leaning, Feuchtwanger was not a Communist; in fact his primary orientation was as a Jew.[77] He was a prolific producer of novels that meditated the fate of the successful Jew in a series of historical periods, ranging from Roman times through several periods of German history extending to the present-day exile. One of the most translated authors in the Soviet Union (Tretiakov pushed for this), nine of his novels, including *The Oppermanns,* appeared in Russian translation, with generous print runs (the latter was also made into a film).[78] He became one of the most popular novelists in the Soviet thirties.[79] In other words, his works became part of Stalinist culture as well as that of the diaspora.

The Oppermanns could be approximately characterized as a Jewish version of Thomas Mann's *Buddenbrooks,* in that it chronicles the decline and fall of a prosperous merchant family (in this case Berlin-based Jews who own a chain of furniture stores), culminating in the death of a particularly sensitive and cultivated male heir. Feuchtwanger's novel, however, rather than taking his family over a long expanse of time, shows a rapid decline over the period 1932–1933. As these dates suggest, a further difference is that the main reason for this decline is the rise of the Nazis and the persecution of the Jews; the young scion of the dynasty, Berthold, does not die of physical causes, as in the case of his counterpart in *Buddenbrooks,* but commits suicide because he cannot take the Nazi persecution.

The novel provides a sociological study of the fate of Germany's Jews, the various family members each representing a different occupation and often a different political orientation as well. Its primary purpose, however, is to establish how the Nazi "barbarians," as Feuchtwanger calls them, are destroying true culture and professionalism. Here the central account is provided in a confrontation between Berthold and his new Nazi teacher at the gymnasium, Dr. Vogelsang. Berthold had intended to prepare a class paper with the title "Humanism in the Twentieth Century," but Vogelsang requires him to write instead about the alleged triumphs of Arminius against the Romans. Berthold's failure to present a sufficiently heroic account of Arminius as the victorious German warrior (together with his being Jewish) make him a marked man for Vogelsang. The Nazi/humanist clash is also played out in a series of hypocritically polite exchanges between Vogelsang and the cultivated gymnasium rector, a friend of the Oppermann family and an anti-Nazi. The rector reproaches Vogelsang for the abominable grammar and general desecration of the German language that he finds in Hitler's *Mein Kampf.* Vogelsang, who has recognized these deficiencies to himself and is embarrassed by them, rather than admit this, retorts that Hitler himself made the point in *Mein Kampf* that oral speech is higher than the written.

The Soviets established their superiority over the Nazis in part with tremendous investment in publication of German books, boasting the largest publishing house of German books outside Germany (VEGAAR) and authorizing 250 titles in German a year at its height, not to mention a lot of German literature published in Russian or Ukrainian translation.[80] The Soviets also prided themselves on publishing versions of the German classics that were free of the bowdlerization to which the Nazis subjected them.

In effect, the Soviets were challenging the Nazis to a battle over texts, over who has the right to claim the title of guardian of *true* culture, which texts represent that "true" culture and which the "false," and who has the right to decide. The claim to stand for "true" literature was, in the logic of the antifascist position, the claim to stand for "true" Europe. For the exiles, it was also central to their claim to stand for the "true" Germany. While the exiles saw themselves as producing and revering great literature, they saw the Nazis as purveyors of trash *(Leserfrass).*[81]

But the noble ideals the antifascists championed—culture, humanism, reason—were all too general, as was perhaps inevitable in a tenuous alliance such as the antifascist movement in culture. The challenge was to specify: which culture? Which humanism? Though some occasionally paid lip service to supporting the culture of the oppressed and colonized from what we would call the third world, others championed European culture and others again a "Soviet-Humanism which has nothing in common with bourgeois humanism."[82] The dilemma was even greater for the Germanophone antifascists.

The Germanophone Diaspora

By 1936 there were forty-six hundred Germanophone refugees living in the Soviet Union, and many more came after the Nazi takeovers of Austria and Czechoslovakia.[83] Yet this group was small in comparison with the one million ethnic Germans who were Soviet citizens, descendants of immigrants from the eighteenth and nineteenth centuries, or with the number of Germans and Austrians who had spent time in the Soviet Union during the First Five-Year Plan, whether as Communists or as workers, engineers, or architects, attracted by the industrialization effort and employment opportunities during the depression. The newcomers were primarily intellectuals or political activists.

The exiled intellectuals were negotiating shifting and competing forces and realities. Obviously, there were economic considerations involved as they sought to continue intellectual activity in emigration. The Soviet Union became the main bankroller of the antifascist movement. Particularly critical for the Germanophone exiles, it provided them with publication outlets (many of them controlled by Koltsov). In addition, Soviet theaters were encouraged to put on plays by Germans, and some Soviet films were projected to be produced under Germans' direction or using their scripts.[84] While in western Europe intellectual periodicals and publishing houses of the diaspora struggled and were often short-lived, a substantial and reliable Soviet budget allocation essentially offered some livelihood for many intellectuals not physically in the Soviet Union. As is clear from the correspondence of Tretiakov, Osten, and Koltsov with assorted Germanophone writers in western Europe, there was a constant concern to arrange publication of their works, both in German and in Russian translation, and even to get food parcels from the Writers Union to them.[85]

Of course all this investment in the antifascist cause served darker Soviet purposes in terms of enticing intellectuals to declare for the Soviet Union, and at times facilitating espionage. But functionally the very availability of this Soviet money and effort was an enabling force in the evolution of a transnational antifascist movement (far from all of whose members were pro-Soviet) with its own narratives, catchwords, and ideals. Each party in it was defining its own identity in the face of impending crisis, and simultaneously formulating a common, transnational cause.

Given such complexities, questions of identity and allegiance among the antifascist intellectuals who began emigrating to the Soviet Union after Hitler assumed power in 1933 were particularly fraught. Were they to be assimilated along with the other German speakers and become Soviet citizens? (Koltsov said at a Foreign Commission meeting of May 29, 1936, that the many German writers living in the Soviet Union were essentially Soviet writers who happened to speak German.)[86] Were they to be a part of the more broadly based international set of antifascist intellectuals and not specifically oriented to the German cultural world? Were they, on the contrary, primarily outcast defenders and preservers of the true German cultural heritage? Or perhaps they were essentially subjects of Moscow's Communist empire?

To varying degrees, the exiles might be characterized as all of the above. These varied orientations and purposes meant that both the exiled intellectuals and their Soviet patrons were inconsistent in their "mission statements."

A key dilemma for the antifascists was how to define their cultural identity, given that they were essentially transnational, diasporic—stateless. Eagleton has argued that "cultures are intrinsically incomplete and need the supplement of the state to become truly themselves."[87] For the Germanophone exiles, defining their own "nation" was particularly problematical because they formed a diaspora of individuals from different countries (Germany, Austria, and to some extent Hungary and Czechoslovakia). Moreover, Germany, which might be seen as potentially the locus and guarantor of their "culture," was not well defined as a geopolitical entity, as was glaringly apparent at this time when the Nazis were laying claim to "greater Germany." The exiles no longer had economic, political, or military power and were scattered over many countries, extending as far as Latin America. To put it bluntly, all they had was language and culture. One is reminded of the Russian émigrés from the Soviet Union who in 1925, after the border was closed and emigration became a finality, pronounced themselves the only true guardians of the Russian cultural heritage and rallied together under the sign of Pushkin.[88]

The German exiles sought to realize a diaspora nation, more specifically a *Kulturnation*. They made language *the* criterion for membership. In a speech that the playwright Ernst Toller made to the German émigré community in New York in 1937, he declared "in reality, no dictator robs a writer of his native country. The language is an organic part of the native land [Heimat], the earth that nourishes it, the earth in which it grows," but he continued: "an artist . . . should not serve nationality but the unity of nations. As long as we émigrés remain true to our ideas . . . we will earn that Deutschtum we believe in."[89]

We will note here a problematic tension between the call of the national and that of the international that also plagued Soviet rhetoric. This was something the exiles never resolved. As James Clifford points out in *Routes,* "whatever their ideologies of purity, diasporic cultural forms can never, in practice, be exclusively nationalist."[90] Translation, multicenteredness, and "multiple adjacencies" are all endemic to the diasporic condition. But for the Germanophone refugees, "decenteredness" had its limits. They needed a narrative to counterpose to the Nazi one, and a cultural identity that accommodated the changed conditions, but they also needed a broader cultural alliance than their relatively small numbers could provide.

Identity dilemmas also plagued Soviet intellectuals in this decade. Were they from the home of the proletarian vanguard, or the home of true culture and enlightenment? Were they Russians, or Europeans, or (multi-ethnic) Soviets? Here I am trying to pinpoint a "horizon of identity," but after all a horizon is an illusion, a chimera, a construction.

The sophisticated Soviet intellectuals that are my focus, somewhat like their Germanophone contemporaries in the antifascist diaspora, effectively had multiple identities. Tretiakov, for example, must have suffered from the problem of competing loyalties. He was personally avant-gardist in orientation. Emerging from the Left Front of Art, the organization of the 1920s that combined several avant-garde groups but was largely dominated by the Constructivists, he continued in the 1930s to plug for German intellectuals of similar orientation. To some degree, they were *his* republic, his transnational coterie. Fortunately, most of them were politically acceptable: Heartfield because he was a Party member and his brother Wieland Herzfelde ran the Moscow-subsidized Berlin press Malik Verlag (after the Nazi takeover it relocated to Prague) and Eisler because his brother Gerhart was on the Central Committee of the German Communist Party. But still Tretiakov was defensive in promoting his avant-garde colleagues' work.

A further complication in making an analogy with a "republic of letters" is the reality that the Germanophone exiles in Moscow and their families were to a large extent ghettoized. Koltsov and Tretiakov periodically called for their literary colleagues to pay more attention to the Germans and help them get works published or staged, but the reality was that they were largely confined to their own German Commission of the Writers Union, the Club for Foreign Workers (a hangout for intellectuals), and giving broadcasts in German over Radio Moscow. They never received as much attention from Soviet writers, nor were their works ever published or produced as much as either they, or their patrons, such as Tretiakov and Koltsov, desired. At a Writers Union Presidium meeting of May 5, 1935, Tretiakov complained about this, remarking bitterly that few writers had come to see Brecht when he had visited that year, but some Russian writers responded that the foreigners were not learning Russian, and even that they were not "Russian Bolsheviks."[91] There was also the problem of the foreign writers' independence and a perceived "willfulness" that sometimes led to their expressing the "wrong" views in print. Koltsov reported at a Foreign Commission meeting of May 29, 1936, that Tretiakov had been assigned to the editorial board of a Soviet German-language periodical (presumably *Internatsionale Literatur*) to keep them in order;[92] and Tretiakov recommended on another occasion that problematical foreign writers be taken into the editorial boards of Soviet journals so that they could be supervised.[93]

The state tried to utilize the newly arrived Germans to raise the level of consciousness and culture among its already existing German minority population, especially in Engels (on the Volga), their main city. But Engels was a provincial backwater, not the cosmopolitan center. The ethnic Germans there spoke an archaic German from the century or so before, when they had immigrated, and were mostly peasants and workers. Nevertheless, Piscator, like Brecht a flamboyant, leftist experimental director in the Berlin theater (he had done *Tai Yang Erwacht*) and one of those assigned to Engels responded with the idealism of the "Author as Producer," even trying to get Brecht to join what he represented as a great opportunity to establish something new and exemplary there, an international cultural center even![94] Brecht was not so moved, but Piscator worked on well into 1936. However, when he was then sent to Paris by MORT, which he headed, he was replaced in Engels and opted not to return.[95]

Of course Darnton, writing his essay for the *New York Review of Books* in 2002 in an excess of enthusiasm for post-Communist Europe, undoubtedly also idealized the extent to which the Republic of Letters ever existed as a harmonious transnational fraternity that ignored national borders. And for the germanophone exiles in Moscow the situation of apartheid was sometimes mitigated by friendships with Soviet colleagues, many of them predating this exile, such as Tretiakov and his Berlin friends, or Vsevolod Vishnevsky and Friedrich Wolf, whom Vishnevsky translated and published, so that several of his plays were put on the Soviet stage.

Among the antifascists, print media and publishing also played an important role in these years in facilitating transnational cultural exchange and bonding, another parallel with the earlier Republic of Letters as Darnton describes it.[96] Newspapers and journals published in Russia and targeted for non-Russian Europeans circulated within the Soviet Union (among the exiles, intellectuals, and the relevant ethnic minorities), throughout the antifascist diaspora and among left-leaning intellectuals outside the Soviet Union. One such periodical was MORP's international literary journal, which began appearing in June 1931 in the wake of Kharkov and was called *The Literature of World Revolution* (Literatura mirovoi revoliutsii) from 1931–1932 and then *International Literature* (Internatsional'naia literatura). It came out in six languages: initially Russian, English, French, and German and later in Spanish and Chinese; the contents of each varied slightly with each issue. In late 1932 Tretiakov, in another sign of his stature after the April 1932 Central Committee decree, was made head of the Russian version of these parallel journals, *Internatsional'naia literatura,* and put on the editorial board of the German edition.[97] Under Tretiakov *Internatsional'naia literatura* published an impressive array of titles from Western European literature, but also provided detailed information about the literary worlds of Western countries and reviewed many of the new translations that appeared elsewhere.

Under Tretiakov's leadership the Russian version of the journal published a lot of Western modernist material, including Joyce's *Ulysses*. The journal initially announced in 1933 that it would publish *Ulysses*, translated by the "First Translation Collective of the Writers Union," but it actually appeared only in 1935–1936, and even then the entire novel did not appear as promised, only episodes 1 through 10.[98] This was a significant achievement nevertheless, given that Karl Radek's keynote address on Western literature delivered at the Writers Union Congress the previous year had denounced modernism, positing as the great alternative facing Soviet literature "James Joyce or Socialist Realism?"[99] Clearly the literary world was far from monolithic, and directives were not always followed; other modernists such as Celine were also published.[100] In reality the literati were deeply divided on the subject of Joyce, as can be seen when Sergei Dinamov, overall editor of the *International Literature* journals, announced with pride at a Writers Union meeting that they had published Joyce, Aleksandr Shcherbakov, then head of the union, retorted "It's some kind of raving. A normal person simply can't take it."[101]

Vishnevsky, Friedrich Wolf's Soviet patron, is said to have been the main figure pushing for publishing *Ulysses*. In 1933 (when *Internatsional'naia literatura* announced that *Ulysses* would appear, but it did not), he made several statements urging that it be published. Though in one he advocated publishing Joyce in order to "know the West," in another he pointed to Joyce's formal achievements and suggested that if Soviet writers could learn from the techniques of a Joyce or a Dos Passos they could outstrip them in three to four years—a version of the Great Appropriation.[102] In 1935, every issue of the military literary journal *Znamia,* where he was an editor, announced that the novel would appear, but it did not. However, while in Paris in 1936, Vishnevsky visited Joyce and was proud to be able to disabuse him of the idea that his works had not been published in Soviet Russia.[103] Vishnevsky himself wrote primarily tough sagas of the Civil War, including the classic socialist realist drama *The Optimistic Tragedy* (Optimisticheskaia tragediia; 1933) and a play about the German revolutionary movement, *Germaniia.* In short, like the main figures in this book, he was a cosmopolitan, and an intermediary, and fiercely patriotic, and, like Koltsov, a Bolshevik and prime mover for the cult of the Civil War as well.

The controversies over Joyce illustrate the general point that one cannot set up a binary of Party writers versus dissident highbrow intellectuals as supporters of Western literature and modernism. Supporters of Western modernism not only came from within the establishment but also persisted long after their cause is generally said to have been lost. Several years later Friedrich Wolf took advantage of the trial and sentencing of Radek in 1937, to revisit Radek's speech at the Writers Congress. In an article in *Sovetskoe iskusstvo* he condemns the attack on Joyce (in 1937!), upbraids Radek for "completely ignor[ing] French and German writers," and relates how after the 1934 speech he went to Moscow's Hotel Metropol to talk to Radek, bringing with him the prominent leftist German writer Willi Bredel and Malraux (both delegates). But "Radek was livid and offhand," Wolf reports, though "Tretiakov, Vishnevsky, and Erenburg were also against [Radek's position]. We all now recognize that we should have taken our criticism farther."[104]

One reason why it was necessary to put out the various versions of *International Literature* in different languages was that most European members of the fraternity did not know Russian and were not likely to learn it. The lack of a single, mutually comprehensible language was a potential barrier to making possible something like a Moscow-oriented, transnational republic of Letters; members of Voltaire's republic communicated in French.[105] The cultural intermediaries we have been following here, Eisenstein, Erenburg, Koltsov, and Tretiakov, were all multilingual and spoke German, but among the Germanophones in the antifascist movement, some resisted learning Russian or mastered it poorly, including Becher, the chief editor of *Internationale Literatur. Deutsche Blätter* from 1933 to 1945, who, though he lived in an apartment building for Soviet writers, *refused* to learn Russian because he wanted to remain German and didn't want Russian to effect his work.[106] Lukács, by contrast, appears to have been able to express himself in Russian to a degree.[107] The central role played by literature in the movement was at least in part because it is more portable—translatable—than language as spoken speech, less mired in idiosyncrasy and irregularity. Though grounded in the local or national, it can transcend linguistic and geographical limitations through publishing and translation.

My account to date has suggested a limited impact from the Germano-phone presence in Moscow. Yet one of them, Lukács, had a major impact on the emerging account of socialist realism. The Soviet debate on social-ist realism, launched when the term was invented in May 1932, ostensibly ended in August 1934 when the Writers Union held its first congress and the term was given official definition. But the definition was somewhat vague, especially in Gorky's address, where he waxed lyrical about "folk-tales, myths, and legends" and the "folklore of the toiling people" as model genres for the new tradition, adding that "myth creation was au fond realistic."[108] Yet in practice the backbone of socialist realism was the novel. What socialist realism might mean in terms of the novel was in ef-fect debated a few months later, on December 20 and 28, 1934, and Janu-ary 3, 1935, when there was a landmark discussion on that genre held in the Literary Section of the Institute of Philosophy of the Communist Academy. This discussion's focus was a critique of Lukács's article on the novel commissioned for the *Literary Encyclopedia*.[109]

Lukács was one of the more prominent examples of the itinerant leftist who, like members of the Republic of Letters, as Darnton describes them, "changed passports as often as he crossed borders." But in post-1933 Moscow he was the man of the hour. Earlier, by contrast, in 1927 Lukács's career as a leader in the Hungarian Communist Party had been cut short when he was expelled for his "Blum theses," which advocated that the Party form alliances with nonproletarian forces in a democratic context. In the mid-1930s, as we will see in the next chapter, that became the new strategy of the Soviet Party (of which he became a member) and of the Comintern.

Since his return to Moscow in March 1933, Lukács had worked mainly on literary theory and aesthetics, but also commented on the roots of Na-zism. Somewhat ambidextrous, he operated both in the Germanophone world of the exiles and in Soviet intellectual life, publishing in journals of both. He had positions in Soviet academic institutions and was at the same time a leader in several Soviet bodies set up for the Germanophone émigrés, such as the German Commission of IVRS (MORP) and the German sector in the Writers Union.[110] But he also played a critical role in the formulation of Soviet literary theory, as is evident in the discussion at the Institute of Philosophy, where all the major names in that field were gathered, ostensibly to critique his article but in practice to endorse it in a virtual act of fealty.

A synopsis of Lukács's article on the novel and this discussion was published in *Literaturnyi kritik* in 1935.[111] The discussion reveals how much, in effect, he and his Moscow coterie inscribed their theory and history of the novel into the Marxist-Leninist model of societal progress while at the same time according socialist realism a transnational, European context.

In his account of the novel and its provenance, Lukács closely follows "classical German philosophy" and primarily Hegel, who, he says, though limited in that he was an "idealist" rather than a "realist," nevertheless "posed the question of the novel more deeply and more correctly than in all the bourgeois theories," orienting his findings around a contrast between the classical epic and the novel.[112] Lukács adduces several stages in the development of the novel, starting with Rabelais and Cervantes, but his high point is the age of what for him were the great realists—Henry Fielding, Sir Walter Scott, Goethe, Balzac—who sought to "assimilate the hero into bourgeois society." They failed to achieve such wholeness, he argues, because of the social contradictions brought about by capitalism. Some of them produced truly great realist novels nevertheless, due to their "fearlessness in exposing contradictions, . . . the truthfulness of their social content."[113]

Lukács posits a decline in the novel after the 1848 revolution, with the subsequent period of reaction. Some writers, he suggests, reduced their heroes to being a mere "average person," a statistical norm, so that the action lost its epic character, while others indulged in an exaggerated subjectivism, a trend that led to the "final disintegration of the novel form in the imperialist era (Proust, Joyce)." With a little casuistry, Lukács is able to include as high realists the Russian novelists of the late nineteenth century (such as Tolstoy) as he argues that in Russia 1905 was functionally what 1848 was in Europe. With the rise of the proletariat, however, a group with strong internal cohesion, it became possible again to create a "positive hero" in the image of the "conscious worker," who destroys the objective causes for the degradation of man." As a consequence, in the Soviet Union the novel was able to "make the most fundamental changes to its nature, re-form itself [perestraivat'sia] in its basics and move toward a rapprochement with the epic." This rapprochement does not involve "an artificial revival of the formal or thematic elements of the old epic (its mythology, etc.) . . . but arises from the classless society." Lukács's conclusion is that since some "survivals" of the capitalist mentality persist in the consciousness, the socialist realist novel must as yet remain "linked with the great bourgeois realist novel. A critical appropriation [usvoenie] and reworking of this heritage therefore plays an extraordinarily important role in resolving the problem of form for the current stage in the development of the socialist realist novel."[114] Several features of Lukács's article need to be highlighted here. First, in that he adduced a genealogy for socialist realist literature that begins in ancient Greece and continues through western Europe in the modern period but finds its apotheosis in a phenomenon generated in Soviet Russia—the socialist realist novel— one sees a parallel between his historical model and the one authoritative commentators advanced for the "socialist realist" architecture of the "new Moscow." In addition, Lukács insists that, given the class-induced limitations of the "bourgeois" novel, it must be "appropriated and reworked" in order for socialist realism to truly attain its status as apotheosis of literary evolution. This is precisely the dynamic I have pointed to in the introduction as a feature of Stalinist culture in this decade. The Soviet product was to become, as Lifshits made explicit in the discussion, "world culture" incarnate.[115]

Second, and as several of the discussants pointed out, by taking as the starting point of his trajectory of literary evolution Homer's oral epics, Lukács is fully in line with Gorky's position at the First Writers Union Congress when Gorky said that socialist realism should be based on the "folklore of the toiling people"; the words "folk creativity" are capitalized in one discussant's contribution, in case we might miss them.[116] Behind Lukács's account of the novel, then, stands a kind of ideal epic, a less "primitive" and mythologized version of the classical epic of Homer; he contends that since the division of labor, when "social contradictions" emerged in bourgeois society, *"struggle within the society"* has been the theme of the novel rather than struggle against external enemies or nature, standard themes of the classical epic.[117] His version of epic functions as a kind of gold standard against which the fluctuations of the novel itself are measured. Its telos is to recover that wholeness of classical epic that Lukács sees as possible only in a unified, classless society. But his account of the original (Homeric) epic as the voice of a unified society is, as Mirsky pointed out in the discussion, idealized, in that Greek society had slaves and hence could not be seen as classless and unified.[118]

Thus Lukács, in presenting a somewhat simplified model of the novel's evolution, pared away of a lot of historical detail that might undermine its neat concordance with the three-stage Marxist-Leninist model of historical development that culminates in a higher stage of unity when the contradictions have been overcome. Many of the speakers faulted Lukács for not bringing into his account the considerable prebourgeois history of the novel or establishing precisely when the genre emerged, and for not differentiating among the several subgenres, in other words for the lack of complexity in his model. Valerian Pereverzev, Lukács's main critic, spoke not only of medieval and Renaissance examples but also of the Greek novel.[119] Lukács's de facto interlocutor, Bakhtin, explored such Greek precedents in some detail in his writings of the late 1930s, such as "Forms of Time and of the Chronotope in the Novel." Another major apparent omission by Lukács also picked up in the discussion was that he did not include in his trajectory Virgil's *Aeneid* (such later epics were labeled "artificial" [*iskustvennye*] as compared with the original, Homeric folk ones).

In the discussion of the Lukács article, a common defense against such carping at his omissions was to expostulate against the notion that any particular countervailing example—a mere "fact," a "contingency"— could controvert any generalization drawn from the writings of Marx, Engels, and Lenin—and, Lifshits and Lukács added in their closing statements, Stalin.[120] In other words, Lukács and others implicitly invoked Stalin's position in his 1931 article for *Proletarian Revolution* (see Chapter 1), which remained authoritative. Lukács's rejection of psychological realism and depiction of the inner self also dovetailed with the current movement of Soviet literature away from the theories of RAPP and in that sense also rendered Lukács a "Stalinist."

Marx had endorsed Homer, but Lukács's account of literary evolution was closer to Hegel. Though speakers made appropriate gestures in the direction of pointing out that Hegel was ultimately inadequate because he was an "idealist," they also insisted on the validity of his account of the evolution of the novel from the Greek epic, in effect justifying the publication of sections of Hegel's *Aesthetics* that had just begun appearing in Russian translation in *Literaturnyi kritik,* starting with number 10 of 1934.[121] Lifshits in his contribution to the discussion talked about "Hegel and Belinsky" as if they were one, thus identifying the Russian tradition with Hegel.[122]

Lukács's sense of Marxism here, his downplaying of economic and class considerations (like Hegel) and his foregrounding of the aesthetic, dovetailed with what he had been advocating since at least 1919, when he became a leader of the Hungarian Communist Party and played a role in its short-lived Communist government. In his article "The Old and the New Culture" of that year, for example, he insisted that the revolution meant the triumph of culture over economics, and even, in another article of that year ("Zur Aufklärung") that political activity is but the *means* to the triumph of culture. In his writings one also detects a progressive weakening of links between the actual workers' movement and the greater cause.[123] In other words, Lukács was an advocate of an updated version of the aesthetic state, but his predilections were refracted through the language of Marx, and even Stalin, so that he appeared to ventriloquate the current line.

In promoting his own tastes, Lukács had to resort to a certain amount of casuistry, especially in admitting canonical European writers of the nineteenth century with dubious class identities to the status of forebears of socialist realism. The greatness of certain novelists in his heroic age of realism (prior to 1848) was, he argues, achieved *despite* their own (class-driven) desires and volition.[124] In particular, "the greatness of Balzac and his central position in the development of the novel is based precisely on the fact that in his images he created the direct opposite of what he consciously planned [zadumannomu]."[125] Engels had made a similar point in his (recently published) letter of 1888 to Margaret Harkness in London.[126]

Lukács, with his insistence on this "despite," is effectively attacking what was called "vulgar sociology," the direct linking of class and literary content, an approach most associated with Pereverzev. As the discussion of Lukács's article evolved, it became increasingly an occasion for attacking Pereverzev and his "sociological" school, which allegedly had the temerity to emphasize the empirical nature of class ("vulgar empiricism") and, worse, downplayed the leading role of the "proletariat" in cultural evolution (read Party).[127] While Usievich, an editor of *Literaturnyi kritik,* and others labeled Pereverzev "Menshevik," his theories "non-Marxist" and "dangerous" *(vrednye),* speaker after speaker pointed to Lukács's Marxist bona fides as one who had recently worked on Marx's manuscripts.[128] By Pereverzev's second speech, he had become apologetic, his erstwhile followers denying their connection to him.[129] Though Pereverzev's school was not completely routed until 1936, this discussion at the Communist Academy endorsed his replacement by Lukács and his associates as *the* Marxist literary theorists, but also swept aside the provincialism of RAPP-era literary policies, effectively expanding the "proletarian" horizon to embrace Hegel, classical German theory, and the western European literary canon. In 1935 Lukács's associate Frants Shiller published his first volume of a new history of modern western European literature, which appeared in three volumes between 1935 and 1937, and was welcomed as a replacement for the old vulgar sociological histories of Vladimir Friche and Petr Kogan, though deemed not sufficiently critical of vulgar sociology.[130]

In the aftermath of the Writers Union Congress, then, the demimonde of the Western cultural tradition had been recategorized as an honored progenitor of the new Soviet one. No longer should Soviet literary theory be "vulgarly" sociological; casuistry could legitimize the Western heritage's problematical status yet also safeguard the Marxist-Leninist comme il faut. But was the Soviet Union marrying into that good family of European *Kultur,* coming out of the demimonde status it had been relegated to as long as it was associated with all that pulp ("proletarian") literature? Or was it the dependable groom all good mothers seek for their daughters, the one who would save the fair "Europe" from the barbarians (a popular reading of Moscow-as-third-Rome among intellectuals in the prerevolutionary years)? Matchmaking at the level of big politics ensured that Western literature and intellectuals would (selectively, of course) be courted and promoted with redoubled effort. As we will see in the next chapter this trend intensified after the Popular Front was formed and Comintern policy shifted.

CHAPTER 5

"World Literature"/"World Culture" and the Era of the Popular Front (c. 1935–1936)

HE YEAR 1935 might be described as the high point of Soviet internationalism. It was the year when the country was in an antifascist alliance with the Popular Front government of France. The culture of the Soviet Union and that of France (which had become socialist) converged in significant respects, though not intentionally, even as both became increasingly nationalistic. And in that year the terms "world literature" and "world culture" were intoned throughout continental Europe as the mantras of the antifascist cause, but nowhere more than in the Soviet Union. Koltsov successfully petitioned Stalin to organize in Zhurgaz a Library of World Literature in mass editions, one of several new initiatives that further expanded the store of translations.[1]

An implicit question remained: how far does the "world" of "world literature" or "world culture" stretch, not just in class and political terms but also geographically and culturally? Does it encompass continental Europe, greater Europe, or the transatlantic world? Does it embrace the non-European, such as the ethnic minorities within the Soviet Union, or the Eurasian possibility? Or does "world literature" (world culture) mean the literature (or culture) of "universal" man? As we shall see, while some in invoking examples of "world literature" or "world culture" were just following the new official line and citing the right texts, others were reaching out for an extralocal perspective. Some enterprising intellectuals used the officially sanctioned further expansion of the cultural horizon to add legitimacy to their veiled critiques of socialist realist practice, though these critiques were now often focused on the performing arts (theater, film) rather than literature per se.

Any attempt at a "world literature" or "world culture" is confronted by the problem of linguistic accessibility, which can be resolved only by using some lingua franca, or by relying on translation, whether in the literal or in the extended sense. But any translation is an act of interpretation and subject to misreadings, or rendering the text in terms more familiar to the translator or his target audience/readers. Translations have also often been made less in the service of expanding the cultural horizons than of forwarding some local agenda. As Soviet intellectuals around 1935 encountered or appropriated an array of foreign culture, issues having to do with language, role, and identity that they had been grappling with for some time were made more urgent, but were also reframed by the new historical moment.

In May 1935 Benjamin wrote two of his most anthologized essays, "Paris, the Capital of the Nineteenth Century," the first of two synoptic presentations of the Arcades complex, and later that year two versions of "The Work of Art in the Age of Its Technological Reproducibility."[2] The latter essay can be seen as a further elaboration of the ideas he had already presented in "A Little History of Photography" (1931), where he first used his trademark term "the aura," and in "The Author as Producer," much of which, though dated 1934, was a response to Tretiakov's lecture also of 1931.

These essays of 1935 were written in a new context. Benjamin had been uprooted, forced to flee Nazi Berlin, and was tenuously existing in Paris, trying to make it as a freelance man of letters. Some of his remarks in these essays on the intelligentsia—such as "to the uncertainty of its economic position corresponds the uncertainty of its political function"; "to dwell means to leave traces"; or "in the flaneur, the intelligentsia sets foot in the marketplace—ostensibly to look around, but in truth to find a buyer"— have an eerie autobiographical ring.[3] Benjamin himself needed a "buyer," but more often than not his publications were rejected.

In that Benjamin wrote these 1935 essays in Paris during the Popular Front, they coincided with a shift of interest in France to "revolutionary" mass culture, a topic he addresses but conceives in a very different way from Popular Front vogues. Benjamin uses a somewhat old-fashioned, Marxist model: a change in the (intellectual) means of production (with the advent of photography and film, enabling mass reproduction) brings about a revolution, a "shattering" or "liquidation" of tradition, ushering in new artistic practices and a new kind of consciousness. This reproduction on a mass scale "jeopard[izes]" the historical testimony relating to "the unique art object," and consequently "the authority of the object, the weight it derives from tradition."[4] *"But as soon as the criterion of authenticity ceases to be applied to artistic production, the whole social function of art is revolutionized. Instead of being founded on ritual, it is based on a different practice: politics."*[5]

In Popular Front France "revolution" was very much in, but it was a very different sense of revolution from the one Benjamin had. As several commentators have remarked, the trauma of the Nazi accession and exile probably contributed to the fact that many German exiles (such as Benjamin) continued to espouse avant-garde ideas of the 1920s at a time when many intellectuals of other Western countries had moved on. The cultural arms of the Popular Front had begun invoking precisely authority and tradition, even in film, the hero-genre of Benjamin's essay on the artwork. Many intellectuals had begun to reject avant-garde experimentalism as jejune and self-indulgent in the face of the world crisis. In their stead, writers were gravitating back toward the grand narrative. The French left focused on a particular event, the French Revolution, which was now seen less as iconoclastic— "shattering," a "liquidation" (terms characteristic of leftist vocabulary of the 1920s—than precisely as a "tradition," an origin and an "authorization." The event essentially acquired an "aura" and became central to public "ritual." The left were now talking about taking back the French Revolution as an institution that had been usurped by the right, arguing that such a mass, popular event, was rightfully *their* patrimony ("tradition," "testimony"). The Communists began to use "The Marseillaise" and the tricolor no less enthusiastically than their "Internationale" and red flag.[6]

Five important thematic elements in Benjamin's essay "The Work of Art"—masses, art, politics, fascism, and war—were key in French intellectual discourse of 1935. But there is another, crucial one that he does not mention: nation. On the contrary, in discussing Baudelaire, Benjamin's *flaneur en titre,* he remarks: "The poetry is no hymn to the homeland; rather, the gaze of the allegorist, as it falls on the city, is the gaze of the alienated man."[7] The national and the international became critical values in 1935, but less as antagonistic than as complementary ideals, complementary because the national cause demanded international action.

The time seemed out of joint. In France they were suffering from a depression. The Soviet Union, by contrast, was enjoying an economic recovery and was able to ease rationing and lower prices for foodstuffs in September 1935, but both countries were preoccupied with the threat of war. The rising danger of fascism propelled the Soviet Union closer to the nonfascist "bourgeois" governments in Europe. Leftist politicians and intellectuals in France, confronted by the fascist menace, had begun circling the wagons, forming alliances against the threat both within and without the country, including, as the Front's name implies, with the masses.

Leaders and intellectuals within the European countries wanted international alliances but argued about which ones to form. In the Comintern, as elsewhere, there was fierce opposition to alliances with the bourgeois West, but Georgi Dimitrov, who had become the man of the hour because of his victory at the Reichstag fire trial, was a proponent of an international antifascist alliance. His position prevailed, and the Comintern revised its militantly anticapitalist stance. A radically more ecumenical policy was announced in Dimitrov's speech to the Seventh Congress of the Comintern in August 1935.[8] Tretiakov and Koltsov had been pushing for some time for more liberal treatment of Western antifascists, and the new policy enhanced their status.[9]

The previous Soviet attitude toward the West was a combination of Dostoevsky's "Europe as graveyard" and Spengler's "decline of the West," inflected by a narrative of capitalism, class, and exploitation. There were two worlds, the doomed capitalist in the West and the rising socialist cum communist in the East. Alternatively, each country was seen as internally riven by a division between its bourgeois population and the revolutionary proletariat. Now the "other [negative] Europe" was generally identified less with the "bourgeois" than with the fascists, though they were said to represent a logical development of capitalism.

Paris had become the center of the antifascist emigration, and of the antifascist movement in general. The Soviet Union, a bankroller (often clandestinely) of much antifascist activity, as well as the most vociferous champion of that cause, played a major role in the Paris activities. Moscow was not to be the hub of antifascism because the Comintern were eager to play down its role, and the Party did not want socialist Moscow polluted by an influx of non-Communist exiles.

Paris replaced Berlin as the center of Comintern European operations. Willi Münzenburg and his cultural outfit, Mezhrabpom, moved there. Erenburg and Koltsov in this new moment essentially each manned one pole of the new Paris/Moscow cultural axis, Erenburg as the principal Soviet corraller of antifascist intellectuals in Paris and western Europe generally, Koltsov as the main cultural functionary for the movement in Moscow.[10] Both traveled back and forth between these poles.

The new axis had an impact on the cultural canon. Now it became common to pair French and Russian writers as the canon encapsulated. Lukács, in his article "Narration or Description" (1936),[11] has now shifted from the broad spectrum of European writers he deployed in his 1934 essay on the novel (see Chapter 4) to foreground works by a Russian and a Frenchman, Tolstoy and Balzac, as positive exemplars. But the Soviet cultural world was ambivalent, at times accommodating Soviet culture in a pan-European, or Franco-Russian, purview but at others insistently operating in a totally Russo-centric tradition, defining socialist realism in terms of Tolstoy and of such thinkers in the radical tradition of the Russian intelligentsia as Vissarion Belinsky, Nikolai Chernyshevsky, and Nikolai Dobroliubov, ignoring the fact that Belinsky, for example, had himself been heavily influenced by such German thinkers as Hegel and Schiller. Hegel's *Aesthetics* was now being published serially and discussed in *Literaturnyi kritik,* as well as in *Arkhitektura SSSR,* while, as if in parallel play, many from the French intellectual elite were going through Hegel under the guidance of Alexandre Kojève, albeit a somewhat different version of Hegel, admixed with existentialism.[12]

An impulse to expand the national purview France-ward can also be seen in the case of Soviet policies on the writing of history. *Pravda* of January 27, 1936, republished two memoranda written in August 1934 by the authoritative triumvirate of Stalin, Zhdanov, and (the now deceased) Kirov that discuss a proposal for a new history of the Soviet Union that had been drafted by the Vanag group (of historians). In these memoranda, the triumvirate criticize the outline for the history on the grounds that it presents the nation's past almost exclusively in terms of the Russians rather than as part of "world" history (sometimes called "pan-European," *obshcheevropeiskaia*). The new, canonical account of modern history should in their view start with the French Revolution (briefly summarizing all that has gone before) and go on to the Paris Commune before switching to the Russian revolutions of the twentieth century, as if in a single, transnational trajectory. The textbook, they insist, should also attack tsarism more strongly than in the prospectus, and not stop the history at 1923 (as projected) but take the narrative forward to 1934. In effect, then, Soviet history would comprise the prehistory of the Paris-Moscow axis, culminating in the Soviet post-Lenin years when Stalin assumed power.[13]

The memoranda also attack the textbook proposal for not showing how Russian radical thinkers were influenced by Western theoreticians, and specifically by the philosophes, the French Revolution's alleged ideologues. This linkage with the philosophes was also a feature of the culture of the French Popular Front and of the antifascists generally. It became fashionable to identify the antifascists with the French encyclopedists, thereby dignifying their cause.[14] At one point an attempt was made to unite some of their leading names in a venture to produce an encyclopedia for the arts and sciences, which was to be for these times what the encyclopedia of Diderot, Voltaire, and Montesquieu had been for the second half of the eighteenth century. In the Soviet Union, Diderot, allegedly an early advocate of realism, featured particularly prominently in translations and scholarship of this time.[15] This plan never got very far but was recurrently talked about; at the London meeting of the Association in 1936, when it was proposed, Brecht (who had a brief affair with Maria Osten while there)[16] and Erenburg were unenthusiastic, while

H. G. Wells rejoined "We are no Diderots or Voltaires."[17] Was this at-tempted identification pretentious, or the mark of a wide-eyed idealism?

Thus Paris became the center of the antifascist movement, and the phi-losophes and the French Revolution its official origins. The philosophes and the French revolution also enjoyed a privileged position in the Ger-manophone exiles' account of their cultural tradition.[18] These precedents were also assimilated in the Soviet national narrative. The fact that the French Revolution had been labeled "bourgeois" by Marx was not sup-pressed, but played down. But now, when the French Revolution was an official milestone used in public ritual and rhetoric of both Soviet Russia and France, it was effectively reweighted to a narrative of military engage-ment in the name of national consolidation.

Darnton identified war ("a royal game, played in the name of dynas-ties") as outside the purview of his Republic of Letters.[19] But war was very much on the minds of the powers that had concluded an antifascist alliance. The left in France were becoming more nationalistic and milita-ristic and shifting the emphasis in their account of revolution by stressing military engagement as its culmination. The battle of Valmy of 1792, an event accredited with assuring the survival of the Revolution when a Prussian army under the Duke of Brunswick was stopped by the French armies of the North and Center from advancing toward Paris, became in many Popular Front representations a culmination point for the Revolu-tion itself. The year 1871, another time when foreign invaders threatened a revolution (the Paris Commune), was a banner moment in Popular Front lore as well. Front ideologues also appropriated the story of an-other French military hero with no ostensible connection to revolution, Joan of Arc. So recently a hero of the right and canonized by the Vatican, she was now described as a military commander from the people and hence more rightly the Front's emblematic hero.[20]

Within Soviet culture at about the same time, there was a cult of the Soviet Civil War as *a,* if not *the,* leading subject of culture, again a rein-flection of the (Russian) Revolution to emphasize not the storming of the Winter Palace but military engagement to drive out the Revolution's for-eign enemies who have ties to the counterrevolutionaries (as also at Valmy).[21] Effectively, the Civil War and the military replaced industrializa-

tion and collectivization as the main themes of fiction and film.[22] The Soviet military and its feats in the Civil War were given increasing prominence
in *Pravda* and *Izvestia* and in state ceremonial and investitures. Koltsov,
the great internationalist, was a prime mover in this trend, a change for
him from writing about bureaucracy and (mis)management of production; inter alia, he edited a prominent collection of articles on the Red
Cavalry that appeared in 1935.[23]

A mark of this shift was that in the Soviet Union, two texts, one filmic,
the other novelistic, were vaulted to the status of the most canonical
works. In film, *Chapaev* (1934), directed by the Vasiliev "brothers," about
a legendary but uneducated Civil War commander of that name, became
the exemplar of socialist realism in film. The novel was Nikolai Ostrovsky's autobiographical work *How the Steel Was Tempered* (Kak zakalialas'
stal'; 1932, 1934), about a Civil War hero (named Korchagin in the novel)
with superhuman endurance who overcomes debilitating wounds to produce a book about his experiences.

Koltsov was particularly important in the promotion of Ostrovsky's
novel. It had not attracted much attention when it was published ob-
scurely in a Komsomol journal but an official cult of Ostrovsky himself
took off in 1935. The "signal" that propelled Ostrovsky from marginal
and local recognition to becoming a national figure was an article on his
life by Koltsov, "Courage" (Muzhestvo), a banner term in 1935, published
in *Pravda* on March 17, 1935.[24] Starting from this article's appearance, an
endless stream of prominent figures made pilgrimages to Ostrovsky in
Sochi, including Lenin's brother and sister, veterans from the Potemkin
mutiny, and the aviation hero Valerii Chkalov.[25]

Korchagin cum Ostrovsky became the model of the revolutionary hero
who wields the sword and the book (the Soviet secret police play a prominent role in the novel). In contemporary Soviet accounts of the new man,
in effect, that he should wield the "sword" (sheer military or coercive
might) *alone* was seen as not enough; that would be barbarism. In the
press of the time, much was made of the contrast with the Nazi, who held
book culture in relatively low regard, seeing it as an impediment to a virile
and victorious nation. An eyewitness report in *Izvestia* about the Berlin
book burning describes how a professor of "political education" in addressing the crowds there drew a comparison between the "intellectual"

brought up on hitherto existing philosophies and the "type of a simple soldier" who was previously considered "uncultured"; "It was not idealist-humanist philosophy that won battles in the world war," the professor continued, "but the silent philosophy of the simple soldier."[26] But in *How the Steel Was Tempered*, the "simple" soldiers are absorbed by literature and stay up all night listening spellbound as Korchagin reads them *The Gadfly* (Ovod; 1897), by the English writer Ethel Voynich. This novel is about an Englishman who fights in the Italian Risorgimento; another inspirational text for Korchagin is the popular prerevolutionary chapbook *Giuseppi Garibaldi*. Both texts have to do with revolutionary movements that are also nation-forming and involve driving out a foreign power, in these instances Austro-Hungary.

A faith in literature was also evident in Popular Front France, where writers enjoyed an elevated status.[27] In the many demonstrations and public rituals, the standard inventory of portraits born aloft comprised assorted philosophes, plus Georges Jacques Danton and Maximilien Robespierre, and writers such as Hugo, Barbusse, Rolland, and Zola. Most of the Front's leaders were themselves in literature's thrall. Leon Blum, the head of its government, had himself played a considerable role in the Parisian literary scene, contributing to a literary journal, writing reviews, and publishing a book on Stendhal.[28]

Literature was also the focus of the great international antifascist meeting held in Paris in June 1935, called the Congress for the Defense of Culture. Mostly writers attended, among them Benjamin, who sat in the audience for many of the sessions. Their belief in the sacrality of literature illustrates yet another way that Benjamin, who believed literature was being superseded by photography and film, was swimming against the tide.

The Soviet Union largely bankrolled and organized the event; here Willi Münzenberg, Erenburg, and Koltsov were particularly active; in fact the Congress was initially Erenburg's idea.[29] The correspondence of Koltsov with Stalin and other leaders regarding provisions for the successive congresses and plenums reveals that he would propose measures for the congresses and the antifascist cause (financing, choosing of delegates and committee members, and publishing initiatives, including initiatives for systematic publication of literature in translation) while the leadership enjoyed the right of approval, ignoring some requests or out-right vetoing them.[30] Despite the Soviet backing, however, it was decided in the Writers Union and MORP that in order to unite the disparate groups attending, the fact that it was a Soviet initiative should not be evident, and there should be no explicit resolutions of support for the Soviet Union.[31] The Comintern organizers were very embarrassed when Gustav Regler, a German Communist writer affiliated with them, put his feet right into it at the Congress and declared the importance of Soviet allegiance.[32]

In MORP discussions in preparation for the Congress, officials advocated that in the speeches and resolutions due respect be paid to the "bourgeois" as well as the proletarian and revolutionary cultural tradition.[33] Consequently, for the Congress such mantras already popular among the antifascists as "reason," "culture," and "humanism," terms that were suitably grandiose but equally suitably vague, were to be yet again intoned as the participants' values, setting them off from the fascists, the alleged agents of Unreason.

The mantra at the Congress, however, was "world literature." The term had a convenient pedigree, in that it originated in a remark by Goethe but was also advocated by Marx and Engels in their *Communist Manifesto*. But what would it actually mean for the antifascists? It was an ambiguous concept, even in Goethe, who to some extent promoted it in the context of getting his works published in other (European) countries.[34] Was it to be a hybrid comprising titles from different cultures? Was it to be a "world-historical" literature, by analogy with Hegel's "world-historical" hero? Or was it to be in some way a literature whose authors had divined the essential for that time, or even for all time, to become the bearers of a universal humanity?

In practice, "world literature" largely meant European literature. And it entailed specific exclusions. These included the problematical Trotsky-ites but also many modernists, especially the avant-garde. The Surrealists, Benjamin's heroes, were not to be entertained, with the exception of Aragon, who had long abandoned Surrealism for socialist realism.

The Soviet delegation to the Congress, headed by Koltsov, was relatively colorless. Erenburg was very distressed about its caliber, and at his insistence they hastily added Babel and Pasternak. Tretiakov was not included, even though he had become a central player in the antifascist cause—because he was considered too avant-garde? He is said in archival sources to have been offended by this, and to compensate Writers Union officials threw him a bone by including him in a delegation of writers to visit Czechoslovakia later that year.[35]

In the wake of the Paris Congress, changes occurred in the transnational literary bodies that had been under the Comintern umbrella. In December 1935 MORP, at Koltsov's suggestion, was superseded by the Association for the Defense of Culture (Association Internationale des Ecrivains pour la Défense de la Culture), and within the Soviet Union by the Foreign Commission of the Writers Union, headed by Koltsov with Tretiakov a deputy, an extremely powerful organization on the cultural horizon and in status above VOKS. Erenburg was close to *Nouvelle revue française,* and there were some efforts to make it a mouthpiece for the Association, committed to publishing a certain number of titles a year.[36] Thus, though Tretiakov's own aesthetic views were fast losing currency, he became increasingly implicated in a campaign whose explicit aim had by 1935 become "world literature." One might assume that for him the antifascist cause and the idea of Moscow cultural hegemony trumped even his commitment to the avant-garde, but it should be remembered that in this year *Ulysses* was appearing in his journal *Internatsional'naia literatura.* He had his own version of "world literature" and Soviet cultural hegemony and continued to work in his various official capacities for its realization.

A second important outcome of the Congress was that in response to one of its recommendations, a new Germanophone journal was established, *Das Wort* (The word; Feuchtwanger's suggested title, its biblical ring in keeping with the sacral role of literature).[37] Founded in 1936 under the Foreign Commission of the Writers Union, *Das Wort* was published in Moscow by Koltsov's Zhurgaz (its financing possible because of the mass popularity of *Ogonëk*) with Koltsov as an advisor but coedited by Willi Bredel, Feuchtwanger, and Brecht.[38] Its editors and sponsors defined it as an "organ of the Popular Front" and successor to Wieland Herzfelde's *Neue Deutsche Blätter,* published in Prague.[39] Though located in Moscow, the journal solicited contributions from all over the diaspora, and its editors were scattered: Bredel had come to Moscow after escaping from a Nazi concentration camp, Feuchtwanger lived on the French Riviera, and the peripatetic Brecht hung out in Denmark and elsewhere. Thomas Mann had been courted as an editor unsuccessfully.[40] This choice of big name, nonresident editors was deliberate because *Das Wort* was targeted to become, in effect, a literary organ of the scattered diaspora.[41] The other two German-language Moscow periodicals, *Internationale Literatur, Deutsche Blätter,* and *Deutsche Zentral-Zeitung* (the latter to some degree a version of *Pravda* for the German population in the Soviet Union) also performed that function, but to a lesser extent.[42] Initially, *Das Wort*'s organizers claimed that the journal would embrace the different positions represented in the emigration. After all, Brecht and Bredel, who had both been attacked by Lukács in 1931–1932 in *Linkskurve,* were far from conventional socialist realists. But over time it became less ecumenical, and the position of Lukács and the like-minded emerged as dominant, even though, as Brecht pointed out repeatedly, he was officially an editor; Lukács was listed only as a consultant on Balzac.[43]

Benjamin was also marginally involved in the journal. It had initially proposed that he contribute articles on French literature two to three times a year, but when he tried to publish his essay "Work of Art" there, it was not accepted.[44] Then he tried to publish two "Paris Letters," but only the first one he submitted appeared.[45] The second letter was on photography and art, but it was not published, though he was told in a letter from Bredel of March 11, 1937, that it would be, and was repeatedly assured that an honorarium had been sent; nevertheless, he never received it.[46] A suggestion that he contribute a review of Brecht's recently published collected works (as Brecht proposed) likewise did not pan out.[47]

As the 1930s progressed, one saw in all three Moscow-based Germanophone periodicals two general trends that were in some senses countervailing, in others complementary. On the one hand, they became more and more obsessed with the German cultural tradition. A regular rubric in *Das Wort,* "Erbschaft dieser Zeit," (Heritage of this time) presented excerpts from German thinkers of the past, chosen to promote an edited version of the German cultural tradition, representing it as both national and "cosmopolitan." Yet at the *same* time, *Das Wort* became ever more Soviet assimilationist, not only by devoting more and more space to panegyrics and apologia for Soviet actions and leaders but also in publishing more and more articles about Russian and Soviet writers.

Moscow intellectuals were also expected to perform verbal acts of loyalty to the state, whether in panegyrics or in intoning the discourse of official spokesmen. But they frequently used these gestures in the service of their particular positions in the bitter debates then in progress as to which cultural forms were appropriate for the new socialist society. The new platform on "world literature" provided an opportunity to frame their arguments in terms of the translated material without engaging socialist realism head on, by critiquing its rigidity in this oblique fashion.

A silent (unpublishable) participant in these debates was Bakhtin, then even more marginalized than Benjamin, in that he was in internal exile in the Soviet Union. Bakhtin's position in his several essays and books from the late 1930s was, as has been analyzed by Galin Tihanov, in many respects a response to Lukács. The terms of his argument drew heavily on the work of Goethe and other German cultural theorists (in some instances he plagiarized), but his discussion of them was refracted via the discourse of "world literature."[48] In other words, Bakhtin, like many contemporaries, was appropriating "world culture" in support of his arguments. Russian literature, which was so prominent in his writings of the 1920s—consider his entire monograph on Dostoevsky—is scantily represented in his writings of the 1930s. But in two of Bakhtin's best known works from this time—his dissertation on Rabelais, the first draft of which he submitted to the Gorky Institute of World Literature in 1940, and the essay "Forms of Time and the Chronotope" (1937–1938)—he, as was becoming typical, presents accounts of literature that ostensibly endorse current Soviet cultural practices but in effect critique the increasingly dry, formalistic, and overly official nature of socialist realism.

I have in mind here in particular Bakhtin's discussion of his key term "carnival" in the dissertation.[49] "Carnival," a highly capacious term, can be related to cultural practices of the time in both the Soviet Union and Popular Front France. In Soviet public life, between 1935 and 1939, as never before or since, "carnivals" were a feature. They were staged throughout the country, in local parks and public squares, in high school halls and factory houses of culture. At the height of each summer a carnival was held in Moscow's Gorky Park in a series that was imaginatively titled "The First Moscow Carnival" (1935), "The Second Moscow Carnival" (1936), and so on. Muscovites cavorted until dawn in masks and costumes. In addition, periodically over the course of the years, some kind of "carnival" or "carnival procession" or "carnival performance" *(karnaval'noe deistvo)* became a highlight of a public celebration, particularly outdoors, but also sometimes indoors in colder months.

At that time, mass festivals (not generally called "carnivals") were also a feature of French Popular Front culture. The peak of the Front's arc is considered to have been a festival staged in 1936, the biggest celebration of July 14 Paris had ever known.[50] Such fare, the organizers believed, would provide bonding experiences, conducing to a more socialistic consciousness among the mass participants, and act as a safeguard against their acquiring a fascist mentality. These festivities proceeded in parallel in the two countries and, though similar, were far from the same. The Soviet versions were part costume ball and part choreographed state occasions, whereas the French ones tended more to be commemorations of revolutionary anniversaries. Both countries in favoring mass festivities were to some extent drawing on the ideas of Rolland (himself an activist in the antifascist cause) whose *People's Theater* of 1902, written in the wake of the Dreyfus affair, had also been the inspirational text for the movement for mass spectacles and popular theater in postrevolutionary Moscow and Petrograd.[51]

The theoretical bases of the popular mass festivals were also explored by those who, in the Paris of 1937–1939, met in an informal College of Sociology, which Benjamin attended sporadically. Most of those speaking there were looking for cultural forms that might be communitarian in ethos without falling into the totalitarianism of fascism. One of them, Roger Caillois, in his address of 1939, "The Festival" (La Fête), advocates a culture centered around mass festivals.[52] It is, of course, unlikely that Bakhtin was familiar with the papers presented at the College of Sociology (though accounts of the festivals promoted by the French Popular Front appeared sporadically in the Soviet cultural press, and Bakhtin may have read them). Caillois, as is particularly evident in his later *Puissances du roman* (1940), warned of the danger that the novel would become a vehicle for pure subjectivity, for closeting in one's room, whether literally or metaphorically. Bakhtin shared this concern but in his dissertation contended that the novel had at times been, *and could still be,* saved by a healthy infusion of culture, or more specifically by the "sense of the world" *(mirooshchushchenie)* that can be derived from "carnival" and popular theatrical forms.

Bakhtin's principal exemplar of "carnival" he sees in Rabelais, not co-incidentally a French writer and one of the authors most cited in these years as a model for "world literature," more often than Lukács's beloved Balzac. But although Bakhtin purports to be discussing "carnival" princi-pally in terms of a novelist, much of his attention is devoted to varieties of noncanonical performance that undermine the status quo, and to bodily gestures and scatological public utterances that contravene all sense of decorum, "free of all norms and limitations of the official world."[53] The orgiastic letting go he associates with "carnival" is not self-valuable, how-ever. It provides the ultimate bonding experience, fusing the "people" *(na-rod),* at that time a key term of official culture. In fact "carnival becomes the symbol and incarnation of the true, universal [vsenarodnogo] festival on the square";[54] in the dissertation he uses *"narodno-ploshchadnyi"* (lit-erally "popular-of the square") interchangeably with "carnival." Though *"vsenarodnyi,"* the Russian word used here, means of all peoples, actually Bakhtin was only talking about European culture. He largely ignores national boundaries and the boundary between the literary and the non-literary as, in his account of its evolution, "carnival" crosses national bor-ders as if unaware of them as it progresses from Rome to France (Paris, Avignon) to Germany (Nuremburg, Cologne), and never quite manages to perfect itself in Bakhtin's own country (Russia).[55]

In the dissertation Bakhtin periodically likens "carnival" to a theatrical performance "without any footlights."[56] His account of Rabelais, in effect, draws on a particular tradition of theater that one might call the ludic, the theater of the street or public square, the traveling theater of the fair-ground tent, theater that tended to be irreverent, exuberant, vernacular, and very likely bawdy. In Chapter 8 he privileges the oral and vernacular over the *"written and printed,"* in effect challenging the basic assump-tions of the Stalinist culture of the "lettered city."[57] His "carnival" is not a mode for reinforcing the status quo, but on the contrary is a mode for debunking it in joyous laughter and fun. Many of his heroes of the carni-val mode, such as the clown or jester *(shut),* wear masks and exult in trav-

esty and taking on disguises, a feature he also emphasizes in presenting
his paradigmatic carnival, the Roman carnival as Goethe describes it in
his *Italian Journey* (Italienische Reise; 1816–1817).[58]

A leading Russian proponent of ludic theater was Vsevolod Meyerhold, in whose studio Tretiakov and Eisenstein met and together in 1922
produced farces in the fairground style such as "Enough Simplicity in
Every Wise Man" (1923). The ludic tradition is also associated with the
career of Molière, who in the Soviet 1930s was often cited as a model for
"world literature" (a four-volume scholarly edition of his works in translation was issued in 1935–1936). In 1933 Mikhail Bulgakov published a life
of Molière in Gorky's *Lives of Remarkable People* series in which he situated this dramatist's career in terms of the traveling theater of the fair-
ground tent.

In 1935 a major controversy arose surrounding Shakespeare, another
dramatist deemed a giant of "world literature." The slogan "Shakespear-
ize More!" (Bol'she shekspirizirovat'!), attributed to Marx, which first appeared in 1932, was now a ubiquitous injunction.[59] So many productions
of Shakespeare premiered that 1935 could be called the year of Shakespeare. The slogan "Shakespearization" was a call to produce a world-
historical literature, raising it to the heights of "world literature," but
what that meant was hotly contested, in this year especially.[60] Was Shakespeare a bard in the ludic tradition, a bard of the "peoples' theater," was
he merely the most prominent of a troupe of itinerant actors who impro-
vised, so that "Shakespeare" was essentially collectively written (another
instance where the "written and printed" was not privileged),[61] or was he
a high-culture writer? Versions of this debate had been going on for decades, both in Europe (consider the controversies surrounding the
Lambs' Shakespeare) and in Russia, but in the Soviet Union it came to a
head in 1935 as critics assessed rival translations of Shakespeare's plays.[62]
The controversy culminated in the "Shakespeare Conference" of November 25–27, 1935, at which Anna Radlova (poet and translator of Shakespeare) and A. A. Smirnov (a distinguished scholar of the Renaissance)
attacked the old translations: "The main idea of both presentations,"
Pravda reported, "was that the old translations did not only distort
Shakespeare textologically, but were done mechanically and moreover in
a language that was not accessible to the contemporary reader and audi-

ence."[63] That comment effectively intones the demand for "simplicity" frequently leveled at modernists, but the intellectuals who praised Radlova were using it casuistically to bolster their call for less bowdlerized versions that might revive Shakespeare's bawdiness. As Osaf Litovsky put it somewhat euphemistically in his 1935 article "The Living Shakespeare," his plays have "the realistic grossness and crudity [grubost'] of a man of the Renaissance, brimming with the joy of life and indefatigable energy and deeply passionate."[64]

Another example of this sort of casuistry would be some of the statements in the *Zapadnyi sbornik* (Western collection—of articles) published in 1937 and edited by Viktor Zhirmunskii, an erstwhile associate of the Formalists. In his foreword Zhirmunskii takes as this book's cue in discussing the influences on Russian literature of Western writers (including, prominently, Shakespeare) a statement of Stalin's concerning the memorandum of the Vanag group (discussed above) on the history textbooks, to the effect that Soviet history must no longer be told in a narrow, Russo-centric framework but rather as part of "pan-European" history. One article in this collection, one on Molière by A. A. Smirnov, argues that some classic writers, including Molière, in large measure overcame their class limitations and, as "humanists" continuing the tradition of the Renaissance, "spoke in the name of all mankind." Molière, he contends, when at his best, emerges as a "lesser version of the great artists and humanist thinkers of the sixteenth century (Rabelais, Erasmus of Rotterdam, Thomas More, and others)." But his greatness consists partly in his *narodnost'*, his use of such great folk genres as the farce, his natural style and sense of freedom from conventional moral constraints in the name of true love, and his closeness to Rabelais, from whom he often took plot themes, and to Rabelais's *Gargantua and Pantagruel.*[65] In other words, here we see embryonically some of the arguments Bakhtin was to make later in his 1940 dissertation on Rabelais, a copy of which he sent to Smirnov, but Smirnov is also using a "humanism" that has a very different inflection from its standard versions in the discourse of the antifascists.[66]

The claim of those who mounted mass festivals and carnivals, whether in Soviet Moscow or Popular Front Paris, that they were introducing more "spontaneous" and "popular" cultural forms, has to be reconciled with the reality that most of those produced were directed at some affirmation of the nation. In the case of France, this is particularly apparent in a film inspired by the movement, Jean Renoir's *La Marseillaise,* originally commissioned by the French Communist Party and intended as "a genuine experiment in collective action."[67] This film purports to represent the spontaneous coming together of Frenchmen from all walks of life (including a Catholic priest) and from different parts of France, who converge on Paris and from there repair to Valmy to defend the Revolution against the foreign invaders. It depicts the formation of the new (or renewed) French nation, now welded, as the many have become the one. But the nation is formed in song, as one after the other these disparate people, seemingly spontaneously and independently, spout snatches of the "Marseillaise," the French national anthem (also the film's title), ignoring the fact that the anthem is well known to have been written by a single author, Rouget de Lisle.

In the same year, 1938, Grigorii Aleksandrov, Eisenstein's erstwhile assistant, directed the Soviet musical *Volga-Volga,* which likewise celebrates the coming together of the nation in the one patriotic song composed by "the people"; in this instance the song is allegedly composed by a musically illiterate simple girl from deep in the provinces who, as she travels toward Moscow with a team of performers, encounters assorted groups of people who, to her bewilderment and without apparent direction, perform her song in multiple variations.[68]

Though *Volga-Volga,* with its theme of the spontaneously generated and bonding national song might seem to have affinity with French Popular Front culture, in actuality its message was, in contradistinction to that culture, inflected by the antiintellectual and antimodernist aspects of the official sponsoring of things "folk." Moreover, and almost paradoxically, it was heavily influenced by the American musical (e.g., *Showboat*), which Alexandrov had been exposed to since he visited America with Eisenstein.

A Broader Reach for "World Culture"?

In drawing on recent American culture, Alexandrov was far from unique. While in this era a Moscow-Paris axis defined a lot of cultural activity, that other behemoth on the horizon, the United States, had become a major influence, suggesting a transatlantic frame of reference for "world culture." In 1933 the United States under Franklin Roosevelt extended dip-lomatic recognition to the Soviet Union, and by 1935 the back-and-forth traffic in intellectual vogues and visitors between Moscow and the United States had increased its pace. At the same time, in the Soviet Union a resolution was made to pursue closer relations with the American literary scene and the John Reed Clubs (founded in 1929 but now allied with MORP).[69] The impact of this was particularly felt in Tretiakov's journal, *Internatsional'naia literatura,* where a lot of American literature and in-formation on American writers was published, and a close relationship developed between the journal and the *New Masses,* to the point where material passed (in translation) from the pages of one journal to the other, giving the impression that they were affiliated.[70] Eisler, newly appointed head of the musical section of MORP and soon to take up a position at the New School in New York, was proud to report that Aaron Copland had written a mass song for the first of May and that his old mentor Ar-nold Schoenberg (in Californian exile), had become disillusioned with capitalism and wanted to visit the Soviet Union.[71]

Among American intellectuals, the Communist cause was becoming ever more popular, especially after the stock market crashed in 1929. The year 1935 was the height of the depression in America and the high point of Soviet-American intellectual convergence. Soviet culture was popular that year. When the Association of American Film critics voted that year on the top ten films, four were Soviet.[72] In April, the John Reed Clubs were ordered disbanded by MORP and succeeded by the League of American Writers (LAW), founded in 1934, in which such luminaries as Dorothy Parker, Van Wyck Brooks, and Erskine Caldwell played a promi-nent role.[73] In May 1935 it held the American leftist Writers Congress, which featured Kenneth Burke, in addition to the more predictable Drei-ser and the Communist writer Mike Gold; in preparation for the Con-gress, *Internatsional'naia literatura* reported, they prepared a book of Marx's, Engels's, and Lenin's pronouncements on literature and art and one on contemporary Marxist literary theory that included Lukács.[74] In June, Edmund Wilson visited Moscow, anxious to extend his visa a fur-ther three months to give himself more time to research the holdings on Marx and Engels in IMEL as part of his work on what became *To the Fin-land Station* (1940).[75] The journal *Partisan Review* and Britain's Left

Book Club were also in *Internatsional'naia literatura*'s sights, suggesting that under Tretiakov's editorship it sought to become a clearinghouse for the left-inclining and modernist literature of the transatlantic world.[76]

The Soviet-American détente also led to extended visits back and forth. In 1935 the Soviet artist Aleksandr Deinecke traveled around America recording his impressions in paintings, and the head of the State Board of Cinematography (GUKF), Boris Shumiatsky, basically an ill-educated career Comintern and Party man but long a fan of Hollywood, spent three months there and came back determined to found a Soviet Hollywood on the Black Sea, while Frank Lloyd-Wright visited in Moscow in 1937.[77] The most famous visit, however, was the motor trip around the United States made from October 1935 to early February 1936 by Ilya Ilf and Evgeny Petrov, already beloved in both the Soviet Union and the United States for their *Twelve Chairs* and *Little Golden Calf*. Ilf and Petrov were sent by *Pravda*, in which they published dispatches on their journey, while photos from the trip appeared in Koltsov's illustrated magazine *Ogonёk*, very much suggesting the hand of Koltsov in this trip.[78]

Ilf and Petrov produced from their impressions the book *One-Storied America* (Odnoetazhnaia Amerika; 1936, published in the United States as *Little Golden America*), which became for decades to come the main source Russians (including Khrushchev) had for understanding the United States. As the title suggests, in this book Ilf and Petrov were trying to present not the racy America of New York or Hollywood (which they visited to make a film of *The Twelve Chairs*) but everyday America, the America of ordinary people, a Popular Front sentiment. This popular book is less stridently anti-American and more informative than earlier writings on America. Ilf and Petrov conclude it by saying that the United States is democratic, unfortunately not socialist but close to "us." Inevitably, there are also criticisms, including a somewhat puritanical reaction to American films and popular entertainment as not only mindless but also exposing too much flesh: "Girls who are half naked, three-quarters naked, and nine-tenths naked dance, or act."[79]

But for Ilf and Petrov, America's besetting sin was its provincialism, the lack of curiosity they found everywhere about the rest of the world. The local paper, movies, and church are "the entire spiritual sustenance that capitalism gives people. Provincial papers are as flat as a pancake."[80] Thus

Ilf and Petrov dismiss the legendary American city with its skyscrapers speeding toward a technological future and taking the rest of the world in its wake, characterizing it as dominated by what Voltaire and others in the republic of letters scornfully labeled the *esprit de clocher* (see Chapter 4).

Ilf and Petrov probably felt able to deliver this verdict on America because 1935, the year they began touring it, was when, thanks in part to the confluence of the Depression and the rise of Nazism, Moscow came closest to realizing the dream of becoming a cultural "Fourth Rome." "Provincialism" in effect was a label for those not reached by its light.

The year 1935 was the highest point of cultural fraternization and enthusiasm abroad for the Soviet Union, with a lot of major names converging on the capital. In February, Moscow hosted the highly successful First Soviet Film Festival, where films were shown from countries like France, England, and the United States. *Chapaev* was awarded first prize at the festival, but at the same time Soviet films were popular in New York, especially *Chapaev,* which broke all records for a Soviet film there with its Broadway run and was also screened in a number of other major cities.[81]

American popular culture also entered the Soviet purview through the Moscow film festival. Several films by Walt Disney were screened there, received prizes, and were widely distributed in the Soviet Union.[82] Shumiatsky decreed that in future Soviet animation should follow Disney's techniques, thereby squelching a distinguished homegrown tradition of animation for decades to come.[83] In March that year, Moscow also hosted an international theater festival that attracted many of the big names in transatlantic theater, including Brecht, Eisler, Piscator, Gordon Craig, Hugh Casson, and Sybil Thorndyke-Casson.[84]

In the Moscow theater itself, *the* event of 1935 was the production of Shakespeare's *King Lear* in the Jewish Theater, Goset, with the famous actor Solomon Mikhoels as Lear (it premiered in February and was featured at the international theater festival in March).[85] Gordon Craig, whose journal the *Mask* (1908–1929) had been at the center of the European movement to revolutionize the theater, came to see the production and gave it his imprimatur.[86] Of all the plays to present in that year of rising militarism, the tragedy of Lear, a king who lost all his territory and descended into madness, seems an unlikely choice, but such was the resonance of Shakespeare, bard of "world literature." In Mikhoels's interpretation, Lear was too individualistic and believed himself all-powerful. He had to learn a more collectivist orientation.[87] In this we see yet another example of translation not just in the literal sense of a rendering in Yiddish but of the kind of "diachronic" translation George Steiner writes about in *After Babel* whereby texts of earlier eras are interpreted in contemporary terms, a process endemic to the Great Appropriation.[88]

For this production, *Lear* had been translated into Yiddish by Shmuel Halkin and was directed by Sergei Radlov, a Russian of German extraction who had originally trained with Meyerhold and was the husband of Radlova. The presentation of a classic of "world literature" in the language of an ethnic minority was symptomatic of the more inclusive sense of Soviet culture and identity that was reflected in the official press and practices of the mid-1930s. In 1936 a new national constitution was promulgated, the so-called Stalin Constitution, one of the most liberal of all time, which assured rights to the ethnic minorities. One sees this greater inclusiveness, for example, in the directives of the Politburo triumvirate regarding the Vanag group's project for a new USSR history textbook (discussed earlier) that the group is to include the history of the minority peoples, not just of Russia. But this injunction could be read in two ways—as oriented toward greater internationalism or toward national consolidation. It was both.

In the mid-1930s, the national minorities began to receive much more attention in culture. In 1935, *Sovetskoe iskusstvo* featured a new ongoing column on the newly formed Jewish Autonomous Region of Birobidzhan. The Literary Institute in Moscow, founded in 1933 to train Soviet writers, began aggressively recruiting would-be authors from ethnic minorities; many of these minorities had essentially had no written or Europeanized literature before. The shift culminated in 1939, when a new journal devoted to the literature of a multiethnic Soviet Union, *Druzhba narodov* (Friendship of peoples), was founded.

This expansion of the cultural horizon raises the question posed earlier about how far "world literature" or "world culture" extends; what would be its compass? Until 1935 the understanding had been mostly in terms of some European variant. But starting around 1935 the purview expanded within the Soviet Union. Symptomatic of this was another Aleksandrov musical, *The Circus* (Tsirk; 1936), a film heavily indebted to

American popular culture, especially the Busby Berkeley musicals. In part the film is an attack on the racism of the United States and Nazi Germany, which is contrasted with the multinational harmony of the Soviet Union, and in that sense implicitly a celebration of the new constitution about to be unveiled in December. (Ironically, in 1937 Kurt Weill and Lotte Lenya in American exile worked on *The Common Glory*, a musical for the Federal Theater Project that celebrated the American Constitution.) Ilf and Petrov exposed American racism in *One-Storied America*,[89] and they wrote the scenario for *The Circus* (though their names were removed from the credits at their request because they were appalled at the popular culture direction the film took). Toward the end of *The Circus*, members of the circus audience, each representing a different Soviet ethnic group, take turns cradling the American heroine's mixed-race (half-negro) child in their arms and singing him a snatch of a lullaby in the language of the cradler's ethnic group (among them Mikhoels singing in Yiddish), thereby demonstrating the lack of racial prejudice in the Soviet Union. This embrace could also be read as a symbolic adoption of a non-European into the "Great Family" of the multiethnic Soviet Union.

Vertov's "Three Songs of Lenin" (1934), one of the Soviet films much admired when it screened in America in 1935, is symptomatic of the switch to incorporating more of non-European Russia in the purview of "world culture."[90] The first of its three "songs" (parts) is about Muslim women of Central Asia throwing off their veils. The key line of its theme song runs "in a black prison was my face." The unveiled, liberated face is a variant on the general Soviet narrative of these years about enlightenment and progress. In the film Lenin and the book are two linked agents that dispel darkness: a shot of copies of Lenin's books coming off a conveyor belt at the printing press provides a visual motif. Thus Benjamin's "Age of Mechanical Reproduction" reaches the Soviet East, bringing with it the promise of the Lettered City (the "stone city"—Moscow—is another motif).

Darkness could of course also be dispelled by a popular uprising. Paul Robeson arrived in Moscow in January 1935 to depict that.[91] His trip was organized by Eisenstein, who had been very impressed by Robeson in the title role of *The Emperor Jones* (1933), and wanted him to play the role of the rebel leader in his projected film on the Haitian revolt.[92] Both

Eisenstein and Robeson were interested in the culture of non-Europeans, the multilingual Robeson in Central Asian and Chinese folk music particularly. He gave Eisenstein for his birthday on January 23 a recent French book about Chinese thought, *La Pensée chinoise* (1934), by Marcel Granet, the pupil of Durkheim and teacher of Levi-Strauss.[93]

This gift had resonance for Eisenstein's role in a more radical cultural détente than was envisioned by the Popular Front alliance, a more encompassing sense of "world culture." The event predated the Paris Congress for the Defense of Culture, but it complicates our sense of the "modernist" or avant-gardist alternative to socialist realism. It also provides a vivid example of a phenomenon mentioned at the beginning of this chapter—the way issues having to do with language, role, and identity that had confronted Soviet intellectuals for some time were reframed in this new historical moment as they grappled with the problem of translation, here in the extended sense.

The Visit of Mei Lanfang

In 1935 a trainload of lavish costumes and performers wended its way from Beijing right across the plains of Siberia to Moscow, arriving on March 12. It was as if an entire court had come to pay obeisance to the Soviet capital. The group was headed by the most famous actor of the Peking opera, Mei Lanfang, an interpreter of female roles. He had made the long trip from Beijing together with his assistant director, Professor Chzhan (Zhang Pengchun), twelve other actors, four musicians, and costumers and other stage assistants, a total of twenty-four in all. The troupe stayed until April 15, staging traditional operas in Moscow and Leningrad.

The visit of Mei Lanfang became a landmark moment in the history of theater. On April 14, the eve of his departure for Europe, at a famous VOKS-sponsored event the Soviet directorial elite paid tribute to Mei Lanfang, followed by a demonstration of his acting.[94] Mei Lanfang's visit also coincided with the Moscow Theater Festival, and some of his performances and lectures were attended by its foreign delegates, including Gordon Craig and Brecht.[95] The experience led to Brecht's first published formulation of his theory of alienation, "Alienation Effect

in Chinese Acting" ("Verfremdungseffekte in der chinesischen Schau-
spielkunst"; 1935).

Had, then, Moscow the periphery (of Europe) become the new center
of "world culture," with Paris just the more pragmatic, operational center
(or front)? Had Moscow become an intermediary between East and West,
realizing a long-standing Russian ambition?

In actuality, though the visit's greatest resonance was to be felt within
culture, the motivation was for both parties, the Soviet and the Chinese,
political. As Carl von Clausewitz might have said, the two nations were
pursuing politics by other means. The Japanese had become a rising
menace on the Soviet eastern front, and the Chinese, ever since the Japanese had invaded Manchuria in 1931, had increasingly been victims of their
aggression. The Soviet and Chinese governments thought it as yet impru-
dent to formalize a political alliance against the Japanese and opted for
the time being for this cultural version of entente.[96] Mei Lanfang had already proved an excellent diplomat for his country, with rave success
tours of Japan (1919, 1924) and the United States (1930). During his six-
month tour of America he became so wildly popular and fashionable that
society ladies rivaled each other in hosting lunches for him, congressmen
were ecstatic, and he wowed Hollywood. Since then he had become active in the anti-Japanese movement in China, and he volunteered to forgo
an honorarium for the Soviet trip as his patriotic contribution.[97]

In view of Mei Lanfang's political significance, the visit was given
prominence in *Pravda* and *Izvestia*. Several articles on Mei Lanfang appeared, including one in *Izvestia* by Karl Radek, the leading Bolshevik
journalist and former Comintern leader, and others by China specialists.[98] Most of these enthusiastic articles provided a lot of background detail on the tradition of the Chinese classical theater and explanations of its
conventions to make it more accessible to the Soviet populace.

Eisenstein and Tretiakov played leading roles in Mei Lanfang's visit.
Both were appointed to the organizing committee, and they accompanied
him everywhere, especially Tretiakov, who, when Mei Lanfang arrived,
boarded the train at the last station before Moscow to accompany the ce-
lebrity into the capital (at that time a standard gesture for most favored
visitors). Eisenstein and Tretiakov also wrote extensively about the visit,
Tretiakov publishing several articles in *Pravda* and *Literaturnaia gazeta*

about the classical Chinese theater and the acting of Mei Lanfang, while Eisenstein, who had been told by Charlie Chaplin while in Hollywood in 1930 that Mei Lanfang represented the height of acting, discussed his work in several of his theoretical writings and also devoted an article to him, "To the Magician of the Pear Orchard," versions of which were published both in a collection of articles put out in the Soviet Union and in an American theatrical journal.[99]

That Eisenstein and Tretiakov should be proselytizers for Mei Lanfang and the Chinese opera is not entirely surprising, given their earlier interest in China. In Tretiakov's script outlines of 1925 for feature films on China and also in his book on his 1924–1925 China visit, *Chungo,* the Chinese theater plays a prominent role. Much of the material there was recycled for his 1935 articles.

Tretiakov and Eisenstein, together with Brecht, argued in their 1935 responses that Chinese theater pointed to a way forward for the theater. But, one might well ask, how in the year after the First Writers Congress, which proclaimed socialist realism as mandatory for all literature and that all cultural effort should be aligned with it, could one credibly argue for a flagrantly nonrepresentational theatrical approach, a theater tradition that, moreover, was historically "feudal," as almost all the commentators in *Pravda* and elsewhere admitted, its performances often set up by some wealthy and probably exploitative patron, whether an aristocrat, a warlord, or a rich merchant, and presented in an archaic language that the contemporary Chinese did not speak? How, at a time when Vertov and others were celebrating women's liberation in the communist age, could one suggest as a model a theatrical tradition that banned women from acting, even from female roles, and slathered the faces of male actors with thick makeup to disguise their gender? One answer has to be that the recurring demand for contemporary themes—sagas of the collective farm and the factory floor—had come up against the demand for a grander, more "universal" culture as befitted "Moscow," world capital. In promoting Peking Opera, they were potentially appropriating for Soviet culture a venerable tradition with a centuries-long pedigree. Eisenstein claimed that Mei Lanfang was modifying the traditional repertoire and including more contemporary themes.[100] But these were not the major rationalizations that he, Tretiakov, and Brecht gave for learning from Peking opera.

In his writings of the 1920s Tretiakov had more or less dismissed the Chinese theater as, like religion, a "narcotic" for the ignorant masses that instilled in them habits appropriate to an authoritarian society.[101] But in 1935 he changed his evaluation, tackling head on the problem of the "feudal" nature of the Peking opera and arguing, as did Eisenstein, that though it "flourished as a court theater," it had now become popular and very meaningful among the "broadest possible masses" and even influenced the revolutionary agitational theater. The Western bourgeois audience was condescending toward such an unfamiliar culture, he continued, but the Soviet audience had been "raised in the spirit of the greatest attention to national culture" (read the culture of the ethnic minorities).[102] For good measure, he added that Mei Lanfang's own career had taken off in 1911, a "revolutionary" year, thereby implying some association between his work and revolution, despite the fact that, as Brecht noted, in Moscow Mei had demonstrated his art before "specialists" in a dinner jacket.[103]

Mei Lanfang himself, in a newspaper interview, also emphasized the importance of Peking opera today for the ordinary Chinese, who, he said, unlike the intellectuals, cannot appreciate European-style dramatic theater because they want the variety and entertainment of the Chinese opera with its acrobatics, sword play, singing, and dance.[104] This was not an innocent statement, given that at the time leftist critics in China were attacking Peking Opera as an elitist feudal relic.[105] But despite Mei Lanfang's claim that this was a popular theater, it could hardly be classified as being in the ludic tradition. The porcelain-doll-like Mei Lanfang, with "her" exquisite hand gestures, would have trouble fitting into its rollicking performances with their Shakespearean "grossness."

Brecht, Eisenstein, and Tretiakov did not deny this preciousness. Tretiakov in his articles stresses how "unfamiliar" to the Soviet audience are all aspects of this theater "born a thousand years ago"—acting, music, costumes, language, the highly codified system of gestures, the unnatural gait of the actors. This theater does not pretend to be realistic, he adds, and thus, for example, stagehands come onto the stage periodically during the action and give actors cushions to rest on or potions to gargle, but are not to be noticed. In addition, the actors' faces are decorated with highly symbolic figures that completely undermine simple representation. The voices seem unnatural, too: "the actors sing but they sing in a way different from ours, in a very subtle, muted falsetto accompanied by two stringed violins and flutes." Indeed, so unaccustomed is the Western audience to this music that they cannot tell whether the melody is intended to be sad or gay. "Don't look in the plots of these plays for contemporary events, people or passions," he adds, concluding: "the question arises, can we learn from an art that is entirely conventional, symbolic, and seemingly incompatible with our premise of an intellectual system? And the answer is yes."[106]

The word used here for "conventional," *uslovnyi,* sometimes translated as "stylized" or "conditional," was a key term in Meyerhold's theories of theater. Meyerhold in his polemical interventions of the early twentieth century argues that theater is necessarily highly conventionalized and belittles the lengths to which Konstantin Stanislavsky would go in trying to render what happens on stage as close to actuality as possible; the like-minded Briusov pointed out in a companion polemical article that the Shakespearean theater recognized this folly and in order to suggest that the action was taking place in a forest would merely put up a sign that read "forest." In 1935 the ongoing controversy about whether Meyerhold's approach to theater or that of his rival Stanislavsky was more appropriate for the Soviet theater was particularly intense, so much so that the Writers Union plenum of that year was dominated by debates over the two theories. Brecht, Eisenstein, and Tretiakov, the three who wrote manifesto-like statements in response to Mei Lanfang's visit, essentially framed them as refuting Stanislavsky; this is most obvious in Brecht, who mentions Stanislavsky both explicitly and implicitly—with references to the theory of the "fourth wall."[107] Eisenstein and Tretiakov, in claiming Mei Lanfang's theater as somehow "revolutionary," were in effect capitalizing on a politically favorable moment to plug for their own "revolutionary"—avant-garde—positions that were currently losing favor. In other words, Mei Lanfang's very "manipulators" and "minders" were using this opportunity to further their own agendas.

But there is a larger context here. Since the early twentieth century, leading theorists of the theater, such as Meyerhold and Gordon Craig, who called for its radical overhaul, had often pointed to the Japanese or Chinese theater as an instructive example for the way forward.[108]

While Mei Lanfang was in Moscow, Eisenstein and Tretiakov actively sought to recruit him for their side in the theater debates. Eisenstein tried to screen *Potemkin* and segments of his other films for Mei Lanfang, but the film kept breaking. The next day, they took him to the newsreel studio of Soiufil'mkhronika, to film his art the equipment kept breaking down. Unfortunately only snippets of the film remain, which is a shame, because almost the only complete film recordings of Mei Lanfang performing were made in the 1950s, when he was no longer in his prime.[109] Despite such snafus by his hosts, Mei Lanfang gratifyingly declared that of all the theatrical productions he saw in the Soviet Union, he was most taken by the two by Meyerhold (though in later People's Republic of China sources, when this was politically de rigueur, he would claim to have been impressed in Moscow above all by Stanislavsky).[110]

The Peking opera was not just "stylized," however, but extraordinarily stylized, what Eisenstein pronounced a "ne plus ultra of theatricality." This was problematical in a country that mandated "realism" in art, if a socialist (politically slanted and hyperbolically Manichaean) realism. Brecht, Tretiakov, and Eisenstein, then, were all three implicitly or explicitly arguing against straight realism, straight representation, what was often called naturalism, for something more *uslovnyi*, what Eisenstein in his article calls a "higher realism," while Brecht calls it a "higher creative process."[111]

Although Brecht, Tretiakov, and Eisenstein were coming out in their articles against Stanislavsky and for a position closer to that of Meyerhold, beyond that the three, though ostensibly of the same avant-garde orientation, presented different accounts of what Mei Lanfang's art represented. Rather as Voltaire used the Orient as a place to go to critique his own society, each was using this "Chinaman" to make his own points about contemporary Occidental, or Soviet, culture. Though Tretiakov and Eisenstein consistently argued against an exoticist reading of contemporary China, they stressed the "otherness" of what Mei Lanfang represented as a pole of possibility, in which they could read lessons for their own art, essentially projecting what they desired onto what they saw.

Brecht in his article finds in Mei Lanfang's acting a paradigm for what he calls "alienation." The idea is that with the "alienation effect," both the audience and the actor have distance on the character being presented, in contrast to the work of the Stanislavskian actor, who must summon up emotional resources and memories from within that will enable him or her to convey what the character he or she is depicting is going through so that the audience can be likewise moved. In "traditional Chinese acting" this effect is applied "most subtly," Brecht claims, because "acceptance or rejection of the [actors'] actions and utterances was meant to take place on a conscious plane, instead of, as hitherto, the audience's subconscious." "The artist observes himself" and at the same time "expresses his awareness of being watched" by the audience. The actor's emotions "need not correspond to those of the character portrayed." Furthermore, whereas "the Western actor . . . persuades [the audience] to identify with him," the Chinese performer rejects this, so that "the audience identifies itself with the actor as an observer, and accordingly develops his attitude of observing or looking on."[112] In point of fact, as several scholars have pointed out, Brecht misread the Chinese theater; although its techniques are highly artificial and codified, inasmuch as the audience was already versed in the plays and their stagings, they came to see a performance equal to their expectations and to identify with the characters, as did the actors, rather than to maintain a distance.[113]

Tretiakov in his articles about Mei Lanfang, by contrast with Brecht, stresses identification, insisting that *despite* the inaccessibility of this art form, the masses in China identify with its stock characters, using them as moral exempla and points of reference in working out their own identity. Brecht's ideas here, however, stand in starker contrast to those of Eisenstein. While Brecht wanted the alienation effect to make audiences think and he advocated a certain "coldness" and calculation in the actor's approach, Eisenstein was more interested in the nonrational aspects of the creative process and its reception, in "understanding the world from the positions of the emotional and figurative thought process."[114]

Brecht's formulation of "alienation" in the theater actually harks back to the Russian Formalists' (and in particular Viktor Shklovsky's) theory of "making strange" *(ostranenie)* from the late 1910s and early 1920s. As Brecht formulated it, "the artist's object is to appear strange and even surprising to the audience"; as a "result everything put forward by him has a touch of the amazing. Everyday things are thereby raised above the level of the obvious and automatic"; here one is reminded of another hallmark Shklovsky concept, "automatization" (*avtomatizatsiia*).[115] Eisenstein had, somewhat analogously, in outlining his theories of filmic "montage" in essays of the 1920s, claimed that by juxtaposing radically unlike material either within a frame or in adjacent shots, these unconventional and unexpected combinations would engender such dramatic "collisions" or "explosions" that they would jolt the audience out of their epistemological complacency and create new meanings, what he called a "dynamization of the inertia of perception."[116] This would bring about a revolution of consciousness, which he saw as in sync with the Bolshevik political cum social revolution. This earlier scenario was closer to Benjamin's formulation of modernist revolution in his essay "Work of Art," where he sees it as a "shattering" or "liquidation" of tradition, ushering in new artistic practices and a new kind of consciousness.

There is more at stake in Eisenstein's article of 1935 than the modernist attack on naturalism. Brecht may have been using the example of Mei Lanfang to make his major statement on acting, but Eisenstein was using it to make a broader statement encompassing as well such topics as the nature of man, of language, and of art. Those who in the twentieth century wrote about the Chinese or Japanese traditional theaters as instructive models for Occidental culture most often moved seamlessly in their discussions from their traditional theater to their art and writing. Gordon Craig, for example, was interested in Japanese woodcuts and the artist Hokusai, which he discussed in *The Mask* even before he began to recommend the Noh theater.[117] Eisenstein, who briefly studied Japanese while at the Institute of Oriental Languages in Moscow in 1920 and had also seen a Kabuki theater during its Soviet tour of 1928, had earlier used primarily Japanese kanji, traditional poetry (haiku), art (Hokusai), and theater in outlining his theory of montage. "Beyond the Shot," of February 1929, which was originally published as an afterword to Nikolai Kaufman's book *Iaponskoe kino*, discusses filmic montage in terms of Japanese art—that is, its writing system and theater.[118] In his discussion of Mei Lanfang and in several of his articles of the 1930s and 1940s, Eisenstein also touched on this range of subjects, now, for obvious political reasons, focusing on Chinese rather than Japanese examples.[119]

In his essay on Mei Lanfang, Eisenstein is effectively entering into a long-standing philosophical discussion that centered around the distinction between the voice and writing in which the Chinese system of writing recurrently functioned as an example. Most Western philosophers of language, and notably Plato and Hegel, privilege speech as more authentic self-expression and relegate writing to a purely derivative function as a second-order system of signs. But in their discussions, most of these philosophers tend to regard the system of writing as practiced in Western cultures, a form of phonetic-alphabetical transcription, as belonging to a higher stage of cultural evolution than the more pictographic or ideographic kinds of writing to be found in several non-Western cultures; their stock examples are the Egyptian hieroglyphs and the Chinese or Japanese kanji. Philosophers like Hegel have identified the Western system of writing as "phonocentric," that is, the letters, generally speaking, correspond to sounds used in saying words.

Among twentieth-century modernists, however, such as, notably, Ernest Fenollosa and Ezra Pound, there was in general a reaction against such conclusions. They seized on the Chinese kanji as an antidote to what they considered the overly rationalist and literalizing effects of the Occidental alphabetical systems.[120] Eisenstein in his essay on Mei Lanfang also reverses the valorization of Hegel's binary of alphabet versus pictogram or hieroglyph. His conclusions are comparable, but not identical, with those of Fenollosa and Pound, but his source is actually Granet. Eisenstein's emphasis on the nonrational nature of Chinese theater dovetails with the theories of Granet in his *La Pensée chinoise,* which Robeson had presented to him in January of that year. Granet's book was not principally on the theater but rather on Chinese thought as derived from its system of writing. Eisenstein's article on Mei Lanfang embraces the same range of subjects as Granet (theater, writing, thought) and, like Granet, points to the visual nature of the Chinese system of writing, a feature Eisenstein associates with the highly codified visual (as distinct from textual) component of the Chinese opera. The visual nature of Chinese writing is not just a difference in the system of writing, he insists; the differences pinpoint differences in the mentality of the Chinese as compared with the Occidentals.

Eisenstein argues, as does Granet, that the fact that a Chinese kanji does not have a standard pronunciation or verbal counterpart opens the possibility of a system of significations that would transcend barriers between those speaking different languages. As Granet put it in *La Pensée chinoise,* "this [Chinese system of] writing can be used by populations speaking different dialects—or even idioms—the reader reading in his own manner what the writer has written while thinking of words that have the same sense but which he could pronounce in a totally different way. Independent of changes in pronunciation in the course of time . . . [and] of local pronunciations which it tolerates, it has served powerfully in the diffusion of Chinese civilization. This is the reason why it has not had to see itself replaced at all by a phonetic [system of writing]."[121]

Eisenstein extrapolates from Granet's "Chinese civilization" to give this observation about the Chinese system of writing a universal perspective. He claims that inasmuch as the Chinese system of writing, like its opera, has been able to overcome linguistic and political divisions, it could provide a model for overcoming the many such divisions in the greater world (whereas Brecht, again by contrast, decries "universalism"):[122] "surely the structure of Chinese writing and of the emotional symbols of the Chinese aesthetic, which serve to link provinces and populations divided by the specific nature of individual national languages, is none other than a unique model for how, through emotional images filled with proletarian wisdom and humanity, the great ideas of our great land must be poured into the hearts and emotions of the millions of nations speaking different languages?" and this "regardless of borders, boundaries and continents."[123] In other words, paradoxically, archaic and national Chinese cultural forms can provide the formula for Moscow's cultural hegemony, though not of course the kanji themselves; rather the principles Eisenstein sees as underlying them.

The Chinese, in Eisenstein's reading, can offer a solution to the problem of language that plagues world unification. He underscores this potential by claiming that theirs is "not . . . a structure of thought defined by national or racial premises."[124] Here he is assigning to the Chinese system an ideal commonly found among the antifascists. The Germanophone diaspora (as discussed in Chapter 4), privileged not race but language as the determinant for "Germanness." Benjamin, one of them, was less interested in "Germanness," but in this antifascist moment he had become particularly intrigued by problems of language and translation and, like Eisenstein, had begun to explore from a Marxist perspective the possibility of a universal language that could transcend race and nation. In one of his less-known articles, "Problems in the Sociology of Language" (1934), which he published in the Frankfurt School's *Zeitschrift für Sozialforschung* in the summer of 1935, Benjamin argues for a materialist, dialectical linguistics that would "invalidate the concept of race, and indeed of peoples, in favor of a history of language based on the movements of classes."[125] Indeed, "typologically distinct languages can be observed in one and the same national formation."[126] In making this argument Benjamin draws particularly on articles by two Soviet linguists, Nikolai Marr and Lev Vygotsky, both of whom actually died the year Benjamin wrote this essay, though he cites not the Russian originals but German translations of one article by each that appeared in *Unter dem Banner des Marxismus* in 1926 and 1929, respectively.

Marr probably appealed to Benjamin because he insisted that the history of linguistic evolution is not about bloodline or race, not even figuratively, and that there are no national languages.[127] Rather, the evolution of language is determined by the process of evolution in economics. Marr, then, substituted class for biology, maintaining that the language of one class will be closer in its typological features to the language of the same class in a different ethnic group than it will be to that of another class in the same ethnic group.[128] He also contended that languages converge when thrown together in economic intercourse and that ultimately, in the classless society, there would be a "single and unified language" *(edinyi iazyk)*.[129] Benjamin also was enticed by the possibility of a single language. In this article (actually citing Piaget here) he talks of "this prospect of a distant future time, when the insights of linguistic sociology will help us not only to understand language but to change it. . . . Attempts to perfect language technically have repeatedly given rise to projects for *lingua universalis*"; his examples are Bacon and Leibniz.[130]

Bacon and Leibniz, two figures from the Enlightenment, were, however, far from espousing the sense of a universal language that informs Eisenstein's article on Mei Lanfang. Eisenstein in formulating his theories in this article (and elsewhere) also drew on the ideas of Marr and Vygotsky, with whom, together with Aleksandr Luria, he was involved in a study group in the early 1930s whose members were committed to establishing a materialist account of language evolution.[131] But while Benjamin wanted to transform language, to perfect it, Eisenstein was more inter-ested in recovering for Western man its a- or pre-logical version. Here Eisenstein picks up from investigations of fellow members of the Marr circle, especially Vygotsky and Luria, who were interested in the survival of primitive forms in contemporary expressive language.

A particular line of investigation for Eisenstein in his search for univer-sal forms was prelogical thought and "inner speech" *(vnutrenniaia rech')*. "Inner speech" was a term used by Vygotsky and Luria to categorize a kind of egocentric speech that splinters off from general social speech at a developed stage. "Inner speech," in Vygotsky's account of it, differs from regular, external speech in that it is highly simplified and predica-tive (i.e., tends to leave out such things as the subject of a sentence). As Vygotsky puts it: "with syntax and sound reduced to a minimum, meaning is more than ever in the forefront." Inner speech also tends to "agglutination"; in it words combine and unite according to different laws from those that govern conventional meanings, and a single word may become completely "saturated with meanings."[132] It is associative, emotive, or poetic in nature rather than logical and works with semantics and not phonetics.

Vygotsky's "inner speech" is, then, close to what Granet, and Eisenstein after him, found in the Chinese system of writing and its traditional the-ater, though they saw these features less as prelogical, as in Vygotsky, than as alogical, as more like the logic of poetry than that of measured exposi-tory prose. Eisenstein and Granet both argue that the Chinese system of writing, and its traditional theatrical arts, are not for abstract reasoning or analyzing ideas, activities more suited to the Occidental system. Rather, as Granet put it, "[the Chinese system] has been entirely constructed with the purpose of communicating attitudes of sentiment."[133]

Eisenstein preferred to view the kanji as providing an alternative sys-tem to one that is "exactly adequate to the realities they designate." He took off from Granet's observations about the noncoincidence between ideogram and word in the Chinese system and the myriad possibilities of their combination to explore how a noncoincidence between sign and significance in Chinese ideograms and theater might give play to imagina-tion and memory in an alternative (nonrealistic) system grounded more in the symbolic than the referential.[134]

In his privileging of the poetic, Eisenstein in effect applies a selective appropriation of Granet to Vygotsky's theory of "inner speech" where "a single word becomes saturated with meanings" and expression is associative or emotive rather than logical. His take on Mei Lanfang provided an alternative strategy for culture to the one then dominant in the Soviet Union. However, in a semidialectical move, Eisenstein suggests that as culture moves toward the socialist realist, the dialectic of the poetico-symbolical and the realistic cum referential or scientific should be resolved in "the unity of what is specifically representative and emotionally effective."[135]

Eisenstein's frame of reference is explicitly much broader than the specific nature of the Chinese theater or system of writing. He claims that "peculiar to the profoundest Chinese thought and the structure of general notions" is the fact that in them "the forms of reflection of consciousness of earlier stages of social development are not replaced by later ones, but are canonized by tradition and enriched by the experience of subsequent stages." Consequently, "the underlying premises of a pre-feudal structure of ideas has been preserved perfectly distinctly." But, he adds expanding his purview, "to some extent, this preservation of continuity is characteristic of any way of thinking. Of artistic thinking, in particular."[136]

Eisenstein is relating here what he reads into the Peking opera tradition not just to the prelogical but actually to prefeudal patterns of thought, *long* pre-Gesellschaft culture systems, such as the mythic and the "primitive." In exploring the relationship between modern and premodern culture systems, he was particularly influenced by Frazer's *Golden Bough* and *Primitive Mentality* (1922), by Lucien Lévy-Brühl, a founder of the French socialist newspaper *L'Humanité* and one of the founders of the Institute for the Study of Fascism, where Benjamin gave his 1934 lecture, but a thinker explicitly rejected by Benjamin in his article.[137] Eisenstein's interest in the premodern is most strongly felt in his earlier work on the film *Que viva México!* (1930–1932), but it lingered well into the 1930s. In that decade he included Vygotsky and Lévy-Brühl in the syllabus for film students at VGIK.[138]

Eisenstein's interest in the "primitive" could be seen as a variant on a well-known paradox of the avant-garde from the first half of the twentieth century: the way they were drawn both to futuristic, technological modernism and at the same time to radically premodern, "primitive" cultural and intellectual practices (consider the Cubists' African masks), though Eisenstein's sense of "inner speech" and the prelogical were not presented as being necessarily "primitive." He had a similar appreciation of Joyce. Eisenstein used Joyce's inner monologue (not the same thing as "inner speech") in his script for Dreiser's *American Tragedy* (1930) and for *MMM* (1932–1933).[139] In Joyce's conversations with Eisenstein in Paris, he explained to Eisenstein that in *Ulysses* each episode was meant to have a color and a semantic motif. In this way the novel became a gigantic symbolic field.[140]

Eisenstein's focus on alogical and "primitive" cultural forms was not only for their own sakes but as starting points for an alternative system of thought and representation that privileged the "gigantic symbolic field." He was intellectually ambitious, and he drew on these examples as he worked up an entire theory of life, art, and thought, no less, that concerned the correspondences between different arts, but also between art, the human, and the cosmos in a metaphysical totality, a reason in itself why in his writings he would constantly dart off in seeming tangents from literature to architecture to film, to music, to art.

But Eisenstein was not interested only in "a certain symbolic association of definite meanings with definite objects" that he saw in Chinese culture. To him "more interesting is the case where the meaning is flexible. Where one and the same subject can have as many different meanings as you like, depending on how it is treated." In the Peking opera "this feature of shifting meanings is perhaps even more striking than the actual use of conventional stage attributes." "And it turns out that the multiple meanings and the flexibility, which we find so amazing in their theatrical accessories, are key features typical of any mode of expression in China."[141]

Rather than rigid correspondences and fixed meanings, then, Eisenstein proposes a language of symbols that not only assumes the Saussurean arbitrariness of the sign but also features multiple and fluid meanings for the signs. All this implicitly challenges the values of the Lettered City, where the written *text* is the dominant and a one-to-one correspondence of sign and meaning is assumed; in Chinese theater as Eisenstein sees it, the text functions more as a motivation for a play of audiovisual imagery and symbolism.

Though Eisenstein's ideas here might seem somewhat quixotic or utopian, he does show recognition that in order for there to be any meaning at all, there must be some fixity in the system of signs. This qualification is particularly apparent in an earlier statement of the same year, Eisenstein's famous address to the Union of Cinematographers of January, where he discussed some of the themes later to be incorporated in the piece on Mei Lanfang but in this instance recommended for cinematographers Lévy-Brühl's findings on the primitive mind from his investigations of the Bororo and tribes of Brazil. Here he repeatedly cites *King Lear* but also stresses Engels's assertion that in the "dialectics of a work of art" one observes a double process: "there is a determined, progressive ascent toward ideas at the highest levels of ideological awareness [vysshikh ideinykh stupenei soznaniia] and at the same time there is penetration through the structure of form into the deepest layers of emotional thinking." Without both being present at once, there is no work of art. There are two essential aspects to a work of art—the "thematic cum logical" and the "emotional forms of thought"—and if the balance tips in favor of either of them, the art is distorted: too much of the thematic and logical renders a work overly "simplistic," "dry, logical and didactic," while a "deviation" *(peregib)* in the direction of the "emotional forms of thought" will lead to "chaos, wanton randomness *(stikhinost')*, and sheer raving *(bred)*.[142]

One aspect of Mei Lanfang's art about which Eisenstein (himself bisexual) is strangely reticent is the fact that it involves crossdressing, making it an awkward model for socialist realism as a tradition very much oriented around male feats. In the Soviet articles occasioned by Mei Lanfang's visit, his acting is generally discussed as if sexually neutral. One explicator, Nikolai Volkov, does engage the topic, saying that "the European theater is familiar with the technique of 'travesty,' but Mei Lanfang is no 'travesty,' he has no intention of deceiving anyone with his likeness to a person of the other sex."[143]

Central to Eisenstein's underlying ideas here is a formulation presented in a topographical metaphor: "as you become more aware of the system whereby these arts were constructed, you seem to penetrate magnificent subterranean halls in whose gilt work you can find a vision of the stratum through which the history of artistic thought has passed." These halls provide "all those strange twists and turns which the process of fantasy and figurative composition undergoes at that most remarkable stage of creativity which occurs after the conception of an idea and before its realization."[144]

Eisenstein's magnificent subterranean halls could be read as a gesture invoking the recently constructed Moscow metro, pride of the nation (or the Christian catacombs). But they are primarily an allusion to memory, the imagination, and other mental phenomena with "subterranean meanings" lying deep within the consciousness. Here we sense what David Bordwell has called Eisenstein's epistemological shift (from his "montage" of the 1920s).[145] Eisenstein is still interested in affect, as he was then, but has gone beyond both the notion that it is brought about by "collisions" and his simpler account of impact on the psyche, then more by analogy with the conditioned reflex: "the Chinese hieroglyph serves first of all as a definite emotional means of making an impression upon the perception through the whole complex of concomitant emotions that it might provoke."[146] The sign itself is not self-valuable but more a trigger to imaginative play (here again in contrast with Brecht, who welcomed the potential of Chinese acting not for imaginative play but for highly cerebral play).

Eisenstein sought in his film work of the 1930s to use complex visual imagery rich in "subterranean" meanings and associations, culminating in *Ivan the Terrible*. But his discussion of the "subterranean" was not only directed at his practice and could also be seen as but a variant of a common figure in philosophical thought. One is particularly reminded of Hegel's figure of the "pit" in his *Phenomenology,* where he posits deep, dark reserves of consciousness that ideally emerge in the authentic act of speech[147]

In the artistry of Mei Lanfang, the intricately painted face and the exquisite bodily gestures are but a trigger to a complex of associations coming up from deep historical memory. The language of the imagination that is thereby brought into play, Eisenstein claimed, is more universal. Consequently, Peking opera "deserves to be considered as part of that structure of thought which is embodied in forms that seem so remote but deep down are somehow close to us and, if they are not always intelligible, are nevertheless in profound sympathy with ours," asserting also:

"that is the only explanation for the magnetic force of creativity which [Mei-Lanfeng] has made famous far beyond his national boundaries."[148]

Thus in this Popular Front moment a displaced antifascist in France (Benjamin) is reading "language" against its Nazi grounding in "blood" and "race" and in doing so drawing on two Soviet theorists. Meanwhile, a Soviet film director (Eisenstein) is reading an exotic theatrical tradition in terms of very different theories of language and the psyche. Though he has drawn them in part from the same two sources as Benjamin (Marr, Vygotsky) and likewise puts them in a Marxist framework, he takes a very different trajectory suggested to him in part by a French book conveyed to him by a displaced American negro artist and in part by a French theorist (Lévy-Brühl).

Eisenstein seeks not Benjamin's linguistic transformation as modernization, not a "shattering" of the old cultural forms, but recovery of the essence within, of "higher" poetic forms locked deep in "subterranean" recesses of the mind, and an idiosyncratic form of linguistic cosmopolitanism. With Lévy-Brühl (whom Benjamin rejects) and Granet, Eisenstein is excited by the possibility of a totally different mentality from the Western, rational, and intellectualized pattern of thought. Yet for him the lessons to be drawn from Mei Lanfang also hold out the promise of world cultural hegemony for the Soviet Union.

As we saw in Chapter 1, in Brecht's *Measures Taken* the Russo-German Communist proselytizers don masks, assume a role, as necessary steps toward dispelling the darkness in "China." But at some level, Brecht's oratorio is a parable about intellectuals dispelling their own subjectivist inclinations and desires for sole "authorship" in the name of the cause, of blending imperceptibly with the masses. Eisenstein in this essay finds a different way of bridging the chasm of cultural and intellectual difference between intellectuals and the masses and between peoples divided by borders of geopolitics, class, and race. While in Vertov's *Three Songs of Lenin,* in an exoticized variant of a typical Soviet narrative, the women of Central Asia tear off their masks (veils) and can "see," can be integrated into the modern world and acquire a socialistic consciousness, in Eisenstein's scheme the Enlightenment narrative is challenged. Veiling/ unveiling and masking/unmasking are not ends in themselves. The face one presents to the world is at best a portal to what lies deep beneath it.

In this year, 1935, Eisenstein was repeatedly attacked for his linguistic "universalism" and seen as not sufficiently patriotic.[149] Indeed, his ideas as outlined here might seem eccentric and a trifle quixotic, all the more so since the Meyerholdian theatrical approach was becoming ever more problematical politically. Yet Eisenstein with his emphasis on going beyond the "mask," the exterior, to recover the essence within (those "subterranean halls") and his insistence on the symbolic character of art, a romantic principle, was in a very general sense actually ahead of the curve of Soviet culture, as we shall see in the next chapter.

CHAPTER 6

Face and Mask: Theatricality and Identity in the Era of the Show Trials (1936–1938)

L ATE 1935 TO EARLY 1936 saw radical shifts in Soviet culture, shifts so radical that the 1930s should be seen as comprising two distinct subperiods. One obvious shift would be the intensification of all manner of repression. The years 1936–1938, as it were this subperiod's establishing shot, are punctuated by the worst purges, called collectively the Great Purge, that ran from 1937 until early 1939, and also by the three show trials, one per year: in August 1936 and in January 1937, with the culminating trial of Bukharin and other members of the "right-Trotskyite Block" in March 1938. In these years there was a tightening up in culture as well, with the secret police playing a greater role. On December 16, 1935, the Committee on Arts Affairs (Komitet po delam iskusstv) was established to further centralize control and integrate all the arts in the one culture. The new dispensation also affected cultural exchange; symptomatically, from 1936 VOKS had to submit all their plans to the People's Commissariat for Internal Affairs (NKVD) and the Central Committee for approval.

The new times presented no small challenge for those pushing for transnational interactions. In late 1935–1936 the influx of foreigners diminished radically, and by 1937 many of those in Soviet exile were dismissed at the institutions where they worked.[1] There were even book burnings of foreign texts! The exiles were also not spared the purges, or the purge mentality. In 1936 a group of the German-speaking exiles (including Lukács) gathered in Moscow for a round of recriminations and recantations—and self-justifications (the transcript has been published in the resonantly titled *Die Säuberung*).[2] This meeting was followed by a wave of arrests, including two months later of Ottwalt, an associate of Brecht who had been attacked by Lukács in the *Linkskurve* article discussed in Chapter 1. During the meeting he had complained that he had been lured to the Soviet Union in 1931 and then jerked around (as evident in Chapter 1, not an uncommon fate). The long list of the Germanophone exiles arrested in 1936 includes Carola Neher, famous for her rendering of Polly Peacham in Brecht's *Threepenny Opera;* she died of typhus in a camp in 1942.

In the Soviet cultural world, the so-called anti-"Formalist" campaign loomed large on the horizon of the initial years in this subperiod. This campaign was launched in January 1936 with two articles in *Pravda* attacking Shostakovich for his opera *Lady Macbeth of Mtsensk* and his ballet *The Limpid Stream* (Svetlyi ruchei), with side swipes at Meyerhold.[3] But the targets were not only in the theater. These articles heralded a whole series of attacks in *Pravda* published over the next month or so in which trends or individuals in each of the different branches of intellectual life were singled out as bearers of an alien "Formalism." The campaign continued for over a year, with intellectuals expected to attend mass meetings at the local branches of their creative unions, at which they denounced fellow members for their alleged formalistic tendencies and called for recantations. A year later, the Nazis staged a similar antimodernist campaign with the opening of their exhibition of "degenerate art" on July 19, 1937, and its attendant commentary; though the Nazi attacks were particularly directed at representations of the body, the Soviet articles also expressed outrage at *Lady Macbeth*'s "naturalism" (i.e., sex— in one scene a large bed dominated the stage). It should also not be forgotten that starting in 1934 the puritanical Hollywood code was implemented, precensoring American movies. The transatlantic world was becoming more conservative and the Soviet Union particularly so.

The Soviet anti-"Formalist" campaign had an approximate analogue in the so-called Expressionism debate, conducted largely on the pages of

Das Wort between September 1937 and July 1938, in which some of the most prominent figures in the diaspora were embroiled.[4] In this debate, Lukács and others of like mind attacked "Expressionism" (essentially modernist trends) and were pitted against Brecht, Ernst Bloch, and Eisler.[5] In *Das Wort* critics picked up from an earlier article by Lukács of 1934 that had attacked Expressionism, claiming that it was linked to fascism (some of the articles were republished in translation in the Russian edition of *Internatsional'naia literatura*). Even though Brecht was ostensibly one of *Das Wort*'s editors, his side had difficulty in getting their rejoinders published, about which he wrote several spirited letters of complaint to his erstwhile associate Fritz Erpenbeck, who was effectively running the journal while Bredel was in civil war Spain. One Brecht letter, of December 1937, expresses outrage that *Das Wort* should be taking this stance "two months after Hitler's speech against Expressionism,"[6] while in another he complains that Eisler's response to Lukács hasn't appeared, adding: "it can't have simply fallen under the table." Eisler and Ernst Bloch had to publish their responses in *Die neue Weltbühne* instead, where they cited the cause of the Popular Front as the main reason why avant-gardism should not be repressed.[7] Brecht proposed to *Das Wort* that he counter the attacks with an article on "Volkstümlichkeit" *(narodnost')*, but after some equivocation appears not to have submitted it.[8]

In Western historiography, these several events are generally interpreted as directed against all manner of avant-gardism and westernizing cultural trends. And generally speaking, they were. However, the attacks were not aimed only at avant-gardists or modernists. In architecture, for example, Ivan Zholtovsky, hitherto a leading Stalinist architect and advocate of styles that continued the tradition of the classical era and the Renaissance, was also vilified, as was what was now branded "Palladianism." And in August 1937 Alexei Shchusev, who designed the Lenin Mausoleum and the Hotel Moscow, was accused of sabotaging Soviet construction and expelled from the Union of Architects, though the Party leadership intervened and he was reinstated in the Union so that he could finish his work on the Hotel Moscow.[9]

The attacks on "Formalism," momentous though they were in their impact, should be viewed in a broader context as indicative of a shift in the rhetorical strategies of Soviet culture that took place around the middle of the 1930s, one in which the purges can be seen as an integral part. This shift more or less "begins," if one can speak in those terms, in mid- to late 1935 (even as the Great Purge was already being prepared). However, another dramatic event and the rhetoric it occasioned actually better capture the shift: the launching in December 1935 of the Stakhanovite movement. For the occasion, Party leaders made bombastic pronouncements to the effect that in the example of one coal miner (Aleksei Stakhanov), a new race of production superheroes had appeared who could defy the dictates of conventional science and their professional advisors to outdo production norms to a stupendous degree. Before long, in lead articles in the Party press and in much-publicized ceremonies, more superheroes, many of them in other fields, such as aviators and mountain climbers, were identified as "new men."[10]

Taken together, these two kinds of events—the emergence of the "new men" and the purges—essentially represent proclamations of on the one hand hyperbolically positive human beings, what I have elsewhere called a "utopian anthropology,"[11] and on the other of hyperbolically negative human beings—supervillains. Soviet political culture has always featured its heroes and villains, so this represents a radical extension of the poles that were endemic. What is important about this shift is not just that the degrees of heroism and villainy have been ratcheted up, that the Manichaean drama has been intensified, but also that the relative muting of sociological factors in establishing the heroes' and villains' respective moral/political identities (the aviator heroes, for example, were not necessarily proletarians and in some instances not even Party members).

Thus Soviet culture had gone beyond its obsession with classification (of subjects) and encyclopedism, as typified the Enlightenment and which also informed Gorky's pet project, *The History of the Factories.* Gorky died in 1936, and most of his projects such as this *History* lost momentum. But they had outlived their day, anyway. Were we to subscribe to the analysis of Theodor Adorno and Max Horkheimer in *The Dialectic of Enlightenment,* we might say that in these years the dialectic was carried to an excess. As the country veered off into "terror," it left the Enlightenment values of the early 1930s in the dust and embraced a singular version of Romanticism.

We can see this particularly in 1937, a vintage year. It was the twentieth anniversary of the Revolution and also the centennial of Pushkin's
death, two events that were commemorated in a major way. It was also
the year when the Union of Soviet Architects held their first congress
(June 16–26), establishing their definition of socialist realism. And it was
a tense and dramatic year in the political arena. At the plenum of the Central Committee of February-March, Stalin made two important speeches
that established the essential narrative and rationale for future show trials
and especially for the Bukharin trial to come (he was arrested on February 27, 1937, during the plenum).[12]

But the overall shift in rhetoric and practices is most evident in the
commentary generated by an event of that year in the international arena.

The Mukhina Statue at the 1937 Exposition

In 1937 the International Exposition opened in Paris,[13] a venue that is particularly remembered for the way Soviet and German (Nazi) rivalry was
played out in terms of their respective pavilions, which were literally juxtaposed. The Soviet pavilion was a banner building of these years, as is
indicated in the fact that its architect was Boris Iofan, designer of the
Palace of Soviets; the Nazi pavilion was designed by his counterpart,
Hitler's favorite architect, Albert Speer, who redesigned Berlin, now to be
called Germania. Like Iofan's Palace of Soviets, the Soviet pavilion was
not just to be functional (in this case, an exhibition space) but was intended as a national emblem. Commentators described it as standing "in
this big international showcase" for "the [Soviet] state as a whole," presenting "the image of the country itself."[14] Indeed, the statue was to out-
live its function as adornment for the pavilion. After the exposition closed,
it was dismantled and transported back to Moscow, where it was reerected
outside the new All-Union Agricultural Exhibition and then adopted as
the logo of the central film studio, Mosfilm, thus becoming a familiar national emblem.

In comparing the two Iofan designs, we sense a shift in architectural
styles, thrown into relief by the fact that these two buildings were planned
by the same architect. Unlike the design for the Palace of Soviets, the 1937
pavilion was not a version of what has been dismissed as "red Doric"; in

other words, it did not use conventions of the classical era for representing the workers' state in an industrial age. But there are important differences not just in these buildings' formal features but also in their conception, differences that catch a significant shift in Soviet culture that took place in the mid-1930s.

The Paris pavilion, as in Iofan's design for the Palace of Soviets, was topped by a gigantic statue, which Iofan conceived in broad outline, giving the further working out of its design to the sculptor Vera Mukhina. This time the statue was not of Lenin but of a worker and a peasant striding forward, bearing aloft the hammer and sickle, emblem of the Soviet nation.[15] A worker and a peasant, a male and a female—how much closer could one get to depicting the Soviet everyman! Yet commentators on the statue from that time do not emphasize the pair's occupational identities. Rather, in the accounts of the Paris pavilion, and elsewhere, new, recurrent epithets and tropes are used, expressions such as "movement," "taking off" *(vzlët),* "genuine" *(podlinnyi),* "organic," "intimate," and "inner truth."[16] Such apparently minor features of the discourse capture a shift in the political culture of the late 1930s away from patterns prominent in the early 1930s, veering into a kind of Romanticism.

"Movement" and "taking off" are said to describe the building's very architecture. The Palace of Soviets was static and vertical in its articulation, comprising an ever narrower series of cylindrical forms, stacked one on the other, adorned with classical columns and topped by a monumental statue of Lenin, standing erect but with his hand outstretched. Iofan's Paris pavilion was, however, oxymoronically, a dynamic statue. The 1937 structure was not really a tower, in that the pavilion itself stretched behind the front section for six exhibition halls arrayed in progressively lower structures (Speer's was taller and featured a tower topped by an eagle). The statue was, by Iofan's stipulation, to blend with the building to make one sculptural form. The entire building with its "stepped pattern of flat roofs that ascend progressively upward" was "dedicated to articulating a sweep both forward and upward that culminated in the statue itself, which continued this arc."[17] In other words, the pavilion presented the Soviet state not in a static construction, as did the Palace of Soviets, but in a dynamic construction of "ascent." Hence the statue atop the Paris pavilion has its ideological dimension, and not just in the capsule representa-

Figure 3. Sketch for the Projected Palace of Soviets in Moscow (reproduced with the permission of the Schusev Museum of Architecture, Moscow).

tion of the Soviet workers moving forward that functions as a symbol of the forward movement of the nation as a whole. This standard narrative has morphed; the statue represents not just "progress" but actually "taking off."

In Soviet iconography, exaggerated movement of leader figures along a diagonal axis, together with some standard waving in the wind, were used conventionally to suggest revolution and the extraordinary dynamism unleashed by Bolshevism; one example would be the iconic representation of Lenin leaning forward as he addresses the crowd, somewhat in the Romantic tradition of historical painting by figures like Delacroix, in other words, a Romanticization of classical conventions.[18] This technique has a near analogue in the feature of Mukhina's statue that most contributes to the sense of movement it conveys—a twenty-meter-long scarf that drapes around the bodies and streams out behind to suggest that they are striding rapidly forward, prevailing over a countervailing wind. This scarf, a dramatic but unrealistic detail for depicting two Soviet working everymen, is unfurled from the palm of the woman's hand and

Figure 4. Side view of the Soviet pavilion for the International Exposition in Paris of 1937 (reproduced with permission from the Schusev Architectual Museum, Moscow).

stretches out horizontally behind the pair, forming, together with their out- and up-stretched hands that hold the hammer and sickle, an arc of a single sweep. The scarf then winds between their bodies and proceeds to drape itself across the male midriff before trailing off behind him in a graceful droop. This festooning of the male worker conveniently covers his genital area and echoes formally the shape of the folds of the woman's skirt, thus feminizing and softening his somewhat angular facial features and dehumanized image.[19] Draping the genital area is in keeping with Stalinist sexual mores but also emphasizes the extent to which the pair are not really individual humans but symbolic figures enacting a drama.

In Mukhina's statue the proletarian male is, predictably, both taller and striding slightly ahead of his female companion. However, he is not merely ahead of her. His front shoe was typically described as "stopping the statue at the very edge."[20] This position inevitably made the statue the subject of many parodies, especially in the post-Soviet period, when lampoons had the pair striding off into nothingness only to come crashing down (shades of one interpretation of the Bronze Horseman statue in An-drei Bely's novel *Petersburg*). But is the worker stopping short, or is he poised to take off?

This question was not irrelevant in 1937, the year the Soviet Union was celebrating the twentieth anniversary of its Revolution. Had the Revolu-tion stalled (or even seen a "Great Retreat") or was it pressing forward apace? Judging from the rhetoric of the time, the country was pushing the pace of change beyond any sorts of norms to the edge of the possible and beyond. Everything—the nefariousness of the "enemies of the people" and the achievements of the country's heroes alike—was claimed to be totally unprecedented: expressions such as "never before in the history of the world" abound in texts. In the press, Mukhina's statue was commonly billed as "going way beyond" *(iz riada von vykhodiashchee)* earlier prec-edents in Soviet and international sculpture.[21]

There was a new dynamic, captured in the commentary about the Mukhina statue, that featured terms like "organic" and "intimate," which are counterintuitive for a statue signifying a worker and a peasant. If in the first half of the thirties Soviet culture held as its model the classical, best exemplified in the attempt to rebuild Moscow as a classical city (and in the design for the Palace of Soviets), in the second half it could be said that Romanticism had succeeded the classical as the dominant cultural trend. This is of course a gross simplification. Romantic trends were al-ways present in Soviet culture—after all, "socialist realism" in practice represents a combination of a trend previously called "revolutionary ro-manticism" with "proletarian realism." The traits I will identify for this shift were all present before.[22] But arguably in the second half of the thir-ties that aspect of socialist realist culture that Andrei Sinyavsky insight-fully called a "classicism" in his essay "What Is Socialist Realism" was superseded as the dominant mode by a kind of Romanticism.

I want to analyze the shift in the late 1930s in terms of a post-Enlightenment moment. Rather as in Europe, in the late eighteenth century and as it entered the nineteenth, it went from a dominance of Enlightenment values to Romanticism, so around late 1935 (I am dating this in terms of the launching of the Stakhanovite movement, though the date is very approximate, since the various changes were not in sync), Soviet Russia drew away from the Enlightenment ideals that had informed so much cultural activity in the first half of the thirties, when the ideal of beauty in urban architecture dominated official rhetoric and practice. In the second half, architecture ceased to be as dominant a cultural paradigm. In addition, within architecture classical or Renaissance models were progressively rejected in favor of the Russian national or Gothic, two styles particularly associated with Romanticism; this shift is evident in the publication plans of the Academy of Architecture for 1937.[23] Literature, as the great novel, also declined in importance, as poetry, painting, opera, drama, and film rose in prominence.

One might well ask whether it is appropriate to discuss Stalinist culture in terms of Enlightenment and Romanticism, given that both have to do with a very different historical moment (and in the case of Enlightenment, place). These classificatory tags are imprecise and multivalent, but they are useful here in that they gesture economically in the direction I want to indicate.

The question arises, precisely which version of Romanticism? Several different ones found echoes in these years. Traditionally, in the nineteenth century, Russian Romanticism had been heavily influenced by versions of the English (Scott and Byron), and also by the conceptual models provided by such Germans as Schiller, Schelling, Schlegel, Fichte, and Herder. These writers and thinkers all had a hold on the culture of the late 1930s and were often cited in *Literaturnyi kritik.* But I am interested here less in the question of "influence" or return to prerevolutionary vogues than in identifying new versions of Romanticism that bear comparison with precedents from the past but were reinflected by the singular cultural milieu in which they arose.

One version of Romanticism that colored the culture of the late 1930s was the historical or adventure romance. Writers like Walter Scott and the Dumas brothers became very popular among readers and critics. In addition, one observes a conscious couching of ideological constructs and narratives in terms of well-known topoi from this kind of romantic literature. For example, "revolutionary passion" was identified as "One for all and all for one," the famous motto of Dumas's heroes in *The Three Musketeers* (1844), popular at that time, while Valentin Kataev called his 1936 novel about worker uprisings in Odessa during the 1905 revolution *A Lonely White Sail Gleams* (Beleet parus odinokii; a film of the same name

was made in 1937), invoking the title of a beloved and particularly romantic poem by Lermontov. Symptomatically, a new opera, *The Battleship
Potemkin* (Bronenosets Potemkin) of 1938, provides a very different version of the Revolution of 1905 from Eisenstein's 1925 film of that name,
which had been a model of Soviet cinema. A *Pravda* review of the opera
praises it for its "profound connection with folk creativity." As if to complement this Romantic notion of "folk creativity," a scene from the opera
was set by the ruins of a monastery, a favorite of the Gothic, and a far cry
from the setting of Eisenstein's climactic scene, the long flight of the
Odessa steps.[24]

Were such apparent citations from the inventory of Romantic culture
just a superficial veneer? I would argue that they were surface signs of a
Romanticism of a more profound order. I will identify four of varieties of
Romanticism that were prevalent in Stalinist culture of the late 1930s, devoting one chapter to each: the turn to the inner, the adventure romance,
the imperial sublime, and the lyric. A fifth variety, to which I have not
devoted a separate chapter, is the insistence on the unity of the individual
and the whole—the state—in an *organic* totality, which in classic Romanticism is in tension with the radical assertion of individuality. The idea of
the "organic" informs much of the Stalinist discourse about the "folk"
(narodnyi), which I do treat periodically, and particularly marks nationalist discourse of the 1930s, though as will become evident it was also deployed in more cosmopolitan contexts. The four varieties of Romanticism
I focus on here are interrelated and essentially were prominent simultaneously but to some extent were also successive. Among them the sublime
was dominant, defining the era.

At the heart of what I am calling a late thirties Romanticism was less
the Gothic than an apprehension of the sublime. Soviet public rituals and
even ideology were inflected with the structure and rhetoric of the sublime. Hence, for example, in the Mukhina statue it might be said that the
pair of Soviet toilers are symbolic figures enacting a drama in the sublime
(as if on a rocky crag, assailed by tempests and negotiating a precipitous
drop). Historically, both theories of the sublime and the Enlightenment
were at their height in the eighteenth century. Thus in some senses they
were not completely distinct movements. Consider Kant, who was a major theorist of the sublime and of the Enlightenment. But Kant actually

preferred beauty, whereas in the Soviet Union of the mid-1930s, Enlightenment values lost currency and were superseded in an all-out drive for the extra-ordinary.

In this chapter I will be concerned with another aspect of the shift to a version of the Romantic: a reorientation in the basic account of the Soviet subject, both implicit and explicit. I mean "subject" here in two senses, one having to do with personhood and the other having to do with being a citizen, but the two were of course closely linked in Stalinist ideology. The shift affected most aspects of Soviet culture and rhetoric (by which I mean such things as *Pravda* editorials, speeches, and public rituals as well as cultural artifacts and their reception).

One can sense this shift in statements about architecture, often a crude index of change. The previous vogue for buildings with elaborate and grand façades was rejected, and architects were enjoined to pay more attention to interiors. The volte-face was effectively proclaimed at what was called a "Meeting on Questions of Construction and the Production of Building Materials," in Moscow, convened in December 10–14, 1935, by the Central Committee of the Party, at which many of the Party leaders made programmatic speeches, their drift reiterated in a series of subsequent articles and speeches.[25]

The general burden of the speeches at this meeting was that Soviet architecture should pay more attention to economy and practical needs. The intricate ornamentation of buildings erected in recent years, their grand façades requiring expensive building materials had, speakers complained, meant prohibitive costs and made problematical, if not impossible, the use of the most advanced technology (so often features were custom made). The elaborate façades also frustrated attempts to standardize components and introduce prefabricated construction methods, further adding to building costs and lengthening construction time. But a second recurrent criticism of architects was that in reaching for grandiose effect, they had turned a blind eye to the need for comfortable and practical interiors, complete with the latest modern conveniences. Rather than praise the grand façades, now most official spokesmen used a new negative term, "façade-ism" *(fasadnost', fasadnichestvo)*. Mikoyan thundered at the meeting: "we have to purge the design process of fantasizers and superfluous excess."[26] Bulganin in his speech to the First Congress of the

Union of Soviet Architects (another event in this series) was even blunter: "The architect must count the kopecks."[27]

It might seem that in architecture, unlike the Stakhanovite movement launched the same month, there was a shift to more prosaic and mundane concerns and away from the grandiose. Yet the same speeches also contain the inflated rhetoric of the Stakhanovite movement. This blunt rejection of "façadism" more or less coincided with the shift from a general horizontal orientation in architecture (ensemble) to a vertical one, a shift that gives material embodiment to the imperative of the new slogan of official rhetoric, "Higher!" and culminates in the Stalinist "wedding cake" buildings of the forties and early fifties.

Starting approximately at the end of 1935, one can detect in architectural magazines a shift to an interest in the interiors of apartments as human, lived-in spaces providing "pleasant conditions for people [chelovek] to spend time in," and in the "everyday." The trend intensified around December 1936, when the infamous Stalin Constitution was promulgated and "care for man" *(zabota o cheloveke)* became a central slogan. In the critique of the interiors, the latest kitchen and bathroom fixtures are stressed, as are the means of waste disposal, and the "niche" *(polochka)* in the kitchen for a housekeeper to sleep. Recurrent terms are "the consumer" *(potrebitel')*, "convenience" *(udobstvo)*, and "comfort" *(komfort)*. The focus on the latest trends was partly about keeping up with the Americans, whose new kitchens and bathrooms were often discussed in the architectural press. But it was not only about that. In commentaries a new and somewhat unexpected value emerges, "intimacy" *(intimnost')* and even the "lyrical" *(lirika)*. One sees this in one contemporary Soviet comment on the Mukhina statue: "on the one hand, she [Mukhina] is a 'purveyor of the intimate' [intimistka'] and the inner life of the model is so important to her that she has striven at all costs to preserve in the statue a trace of the precious life of another caught unawares [otpechatok zastignutoi vrasplokh, sokrovennoi chuzhoi zhizni]; on the other hand, she is a monumentalist, and any of her works, any statue, is executed [to convey] relationships [vypolneny v sootnosheniiakh] that demand huge dimensions."[28]

The notion of capturing an individual's "precious" inner thoughts seems out of keeping with such a poster-like, idealized representation of the typical worker and peasant. Benjamin noted in his Moscow diary of 1927 that the Bolsheviks had abolished private life.[29] Might it not seem that by the midthirties they had brought it back? But such banner terms of this time as "the lyrical," "comfort," and "intimacy" were not really used by authoritative figures in the Soviet architectural press in the same sense as would have been the case in the West. As Jochen Hellbeck has argued, "the problem of applying a public-private binary to Stalin era . . . subjectivities is that it projects a liberal understanding of selfhood into the Soviet context." Rather, "under socialism, any notion of the private was [to be] rendered anachronistic."[30] By "intimacy," for example, commentators did not mean sexual intimacy or even, really, personal intimacy. Rather, "intimacy" identifies one side of the division of space: a building's exterior is intended for public view and edification and is as such contrasted with inner space, the realm of comfort (one of the privileges of the New Class) and of sensibility.

The redirection of attention and prestige away from the exterior, or façade, of a building to what is within is also a redirection to the space where the individual is not merely reacting to public spectacle but also thinking and feeling; the apartment is the domain of a more private, even inner, self. But this was in no way to mean a particularized—let alone an eccentric—self. The turn to the "inner" points to a reweighting within the society. In writing about apartments, commentators stressed that they were to provide a study, but there was rarely any mention of rooms for children. In other words, the new apartments were effectively privileging the man of the household, the master, over the wife, and privileging some sort of eternal or a historical state over the life stream (procreation). The stress on providing studies was also symptomatic of the increase in stature of intellectual activities in the "lettered city."

Interiors also entail divisions (for example, the study that the children cannot enter while the master is at work). At this time secret, or taboo, spaces became a feature of writing about buildings. Thus, for example, whereas in early discussions of the Palace of Soviets stress had been laid on its role as a place for mass meetings, now it was stipulated that there should be a whole series of separate spaces such as cloakrooms and elevators for particular categories of people, spaces from which in effect the masses were excluded.[31] A similar pattern obtained at the new Exhibition of Agricultural Achievements (a sort of socialist theme park), where particular spaces were stipulated to be off limits to all but a few. Vyshinsky in the Bukharin trial, we might recall, kept alluding to transcripts of the interrogations that were held behind closed doors, accessible only to the most august. Here we might revisit the Govorkov poster of 1940, "Stalin in the Kremlin Cares for Every One of Us" (discussed in Chapter 2) and note that Stalin is now depicted not on the podium but in a small, "intimate" study, separated from the outside world.

The policies that came in with the reaction against "fasadnost'" had contrary thrusts. On the one hand there were very pragmatic considerations, with a stress on the quotidian and material well-being, and de facto a shift to what Vera Dunham called the "big deal," rewarding the bureaucrats and professionals, the "new class," whose loyalty and efforts were to be crucial in establishing a "fourth Rome." At the same time there was a thrust away from such trappings of the good life to a desire for some transcendent, the extra-ordinary, the intensity of passion, the Romantic.

Stanislavsky, the Show Trials, Face and Mask

Two moments bring out some of the distinctive features of the shift I find in the culture of the second half of the 1930s. Both were at their height in 1938. The first of these is the trials themselves, or more specifically what is called the Great Purge Trial, that of Bukharin, Aleksei Rykov, and other members of an alleged Trotskyite-Rightist Bloc that took place in March 1938. The second is the canonization in the same year of the great director Konstantin Stanislavsky,[32] a cofounder of the Moscow Art Theater, best known in the West as the guru of Method acting (he called it a "system").

It might seem that the theories of Stanislavsky on the one hand, which were developed over a long period of time, and the purge trials on the other come out of different traditions and are essentially quite distinct, that the prominence of both in 1938 was essentially a coincidence. One might argue that the Great Purge Trial was about Party factionalism and political maneuvering, whereas the lionization of Stanislavsky in the same year was essentially about the rejection of all varieties of modernism and the avant-garde ("Formalism") and the return to an earlier cultural vogue, seen, for example, in the cult of Pushkin the previous year. Yet the principal texts generated by these two phenomena—the transcript *The Great Purge Trial* plus auxiliary writings in *Pravda* and so forth on the one hand and Stanislavsky's writings on the other—throw into relief the new mode of rhetorical discourse in the mid- to late thirties and the new sense of the subject.

Stanislavsky was largely canonized in 1938, the year of his death at seventy-five and the fortieth anniversary of his Moscow Art Theater (MKhAT). That year, he received the highest Soviet honor, the Order of Lenin, and it was proposed that an entire network of theaters in the MKhAT mold be set up all over the country.[33] Both Stanislavsky's writings and the practice of MKhAT, in one of the most striking cases of the dominance of Moscow over Soviet culture (discussed in the introduction), became dogma for all Soviet theaters, and MKhAT was sent to Paris in August 1937 to showcase Soviet cultural achievement at the time of the Paris Exposition.

By contrast, Meyerhold was subjected to repeated attacks; his theater was closed, in 1939 he was arrested, and he was shot in 1940. Yet there is no sign of Marxism-Leninism in Stanislavsky's "system"; in fact, in his work in MKhAT during the Soviet period Stanislavsky long resisted staging politicized, pro-Bolshevik plays, rather longer than did Meyerhold, who joined the Party in 1918 and proclaimed a "theatrical October" in 1920. Nevertheless, the beneficiary of the demise of the Meyerhold school was Stanislavsky.[34] This is not to suggest that he sought such preference; in fact he was generous toward Meyerhold when Meyerhold was persecuted in 1936 and appointed Meyerhold as an assistant. One could be cynical and say that Stanislavsky was canonized only because once the Meyerhold School was eliminated he was the only towering figure left whose theories might be nominated "socialist realist," but I would argue that his theories in some of their quirkier aspects actually matched the historical moment well, though far from perfectly (one problematical aspect for Soviet officialdom can be sensed in the authoritative introductory note to *An Actor*, "From the Publisher," whose anonymous author insists that the central role Stanislavsky gives to the "subconscious" is deceptive and does not represent his position accurately).

When Stanislavsky died in 1938, he had been working on a multivolume, systematic account of his system, of which only two full-length books were completed, *My Life in Art* (Moia zhizn' v iskusstve), produced in 1922–1923, and a book that appeared posthumously in 1938, *Rabota aktëra nad soboi* (An actor's work on himself; hereafter *An Actor*).[35] With his canonization in 1938–1939, these two books, but particularly *An Actor*, became the most authoritative texts for acting and directing; allegedly they provided *the* source for the socialist realist tradition in theater (as more of Stanislavsky's writings were published, they were added to this canon, but these two works were at its center).

At a superficial level, theater or theatricality might seem to be a common feature of both the purges and the writings of Stanislavsky. As many have remarked, in the mid-to late 1930s the theatrical element to be found in most areas of Stalinist culture became particularly pronounced (the many examples include the mass parades, the show trials, rituals on the eve of these trials involving displays of caricatured effigies of the accused, public confessions, and the use of mummers and "carnival" for mass celebrations at such places as Gorky Park). Moreover, this period was one when theater itself was in vogue, together with opera and cinema, which in sources such as *Pravda* supplanted literature as the center of attention. Theater also captivated the populace. It was not uncommon for Muscovites to queue up all night to get tickets for a new production, especially for one staged in Stanislavsky's MKhAT.[36]

That theater should be so popular at this purge time is perhaps not surprising. It had been in vogue during the two most revolutionary—or extremist—moments of the twenties, that is, during the immediately postrevolutionary phase and during the cultural revolution of the late twenties. In the midthirties, however, one sees not just a shift to the theater but also a shift in theatrical modes. Whereas in the postrevolutionary days, a time of millennial fervor, the characteristic theatrical form had been the open-air mass spectacle, now a dominant mode was melodrama. Even productions of theatrical classics were colored by it. This development might be seen as having its own logic, in that many theater historians see melodrama, which originated in France, as having been historically an heir to the popular pantomime or tableau of the revolutionary theater spawned by 1789.

Definitions of melodrama vary from critic to critic as different aspects are stressed. While one scholar, Robert Heilman, insists that "in all versions of the melodramatic genre . . . there is some variation of the conflict between man and elements outside himself (hero versus villain, man versus nature),"[37] another, Robert Lang, asserts that "the family is the melodrama's favorite milieu" because "there one finds the most vivid and troublesome contradictions of melodrama's ideological context . . . intense primal emotions that are always in some sense in excess of the situations that produce them. To the degree that the melodramatic text is hysterical, neurotic or paranoid, so is the family."[38] Lang also argues that melodrama "is first a drama of identity."[39] As I have argued elsewhere, the pitting of man against the elements and of man against enemies, in both instances framed by a "familial" context (the Stalinist myth of the "Great Family"),[40] were core narratives of High Stalinist culture. Arguably, these narratives were essentially figural representations of what is at their heart a drama of identity played out more often than not in the melodramatic mode.

The element of melodrama was certainly prominent in the show trials, which seem substantially scripted by its conventions. Many of the elements of the melodramatic repertoire are featured in the transcript of Bukharin's trial, where political maneuvering within the Party and ideological differences have been transposed into a narrative of dark plottings, secret societies, and individuals seething with a lust for revenge that they attempt to effect clandestinely by all manner of dastardly deeds, including resort to that old favorite of melodrama, slow-acting poisons. In the hyperbolically Manichaean world projected by the prosecution, exposure—revelation that those on trial are masquerading with a false identity—is the basic move. Their true identity is represented in terms of villains from a range of popular genres in the melodramatic vein. Political life became a sort of primal drama that pitted the true offspring of the noble line (of Marxism-Leninism) against the blackguard-imposter, a stock villain of melodrama. Even the audience at the trial is scripted as witnesses to a melodrama. Koltsov reported that "A shiver ran through the entire hall as Vyshinsky [the chief prosecutor] asked Bukharin. . . ."[41] Of course there was always a melodramatic strain in Bolshevik rhetoric, which featured a Manichaean account of the world. But in these texts, that dichotomy is even more starkly present, and the account has the breathless intensity of melodrama.

In comparing the trial transcript and such related texts with the theories and practice of Stanislavsky, I am not going to suggest that he was an advocate of melodrama per se (though Lunacharsky, a great supporter of MKhAT, had recommended melodrama when he headed culture in the 1920s). But there was a disparity between Stanislavsky's customary choice of plays to stage and his training techniques for actors. Soviet commentators from the thirties generally classified his approach as some form of "scenic realism"[42] or better still, socialist realism. But a reading of Stanislavsky's programs for training actors makes problematical any claim to a "realism" in the sense of trying to depict ordinary reality.

Stanislavsky insisted that "emotional truth," the "truth of passions" *(istina strastei)* was more important in the theater than any objective account of reality.[43] He repeatedly emphasized catching the essential rather than the realistic in theater work, and giving priority to passion rather than contemplation or reason.[44] In his introduction to *An Actor,* he tells the reader that in writing this text he did not want to be "scientific" or "philosophical." "I sought some special form for this book," he continues, "that would help the reader *feel* what is said in its printed words."[45] And the extract from *An Actor* selected for publication in the *Pravda* issue commemorating Stanislavsky's seventy-fifth birthday contains the statement "after all, I am no statistician who needs to be accurate. I am an artist and for me the emotions are important."[46]

As this emphasis on "truth," albeit "emotional truth," suggests, the crucial affinities between the trial transcript and Stanislavsky's theories must be found at a deeper level than standard motifs and plot conventions. Many recent theorists of melodrama have argued that while it ostensibly thrives on suspense, peripety, and dastardly deeds, its purpose is in fact to reveal an *inner* reality, an essential moral essence or universe obscured by both the quotidian existence of the characters and by their ostensible actions and motives. Melodrama, argues Peter Brooks in *The Melodramatic Imagination,* seeks "the creation of drama, an exciting, excessive, parabolic story—from the banal stuff of reality. States of being beyond the immediate context of the narrative, and in excess of it, have been brought to bear on it, to charge it with intenser significances. [The audience is led] through and beyond the surface of things to what lies behind, to the spiritual reality which is the true scene of the highly colored drama to be played out . . . a superhuman drama involving life and death, perdition and redemption, heaven and hell, the force of desire caught in a death struggle with the life force. . . . this essential drama [goes] beyond the surface of the real to the truer, hidden reality, open to the world of spirit.”[47]

Stanislavsky's writings, including many from well before 1938, are full of passages about this. For example, in a section of his autobiographical work *My Life in Art* about Chekhov's play *The Seagull*, we read: “performances of Chekhov's plays are all about . . . revealing [characters'] inner feelings,” about “delving [actually “raskopki,” as of archeological excavation] into the depths of [their] souls.” “The more you read him,” Stanislavsky continues, “the more you sense layers [zalezhi] deep within,” where the “complex inner action is hidden [taitsia].”[48]

It is this aspect, strongly present in the show trial transcripts, I want to focus on in advancing Stanislavsky's theories as dovetailing in many respects with the distinctive culture of the purge years.

It will be noted that *My Life in Art* is actually an autobiography. *An Actor,* moreover, is not a systematic outline of the director's theories with appended accounts of the famous Stanislavskian exercises, as one might expect. Rather, the material is presented in the form of a diary kept by a young acting student called Nazvanov to record the entire course of his training as an actor in the school of a certain Tortsov and his assistant (Nazvanov has supposedly been a stenographer and therefore is able to record accurately the remarks of the students and teachers). In his introduction, Stanislavsky warns the reader that the “diary” deals with fictive characters at a fictive school of acting. In the text he simulates the diary genre by having everything take place in the town “N” in the year “19.”; each “diary entry” has the same, incomplete date above it.

Stanislavsky's use of the diary form seems unexpected at this most Soviet of moments, when a collective sense of identity was mandatory. In actuality, however, writing one's diary was a popular activity in this decade, and the diaries and autobiographies of Tolstoy and Herzen, as if to provide models, were republished in the mid-1930s.[49] Moreover, what we find in both Stanislavsky's writings and the rhetoric of the purges is a strange case of the personalized impersonal.

Those who promoted Stanislavsky in 1938 proclaimed that his writings, such as *My Life in Art,* were attacks on the Formalist position.[50] Indeed, in *An Actor* he criticizes those who believe that "surface form" is enough in acting, dismissing it as a mere "mask." This remark is an implicit attack on the theories of Meyerhold, who scorned attempts to represent "reality" or the workings of the inner psyche on the stage. In some instances, he had his actors wear masks. Where Meyerhold promoted the mask as an aid to true theatricality, Stanislavsky saw it as an empty sham. Such "acting techniques," he insists in *An Actor,* "have lost that inner essence that gave rise to them and have become sheer stage mannerisms [here he uses Meyerhold's key term "uslovnost'"], which have nothing in common with real [podlinnoi] life."[51] In thus implicitly dismissing the theories of the Meyerhold school, he continues: "standardized routines for the external [of the body]"—read Meyerhold's system of Biomechanics—"[are just] a dead mask of nonexistent feeling."[52]

The attacks on Meyerhold and "Formalism" can be seen in a broader frame of reference than that of rival theatrical schools. In the midthirties we see in so many manifestations of culture and rhetoric in the Soviet Union a rejection of surface form for lived experience, of outer semblance for the "true," or "authentic," inner self, what was called the *pravdivyi,* the *podlinnyi,* favorite adjectives both of Stanislavsky and of Bolshevik rhetoric at this time.

There was also a shift in the categorization of citizens, which *could* be seen, at some level of generality, as analogous to the rejection of fine exteriors for architecture. Prior to this, much of Stalinist culture could be seen as having given priority to the "mask" over the "face" beneath; if you will, to the category or "form" of the thing over its actuality, the plan or design over its execution, the façade or veneer over the inner reality. In the late twenties and early thirties, surface markers of identity such as class and political record determined an individual citizen's fate in many ways, including whether one was given entry to some institution of higher education, or was to be purged. As Igal Halfin, Sheila Fitzpatrick, and others have argued, these "class" identities were to some extent constructions—*uslovnye,* if you will. During the course of the thirties, however, both the sociological category to which an individual belonged and even such factors as Party or Komsomol service became increasingly less operative in deciding an individual's official identity and therefore fate.[53] In effect, the number of sociological categories shrank, and a hyperbolically Manichaean classification developed whereby there were just two categories of personhood: villains (now dubbed "enemies of the people") and citizens. Within each, there were further divisions by degree of positivity or negativity.

Those previously regarded as social aliens were now effectively deemed villains who had to be exposed by the forces of purity and righteousness. Stalin claimed in his speeches to a 1937 Party plenum that the Trotskyites "had already stopped being ideologically committed," for they had "turned themselves long ago into highway brigands."[54] At the show trials and in official writings of the midthirties, whenever an "enemy of the people" was exposed, a sociological category could be used to establish that person's negative identity, but what was most important was no longer social origins, or Party membership, or work record, or even public statements—all these could be "masks." The essential criterion was the moral/political identity of the inner self.

The show trials of the Great Purge were intended to expose the semblance, or veneer *(maska),* of Party dedication among the accused. How else could one explain the fact that so many of them had been Party leaders for so long? Stalin addressed this issue in speeches to the 1937 plenum that set the framework for the Great Purge Trial and its accompanying rhetoric. In these speeches he insisted that there had been a qualitative change in the nation's enemies, who were now less readily discerned than those tried earlier (at, for example, the Shakhty Trial of engineers in 1928). "How," Stalin asked, "can one explain the fact that our comrades in leading positions who have had invaluable experience in combating all manner of anti-Party and anti-Soviet tendencies turned out in this instance to be naive and blind and were not able to discern the true face of the enemies of the people, were not able to recognize wolves in sheep's clothing, were not able to tear off their masks?"[55]

This theme of the false mask and true face was picked up in such places as the series of *Pravda* editorials that came out at the time of the 1938 show trial and in the rhetoric of the trial itself. There, for example, the procurator of the Soviet Union, Vyshinsky, in summing up the case for the prosecution, invoked this theme repeatedly, typically describing the Trotskyites and Bukharinites as

> people . . . who have been walking around all their lives with masks on [pod maskoi]. . . . who have been hiding their real face [nas-

toiashchee litso], the face of sworn enemies of the Soviet people, behind a skilfully constructed guise [iskusnaia lichina] . . . [his ellipsis]
The mask has been torn off. Their true face [nastoiashchee litso],
their true profile [deistvitel'nyi oblik], is clear now to everyone.[56]

In the Russian of this passage, besides the word for "mask," one finds
several words formed from the cognate roots *lik-*, and *lits-*. Most of them
denote the face, but one—*iskusnaia lichina*—denotes something more
mask-like and negative (because deceptive). In Russian the word for face,
litso, can be used for a range of meanings, including role, or theatrical
role—and façade. Hence the opposition "real face"/ "assumed guise" that
is implicit in the doctrine of tearing off the masks is somewhat blurred
lexically, a fact that foregrounds the problem that for the truly paranoid
imagination, under each mask we might not find the "true face" but just
another mask. The task, then, was to dig deeper, to uncover the true essence that might well not be on the surface, but hidden within.

Stanislavsky and his acting school maintained that to be effective on
stage, one must act not from one's outer, surface self but from "deep"
within. Thus his attack on giving priority to surface form in theater dovetailed not only with the anti-"Formalist" campaign of the midthirties but
also with the rhetoric of "vigilance" in "tearing off the masks" that was
central to the Great Purge time in which Stanislavsky was so venerated.
At this time his theories struck a chord. In the selection from *An Actor*
published in the *Pravda* issue commemorating Stanislavsky's seventy-
fifth birthday, he says: "people rarely open up and show their souls as
they really are. Most often they mask their feelings, and then their external appearance [lichina] is deceptive; it is unhelpful to the outside observer, who finds it all the harder to guess what feelings lie hidden."[57]
Thus there is in some aspects of Stanislavsky's theories—foregrounded,
not surprisingly, in the selection from his writings—an element of surveillance, of "unmasking" surface appearance in the service of uncovering the
"true" person. The actor functions as a sleuth trying to uncover and expose
what lies beneath. Indeed, it is something of a clichéd observation that
Stanislavsky's school had some affinity with the NKVD, and even that the
Method school in the United States had some affinity with the CIA.[58]

The subtitle of *An Actor*—essentially a fuller version of the title—is *The*

Work of an Actor on Himself in the Creative Process of Experiencing. My deliberately literal, if awkward, translation foregrounds the three central elements of his system—an actor's work on himself, experiencing, and experiencing not as a passive activity but as a creative process.

The word used for "experiencing" in the book's title, *perezhivanie,* could also be translated as "feeling" or "reliving," translations that are perhaps more apt, because a central preoccupation of Stanislavsky's system was training in the use of "affective memory." In order to represent an emotion or mood, he believed, the actor should experience it himself or herself. Consequently, he developed a series of exercises whereby in order to act out a scene where one was to express a particular emotion, one either recalled a past moment of emotional intensity when a comparable emotion was experienced or, if it had not been experienced, one developed the imagination to the extent that one could experience this moment "as if" it had. The moment was to be summoned up in the memory in all its detail (sights, sounds, smells, and even the slightest details of the setting), and then the actor would be able to act out a comparable moment in a text "truthfully" *(pravdivo)* and "authentically" *(podlinno).* The alternative, in Stanislavsky's system, is wooden ("Formalist") or ham acting, acting that rings false. The greatest impediment to transcendent acting is, he contends, to be found within the actor himself or herself, in having too high a degree of self-consciousness.

Early in *An Actor,* the narrating apprentice actor, Nazvanov, experiences his first moment of triumph, takes his first step toward mastery. But this is a step he makes by himself, unguided, and virtually inadvertently. His first exercise at the drama school has been to prepare, with a handful of fellow students, a section of Shakespeare's *Othello* (a play on which Stanislavsky worked extensively himself as a director and about which he wrote). Nazvanov in successive diary entries chronicles his trials and errors, his emotional highs and lows, as he tries (mostly at home by himself) to practice his role as Othello. Then comes the day when they put on a performance in costume before their teachers and other pupils. Nazvanov gives a running commentary on his acting as if it is in progress, listing the inadequacies he senses and his recognition that "inside, I felt all was empty as never before."[59] "I was ashamed of every word I uttered, of every gesture I made, which I immediately criticized,"[60] he continues.

But then, suddenly, in my helplessness and confusion I was overcome by anger [zloba]. I myself don't know at whom it was directed—perhaps at myself, perhaps at the audience. At that point for several minutes I felt cut off from everything around me and became unrestrainedly [bezuderzhimo] bold. That famous phrase "Blood, Iago, blood" . . . . I wrenched out of myself against my will. It was the cry of a frenzied sufferer. How that happened I myself don't know. Perhaps in these words I sensed the offended soul of a trusting human being and felt genuine pity for him. . . . I had the feeling that for an instant the audience pricked up their ears and that a murmur passed over the crowd like a rustle of wind over the crowns of trees. As soon as I sensed approval, a great energy welled up in me [zakipela] so strong that I did not know where to direct it. It carried me on. I don't recall how I played the end of the scene. I just remember that the footlights, and the black hole of the portal disappeared from my attention, that I was free of all fear, and that on the stage was created an intoxicating [upoitel'naia] life that was new to me and unknown. I know no higher joy than these few minutes that I experienced on the stage. I noticed that Pasha Shutov [a fellow student playing Iago] was amazed at my rebirth [pererozhdenie]. I fired him up and he began to act with great animation [odushevlenie]. . . . When I left the stage triumphantly . . . it seemed to me that everyone was looking at me with rapturous eyes.[61]

In fact, Nazvanov's impact was less dramatic than he imagined. However, when his teacher Tortsov later sums up his impressions of the various performances students had made that day and singles out two moments as examples of "the art of living through experiencing [perezhivanie]," one of the two is this high point of Nazvanov's performance. "Both you, as you were acting," Tortsov comments, "and we, as we were looking on, gave over our entire beings to what was happening on the stage, we died, and were revived again, in the one sweep of emotion [volnenie] that was common to all of us."[62] When Nazvanov later admits that he had "acted subconsciously," Tortsov responds that this would be "very good if the subconscious led you on the true [vernyi] path, but bad if it was mistaken,"[63] maintaining that it is best if an actor is so caught up in the play that he does not notice how he feels or what he is doing. But in order for the actor to guarantee that in giving rein to his subconscious he is not on the wrong path, he has to learn both to "arouse it and to direct it." Hence the fundamental principle of the system is "subconscious creativity through a conscious use by the actor of psychological techniques [psikhotekhnika]"[64]—in other words, by means of the entire "system" of Stanislavskian exercises and techniques.

The basic content of the Stanislavskian "psychotechnical" exercises involves, besides routines specifically designed to relax the body (many of which are derived from yoga), set "études" and other strategies aimed at helping the actor experience, or reexperience, very particular, private moments of great emotional intensity (such as the death of a loved one) or of banal, domestic experience.

Although Stanislavsky generally did not favor melodrama in his choice of plays, generally from high culture, many of his études (training exercises for actors) involved that curious combination of banal domestic situations with the hyperbolically dramatic and emotional that is the stuff of melodrama. One such example would be an étude in which the father of the household is at his desk by the hearth sorting out key financial documents while the wife bathes their child in the bathroom. She summons him, but in his absence her simpleton brother starts messing with the papers and throwing them into the fire. The husband is so enraged on his return that he hurls the brother-in-law at the wall, and the impact proves fatal. The wife, hearing the screams, rushes in from the bathroom, and the neglected baby drowns in the bath.

Stanislavsky's alleged "scenic realism" means, in effect, achieving "authenticity," one of Stanislavsky's favorite terms, together with "genuine feelings" *(podlinnye chuvstva)* and the "true" *(pravdivyi or vernyi),* contrasted as such with mere semblance of truth or surface realism *(pravdopodobie)*. Essentially, these are terms of a reflective aesthetics. In the theater, an actor can produce a good or bad imitation, depending on how close he gets to the "truth" of certain basic emotions. The actor has to make his truth merge with the truth of what he is representing. Then his acting will be "authentic."

How could any system that became mandatory practice in the Soviet Union of the late thirties prioritize "lived experience," personal emotion, and banal or melodramatic situations? Likewise, how could any system that posits one's "rebirth" as coming from "within," by working on one's self, assume that status?[65] In the land of militant collectivism where the "self" was so highly depersonalized, how could the actor be the witness to the mask of the authentic, and therefore its mediator? Arguably, this was not just because Stanislavsky enjoyed a kind of "poetic license" as a long-standing authority figure in the arts.

The Stanislavskian system is based on a theory of primal emotions and their universality. As Stanislavsky said in his introduction to *An Actor:* "What I am writing about in my book does not just concern a particular epoch and its people, but has to do with an organic nature common to all people of an *artistic* cast of mind, to people of all nationalities and all epochs."[66] The particular dynamic represented in Nazvanov's account (quoted earlier) of his first public performance in the acting school presupposes empathy, and the notion that true art "infects" the reader/audience with the feelings that the creator has experienced and embodied in the work of art (a theory presented in that canonical source, Tolstoy's essay "What Is Art?"—canonical in Soviet Russia in part, but only in part, because of Lenin's love of Tolstoy). Stanislavsky, in the final, sixteenth chapter of *An Actor,* which he pronounced his most important ("The Role of the Subconscious in the State of the Actor on the Stage"),[67] has Tortsov congratulate Nazvanov for his final mastery of acting, which Tortsov senses, even though, as he also admits, he does not "know what's on your mind." As Nazvanov, fired by this encouragement, begins his acting assignment for the day, he becomes completely engrossed in working through in his mind a fantasy scenario involving himself. Tortsov urges the other students to "Pay attention. Nazvanov is not doing anything [as he acts], yet we sense that within everything is seething [burlit]." "At that moment," comments Nazvanov, in a description that could have been lifted from a Barbara Cartland romance, "my head began to spin. I lost myself in my role and had no sense of where I was and where was the figure I was depicting."[68] Nevertheless, Nazvanov *within* is still not living out his role from the script so much as continuing the same fantasy narrative in his imagination.

It might seem here that Stanislavsky is advocating a virtually solipsistic retreat into private fantasies, but in fact he is not. Though the onlooker cannot read the specificity of what goes on inside the actor, the end achieved is expression in its universalist form. Form passes away, and you get essence. Stanislavsky's system, then, is directed at an effect, at creating a contact between the inner life of the actor and the role he is playing on stage, and then, at the same time, with the audience, so that they are all threaded into a oneness. This oneness, however, is guaranteed in the primitive recesses of the actor's memory—the agent of his or her magic.

Stanislavsky's sense of how memory operates is vaguely similar to that of Henri Bergson. Over time, as he elaborated in *An Actor,* the memory of an experience is not passed on into the general memory store of an individual intact. Rather, the aspects of the experience that most affected the individual are transmitted. In addition, over time other snatches of memory accrue to them, snatches that come from other experiences that have some affinity with the original one. The main example Stanislavsky provides of this process is an experience of Nazvanov. While walking around town, Nazvanov witnesses a terrible accident: a man is mown down by a tram. But he discovers that in time, the sheer "naturalistic" horror of this event is displaced in his memory by other less grizzly memories associated with trams, which have more affective weight for him because, as he explains, he experienced them himself, not as a mere observer.

When Nazvanov recounts his thoughts on this to Tortsov, Tortsov takes the occasion to expound an important principle. What Nazvanov experienced, he contends, was a "process of crystallization which happens to memories and feelings in the emotional memory. Every man experiences over his life not one, but many catastrophes." He continues:

> recollections of them are kept in the memory but not in all their detail; only those particular features that had the most profound effect are preserved. From many such lingering traces of what one has experienced a single memory is formed from analogous experiences— one big, condensed, broadened and deepened memory. In this memory nothing is superfluous; [it comprises] only the most essential. This memory is a synthesis of all analogous feelings. It is related not to the small, individual, and contingent occurrence, but to all like occurrences. It is a form of large-scale memory. It is more pure, more dense, compact, has more content and is sharper than even reality itself.[69]

In this account of Nazvanov's experiences and Tortsov's response, we will note the displacement of violence into a less disturbing narrative, a common trend in Soviet culture. We also note that the two key features of Tortsov's account of memory are crystallization and emotional intensity. This created memory is allegedly purer than the experience-based memories on which it draws, though more remote from actuality, and in fact a hybrid. But Stanislavsky's ideas, as expressed in Tortsov's injunction to form a "single memory" purged of the "contingent" and the "superfluous," fit in with Lukács's stipulations for the novel in "Narration or Description" and with Stalinist ideology in general.

This theory of memory formation, which is central to Stanislavsky's system for actor training, is in some respects comparable to the modes of characterization to be found in the rhetoric of the purge trial, although the genres and intentions are quite different. In the prosecution's accounts of both the accused themselves and of their actions, we can note an even greater downplaying of particularity and a generic indiscriminateness of a degree that one might call hyperbolic antiparticularism.[70] Essentially, different categories of personhood and different categories of crime, different both in degree of iniquity and in the sense that they came from different discourses or genres, are lumped together, undifferentiated.

One striking feature of the show trials is the disparity between the augustness of the occasion and the content of the defense, which reeks of melodrama and other varieties of popular culture, such as the religious chapbook or the adventure tale. The accused at the Great Purge Trial, the alleged Trotskyites and Bukharinites, are often identified with the devil, or with some subhuman creature: attributions include all manner of wild beasts (such as "a nest of vipers") or some "beast in human form." There was even a suggestion of the grotesque freak, as in Gorky's then often invoked expression "an accursed mixture of the vixen and the pig." Another popular version had the accused as a band *(banda)* or gang *(shaika)* of "wreckers, saboteurs, spies, and murderers," sometimes with "thieves" thrown in for good measure, or as "the Trotskyite-Fascist terrorist gang." Every one of the accused is to an extraordinary degree an amalgam of interchangeable categories—wrecker, spy, highway bandit, and so on—that are strung along in lists that have an implicit sign of equivalence between them. Any one of the accused could, *as accused,* potentially have the *en-*

tire inventory of negative characterizations leveled at him, or be accused of all the crimes that are "revealed" in the course of his questioning. Similarly, there is a marked indiscriminateness of time and place; each discrete "event" cited at the trial is, although pinpointed as to time and place, essentially ahistorical.

The third part of Stanislavsky's descriptive subtitle for *An Actor* is *The Creative Process of Experiencing,* but as noted, experiencing, in his view, is not a passive activity but a creative process. The actor should not just "depict, but create an inner life." Then and only then, stipulates Stanislavsky, can he exclaim "I am" (in Russian Stanislavsky uses the biblical *ia esm'*).[71]

Thus Stanislavsky's "system" does not only turn on moments of great emotional intensity but also on moments of, if you will, existential or even ontological intensity. Nazvanov's account of his first performance is structured as a conversion experience (it is called a *pererozhdenie,* or "rebirth"). As the actor "focuses" intensely on the particular or banal experience, he or she experiences a kind of epiphany and is transformed.[72] However, not all are able to have such an experience. Great acting comes from an inborn talent and wells up from a "genuine artistic subconscious." Though Stanislavsky believed that his techniques would facilitate that process, he also believed that without such latent talent, the desired result is not always amenable to "conscious control."[73] There is, effectively, a hierarchy in humans that privileges the creative ones (though such persons are found throughout the universe). However, they do not necessarily know that they are chosen. Role and essence have to coincide (tear off the mask). The creative ones are, thus, vaguely analogous with the chosen ones in Calvinist doctrine.[74] Rather than a religious morality, however, what we have here is closer to a secular eschatology of the aesthetic.

In the second half of the thirties, Stalinist culture also effectively operated on a hierarchy of the chosen/nonchosen. The Stakhanovites, for example, were also represented as having a kind of inner genius. They were not just production heroes in the sense that they achieved by dint of sheer effort and will. Though in actuality their production feats were directed by the Party and were often made possible by assigning them an auxiliary crew of workers, their achievement was said to have been directed from *within,* to the consternation of bureaucrats and "experts" who drew up what proved to be anemic production quotas.

In Stalinist culture, this represents a simplification as compared with the first half of the decade, when more categories of person, effectively, operated (then, the division was much more by occupation or sociopolitical category). In this later period, the categories were more general; there were essentially three of them, organized in an ascending hierarchy: member of the masses; "new man"/creative person; and leader. There was also essentially only one negative category, "enemy of the people," though there were gradations of nefariousness. However, by the mid-thirties, belonging to that category of person was both more determining than it had been, and irreversible; enemies of the people were no longer regarded as redeemable, as they had been earlier, in the Belomor Canal project. Yet, paradoxically, that someone belonged to that category was not necessarily as "readable" either on the surface, or even by the individual looking within. Only if that person or his or her observer went "deeper"—if they plumbed the ultimate degree of withinness—would his or her status as an enemy be surely revealed. In that inner self, one would discover not only ill intention but also that this person had no inner gold—was not chosen.

According to Stanislavsky's theories, the truly creative actor must find guidance within. By following recommended routines, one purges one's self and realizes that more authentic potential that is within, though one does not know it. This is the ultimate in self-realization, but it also involves casting out the dross from within to make a unified whole, a purification in a kind of distillation. Once the essence has been found, the dialectic of inner and outer is resolved.

The question remains, how can the gap be bridged between creator and created? An answer has to be that we are all creating, but creating in the act of being created. In Stanislavsky's system, the actor experiences a falling away of the barrier between narrated self and narrating self and becomes just a pure, quivering self.

This fictive diary of Stanislavsky *(An Actor)* points to a somewhat unexpected way our exploration of the "face"/"mask" binary can be extended. We see how "totalitarianism" can operate, not just by the coercion of an "atomized" populace but also through the attraction of the illusion (to which so many of its "Stalinist" actors were subject) of being able to recover a primal state so basic that in it one can enjoy one's true essence as a creator. Then the "face," or obscured self, can strike through the mask in an act of self-affirmation *(ia esm')*. Yet this primal state is also so basic that the particularity of the individual is lost in an ahistorical self.

The canonization of Stanislavsky in 1936–1938 potentially points to another aspect of the evolution of Soviet culture that many scholars have remarked—the increasing cultural autarchy, or more specifically the increasing emphasis on the Russian national tradition to the exclusion of Western models. But as Stanislavsky himself says in his introduction to *An Actor,* most of the book's theory was worked out in 1907–1914, before the Revolution. Furthermore, he mentions that he has been working on this book since 1927 (i.e., not in the mid- to late 1930s moment I am discussing here), though he continued to revise and rewrite until death made further revision impossible. What Stanislavsky did not add, but should have, is that in formulating his system he was strongly influenced by, inter alia, yoga, and Theosophy, then popular in the West, and the thought of several prerevolutionary French philosophers and psychologists, and particularly by the work of the psychologist Theodule Armand Ribot and a work he influenced, Bergson's *Matter and Memory* (Matière et mémoire; 1896).

Any insistence that the Stalinist cultural horizon was now largely circumscribed by an officially sponsored nationalism is problematic, given that during precisely these years (1936–1938) the international effort in the Spanish Civil War captured the imagination of the entire populace, and of intellectuals particularly. In so responding they were, as Stanislavsky recommended actors do, giving priority to passion rather than contemplation or reason, as we shall see in the next chapter. Koltsov, one of the most prominent Soviet participants in that war, crafted his best-seller *Spanish Diary* (Ispanskii dnevnik), which fed this frenzy, not as a melodrama but as an adventure romance.

CHAPTER 7

Love and Death in the
Time of the Spanish Civil War
(1936–1939)

THE SPANISH CIVIL WAR, in its early phases at least, attracted the antifascist left to its cause. Enthusiasts who fought there sought to recapture some of the élan of revolution, prepared to go all the way even if this meant death. Many of them looked to the Soviet Union as the one country prepared to stand up to the fascist advances. In consequence, perhaps, in the memoir and fictional works by the Western activists I will discuss, we see the closest the Soviet Union ever came to getting major writers, such as Ernest Hemingway and Malraux (as distinct from Western Communist writers like Mike Gold), to adopt conventions of socialist realism, and in that sense the closest Moscow came to being a cultural "Fourth Rome." But, as we will also see, even if intellectuals could be construed as incorporating some Soviet conventions in their works, it was only very tentatively; they resisted subordinating the text to the totalizing socialist realist masterplot, and at times, on the contrary, they parodied its clichés.

The war itself was fought roughly between the left who had gained power in elections of February 1936—the Republican side—and the "Nationalists" or "Falangists," who under General Franco sought to wrest power from them. It lasted from his *pronunciamento* of July 17, 1936, until the Republican troops surrendered on April 1, 1939.

In the Soviet Union this war captured the imagination of intellectuals and of the populace at large. Schoolgirls plotted to run away there and fight for the Republicans; ordinary people dreamed they were on its battlefields ramming bayonets "into fascist stomachs."[1] The dramatist Aleksandr Afinogenov whipped up a play *(Saliut, Ispaniia)* in a mere two weeks to respond to the war, Shostakovich providing the music; at the November 1936 premiere, while Madrid was under siege, the audience "shouted, screamed, cried, waved their arms," as the author found himself caught up in the emotion and fought back tears.[2] And in 1936–1937 Muscovites queued up around the block to see the latest installment of Roman Karmen's newsreel series "On the Events in Spain" (K sobytiiam v Ispanii),[3] while in 1938 Koltsov's *Spanish Diary* (Ispanskii dnevnik) was probably the most widely read book in the capital.

This ecstatic identification with the Republican cause was not only felt in the Soviet Union. From all over the world, idealistic young writers, artists and activists, together with *thousands* of workers and communists, came streaming over Spain's border with France to join the International Brigade (set up as a result of a Politburo decision of August 28, 1936, with Dimitrov present, and formed in October 1936).[4] They were intent on fighting for what some have called "the last just cause," often compensating for the neutrality of their own governments. For intellectuals this theater of war was such a mecca that the list of those who went to it was a veritable who's who of left-inclining, including many of the usual suspects from the antifascist talkfests. Some came to fight, others as journalists, or just to bear witness.

Was there ever such an intellectuals' war?—one in which, on the Republican side, writers became soldiers and even commanders, many of them deciding policy and tactics! While Malraux organized and led an air squadron (of superannuated planes), Máté Zalka, the Hungarian writer, commanded an International Brigade as General Lukács, with Gustav Regler as his political commissar and Ludwig Renn, another German writer, heading one of its battalions.[5]

Koltsov was not technically listed in the International Brigade, but this pattern of the intellectual warrior holds particularly true for him. As his *Pravda* colleague David Zaslavskii recalls in a memoir, "he was not only a writer but also a military commander. He had not only a pencil but also a pistol."[6] With Stalin's approval Koltsov left for Spain on August 6, 1936, as one of the earliest Soviet emissaries to the war and arrived before there was a major Soviet military or diplomatic investment, staying until November 1937, except for a trip back to Moscow that spring. Though officially in Spain as a special correspondent of *Pravda,* he was in fact often reporting on operations he himself was running. His political functions allegedly made him a more important figure than the ambassador, and he sent daily dispatches from Spain to the Kremlin.[7] The battle for Madrid in October–November 1936, a time when Soviet military aid (tanks, planes) and the International Brigades made substantial contributions in staving off the capital's fall, was the high point of Koltsov's career in Spain. Faced by that imminent danger, on November 5 the Republican government of Largo Caballero decided to leave the encircled capital for Valencia; in this power vacuum, the Communists and the Russian advisors rapidly assumed executive functions abandoned by the regular civil servants, forming a junta of defense. Koltsov was in its early days its chief inspiration and a political actor, organizing everything from military tactics to counter-propaganda.[8]

Erenburg also played a significant role in the war beyond his literary and journalistic work. He arrived in August 1936 as a correspondent for *Izvestia,* staying until December 1938, and was allegedly able to talk "frankly with the highest officials in Spain, and to determine their views of the political and military situation." His dispatches, relayed to the Politburo via Marsel' Rozenberg, the Soviet ambassador to Spain, provided crucial intelligence to the leadership as well as advice on political strategy.[9]

The concern here, however, is not the political or military history of the war. Rather, I will treat the narratives and films generated by a coterie of non-Spanish enthusiasts for the Republican cause.

Most of the big names among the antifascist intellectuals in Spain at some point or other intersected with Koltsov, Erenburg, Karmen, and each other. This includes Malraux, Robert Capa, Endre Erno Friedmann, Joris Ivens, Hemingway, Regler, Paul Robeson, and Langston Hughes (who was in Spain as a correspondent for the *Baltimore African-American*). Despite language barriers, they became friends in a transnational camaraderie that led to a series of collaborations (Luis Buñuel, for example, appropriated some of the Karmen documentary footage for

Madrid [1936]). The main link for all these figures was a succession of Madrid hotels where they stayed when not at the front and in which, as most accounts run, in smoke-filled rooms whose walls were pockmarked with scars of war, they drank and talked the night away.

The Spanish Civil War was a high point of their association. By the end of the decade, this group were dispersed both geographically and politically. In Spain many of the intellectual volunteers had become progressively disillusioned by the dirty politics on the left and the infamous purges both in the Soviet Union and within their ranks. It has been fashionable to write off this heroic moment of the war as one in which witting or unwitting intellectuals were pawns of a cynical or power-hungry Stalin, who covertly indulged his imperial ambitions. I am not going to enter the "last just cause"/"manipulated pawns" debate of historiography. Of course Stalin practiced Realpolitik. Undoubtedly there is much truth in such accounts, but they are also overly Manichaean. For a start, as recent publications from the Soviet archives reveal, for much of the war the Party leadership were advocating that Communists in Spain resist taking over and instead provide support for the Popular Front groupings. Stalin, preoccupied with the purges and show trials, was somewhat reluctant to commit, while it was figures like Koltsov who lobbied him for more aid. In addition, such accounts presuppose that the "manipulators" were operating dispassionately and were not themselves caught up in the Republican cause. Their own depictions of the war emphasize the frenzy of engagement.

It is the headiness these writers and filmmakers convey, a marker of the cultural ethos of the Civil War years, that I want to pinpoint first. But I want to argue that these works, despite their authors' immersion in the Spanish cause, should be seen in a context broader than the war itself and its reception, or even than the antifascist cause they served: the cult of all-out passion that marked the culture of mid-1930s Europe generally.

Love and Death

In the Moscow of 1937, as the Spanish Civil War was at its height, *the* cultural event was a stage adaptation of Tolstoy's *Anna Karenina*, directed at the Moscow Art Theater by Vladimir Nemirovich-Danchenko,

Stanislavsky's cofounder of that theater and now archrival.[10] People stood in line all night to buy tickets to it, and other productions of the play sprang up all over the provinces.[11] The Nemirovich-Danchenko *Anna Karenina* was also showcased at the Paris Exposition of 1937. In fact its Moscow premier on April 21 of that year, attended by Stalin, Molotov, Kliment Voroshilov, and Zhdanov, was timed so that the production would reach its artistic peak when at the Paris Exposition, two facts that are in themselves indices of its tremendous importance for Soviet officialdom.[12]

This play was emblematic of the times and throws into focus some of the paradoxes of late 1930s Soviet culture. We could ask why a prerevolutionary classic by a nobleman and set in the world of his class dominated the cultural skyline, but we could equally well ask why a love drama of fatal passion was so prominent at this time of national and international crisis. This question is particularly apt because the stage adaptation drastically simplified the novel's plot, leaching out the great political and moral issues that beset its main hero, Levin. Essentially, and as was picked up in the reviews, the stage version of the novel had become the story not of marriage and families, and not of the right path for Russia, but one of grand passion, of how Anna's great love for Vronsky led to her tragic suicide. The production ended with a life-size "train" advancing toward the audience, bearing down on Anna lying on the tracks.[13]

This focus on the love life of Anna and Vronsky was not untypical of Soviet culture in the late thirties. Despite the increasingly constrictive sexual morality, one finds then a vogue for plays, operas, and ballets centering around extramarital sex and adultery. They were far from moralizing exercises, and in them the heroines, those indulging in illicit sex, are given sympathetic treatment. Examples include the play *Emma Bovary*, an adaptation of Flaubert's novel, the ballet *Prisoner of the Caucasus* (1938, based on Pushkin), and both the ballet (by Prokofiev) *Romeo and Juliet* (1936–1938) and the Shakespeare play of that name, which Nemirovich-Danchenko used as one of his frames of reference in working on *Anna Karenina*.[14] In addition, in terms of the Shakespeare repertoire, rather than stage his historical dramas, directors chose tragedies in which passion led to the protagonist's demise—*Othello, Romeo and Juliet*. Little attention was given to his historical dramas, all those Richards and Henrys.

Were these revivals symptomatic of the reembourgoisement of Soviet Russia? Not according to Nemirovich-Danchenko, who insisted that his production of *Anna Karenina* was to be staged in the great tradition of classical tragedy with Euripides and Shakespeare as his models. During rehearsals he instructed Alla Tarasova, who played Anna Karenina, to act as if she was wearing a toga and playing a great tragic role such as Euripides's Phaedra, or possibly Medea.[15]

Anna Karenina culminates not in a heroic death but a suicide, as is true of *Emma Bovary* and of Juliet in Shakespeare's play, and also of the 1937 stage adaptation of Feuchtwanger's antifascist novel *The Oppenheim Family,* which cut out the second half of the novel to end with young Berthold's suicide.[16] But it was not just in Soviet Russia that the tragic themes of fatal love and suicide had become so much in vogue. This was also true in France, where a hit at this time was Anatol' Litvak's film *Mayerling* (1936), which treats the suicide pact in the late nineteenth century of the heir to the Austro-Hungarian throne, Archduke Rudolph, and his great love, Marie.[17] In this film the love plot is complemented by scenes showing how Rudolf is attracted to dissident intellectuals and restive students, partly because he feels so deeply the constricting society in which he lives and the constant surveillance to which he is subjected. In Marie he finds an authentic love that liberates him from this oppressive society, and when his attempts at having his marriage of political convenience annulled to marry her are thwarted, he and Marie enter a suicide pact, and he shoots them both at his hunting lodge, Mayerling.

A useful theoretical model for analyzing this vogue and its implications can be found in a book written in 1938 by the French theorist Denis de Rougement, *Love in the Western World* (L' Amour et l'occident; published 1939). The book posits an inextricable link in the Western tradition between passion and death, Eros and Thanatos, arguing that "[love] requires death for its perfect fulfillment."[18] For him the legend of Tristan and Iseult, who followed passion blindly to their deaths, provides the paradigm for this linkage. De Rougement traces that story forward in its many variations in Western culture, picking out *Romeo and Juliet* as another high point.

Though the world of Tristan and Iseult, and for that matter of Romeo and Juliet, might seem remote from that of the Soviet late thirties, this motif had particular resonance there, though in modified form. Since the scandal of January 1936 when Shostakovich's opera *Lady Macbeth of Mtsensk,* which reeked of sex, was attacked in *Pravda* after Stalin was affronted at a performance by, inter alia, the giant bed that dominated the stage for an entire act, sex, always problematical in Soviet culture, had been all but purged from it.

But in a sense, and as de Rougement brings out, Tristan and Iseult is not *about* adultery either, though the plot keeps providing the couple with occasions for practicing it. It is about fatal passion. The lovers' consummation is constantly frustrated or delayed by obstacles, for "what stirs lyrical poets to their finest flights is neither the delight of the senses nor the fruitful contentment of the settled couple; not the satisfaction of love, but its *passion.*"[19] The couple are doomed never to live in ordinary time and remain locked in a fevered state.

The Soviet reviewers of the various dramas of passion then in vogue insisted that they were not about sex or adultery. Commentary on them developed a common narrative to explain the illicit liaisons: a woman consumed by a genuine passion is trapped by constraining society, leading to her demise.[20] *Anna Karenina,* reviewers insisted, was not "naturalistic" (a code word for sex). Rather, in the play Anna and Vronsky are pitted against "high society" *(svet).* "I was ecstatic," reported one reviewer on the acting of Tarasova, who was "quivering in the heat of passion, tormented by the artificiality and hypocrisy of her milieu, protesting, and in her death taking revenge for her broken life and the slavery of women without legal protection."[21]

The vogue for passion and overcoming society's constraints emerged even as the Soviet Union was becoming more conformist, the New Class was becoming entrenched, and "comfort" *(konfortabel'nost')* was becoming a new recurrent in public discourse.[22] Women of unbridled passion were being featured in culture at a time when in reality, Soviet women were being shunted back from careers into auxiliary domestic roles. Does this standard narrative in the reviews, then, represent casuistry on the part of critics, enabling popular taste to count despite official attitudes to sexual mores? Are the explanations in terms of an oppressive, class-stratified society merely a fig leaf to make more respectable the vogue for dramas of love and passion? Are these dramas of the illicit staged in compensation for the creeping conformism?

Rather than discussing these productions in terms of their attitudes toward adultery, one might see them as particular examples of the general European cultural trend. There was, for example, a cult of death among the Nazis, too. Friedrich Wolf noted this cult in articles he published in Moscow at the time, reporting that the Nazis had rewritten death in military combat, making it a joyous event.[23] Moreover, in the same year that de Rougement wrote this book (1938), the Wagner cult, fostered by the Third Reich, was reaching its apogee in Germany,[24] especially his *Tristan and Isolde,* which conflates the themes of fatal passion, a constricting society (here a court), and suicide. De Rougement, who had himself recently worked in Germany, reads the famous third act of the opera as representing "far more than a romantic disaster . . . the repressed longing for death."[25] And at about this time Freud wrote *Moses and Monotheism* (1936/1939), in which he revisited the theories of Eros and Thanatos that he had effectively engaged in *Beyond the Pleasure Principle* (1920).

The narratives of fatal passion that abounded at this time gestured toward a version of Romanticism. It is perhaps no accident that Goethe's *Sorrows of Young Werther* (Die Leiden des jungen Werthers; 1774/1787) experienced a revival in the late 1930s; Max Ophuls, in Paris exile from the Nazis, directed the film *Le Roman du jeune Werther* in 1938. The novel was also published in translation in Soviet Russia in 1937 with an introductory essay by Lukács.[26]

Werther was a (somewhat effeminate) male. But in these Stalinist dramas emotional intensity was generally assigned to the female roles. In the stage version of *Anna Karenina,* Vronsky, the honorable Russian military officer, is a somewhat wan presence, as critics remarked, more an essential prop enabling Anna to experience grand passion than a figure of comparable stature. For the scene at the horse race where Vronsky falls with his horse, Nemirovich-Danchenko stipulated that the actress would depict an anguished Anna as losing self-control. By contrast, one of the main criticisms of Meyerhold's production of *One Life* (Odna zhizn'), based on Nikolai Ostrovsky's novel *How the Steel was Tempered,* is that its protagonist, Pavel Korchagin, is too hysterical and sees his life as a sacrifice when it should be represented rather as a joyous struggle.[27]

In such works of the late 1930s there was something of a gender divide. While women were shown in the throes of passion, men invested that intensity in exuberant military engagement. Libido was harnessed and Eros displaced.

This link between grand passion and war was also pointed to by de Rougement, who argued in "Love and War"—the title of a lecture he gave at the College of Sociology in May 1938 and then included in part 5 of his book—that the "repressed longing for death" that he identifies with Western civilization "beyond question manifests the most tenacious root of the war instinct we nourish."[28] "The danger of annihilation, for which they volunteer . . . parallels the 'obstructions' sought by lovers."

Self-willed death, like adultery, is a form of transgression, going beyond the limits of conventionally sanctioned experience. As de Rougement put it: "the prospect of a passionate experience has come to seem the promise that we are about to live more fully and more intensely." Boundless passion was in vogue, an extremism to go with the extreme times.

One should not forget that these Soviet plays and films were appearing during the Great Purge and the show trials; several laudatory reviews of *Anna Karenina* appeared in the cultural press alongside material on the trial of "Trotskyites."[29] The many Soviet works that claimed to feature authentic emotion and authentic human beings contrasted implicitly with the *inauthentic* Communists who were on trial. In dealing with *them,* it was widely felt, the country must go to the limit: "Annihilate!" *(unichtozhit')* was the recurrent headline in the press as citizens clamored for the highest measures.

In many reviews of these Soviet dramas of love and passion, a claim of authenticity is made about the protagonists' doomed love, a claim derived from the extreme nature of their experience. It is in this area that the cultural vogues of the Soviet midthirties intersect with the narratives about the Spanish Civil War (consider the sobriquet given the Spanish Communist Party leader: La Pasionaria). The foreign intellectuals often wrote of going to Spain in terms of setting themselves up for death. W. H. Auden expressed it in his poem "Spain 1937":

What's your proposal? To build the just city?
I agree. Or is it the suicide pact, the romantic
Death? Very well, I accept, for,
I am your choice, your decision. Yes, I am Spain.[30]

The cosmopolitan adventurers in Spain were the Anna Kareninas whom a fatal but authentic passion, the passion for true revolution, was driving to throw themselves under the "train"—to sacrifice themselves to the increasingly inexorable (train-like) onward march of Franco's war machine, or to place themselves in the way of the brutal bombing by Hitler's Condor Squadron.

To say so much, however, is to render their commitment an individual action, almost narcissistic—as de Rougement saw fatal passion as ultimately being. Though the literature and films generated by the war are all about the experience of war for an individual in the thick of it, given that it was fought over rival political systems (many describe it as a tussle between fascism, communism, and democracy, though the picture was more complex, and there were shadings of each), in them the war became the fitting stage for a drama of commitment and ideas.

Here I will discuss some of the most famous films, novels, and memoirs about the war produced by non-Spanish participants committed to the Republican cause. Among the texts I am looking at are Malraux's novel *Hope* (December 1937) and its film version (1939) of the same name (to avoid confusion I will use its French title, *Espoir*); Hemingway's novel *For Whom the Bell Tolls* (1939–1940, based on his time in Spain from March 1937 to May 1938); and Regler's novel *The Great Crusade* (Das grosse Beispiel, 1940), which is virtually a memoir and draws on his experiences with the Twelfth International Brigade, as well as memoirs written at the time, such as George Orwell's *Homage to Catalonia* (1938) and several works by Arthur Koestler that draw on his experiences working as a Communist journalist and Comintern emissary in Spain, beginning with his propagandistic *L'Espagne ensanglantée* of January 1937, then *Dialogue with Death* (written in the fall of 1937) and *Spanish Testament* (1938). From the Soviet side, the main literary text is Koltsov's *Spanish Diary* (1938) and Erenburg's *No pasaran! Grazhdanskaia voina iul'-dekabr' 1936 goda,* volume 2 of *Ispaniia* (1937), which features a photomontage by John Heartfield and photos by Capa, and *Ispanskii zakal. Fevral'-iul' 1937* (1938). The films were partly intended to counteract the newsreels, which were generally slanted in favor of Franco.[31] Among them, besides Malraux's *Espoir,* there is Joris Ivens's *Spanish Earth* (1937), with a voice-over written and delivered by Hemingway, and the Soviet film *Spain* (*Ispaniia,* 1939), put together by Esfir Shub, with a text by Vsevolod Vishnevsky but drawing substantially on newsreel footage shot by Karmen and his cameraman, Boris Makaseev, in 1936–1937.

Almost all these texts are based on their author's or filmmaker's recent experiences in Spain.[32] Not only do they thus come out of the thick of things, but most were produced as part of the propaganda effort for the Republican cause (Martha Gelhorn pulled off a screening of *Spanish Earth* for President Roosevelt at the White House, in vain hopes of persuading him to support the Republicans).[33] A major exception is Orwell's *Homage to Catalonia,* which chronicles his progressive disillusionment with the Republican forces. But all, including *Catalonia,* seek to bear witness to the experience of war, to provide an authentic account, as Erenburg put it, "from the eyes of a witness"; his most characteristic expression is "I saw."

War, as Paul Virilio has pointed out, is not only about routing the enemy by means of physical weapons: "Weapons are tools not only of destruction, but also of perception."[34] It was the task of the authors and filmmakers I will be discussing to wield their weapons of mass perception on an international battlefield.

Each of these texts derives its right to make a stand on the war itself, on war in general, and implicitly or explicitly on the rival belief systems at issue, from its claim to the "immediacy of its act of witnessing," somewhat as has been said of Goya when he responded to an earlier Spanish war with his series "The Horrors of War": that he "produced [the series] with the stench of destruction in his nostrils."[35] The films were shot even as the war was in progress, and the literary counterparts discussed here are diaries or largely based on diaries. The diary is a genre whereby (as the term itself stipulates) the author writes about the events that occurred the very day he or she is recording them. He or she is not meant to be privy to what happens next day. But in committed art, immediacy, a perspective so in the present moment that one does not see beyond it, has its limits. Sooner or later, the narrative has to provide some interpretation and structure. These various competing demands were worked through in different ways in the films and writings of the Spanish Civil War.

At the point when these writers and filmmakers recorded their impressions of the war, most of them were to some degree oriented toward the Soviet Union. Some, such as Koestler and Regler, were connected to the Comintern. Others, such as Hemingway, were not institutionally involved but had personal links (Hemingway with Koltsov, who got several items by him into *Pravda*) and were exploring the possibility of closer commitment, while Koltsov, Erenburg, and Karmen were on assignment from the Soviet government. All their works, as I will show, bear the marks of their closeness to the Soviet Union in that, to varying degrees, they use the discourse and symbols of Stalinist culture. Whether or not they were adopted consciously must remain moot, but if nothing else, the similarities among all these works point to the extent to which the intellectual and cultural universes of Soviet and Western leftist intellectuals were converging during this historical moment, dominated for them by the looming threat of fascism.

In the narratives and films occasioned by the Spanish Civil War you see much commonality. One standard theme, found in de Rougement as well, is that authenticity is best achieved in extremis, the extremis of an all-consuming, fateful passion, the extremis of facing death.[36] In these texts there is often an implicit claim to representing greater political truth by showing those facing death. In Joris Ivens's *Spanish Earth,* this idea is virtually explicit when Hemingway in voice-over comments at one point that the audience is seeing a true representation, because "men cannot act before the camera in the presence of death." This had been a major theme for Hemingway. In much of his earlier fiction, he showed his characters facing up to death, whether in a bullfight, in big game hunting, or in war. Even his descriptions of sex were often structured as taking the lovers to some sort of brink or beyond, as a form of dying, to return only after the love act is over.

The challenge was to represent war, but more particularly death, accurately, nonmelodramatically, so that it would seem all the more authentic. Though an elegiac tone was used at times, death and dying are generally depicted not as a heroic sacrifice but either in a very understated way, so as to enhance the author or director's claim to objectivity, or with exuberance.

Exuberance is a common general trait of the fictional narratives. They avoid showing fixity and stasis, so caught up are they, as in the Mukhina statue, in the frisson of frenetic movement. But this also characterized the lifestyle of their authors. The prototypical intellectual who found himself in Spain was the peripatetic leftist, the restless adventurer, such as Erenburg or Hemingway. Of Joris Ivens it has been said that "as a 'Flying Dutchman' he traveled from one country to another to record their revolutions, but he rarely returned to any of them, except China. He was a fleeing and fleeting Dutchman, always looking for a country where his utopian dream might match the historical moment";[37] Malraux has been characterized as "a heroic fugitive from the commonplace."[38]

Regler, who had gone to Spain from Moscow, suggests in his later memoir *The Owl of Minerva* that he and many others rushed off to Spain in the hope of recapturing the true revolution that they felt was being so hopelessly distorted in Soviet Russia with the arrests and show trials. At the time it was widely believed, he reports, that only from outside Russia could any renewal come.[39] Regler suggests that Koltsov, with whom he associated both in Moscow and in Spain, also sought this.

In this account, Republican Spain was seen as a bulwark not only against fascism but also against what is glibly labeled Stalinist "totalitarianism." Ex post facto accounts are often rationalizations of behavior, casuistic and self-serving, particularly suspicious in one such as Regler, who had in the meantime changed sides, so that we cannot necessarily assume that this account of the quest for the true spirit of revolution represents his motivation at the time. After all, both he and Koltsov were sent to Spain on a Party or Comintern assignment (a fact that in his novel *The Great Crusade* he leaves out of the sketch of the biography of Commissar Albert, a character who largely represents Regler himself).

Yet, true or false as Regler's account may be in his or other individual cases, it has its own logic in that from the very beginning intellectuals had welcomed Republican Spain as an antidote to constricting, bourgeois Europe (or Soviet Russia). In *The Owl of Minerva,* Regler cites the increasingly puritanical legislation of sex in the Soviet Union as one of the reasons for fleeing to the Spanish Civil War. Just as in so much Soviet theater, film, and opera of the late thirties, such as the stage version of *Anna Karenina,* women in the throes of authentic passion were counterposed to the hypocritical and constraining society in which they lived, one dominated by a retrograde church, in the Spanish Civil War the Republican camp represented, in the imagination of many supporters, the site of authentic revolutionary passion that would confound bourgeois Europe and the stultifying, bureaucratic Soviet Union where the Revolution was if not "betrayed," as Trotsky had accused it of being, at any rate compromised and stale. The new regime in Spain promised the recovery of a secular, cosmopolitan, enlightened culture.

The Republicans in Spain, many of them anarchists, saw themselves as pitted against pillars of the old order. They were particularly against the Church, with an anticlericalism that was expressed in an orgy of destroying churches (the Nationalists represented their own campaign as a religious crusade, taking as its precedent the Christian reconquest of Spain from the Moors).[40] The atrocities against priests were rationalized by tales of sexual exploitation, rape, and other heinous atrocities perpetrated by the clergy or Franco's forces. Many also rejected the rigid Catholic sexual morality with its emphasis on conventional marriage; de facto marriages or temporary liaisons were the order of the day, and some women gave birth at the front to the fruits of casual liaisons (for example Paquita in *The Great Crusade*).

The Republicans were also against conformism and crass materialism (not in any case very possible during a wartime of critical shortages). While Soviet architectural journals waxed lyrical about garages for cars, furniture, kitchen fittings, and modern conveniences such as those found in affluent American homes (as was often explicit), in Republican Spain, by contrast, everyone operated in very rudimentary conditions and took pride in that fact. In Barcelona, Hugh Thomas in his classic history of this war reports, no one dared be seen in middle-class clothes. To wear a tie was to risk arrest.[41] The mono, a worker's one-piece overall, became an unofficial uniform of the Republican as an antibourgeois statement.

In both the memoirs and the fiction of the antifascist intellectuals who went to Republican Spain, the story is one of constant comings and goings, of moving around from one front to the other, and of sporadic and brief intersections with one or another fellow traveler. This made for exciting stories, one reason why these works were so popular. Intellectuals who wrote about their experiences there could represent themselves as men of action, reversing the long-standing convention for representing intellectuals in communist literature as weak, shiftless, and unreliable.

Nowhere is this frenetic movement more apparent than in Koltsov's *Spanish Diary*. Koltsov began his *Diary* in December 1937, immediately after his final return from Spain that November, at a time when the fate of the war was to a degree decided. He called his memoirs a diary, and indeed the text has the diary format, with dated entries, but it is in fact a reworking of a selection of his *Pravda* dispatches from the front. Another difference from a genuine diary is that Koltsov introduced into the narrative a second persona for himself, that of a Mexican journalist named Miguel Martinez. As Koltsov makes explicit, his choice of country is because Mexico had a revolution, too, and Miguel is of course a Spanish version of Koltsov's name, Mikhail; in fact Miguel was his own nom de guerre in Spain, and the physical description of Miguel resembles Koltsov, right down to the headaches.[42] Thus, the diary's ostensible author has two personae; he is both a writer and a politician cum commander, as was true of Koltsov himself. One cannot differentiate between the two, and probably Koltsov himself did not either. He was both a Soviet functionary and a revolutionary Romantic and cosmopolitan.

The actual trajectory of Republican Spain was one of increasing loss of territory to Franco's forces, but this aspect, though not omitted, pales before the representation of the struggle in these texts as an adventure narrative. Koltsov, and several of the other authors discussed here, contrived to give the events in Spain the aura of romance. Suspense, intensity, and bravado are hallmarks of their texts. Koestler's *Dialogue with Death* provides suspense as the autobiographical protagonist waits in a Nationalist jail for the moment when he will be taken out and shot. Hemingway in *For Whom the Bell Tolls* derives intensity less from military escapades than from sexual encounters (between his protagonist, Jordan, and the simple Spanish girl Maria) that in the jaws of death become so intense that "the earth moved." In most accounts of this war, however, the erotic has been leached out in favor of the vertigo of combat. Jean-François Lyotard has said of Malraux flying with his squadron in Spain: "with bombs and machine guns on board and with enemy fighters hurtling down out of the clouds: paradise!"[43]

As the largely autobiographical protagonists of these writings experience the war, they pass from dramatic situation to dramatic situation in an accelerating succession. The rush of events makes Koltsov's diary chronicle of civil war Spain seem more genuine, as if he is taking his readers through an uncharted course. He gives them the impression that they are in the thick of events, using standard conventions for oral narration in Russian such as switching from the past to the present tense for all dramatic moments, often using such temporal markers as the adverb "now." As the action reaches a climax, he adopts a telegraphic style with very brief sentences, some without verbs or subjects. Malraux in *Days of Hope* used similar techniques in his account of the bombing of Madrid told from the point of view of a dazed eyewitness struggling to find any bearings in the smoke and flying debris.

Koltsov's *Diary* features hair-raising trips by plane and car. In one of its more exhilarating mad dashes by car, he and his chauffeur, a "pair of crazies [oderzhimykh]," cheating death at every turn, hurtle down a road recently overtaken by the Nationalists and subject to enemy fire. When they reach the most dangerous section, he instructs the chauffeur to "give it everything you've got," and they proceed at breakneck speed, the bullets whizzing past but miraculously missing them.[44]

Regler's *Great Crusade* and Malraux's *Days of Hope* likewise get a lot of voltage out of escapades in cars or planes. In *The Great Crusade* a soldier comments as Dr. Werner's car speeds past: "The crazy fool—he eats up bullets."[45] *Hope* has two protagonists, Manuel and Magnin (both names, perhaps not coincidentally, begin with the letter *M* as does Malraux), and its narrative alternates between accounts of one and then the other. Much of the Manuel plotline concerns dramatic events associated with cars (wrecks, suicidal crashes), and Magnin, like Malraux, is a commander of an air squadron. For the film *Espoir,* a radically pared-down version of *Hope,* Malraux took out many incidents and characters, but two that he kept from the novel and around which he built the film are a suicidal head-on car crash and a plane crash at Teruel.

The cult of death-defying speed in cars and airplanes, sometimes ending in the most glorious of crashes, is not just a heady Romanticism but also potentially participates in myths of the European avant-garde. Since at least Filippo Tommaso Marinetti's "Founding and Manifesto of Futurism" of 1909, which opens with exuberant Futurists setting off in a car at breakneck speed, only to crash into a ditch to general merriment, speeding by means of new means of transportation, riding the technological marvels of the new age such as the motorcar and the airplane, had been an avant-garde signature.

The protagonists' bravado in these texts could also be seen as representing the appropriation of techniques from popular Western films and novels to serve the ideological cause. But this bravado also fits with the overall Soviet narrative of movement forward at a revolutionary pace. Prowess in aviation and long-distance motorcar races were features of Stalinist official culture. In fact Karmen had been dispatched to the Spanish engagement straight from filming a long-distance motorcar race over three thousand kilometers from the deserts of Kara-Kum to Moscow.[46]

The dizzying pace in these works renders them hyperbolically antistasis and contrasts with the representation of the war in George Orwell's *Homage to Catalonia,* where nothing much happens for long stretches of time. The soldiers in his unit, confined to one place, experience the war largely as an endless everyday round of mud, filth, rats, and malfunctioning equipment. Not coincidentally, perhaps, Orwell's account is that of a disillusioned leftist and consequently he demythologizes and chronicles the unraveling of Republican spirit, while the writers who as yet remained enthusiasts indulged in adventure romance.

Though the films were generated from within the same milieu as the fictional and nonfictional writings, they present an interesting contrast in this respect. Far from exultation in speed and adventure, their hallmark was the understatement. Their commentaries present the atrocities in a strikingly dispassionate way, particularly marked in the laconic style of Hemingway's voice-over in *Spanish Earth.* The anguish of the bombing victims is often left to the audience to sense. For example, pedestrians walk over or around bodies in a matter-of-fact way as if they are not there.

The Soviet documentary film *Spain* is, however, more overtly propagandistic than *Spanish Earth* in condemning the violence outright. By contrast with Ivens, Karmen deliberately sought to capture the terror on the faces of citizens during the bombing raids, in one scene focusing on a woman with a baby carriage, in homage to the famous scene on the Odessa steps in Eisenstein's *Potemkin* (screened in Spain during the war).[47] But the text that expresses the most outrage at the carnage is *A Diary of My Times* (Les grands cimitières de la lune; 1938) by Georges Bernanos, a Catholic and monarchist; the book, part of which was published in translation in *Internatsional'naia literatura* for 1938, is a diatribe against the Falangists for their needless mass slaughter of defenseless Republicans on Majorca, and of the Catholic Church for condoning it.[48]

In a sense, representations of war, if they are to be "authentic," should be intrinsically episodic, but this makes the propagandistic function of most of these texts more problematical. Indeed, they were being produced at a time when the problem of how to reconcile the reality of contingency with the requirements of narration (as I have brought out in earlier chapters in discussions of Lukács) was a major issue in literature and literary theory. The problem of contingency, both in reality and in fiction, had acquired greater philosophical cum literary-theoretical urgency with *Nausea* (La Nausée), which Sartre, the emerging young leftist writer, had completed in 1936 and published in 1938. Its protagonist, Roquentin, thereafter in Soviet criticism a paradigmatic negative example and counterpoint to the socialist realist positive hero, posed the problem of giving coherence to the contingency and absurdity of existence, one that was not preprocessed and illusory. Benjamin's essay "The Storyteller" (published October 1936) provides another way of addressing this problem.

Different narrative strategies were used to give these novels and films about Spain cohesion and to channel the chaos and randomness of the war experience into a desired ideological framework. Most of these strategies are comparable with particular stock features of socialist realism. A common one was the plot of increasing maturation and self-awareness, *Bildung*. In both Hemingway's and Malraux's novels, death and danger are the forces that propel protagonists toward this. The act of writing also played a central role in these fictions, participating in the common assumption at this time that there was a link between writing and self-formation.[49]

The idea that by writing one can transcend the problem of the randomness of existence is particularly evident in the case of the protagonist in *For Whom the Bell Tolls,* Robert Jordan, who is a professor of Spanish but also an aspiring novelist. Jordan hopes to produce a novel from his Spanish experiences, but in a reprise of the ending of Hemingway's short story written shortly before the Spanish war began, "The Snows of Kilimanjaro" (1936), he dies before he can write the great book.

As Hemingway describes this novel project in *For Whom the Bell Tolls,* it would have given Jordan's life coherence. Hence it is a novel about a novel that will not be written, or as Denis Hollier has put it, "death blocks the hero's conversion into a novelist." Hollier musters such elements in the plot as bridges being blown up and messages failing to get through to headquarters in support of his dramatic conclusion that "the action must take place in the absence of any contact with 'narrative headquarters.'"[50]

Hemingway's protagonist wants to rewrite his life as a book, collapsing the distinction between reporting and fiction. By writing one can triumph over death, give one's life order. Robert Jordan could have written his novel, rerun the tape of his life, but death intervenes, and he does not pull it off. Actually, in Hemingway's novel there were two tandem writing projects. Another character, Karkov (based on Koltsov), is also going to write a book about his Spanish experiences, and he and Jordan discuss this. Karkov is more than just another aspiring novelist, however; he is also a potential version of Jordan's "narrative headquarters." In Jordan's ruminations about his life in the partisan group, Karkov functions as an important point of orientation as Jordan tries to think through the meaning of what he is undergoing. Potentially, Karkov is the "mentor," a character function in the standard socialist realist novel, the older and more politically conscious character who guides the young hero's political maturation.

If for much of the novel Jordan's point of reference is Karkov, Karkov's is Moscow, the place that might have provided for Jordan a "narrative headquarters." Karkov suggests that possibility to him; he proposes that Jordan read specific Marxist texts and that after the war he go to Moscow to study or work. In other words, Karkov is proposing for Jordan the program that over the course of the decade many foreign intellectuals had followed at Koltsov's instigation; one is tempted to assume that this section of the novel is fairly autobiographical and replicates the kinds of conversations Hemingway had with Koltsov. Jordan shelves his response, though the reader presumes he would not take Karkov up on the offer; and he is killed, anyway (actually, Hemingway originally wanted to make Jordan a communist but was dissuaded by his publishers).

In much of the fiction of this time, this existential theme of individual growth and self-awareness in the face of death has been conflated with the theme of growth in political consciousness that was central to the plot of the socialist realist novel. A case in point would be *Days of Hope,* where Malraux shows Manuel's progressive development from uncommitted intellectual into disciplined leader of a Republican unit, thus following the general course of the typical socialist realist plot, if in an abstracted version that makes no specific references to Marxism or Bolshevism. At the time Malraux was advocating a "reconditioned" novel, one constructed not on the basis of individual psychology but on the basis of what he called "third person psychology," so that "the character . . . is reduced to the role of novelistic accessory."[51]

Malraux, however, structured his hero's progress in consciousness much more loosely and episodically than would have been the case in a Soviet novel of this period. Manuel enters the cause only fortuitously. A friend commandeers the car he has bought to go skiing in the Sierras, because the Republicans need it to transport dynamite for blowing up bridges. As Manuel travels with the car and interacts with the Republican combatants, "suddenly" he does not care about his car any more and is caught up in the frisson of the action. The car soon crashes anyway, and Manuel becomes a Republican fighter. At the end of the novel, his political maturation is proclaimed.

Thus there is in Malraux's novel a progression from the war as an arena of adventure to war as the place where self-control and discipline are achieved. Among those who have written about this novel, there has been a debate as to how unambiguously this progression is charted.[52] Subjecting the self to "narrative headquarters" is particularly problematical for an intellectual (as discussed in Chapter 1), yet in the fiction treated here the central character is a version of the intellectual. This is not so in the films, arguably not a fortuitous difference. Malraux in *Days of Hope* repeatedly explores this problem; in one section he reflects that in order to truly engage in this war one has to have a Manichaean outlook, but intellectuals see greater complexity and have a hard time achieving this.[53]

In adapting his novel for the film *Espoir,* Malraux dispensed with its overriding narrative structure and provided no trajectory of the heroes' development and little dialogue. Neither Manuel nor Magnin emerges as a protagonist; they are just unnamed figures moving with others over a busy canvas. Malraux left out the sections where Manuel agonizes over, for example, the meaning of commitment and the morality of the purges among the Republican forces (in Hemingway we see a similar pattern, in that he shows Jordan's inner torments about the conduct of the war in the novel, but this is totally absent from his text for *Spanish Earth*). For most of *Espoir,* Malraux focuses on just two episodes selected from many in the novel: one culminates as Republican volunteers drive a car straight at a Nationalist cannon in a suicidal gesture that silences it; in the other (the penultimate episode in the novel), (Malraux's) daredevil squadron bombs a hidden airfield, destroying many enemy planes. Then one of the Republican planes is hit and crashes into a mountain. The local peasants rally to carry the dead and injured down from the mountain on stretchers in a sort of inverted road to Calvary, while unrealistically large numbers of them line the winding path down; the men raise their fists in a Republican salute.

In *Spanish Earth* Ivens adopted another strategy to give the chaotic reality of war he depicts coherence. He used as the film's climax the completion of an irrigation project in the village of Fuentadueña, the progress of which he had been presenting intermittently over the course of the film. An irrigation project was a natural subject for Ivens, whose films' dominant motif was some version of water (rain, a river, dykes), but in this film the project functions rather as, in the socialist realist novel, a particular task in construction or production provides an overarching structure. But in Ivens's film, in contrast to the conventions of Soviet socialist realism, the project of building the irrigation system, though a collective effort, has no commanders. However, just as in socialist realism the narrative of construction or production is not self-sufficient but a vehicle for an allegorical enactment of Soviet progress toward communism, here the trope of bringing "water" to a parched land stands for the promise of national fulfillment.

Some such allegorical element was commonly found in these texts about Spain. Though ostensibly based on the author's or scriptwriter's own experiences, they tended to elide the personal. This is especially true of Koltsov's *Diary*. We have a "diary" but little self. Such inner thoughts as are represented are typically speculations about what might be happening on the Red Square during a parade, yet in Koltsov's personal life at this time a drama was unfolding. After Maria left Spain in the fall of 1936, she began an affair with Ernst Busch (the German singer and composer who performed in *Measures Taken* and visited Moscow with Eisler in that connection in 1931). When she returned to Spain in the spring of 1937, it was with Busch, creating tensions suggested in *For Whom the Bell Tolls,* where she appears (unnamed), but they are nowhere to be found in the *Diary*.

In the *Diary* Koltsov seems most emotionally invested in the tragic deaths from wounds of two combatants with no personal ties to him, first the tank driver Simon,[54] then the air ace Antonio (perhaps not coincidentally, one performed feats in a land vehicle and the other in a plane). Koltsov presents the two as if each was his kin, or at least a close buddy, describing over several diary entries his visits to them in hospital and his anxieties about whether they are going to recover, raising the reader's suspense about whether they will die as he digresses to another topic, returning to the wounded fighter only an entry or two later.[55] It would appear from Hemingway's novel that Karkov's avuncular concern was actually because he had been instructed that if Madrid fell, he was to shoot Antonio rather than have him fall into enemy hands. In the diary, when Antonio dies, the narrator attends the funeral, and when the cemetery official asks if there are any kin present, he steps forward. But when the official asks the Koltsov protagonist to suggest an epitaph for Antonio, he rejects the request: there is to be no epitaph because Antonio is to be written about in *Pravda* and this will be his epitaph. This exchange highlights the fact that Antonio, like so many others whom Koltsov describes, and despite the diarist's apparent personal concern, exists not as an individual but as a symbolic figure of Soviet rhetoric.

The "tank driver Simon" and the pilot Antonio stand for the Spanish conflict as both transnational and transpersonal. By their names both are implied to be western Europeans, but they were actually Russians. Simon's real name was Semyon, and he was a Soviet soldier who was posthumously given the honor of Hero of the Soviet Union, while Antonio was Sergei Fedorovich Tarkhov, who used a Spanish name, Antonio, as his alias in Spain (a common practice).[56] This reticence about their actual nationalities is symptomatic of the degree to which Koltsov plays down Soviet involvement in the war, preferring to represent it as a struggle of the Spanish people (in keeping with Soviet government's policy to minimize public acknowledgment of its contributions). Thus, for example, though in several histories of the war the moment when the International Brigade first appears in the narrative as new defenders of besieged Madrid is foregrounded, as it is in Regler's *Great Crusade,* in Koltsov it is only mentioned at the end of a paragraph, and the brigade fighters are not accorded the typical heroic billing but described as young, inexperienced, and not knowing know how to use weapons.

The non-Soviet writers I am discussing were poised on the cusp of Soviet commitment, but just as Robert Jordan in Hemingway's novel shelves the idea of going to "Moscow," they are at their most fuzzy and ambiguous when it comes to endorsing Soviet actions. Malraux and Regler flounder somewhat when their novels touch on the problem of the Moscow show trials and the purges. In *Hope,* in one particularly ambiguous section, when a protagonist encounters a friend among those to be purged, he brushes aside the doomed man's entreaties to save him and walks on, while in *The Great Crusade,* Regler has a troubled soldier of the International Brigade rationalize these events to himself in terms of characters in Dostoevsky![57] Koestler in *Dialogue with Death* took this ambiguity to a greater extreme; he largely eschews socialist realist plot functions in favor of psychological exploration and irony. As if to debunk the heroic clichés of Bolshevik narratives, in one jail scene, when some prisoners sing the "Internationale" while one of them is being led to his execution, this gesture is seen as pitiful; as if unaware that this is their cue, the other prisoners do not join in.[58]

In representations of the war in Spain made by the antifascists, the point is almost invariably emphasized that the Republicans are fighting to preserve Spanish, and by extension European, culture. This culture is standardly represented in terms of El Greco, Goya, and especially Cervantes, some mention of whom was virtually de rigueur (the author of *Don Quixote* might seem a strange choice, but he was the Spanish national writer, and his play *La Numancia* [1582], about Spaniards resisting a Roman siege, was staged in besieged Madrid).[59] The indomitable statue of Cervantes functions as a guarantor, as it were, that "Europe," "culture," or "civilization" will prevail, withstanding the barbaric assaults. In *Spain,* for example, his statue is shown both near the beginning and near the end so that it provides a frame. For all the frenetic movement, for all the chaos of the bombing, there is something immutable, eternal.

There is a whiff of racism in these writers championing European-ness, in that they represent the Nationalist forces more often than not as Moroccans or Moors. This is historically accurate, since Franco used Moroccan units, but not to the degree that they are so identified in this fiction. Regler's novel, with its unfortunate English title *The Great Cru-sade,* is intermittently offensive, with expressions such as "black figures . . . Moroccans," "that line of black men," and "Moors, herd of beasts." The protagonist, Albert, warns: "they will make niggers out of you, you people of Cervantes and El Greco," and reminds his soldiers that "Madrid is not Addis Ababa."[60]

These texts also periodically invoke particular places or dates, gen-erally from the inventory of leftist mythology, as precedents for the struggle around which the Republican fighters orient themselves. For ex-ample, Madrid, the center of Republican Spain that the combatants are attempting to keep at all costs, is commonly represented as a mythic city, a place of revolution. In Regler's novel *The Great Crusade,* as his battal-ion of the International Brigade marched toward the besieged capital,

> at every turn on that nocturnal march they looked for the city . . .
> [with] a city soviet elected by the citizens. . . . They . . . marched on,
> faithful to the picture in their minds. Madrid was big. Madrid was
> beautiful. In Madrid's streets people strummed guitars, sang revolu-
> tionary songs; workers danced with their women around the Repub-
> lican flagpole. Children fetched stones to build the barricades.
> Young girls stood with their rifles at the loopholes.[61]

The idealized Madrid that we see in Regler is a composite of the revo-lutionary city, combining elements from the French Revolution (dancing around the flagpole), especially in the image of it that was promoted by the French Popular Front government at this time, with its mass revolu-tionary commemorations in the streets, and to some extent the Paris Commune and the Bolshevik revolution as well (electing a soviet). But this "Madrid" proves elusive, not borne out in reality. The mirage is shat-tered with the death of the brigade's beloved commander, General Lukács.

In Koltsov's "diary" another city, Moscow, functions throughout as a sort of beacon to guide both his protagonist, Miguel, and the Republi-cans generally through the dark night of the Francoist onslaught. He presents Moscow not as all those new, stolid stone buildings but, using a common trope of these years, as a "brilliant sea of lights," as if it were vis-ible from Madrid, beckoning as the home of revolution.[62] Moscow is also twinned with Madrid as an ineluctable pair—"all the world is now Ma-drid and Moscow."[63]

Moscow is in Regler's memoir *The Owl of Minerva* the dystopian state to be fled, but in Koltsov's narrative its very stability in effect makes it the dependable beacon, the guarantor, that enables the randomness, chaos, and confusion of Civil War Spain to acquire coherence. In much of the diary, events rush headlong. This very randomness not only implicitly engages the unjustness of the enemy attacks but also provides a justifica-tion for foregrounding the constancy of Moscow and the virtues of the Soviet Constitution. Koltsov largely contrives to keep the cult of Stalin out of the diary, and these two may be seen as substitutes.[64] "Moscow" is represented less as a material actuality, a place, or a political power than as the site of revolutionary ritual. Parades in the Red Square punctuate the text, giving it structure.[65] In Erenburg's *Non Pasaran!*, by contrast, there is a portrait of Stalin on the table of a Spanish officer who declares "I have read about Tsaritsyn"—the victorious battle in the Soviet Civil War whose success was accredited to Stalin.[66]

In these books, then, Moscow, Paris, and Madrid function as spatial icons, but the references are really temporal. Time and space are merged in a chronotope of revolution. Space (Paris, Moscow) is time (revolution-ary France, revolutionary Russia). Many of the participants in the conflict from the Republican side used other historical precedents for civil war being a time of revolution and of resistance to a foreign foe, such as the rising in Spain of 1808 to oust Napoleon or 1848, a time of revolutionary uprisings in several countries of Europe that interested Marx. For Koltsov, however, the main frame of reference for the Spanish conflict is less the actual Bolshevik revolution than the Soviet Civil War of 1917–1921, represented in the recurrent parallels he draws to it as a time of resistance to counter-revolutionary forces and to intervention by foreign troops. This war, rather than 1808 or 1848, was promoted by Soviet emissaries in Spain as *the* precedent for the Republicans' cause. Soviet films about it were shown all over Spain, in towns and villages, and at the front. Erenburg, who drove in from Paris in a van with a mobile screening unit, was a leader in this effort.[67]

In all, some three dozen Soviet films were shown in Republican Spain during the war. But two recent ones formed the mainstay of the Soviet cultural effort there. First, *Chapaev* (1934), by the Vasiliev "brothers," was *the* classic socialist realist film that extols the feats of an eponymous and legendary commander from the Civil War, and was the most frequently viewed film in the Spanish Republic. Many soldiers saw it repeatedly.[68] Second, Efim Dzigan's film *We Are from Kronstadt* (My iz Kronshtadta) of 1936 depicts the 1919 heroic defense of the naval base in Kronstadt in an effort to prevent the fall of revolutionary Petrograd to Yudenich's forces. The two were essentially part of the common cultural landscape of the antifascist intellectuals and were also hits in Paris.[69]

We Are from Kronstadt had been selected by the Soviet authorities to be a centerpiece of their Popular Front cultural offensive. In 1936 Vsevolod Vishnevsky, whose classic play about the Soviet Civil War, *Optimistic Tragedy*, was also performed in Madrid, wrote the script and essentially acted as the codirector.[70] He took the film on a big promotional tour around Europe whose highlight was a premiere in Paris, where he met a plethora of intellectual giants, including Man Ray, Picasso, and Joyce, the publication of whose *Ulysses* he had promoted in the Soviet Union.[71]

Vishnevsky received a big award for *We Are from Kronstadt* in the New Year's honors for 1937, and articles occasioned by this award mention how effective the film was in raising morale among combatants in Spain, where it was allegedly "taken above all as a directive for action," citing as evidence sections of Koltsov's *Spanish Diary*.[72] Then Vishnevsky was commissioned to write the text for *Spain* when Esfir Shub was recruited to direct it, using Karmen's newsreel footage. Eisenstein also negotiated with Vishnevsky at one point to do the script for a film called *Ispaniia* that would star Paul Robeson as a Moroccan negro who deserted from

Franco's forces, one of the many Eisenstein projects of this decade that never materialized.[73]

Chapaev and *We Are from Kronstadt,* though films rather than novels, both follow the standard Soviet narrative about how the protagonist grows in political consciousness. In fact all these literary texts on Spain emphasized the Spanish fighters' childishness, lack of organization, and apathy and the need to "establish organized and disciplined units."[74] But many commentators allege that the main message that Spanish viewers took from *Chapaev* and *Kronstadt* was "never retreat"; both films show the way troops who start to flee in the face of overwhelming enemy forces are turned around by their commander, face the foe valiantly despite the odds, and prevail. Koltsov "reports" in his *Spanish Diary* entry of October 25, 1936, that when the demoralized Republicans were in a tight spot as they fought the Falangists they gained courage from thinking about *We Are from Kronstadt* and threw themselves back into their battle with redoubled efforts, starting to throw hand grenades.

Several of the non-Russian texts I am discussing here also pick up on these two films. Protagonists replicate moments from them, mutatis mutandis (especially in *Hope* and *Espoir*), or watch one of them and model themselves on its fighters, looking up to its hero commander. In a scene from *Hope* that Malraux might have lifted from *We Are from Kronstadt,* "order is restored as soon as [the commander's] words are heard; the troops rally and advance."[75]

In Regler's *Great Crusade,* the precedent of the Soviet Civil War is never far from the narrative. Soldiers compare the physical attributes of their commissar with those of Chapaev's commissar in the film, and in one scene, as General Paul addresses the troops in a hall near Madrid, while the troops "listened to him open-mouthed. Something of the spell of a certain distant army wafted through the bare hall. Voroshilov on a sleek white-footed bay, galloping out of the turreted Kremlin."[76]

Almost all these texts want to stress the heroic determination of the Republicans and use the bombing of Madrid as a high point. That occurred in October–November 1936 and the war then had more than two years more to run. But the next year was in crucial respects a different historical moment. The Great Purge began, and in late 1937 the considerable Soviet investment in the Republican side lessened appreciably.[77]

These shifts had their impact on texts on the war produced later, most clearly on *Spain,* which was largely put together after the Republican cause had been lost and which is the most "Stalinist" of these texts, a distinction that affected the film at many different levels. For example, it represents an exception to a general pattern in these works of textual sparseness and understatement, particularly compared with *Spanish Earth.*

The later moment when *Spain* was finished and its voice-over added made it possible to cover the entire war, something that in itself makes the film less open-ended than the other works I have been discussing. When Shub took over, she had several Spanish cameramen shoot contemporary material in Spain, including Spanish and International Brigade soldiers retreating across the border to France, and scenes from Franco's capital, Burgos, which she added to the Karmen material.

The voice-over in *Spain* emphasizes the heinous acts of the fascists, using the discourse of the purges, not surprisingly, given that the Great Purge (1937–1939) had only just come to an end when the film was completed. Even the Republican defeat is accounted for in a narrative of treachery: "let it be that the traitors have opened the gates of Madrid to Franco, the struggle will continue . . . mercilessly." Here and elsewhere, the epithet *besposhchadnaia*—merciless—is used, *the* standard epithet of the purges.

Koltsov's *Spanish Diary* was also affected by the new times, especially in the more "Stalinist" second part that begins on New Years Eve 1937. Breathless travel, adventure, and a somewhat bohemian existence become less and less features, and the Miguel figure fades from view. One finds recurrent use of the rhetoric of the purges, such as "vigilance" and "keen eyes," an obsession with Trotskyites, and speculation that spies may be the reason for the setbacks at the front.[78]

One could assume that all of Koltsov's public incantation of the official line on the purges was simply unavoidable while the inner Koltsov was appalled, or at least disquieted, by them. But some evidence, such as a letter of Koltsov to Maria Osten of March 11, 1938, about those condemned at the Bukharin trial, casts doubt on this: "what horrendous terrible conspirators, what thugs, what base and bloody criminals! One breaks out in a sweat when one hears how a Yagoda or a Khrushchev calmly talks about the murder of Gorky and his son."[79] One can only speculate on the extent to which this letter expresses his genuine reaction, given that he would have assumed that it would be read by agents. It is impossible now to second-guess intentions, the "deep down" responses or mental set of a man who consistently endorsed in print the various purges, including those of assorted anarchist, socialist, Trotskyite, and even communist groups and individuals in Spain. A climate of suspicion and denunciation prevailed at that time, and few intellectuals, including the left leaning but relatively independent, were free of it. One sees its marks in plays, films, and novels throughout Europe of this time (such as *Mayerling,* as mentioned), including the literature and films that came out of the Spanish Civil War, such as other works by Hemingway.[80] Even Hitchcock's 1936 British film *Sabotage* is about a conspiracy of "wreckers" with links to foreign powers (a favorite Soviet accusation of the purge era) who seek to bomb London; they must be watched clandestinely by the secret police, who look to ordinary citizens for intelligence on them.[81] In addition, at the center of Eisenstein's film project of this time, *Bezhin Meadow* (Bezhin lug), is the story of Pavel Morozov, a new official hero and example for Soviet youth, who in 1932 was allegedly killed by his own father for having denounced him to the Soviet authorities as part of a kulak conspiracy to sabotage their collective farm.[82] Babel, who wrote the second version of the script, called the father a "wrecker." Thus this film represents yet another case where Eisenstein could be seen as an apologist for the purges, but the reality is more complicated. *Bezhin Meadow* did not please the authorities, and in March 1937 the film was confiscated and shooting was stopped.[83] When this was threatened, the film's supporters enrolled Feuchtwanger in the cause during his Moscow visit of 1937, and to the considerable annoyance of officialdom, he included a positive account of the film in a statement published in *Sovetskoe iskusstvo* that more or less supports the show trial of the "Trotskyite Center" that he witnessed in Moscow.[84]

Feuchtwanger was in Moscow to collect materials for what was to be called *Moscow 1937,* intended as a rejoinder to Gide's negative assessment of Soviet Russia, *Return from the U.S.S.R.* (Au retour de L' U.R.S.S.), which came out in late 1936.[85] With Gide's visit, Soviet authorities had counted on getting another prominent endorsement of the Soviet cause, and in Moscow Gide had been taken to see Babel, Pasternak, and other writers, all under Tretiakov's and Koltsov's tutelage.[86] When he proved turncoat (in Soviet eyes) officials stopped the several ongoing publications of his texts in translation.[87]

To denounce the Soviet Union at the height of the Popular Front, when the fascist menace was becoming ever more apparent (especially in Spain), was something most antifascist intellectuals hesitated to do, even though many of them were deeply disturbed by the show trials (Koestler, for example, originally had an agreement with the Party when he left it in 1938 not to attack Bolshevism openly).[88] Many in France, including Erenburg, tried to talk Gide out of publishing his book, at least until after the Spanish war was over, and Koltsov in the *Spanish Diary* relates how in Spain he met Paul Erbar, Gide's secretary and relative, and asked him to dissuade Gide when he returned to France, but in vain.[89] *Return from the U.S.S.R.* almost instantly made Gide a bête noire among the intellectuals of the Popular Front.[90] Koltsov was under pressure to write a book in response, but in the event it was a "Greek" (foreigner), Feuchtwanger, who did so with *Moscow, 1937*.[91] Though archival materials on Feuchtwanger's visit to Moscow reveal his dissatisfactions with the conditions he encountered in the Soviet Union and his distress at the purge trials, he largely suppressed his doubts and reservations for the book, which was translated into Russian for mass editions.[92] The disaster for Moscow of *Return from the U.S.S.R.* was also to some extent mitigated by the bombing of Guernica on April 26, 1937, which gave antifascist intellectuals a renewed sense of the urgency of their collective efforts.[93]

Koltsov was not in Spain at the time of that bombing (though he mentions it at the end of part 2) because he had been recalled to Moscow and asked to prepare the new Congress for the Defense of Culture, a sequel to the Paris Congress of 1935, this time held in Spain from July 4 to 7, 1937, and finishing in Paris on July 17. (In 1936, before the war broke out in Spain, Malraux had been in Moscow to help organize this congress.) One may assume that another reason for Koltsov's recall was to discuss the Gide debacle, and doubtless to exculpate himself, as unfortunately for him, he was centrally implicated in Gide's visit. When he returned to Spain in May 1937, en route he visited Feuchtwanger in France for two days, an event to which he gives particular emphasis, in that it opens book 3; the visit was doubtless to influence the book Feuchtwanger was writing, based on his trip to the Soviet Union of December 1936–January 1937.[94]

The 1937 Writers Congress that Koltsov had returned to Moscow to prepare, had its pathos, in that it took place when the antifascist cause in Spain was palpably imperiled, if not hopeless (the delegates needed no reminder of this, for at night they had to take shelter in the hotel basement as bombs fell all around).[95] But it was not conducted in the spirit of the 1935 Congress. Almost all the Soviet delegates denounced Gide, as well as the recently purged high-ranking Soviet military officers Mikhail Tukhachevsky and Yona Yakir. (Feuchtwanger did not actually attend.) Koltsov in his speech lumped Trotskyites together with Hitler, fascist Italy, and militaristic Japan.[96]

Though Erenburg attended the conference, he was already distancing himself from this version of the Soviet antifascist cultural front, and he wrote to Koltsov on July 16, 1937, after the Congress, asking to be excluded from the secretariat of the Association for the Defense of Culture.[97] He was beginning to experience the new times himself; in late 1937, he was denied an external passport to return to Paris from Moscow, securing one only after his second petition reached Stalin (he had been forced in the meantime to attend the show trial of his friend Bukharin). Koltsov was in any case no longer working on the affairs of the Association after July 1937.[98] The days when each manned one pole of the Moscow-Paris antifascist movement were over.

Koltsov's role and intentions in Spain and in the 1930s generally have been subject to diametrically opposite interpretations. Some Western historians of the war dismiss him out of hand as an NKVD agent or even claim that he was involved in the purges within the Republican ranks in Spain.[99] But Koltsov, who was deeply committed to the Republican cause and was one of the Soviet Union's leading advocates of internationalism, should not be written off completely in such terms. Indirect evidence of his not being solely "Stalin's man" comes in the fact that, as Daniel Kowalsky reports in his history, some of the Karmen newsreels, which Koltsov largely supervised and for which he wrote many of the captions, "giv[e] prominence and respectability to Spanish anarchists, while . . . [in] another a caption refers to 'Barcelona: center of revolutionary Catalonia' (this despite the Soviet advisors' well-deserved reputation as fierce enemies of popular revolution in the Catalan capital)."[100] In addition, almost all the foreign intellectuals who crossed paths with Koltsov in Spain give him a good press, some drawing a distinction between him and other Soviet emissaries of whom they were wary.[101] The list includes Hemingway, but also even those such as Regler, who had become disillusioned with communism. Rather than choose one of these characterizations as correct, I would suggest that there was a blurring of roles and identities in Koltsov himself—as an exotic, freewheeling intellectual, a drinking buddy of Hemingway, and at the same time a Soviet apologist, "Stalin's man," or a Comintern agent.

The Good Prince

While all-out passion and mad, headlong dashes were features of Soviet culture in this period, Stalin favored a sudden reversal extricating the subject from his death course. He generally wanted the good guys yanked from the brink, rather as in silent movies the heroine is always yanked from the tracks just before the approaching train reaches her. In the production of *Anna Karenina* the curtain came down before the "train" reached the heroine, and in a sense in the purge trials, the country was effectively shown to have been yanked from the brink of being sold out to the capitalists and fascists by "enemies" working within. Many of the publicly staged dramas, especially those in the Arctic North, such as the Chelyuskin or Papanin expeditions (see Chapter 8) featured entire expeditions on the brink of perishing when at the last moment a Stalin-organized rescue force arrived and they were saved. And though Eisenstein had originally planned to end *Alexander Nevsky* (1938), another text marked by exuberance in battle, with Nevsky dying a martyr's death while returning from a diplomatic mission to the Mongol khan, Stalin apparently protested that "such a good prince must not die," prompting Eisenstein to finish the film with the ceremony celebrating victory in the Battle on the Ice."[102] In the script of his earlier film project *Bezhin Meadow*, Eisenstein had been able to resist instructions that at the end the young hero not die; instead, as he dies, his Komsomol mentor keeps his spirits up by talking of the new Moscow, all lit up (like Koltsov's vision of Moscow in *Spanish*

Diary) and transformed, with its grand houses and theaters and the stars on the Kremlin towers burning. Do such examples suggest that the intellectuals were caught up in a romantic infatuation with death but not the state?

Actually, at this time among intellectuals, death from fatal passion and death from military engagement were controversial options for a work's plot. In the initial libretto for Prokofiev's *Romeo and Juliet* (which premiered in Brno in December 1938), written by Sergei Radlov, who had directed the 1935 production of *King Lear* in the Yiddish theater, the lovers were spared from death by the friar appearing at the last moment and preventing Juliet from committing suicide, but this resolution sparked fierce debate among intellectuals and was ultimately reversed in the libretto.[103]

As we well know, in reality not everyone was yanked from the brink, not everyone rated as a "good prince." Many intellectuals were purged in 1937, among them Tretiakov. He was arrested while a patient at the Kremlin Hospital on July 26, 1937, even as the Madrid Congress was proceeding, and shot on September 10, not to be rehabilitated until 1956 after Khrushchev came to power. Brecht was distraught when he heard the news and wrote his poem "Is the People Infallible?" questioning the judgment.

Arosev, the head of VOKS, was arrested in June or July 1937, about the same time as Tretiakov. But several other writers arrested in 1937 were from the opposite camp to Tretiakov, former members of RAPP who were now accused of being Trotskyite. One of them, Afinogenov, the enthusiast who wrote *Salute, Spain,* was not arrested but was thrown out of the Writers Union and the Party and spent most of the year in anguished limbo.

The main charge against Tretiakov was that he had lost heavily at cards while in Vladivostok in 1919 and that when he was confronted, in 1924 in Harbin, by a document about a debt he could not pay, he was forced to spy for the Japanese (his wife, however, as is evident from her interrogation transcript, refused to endorse this narrative).[104] Rather than investigating Tretiakov's work on the Foreign Commission, the accusers supplied a fantastic narrative of spectacular gambling debts, honor, and revenge in an exotic clime (particularly fantastic, since Tretiakov was so puritanical that it was far-fetched that he would even be playing cards). Such a narrative could have been lifted from a Romantic prose work from the nineteenth century by Pushkin or Lermontov, though updated, in that instead of the protagonist being forced to fight a duel, he is made to spy. Tretiakov, the theorist of "Literature of Fact" who (as we saw in Chapter 1) in the late 1920s and early 1930s denounced novels and fiction as inappropriate for the new Soviet age was forced to compose the last text of his life in that mode.

The Romantic adventure tale closely linked to the drama of all-out passion was but one variant of the return of the Romantic at this time. The fantastic tales generated by the state needed settings and tropes adequate to their import. As we shall see in the next chapter, the dominant mode was a version of the sublime.

CHAPTER 8

The Imperial Sublime

W E HAVE ALREADY seen how the new emblem for the nation, the
Mukhina statue atop the Soviet pavilion at the 1937 Paris Exposition, ostensibly representing a worker and a peasant, extended the dynamic upward sweep of the pavilion and transposed its subjects from the
workplace where one might have been expected to find them to a sublime, naturalized world. But sublime images dominated late 1930s Soviet
culture generally. Breathtaking panoramas and wild nature abounded in
novels and films, even those ostensibly about production.[1] And landscape
painting, with which much eighteenth-century writing on the sublime
and the beautiful is explicitly associated but which had not before been a
significant genre in Soviet art, came into vogue.

The new vogue for dramatic landscapes was not just a matter of taste.
The sublime provided inspiring tropes for allegories of national identity.
A similar trend has been observed in late eighteenth-century England
and in mid-nineteenth-century America, when painting emerged as a preeminent art form and "images of the landscape and ideas of the nation
were deeply intertwined."[2] In the Soviet Union of the late 1930s, film also
assumed a key role in shaping and articulating identity with images of
wilderness and of towering peaks.

At this time, with fascism a rising menace to the west and Japanese expansionism to the east, Soviet culture became increasingly obsessed with national consolidation, and the sublime proved useful in providing tropes for articulating power relations. Early nineteenth-century Russian literature had presented the Caucasus as a sublime, especially in the work of Pushkin and Lermontov, whose Caucasian fiction and poetry has been analyzed in terms of Russian imperialism and the southward thrust of conquest.[3] Now these writers were in vogue once again.

Here, however, I am not exploring the influence of nineteenth-century Romanticism on Stalinist culture. Rather, I am proposing the theory of the sublime as it has been classically formulated, primarily in texts of the eighteenth century, as a heuristic model for discussing characteristic narratives and tropes of Stalinist culture. More, I am proposing the sublime as a dominant that structures these tropes and narratives in a poetics of space.

I would like to suggest that instead of invoking the timeworn idea that Stalinism was essentially a new variety of the Christian religion, we might entertain the possibility that it would be more appropriate to classify the culture of the late 1930s as a version of the sublime. But first some sense of what I take the term to mean.

The Sublime

There are several different versions of what the sublime means, even in the classic formulations of Kant, Hegel, and Schiller, Longinus and Edmund Burke,[4] but there are a few generally agreed-on features. The first of these is that the sublime is iconically found in some dramatic natural formation—a looming crag, a deep ravine, a crashing waterfall, the toppling boulder, a raging torrent. This is a formation that the viewer comes across suddenly, and most often in a place far from his or her humdrum everyday world. Though conventionally found in nature, the sublime is not confined to it; Burke, for example, said that the sublime can be found in anything earthly, including human constructions, if its dimensions are "huge and grand."[5] The Soviet Union with its colossi already had what might be classified as a technological and architectural sublime, but in the late thirties imagery from nature was more often used.

The sublime is also usually associated with scenes with potential for adventure and suspense. A typical array of sublime settings, one said to characterize the paintings of a noted artist of the sublime, Salvator Rosa, encompasses places of "desolation, solitude and danger, impenetrable forests, rocky or storm-lashed shores . . . lonely dells leading to dens and caverns of banditti, alpine ridges, trees blasted by lightning or sapped by time, or stretching their extravagant arms against a murky sky, louring or thundering clouds, or suns shorn of their beams."[6] Such sights contrast with landscapes of beauty, said to exude harmony, symmetry, and order (values more readily associated with architecture). The sublime violates the norms of beauty, but it thrills the beholder with what Schiller, in an access of Sturm und Drang enthusiasm extolled as "bold disorder."

Thus, no matter how immobile its elements may be, a sublime scene is fundamentally dynamic. It is all about affect and elicits an emotional response. The sublime is a site of drama, derived in part from the very dimensions of the phenomena presented. The term itself, "sublime," corresponds to the Greek *hypsos*, height, and a dramatic verticality—towering cliffs, craggy towers, giant trees—is crucial to the notion of the sublime (in the eighteenth-century, mountains, following in part Rousseau's apostrophe on the Alps in his *Confessions,* were added to its inventory).[7] But along with a marked verticality goes an extreme horizontality, either implicitly or explicitly an affect of this verticality. The heights afford a panoramic vision stretching almost endlessly. Indeed, all the dimensions are hypostasized, including depth (deep caves, steep ravines falling away).

So tremendous are the dimensions that the sight of the sublime overwhelms the viewer, giving him or her an apprehension of infinity. Burke, in his classic source on it, *A Philosophical Enquiry into Our Ideas of the Sublime and the Beautiful* (1757), elaborates: "the eye not being able to perceive the bounds of many things, they seem to be infinite, and they produce the same effects as if they really were."[8] One will note here the "as if" suggesting that essentially invocations of the sublime are tropological rather than about actual natural formations. But it is also generally "as if" in the sense that the beholder experiences the vertiginous danger vicariously or at a distance, perhaps only in a sublime scene in art.

Characteristically, the beholder comes across a sublime scene suddenly, triggering an epiphanic moment. Some of the most famous examples are to be found in the poetry of Wordsworth and Byron. A paradigmatic moment comes in Wordsworth's autobiographical poem *The Prelude or Growth of a Poet's Mind* (1805) when the protagonist is tramping on Mount Snowdon and "like a flash" the light of the moon illumines the terrain to reveal a boundless stretch of dramatic crags stretching to the sea.[9] As in other similar passages of this work,[10] Wordsworth intimates here a power that transcends both nature and the senses. His epiphany involves not just being able to see revealed that which was obscured by the mist and dark but, more important, a revelation about the human mind and the capacity of the imagination. In "higher minds," a creative capacity puts them intimately in touch with a realm beyond sensuous reality, an effect also achieved in Caspar David Friedrich's paintings, which often direct the viewer's gaze into a limitless space.

When in such texts the viewer is suddenly afforded the panoramic view, he or she senses a greater power or reality, a transcendent. Several classic theoreticians of the sublime stress its relation to the Absolute, to God. Hegel in effect did away with the props of the sublime (all those crags and crashing waterfalls) and discussed it in terms of the relationship between God and man, the infinite and the finite. To him, God is "incapable of expression in his *positive* essence in anything finite and mundane."[11] And despite the sublime's secularization at the hands of some of the Romantics, it retained its association with transcendence and the Absolute. As Weiskel has observed, whether or not God is inferred, the Sublime involves an apprehension of power and a "massive transposition of transcendence into a naturalistic key."[12]

In Stalinist Russia, the sublime was very functional as a source of narrative strategies for, effectively, naturalizing Stalinist power. Most paradigmatically the encounter with Stalin himself was presented as an encounter with a sublime figure, especially in film. One common topos is the visitor to Stalin who is struck dumb and cannot express himself or herself in words at the sight of the leader whose person exceeds all norms. This is in the tradition of the sublime whereby, as Terry Eagleton puts it, "[God] defeats all representation and strikes language dumb—which is to say, in aesthetic terms, that he is sublime."[13] In Grigory Alexandrov's fourth musical film of the 1930s, *The Radiant Path* (Svetlyi put'; 1940) the heroine when presented with an award by an eminence in the Kremlin, a personage too overwhelming to be represented on the screen and only inferred, she swoons and is transported by a magic-carpet-like car ride to a sparkling white world.[14]

But in classic theories of the sublime, an important affect is not just the vertiginous thrill experienced by the beholder but also terror. Kant and, especially, Burke stressed this aspect. Sublime power so transcends the bounds of the finite and the mortal that the individual encountering it is gripped by a sense of being threatened with obliteration; its "thrill" can be terrifying. As Burke explains: "when we contemplate the Deity, . . . so vast an object . . . we shrink into the minuteness of our own nature, and are, in a manner, annihilated before him . . . if we rejoice, we rejoice with trembling." But as we sense here, the sublime was often seen as having a contradictory character. Burke wrote of its "delightful horror,"[15] while Schiller, remarked its dual nature: "the feeling of sublimity . . . appears as horror, and of *joyfulness,* which can amount to transport."[16]

It hardly needs pointing out that the late 1930s were in the Soviet Union an age of terror in the most literal sense, an age when, as Eagleton defines the sublime in *Holy Terror,* "reason flips over into madness."[17] "Terror" and "trembling" were dominant emotions, "trembling" before the might of Stalin but also "trembling" at the ever-present danger of being arrested, as people were overwhelmed by the sheer scale of the arrests (though as Burke stresses, a certain distance from the pain is necessary for the experience to be truly sublime). But at the same time, much of Hegel's *Aesthetics, the* source for his account of the sublime, was appearing in Russian translation and was being promoted in *Literaturnyi kritik* and elsewhere by members of Lukács coterie.[18] Even Kant's aesthetics were explicated extensively in this journal (if critically),[19] and examples from Hegel and Schiller, who had long been important in Russian intellectual discourse, together with Belinsky and others influenced by them, were recurrently cited in its critical and theoretical articles.[20] The collection of Schiller's articles on the aesthetic published in 1935 (mentioned in the Introduction), a collection that opens with a long introductory essay by Lukács, includes both of Schiller's essays on the sublime.

It could be said that the appropriation of sublime imagery by the Soviet rhetoric of the late 1930s was a move to make Soviet "reality" adequate to the terror. These extreme times demanded a Stalin and a nature (reality) of hypostasized, awe-inspiring dimensions. But the terror, the purges, can be seen not as a separate phenomenon for which sublime imagery is necessary, in compensation for the terror, as it were, but actually as integral to this dominant mode of the sublime. Though bureaucratic procedures continued with mandatory protocols of interrogations, transportation lists, and so on throughout the purges, such practices were secondary to the drama of the sublime with its fantastic tales of nefariousness, which citizens could contemplate with thrill or "terror."

The rhetoric about the nation's enemies had changed. In the early 1930s, speeches and editorials enjoined the populace to get rid of the enemies as "vermin," as unclean elements, as it were, threatening the "city of light." But in the transcripts of the show trials, "enemies" are referred to as wild beasts and brigands, as characters from a Romantic adventure tale, or as figures that might be conjured up by the imagination at the sight of a sublime landscape (though admittedly some Christian imagery was used as well, such as "Judas-Trotsky").

Theoreticians of the sublime promoted its pedagogical potential and proffered the possibility of a higher order self-formation, what Hegel characterizes as an *"elevation* of the mind." In the accounts of Hegel and Schiller the sublime functions as a way of overcoming the old dualism between the material and the "spiritual" or mental, of breaking down the distinction between the subjective and the objective, as Lukács emphasized in his introduction to the Russian translations of Schiller. In the scenarios they outline, there is a tripartite drama involving the inner man, the external world, and the Absolute or transcendent. Hegel discusses this in terms of Romantic art in general. In his *Aesthetics* he identifies "spiritual elevation" as the fundamental principle of Romantic art. This "elevation" was to be achieved by tuning in to the Absolute, and rejecting the "external contingency of existence" in favor of "the inner life which shines in itself," bathing in its "inner bliss."[21] As he explains:

> The entire content [of Romantic art] is therefore concentrated on the inner life of the spirit, . . . the inner battle of man in himself and his reconciliation with God. . . . But since this absolute content appears compressed at one point, i.e., into the *subjective* heart, . . . the

scope of the subject matter is therefore also *infinitely* extended again. It opens out into a multiplicity without bounds.[22]

The contradictory nature of the Sublime with its simultaneity of two extreme reactions in the beholder—joy/terror—is paralleled by the absolute contrast of the two key poles of the narrative: the extra-ordinary extension of sublime phenomena in the physical world and its locus in the inner, "intimate" sphere. In Hegel's scenario, the subject has incorporated the sublime into his inner being, but this sequence can be achieved only by the mediating function of the Absolute. In Stalinist culture, somewhat analogously, a hyperbolic extension of all possible dimensions in the external world was twinned with its logical opposite, an "intimate" innerness as the subject comes to recognize that true sublimity resides within the self, but a self that has sought out and internalized a transcendent.

The motif of incorporating the sublime within the mental life of the self was also central to Schiller's scenario for individual encounter with the sublime. His account, though different from Hegel's in significant respects, was perhaps even closer to the Stalinist appropriation of the sublime. In Schiller's version, the subject engages with the sublime, and this very engagement frees him from the humdrum in scenarios not unlike the ones we saw in chapter 8 where the Anna Kareninas and Emma Bovarys chose passionate engagement over dull conventional existences: "the aspect of boundless distance and immeasurable height, the wide ocean at his feet, and the great ocean before him, rescue his spirit from the narrow sphere of the actual and the oppressive confinement of physical life. He is presented with a larger unit of measure by the simple majesty of nature, and, surrounded by her noble shapes, his mind no longer brooks the mean and narrow."[23] Schiller, then, rather than seeing the sublime as an alternative to beauty but lesser, privileges it, giving it a central role in his epistemological and anthropological system. To him, beauty, harmony, a refined taste, and so on can satisfy only until the individual has come face to face with "bold disorder," something outside the neat systems of "connections" that hold sway in "the saloons and students' cells" but are essentially tame, boring, domestic, and even "counterfeit."[24]

In Schiller, the reward for facing "bold disorder" is "freedom," breaking out of the confines of the "mean and narrow" that characterize the "dweller in the cities" who applies himself "so readily to trifles" and becomes consequently "stunted and withered." "Freedom . . . is a spectacle for noble minds, infinitely more interesting than welfare and regularity without freedom, where the sheep patiently follow the shepherd, and the self-ruling will is degraded into the subservient fragment of a machine."[25] Such notions as the "self-ruling will" and the deprecation of "welfare," "regularity," and characterizing citizens following societal norms as "sheep" were of course problematical in a Stalinist context that took pride in its "socialist" identity but also expected political conformism, yet Stalinist political culture featured narratives akin to Romanticism's one about breaking with the tame and ordinary, the petty and domestic, and even the dictates of common sense in the name of a possibility that could simply take the breath away.

What Schiller called the "bold disorder" of the sublime does not in his view submit to ready tabulation or categorization. Consequently, though scientific discovery has been involved in the conception of the sublime, the sense of science that has been favored in that conception has not been that of faithful recording, exactitude, and classification, values that were typical of the Enlightenment era. The grand and commanding conceptions produced by the sublime are not subject to rational disquisition. Most theoreticians of the sublime (Burke, Hegel, Schiller, etc.), in attempting to define it, spoke of an experience of a power that exceeds the quantifiable and the usable. Something comparable can be seen in Stalinist science, where the pressure was on to pull off something extraordinary, something that defied all previous conceptions and measurements, even the received laws of nature.

One example can be seen in the Stalinist hero-scientists who worked in agriculture. One of them, Ivan Michurin, was featured in a documentary film selected for screening at the Paris Exposition in the Soviet pavilion that featured the Mukhina statue. This film, *The Transformer of Nature* (Preobrazovatel' prirody), presented Michurin as "a man who spent sixty years of his life reconstructing nature."[26] His "reconstruction" and denial of genetic determinism had been picked up by Trofim

Lysenko; *Pravda* boasted in 1938 that no writer of fantastic fiction had been able to match his feats in agriculture.[27]

Stalinist culture featured individuals who were alleged to have pulled off scientific feats in a sort of literalization of the sublime model of the "self-willed" individual who engages that which does not fit in with the neatly ordered and interconnected conventions and who is thereby "elevated" to a higher order of humanity. The best known of these, the Stakhanovite, the exemplum of the Soviet production hero of that time, was the titanic figure who with his own hands performs extraordinary feats that go way off all the charts for norms of production, thereby defying rational, "exact" science and confounding the calculations of the possible made by engineers and other trained professionals. In a sense, the narrative about the Stakhanovites is a bowdlerized version of the Schillerian Promethean. Stakhanov might seem a curious emblem for a society committed to large-scale, modernized industry. Just as the sublime in the account of Romantics is "ultimately about intuition,"[28] his feats involve a version of the Romantic notion of the inner genius. Though the Stakhanovite's feat was basically one of brawn, it was cast as epistemological. Typically, Alexei Stakhanov's name would appear in a list of some of the greatest Russian scientists, such as Lomonosov, Mendeleev, and Pavlov.[29]

The late thirties, when arguably the Sublime became dominant in Soviet culture, coincides with the time when Stalinist ideology was codified in its final form. At this time ideology, too, became naturalized. The year 1938, the year of the Bukharin trial, saw the publication of a landmark text, *The History of VKP (b): Short Course* (Istoriia Vsesoiuznoi kommunisticheskoi partii [bol'shevikov]. Kratkii kurs). This book was allegedly "edited by a Commission of the Communist Party," but Stalin had a major hand in its writing;[30] between 1938 and 1940 it was published in forty-eight languages and 16.2 million copies.

A political primer might seem an unlikely candidate for the sublime, but we actually find a version of it in the text's crucial fourth chapter, whose second section, "On Dialectical and Historical Materialism," drawing on copious quotations from Engels, Marx, and to a lesser extent Lenin, outlines the basic structure of revolutions.[31] This chapter, as was conventional in Marxist writings, attacks the "idealist" philosophical tradition—precisely the tradition represented by Kant, but also Hegel and

Schiller—yet there are affinities between the two philosophical systems in the way this chapter naturalizes political revolution in a narrative of the sublime, though the *Short Course* alleges that its account of reality as being in constant movement contrasts with the Idealist model of alleged "peace and immobility, of stagnation and immutability."[32] This section figures revolution in terms of a shift from quantitative to qualitative change, using as its primary example the moment when water, after a progressive (quantitative) change in temperature suddenly changes in composition: heated water turns to steam, or cooled water to ice. All things in the world are interrelated, the account insists; what happens in nature also happens in the societal sphere. Phenomena in society can be "natural and inevitable" like these processes in nature. Major societal shifts occur when the class struggle heats up, as it were. History progresses not in a continuous line but rather in bursts or leaps—here the text uses Engels's term "qualitative leap" *(kachestvennyi skachok)*—whereby "qualitative changes occur not gradually but rather quickly, suddenly, in the form of a leap-like shift [skachkoobraznogo perekhoda] from one state [sostoianie] to another. They occur not by accident but in accordance with laws."[33] In other words, political revolutions are organic, though there is some equivocation on this, as the account in this section quickly backtracks and gives priority to productive forces. The model for historical progress is articulated as a form of dramatic sublime. Changes occur "suddenly," in "leaps" to a radically different "state," a transformation that transcends incremental, quantitative change.

Shortly after the *Short Course* appeared, Eisenstein published in *The Art of Cinema* (Iskusstvo kino) an article somewhat misleadingly titled "On the Structure of Things" (O stroenii veshchei). Its last section (dated January 1, 1939) is on "pathos" in cinema. Pathos was a favorite concept of Schiller, who dedicated a long essay to it of 1801 (later translated into Russian),[34] but Schiller's ideas in turn influenced Belinsky and other Russian intellectuals of the nineteenth century, who also explored the notion of pathos. Eisenstein's interpretation of "pathos" was, however, very different from Schiller's. He had been writing about pathos since the late 1920s, when he read Engels, but in this 1939 article he formulates it using a model and some vocabulary that seem to derive from the *Short Course*.[35] "Pathos" as he uses the term is in some respects comparable with "ecstasy," another term that he discusses here and that, as he explains, comes from "ex-stasis," coming "out of a state," but the word used for "state" here, *sostoianie*, is the same one used in the *Short Course* for the shift from one state to another in the "leap" from quantitative to qualitative change. In the Eisenstein essay, both "ecstasy" and "pathos," though not identical, involve going from "one's customary state" to something radically and qualitatively different, at one point explicitly identified as involving the "leap [skachok], the shift from quantity to quality." Here Eisenstein uses the *Short Course* images of water to steam or ice, iron to steel.[36] As with the sublime, then, both the "leap" and "ecstasy" have to do with epiphanic moments.

More than *skachok,* or "leap," the key term of the late thirties was, as we have seen in the rhetoric occasioned by the Mukhina statue for the Paris pavilion, *vzlët,* effectively a translation of a phenomenon from the physical world into the terms of the dramatic sublime. *Vzlët* means "takeoff," as with airplanes or birds, takeoff in flight, but it can also be used for taking off in a flight of the imagination. A telling moment came in December 1935, precisely when the culture was "taking off," when aviators paid a ceremonial visit to Stanislavsky (in itself a setup) and he was reported to have said: "you fly to the Arctic but we fly in our imagination."[37]

As in Romanticism, in the late 1930s the Sublime was privileged over beauty. The Romantics reversed the order of prominent predecessors such as Kant and Burke whereby beauty was above the sublime (though all agreed that both were valuable). But Schiller did not share their preference, as can be sensed in his disparaging comment "who does not rather linger amid the spiritual disorder of a natural landscape, than in the insipid regularity of a French garden."[38]

Stalinist culture of the late 1930s to a marked degree favored settings well away from the cities, in untamed nature. That they were generally remote makes them in a sense an alternative to a utopia: both are cut off from the outside world and idealized, but the utopia is generally an urban space. In the sublime scene we find potentially a spectacular venue for enacting revolution without the torpor of the humdrum world of offices and apartments. A feature of late 1930s culture, whether in novels, films, paintings, or the rhetoric surrounding such central public events of the political culture as the long-distance flights by aviators, was a setting that dazzled its beholder with improbable horizontal and vertical expanses.

"Height" was the central symbolic value of Soviet political culture of the 1930s, encapsulated in the phrase "Ever higher and higher." In the political culture, however, "height" was represented principally not in the workplace but in such central gestures as the feats of aviators (the sublime had been updated for the airplane), which were celebrated in the cinema, in literature, and in art. The vertical has conventionally been associated with power, and press reports on the aviators' flights established a link with Stalin that could be seen in such rituals as their planning the route under his guidance and being met by him on their triumphal return.

Stress was also laid on the nation's vast dimensions, its broad expanse. In the sagas of aviation the two dimensions, the vertical and the horizontal, are both present, whether implicitly or explicitly: the aviators went "ever higher," but their main feats were in breaking records for long-distance flight. The country's great breadth is also emphasized in the hit song of the 1936 musical *The Circus* (Tsirk), directed by Eisenstein's erstwhile collaborator Grigory Aleksandrov. The film is set in Moscow, but the tropes of its theme song come from the natural world, as it opens: "Broad is my native land / Many has it of fields, woods and rivers" (Shiroka strana moia rodnaia / Mnogo v nei polei, lesov i rek). My stilted translation is deliberate to bring out the syntactical arrangement of the two lines that has been organized to emphasize might and power ("Broad . . . / Many . . ."). In Aleksandrov's next film, *Volga-Volga* (1938), now set largely in nature, the corresponding song is the "Song about the Volga," the central artery of Russia. The culminating line of its refrain is similar, though the reference to power is more explicit: "broad, deep, strong" *(shiroka, gluboka, sil'na)*. Once again, the epithet "broad" is placed first in a line to emphasize the vastness of Soviet space.

In *The Circus* the theme song is composed by the film's hero and heroine while seated at a grand piano in a stateroom of the Hotel Moscow, located in view of the Kremlin. This placing is made explicit with a shot of the Kremlin tower, a figure for Soviet power (see Chapter 2), looming unrealistically close to the hotel window. The song that the protagonists compose in that setting became one of the main Soviet hits of the decade, but also enjoyed the status of an unofficial auxiliary national anthem; the tune of its opening line was adopted for the Kremlin chimes. The chimes, in turn, were broadcast by radio over the entire Soviet Union when it went off the air at midnight, to shut down the nation for the night, as it were, sending its citizenry to sleep confident of the greatness of their (vast) country.

One aspect of the Romantic notion of the sublime that was potentially problematical for the Soviet Union was the sense of a superior order of man, what Schiller called "noble minds" or "men of elevated dispositions" who tower above the mere "sheep." Yet Soviet political culture of the late 1930s featured precisely this sort of hierarchy in anthropology. The Soviet system had (symbolically at any rate) produced a higher order man, as in the extraordinary Stakhanovite and other national heroes. But essentially these figures from narratives of the sublime were not self-valuable; they were only actors in symbolic dramas. What Stalin is afforded in the narratives about the aviators and mountain climbers is a magisterial gaze from the "heights," even though in actuality it is these surrogates who undertake the journeys. The "heroes'" function, as with the function of the figures on the Mukhina statue, was to attest to the higher order—the extraordinary—nation they represented. In most classic theories of the sublime it is gendered, associated with the masculine, while beauty was said to have more feminine attributes.[39] Schiller, in a condemnation that seems to anticipate Nietzsche, dismisses those who cling to the illusory world of "beauty" and refinement as "weak" and "effeminate," too captivated by the sensuous world of women and the domestic. The urban, similarly seen as domesticating, was also scorned. Schiller remarked that "history declares that nations have declined according to their aesthetic culture. Enervation and loss of freedom have followed close upon refinement." But on the Mukhina statue, the new national logo, there were virile figures for a virile nation no longer captivated by effete "beauty" and harmony but prepared to face "bold disorder," to step up to the very brink, and even go beyond.

The Imperial Sublime

Though the theme songs of the Alexandrov films use crude versions of the platitudes of the sublime, the extreme physical extension they attribute to Russia is not just, as in some theories of the sublime such as

Hegel's, a prop or a trope. These films are about dominion and dominance. The "broad" expanses of the country extolled in the Alexandrov films also have to do with expansionism, in fact "broad" indicates not only the magisterial but also the encompassing. It suggests both the sublime in the vast spaces (in *The Circus* reaching the stratosphere) and the expansive in another sense of the Russian word used, *shirokii,* which not only denotes a physical quality but can have a more metaphorical meaning as a human trait. A person who is *shirokii* is expansive and generous by nature; the *shirokaia strana* (broad country) is evident in one of the last scenes of *The Circus,* which, as argued in Chapter 5, provides an allegorical representation of the way the country reaches out its broad arms to encompass its many ethnic minorities under the one great, *shirokii* Soviet "tent" (the film was based on Ilf and Petrov's *Under the Big Tent of the Circus* [Pod kupolom tsirka]). Not only are these ethnic minorities embraced by its capacious canopy, but so is the heroine (Marion), who has fled racist America with her black child; her villainous German lover-manager, Kneischits, a caricature of the Nazi, has no place there, however.

This was, then, an imperial sublime,[40] a sublime that celebrated Soviet dominion over the lands and peoples the Russians had conquered earlier in forming their empire. Starting around 1935, one notices an exponential increase in *Literaturnaia gazeta* and other cultural organs, including the cultural coverage of *Pravda* and *Izvestia,* of material on or by figures from non-Russian nationalities;[41] this includes their national epics, generally (this smacks of tokenism) with one bard or classic epic promoted for each major ethnic minority, and includes somewhat pseudo-"folk" epics recounting the feats of Soviet heroes.[42]

There was an expansion of the Soviet citizen's sense of the national horizon. The country's geographic periphery (largely the locus of the ethnic minorities) became central to its political culture. This represents the culmination of a gradual process whereby the focus of culture spread out ever farther from the capitals and European Russia. During the First Five-Year Plan, one can already sense the purview broadening, with theater and dance festivals in the capitals incorporating troupes from the republics and leading avant-garde architects beginning to design buildings for republican capital cities. Progressively, also, national cinema studios were opened in the republics (though initially largely manned by Russians).

But the central myths of Soviet political culture remained as yet largely untouched by this progressive incorporation of the non-Russian republics into the mainstream cultural sphere.

During the Plan years, the sense of periphery was Eurocentric. Magnitostroi, the banner project of the time, about which several novels and films were generated, including Ivens's *Komsomol: Song of the Heroes* (discussed in Chapter 1), had been billed as arising as if magically on a remote windswept plain. But in reality it was located only *just* outside the border of European Russia, south of the Urals, with virtually all of Siberia stretching to the Pacific left unheralded. By the late 1930s, however, the purview of literature and film extended out into Siberia and to the Soviet Far East, south to the Pamir Mountains, and north to the Arctic. Symptomatically, on May Day, 1937, in what was to be Tretiakov's final radio broadcast direct from Red Square for the revolutionary parades (a series inaugurated in 1931), he first put on the air a live report from embattled Madrid, and then one from the Komsomol pioneers setting up the new giant city of Komsomolsk in the far eastern wilderness: Moscow, metropole of the fourth Rome, receives reports from its far-flung reaches.[43]

The new sense of the periphery was largely conveyed in terms not of construction sites but of a grandiose natural landscape. Landscape, in W. J. T. Mitchell's suggestive phrase, can function as the "dreamwork" of imperialism.[44] The increased attention paid to the republics in the cultural press was given less to the indigenous peoples in the periphery than to its sublime terrain. In Soviet cultural representations of the late 1930s, the nation is forged in remote and dramatic nature, in its periphery. The Soviet government was ideologically committed to realizing a postimperial polity, yet the non-Russian republics and ethnic groups remained subordinate, while their territory beckoned for exploitation. As recent historians have remarked, those who painted the American West in early nineteenth-century America (a fitting comparison given that, as with Russia, the empire/nation was secured by exploring and settling contiguous territory) were often attached to groups surveying its natural resources with a view to exploitation. This aspect was downplayed in the paintings, where natural settings were depicted with sublime features, sometimes inspired by Byron's poetry.[45] As it happens, just as the most dramatic

American scenery tends to be located in its West, the only significant Soviet mountains were located in its periphery.

Sublime nature in 1930s representations was, however, less likely the crags, rushing streams, or cascades, as in Pushkin and Lermontov, the German sublime and in much English and American poetry and painting of the sublime. Even what Susan Layton has called "the poetic discourse of Caucasian sublimity," which had been so much a feature of nineteenth-century literature, was less common. The loftier Pamir Mountains of Central Asia largely supplanted the Caucasus.[46] In fact the "first Kazakh film," *Amangel'dy,* with a scenario by the established Russian writer Vsevolod Ivanov and the Kazakh Ganita Musrenda and based on an historic uprising from 1916, transposed the action from the flat lands where it actually took place to the "beautiful mountains of Ala Altu."[47]

The paradigmatic periphery of Stalinist culture was, however, the frozen wastes, to be found in Siberia but most dramatically in the Arctic region. Their vast expanses of snow and ice were seen as a more specifically Russian landscape (though they were part of the repertoire of the German Romantic artist Caspar David Friedrich, e.g., *The Polar Sea* [Das Eismeer, 1823/1824]). A frigid terrain is associated with Russia's victory over Napoleon, the great victory over an expansionist empire. But the frozen wastes also provided a mythic space, a place of extremes, an absolute beyond. Around 1937–1939 a spate of fictional works and films appeared featuring hair-raising rescues.[48] These expanses provided a virgin territory, despite the presence of an indigenous local population. As wastes, they represent a sort of infinite nothingness, but also a potential; it is Stalin who gives them meaning, especially since they are associated with Stalin's prerevolutionary exile within the Arctic Circle. Mikhail Kalatozov's film *Chkalov* (Red Wings) of 1941 about an aviation ace has as its climactic scene Chkalov wrestling with, and prevailing over, an Arctic cold that penetrates his plane.

The preeminence of snowy wastes among versions of the sublime is evident in Eisenstein's *Alexander Nevsky* of 1938, which has as its centerpiece the famous battle on the ice of Lake Chudov (in that medieval time a periphery). Here it is ice, and mastery of the ice, that defeats a foreign foe, not superior military hardware. *Alexander Nevsky,* incidentally, was enormously popular (untypically for Eisenstein), suggesting that its battle with the elements struck a chord with the Soviet public. The battle scene itself is presented as an infinite horizontal expanse of ice, while Nevsky controls events from an elevated rock that juts up incongruously in the snow. This incongruity is dictated by the scene's visual referent, medieval paintings of battles that feature similar rocks, but Nevsky's vantage point also enables the magisterial gaze afforded by the sublime. In this battle the Russians are trying to rid their borders of the alien; here it is the Livonian Teutonic knights—read Germans—but the opening scenes prefigure a future battle with the Mongols, suggesting the then current Soviet confrontation with the Japanese. The battle on Lake Chudov was a particularly propitious choice at this time (Eisenstein was far from the only one to depict it)[49] because an actual battle on a lake took place that year (July 29–August 11, 1938), the Battle of Lake Khasan, where Soviet forces engaged the Japanese in the Soviet Far East; Eisenstein himself pointed to this link in a speech he made when the film was released in Leningrad.[50]

The imperial sublime, as mentioned, has to do with not only securing territory but also exploring its potential. On May 21, 1937, four days before the Paris Exposition opened, a group of four led by Ivan Papanin were deposited by plane in the North Pole region to spend nine months conducting scientific investigations. The four drifted on an ice floe southward along the coast of Greenland, taking scientific measurements of the sea depth, gravity, and the magnetic field, but by early 1938 the expedition was in a perilous position, as the ice floe on which they had been stationed for the winter began to break up and their tent was submerged. Their cliff-hanger air rescue on February 29, 1938, stirred the entire country. When the expedition reached Moscow they were treated to a ticker-tape parade, and a series of books was generated on the drama.[51]

A *Pravda* article of February 1938, "An Unprecedented Feat," makes clear that the expedition's official significance lay not just in the extraordinary risk and daring but also in its contribution to science. The Arctic theme had been prominent in Stalinist narratives of heroism since at least 1934, with the Chelyuskin expedition (Tretiakov had edited a book in German on it).[52] But in this article, the sublime and science are inextricably bound up with one another, symptomatic of the "drift" science itself was undergoing. The foreigners, such as America's Commander Robert Peary, who had previously visited the pole, the article claimed, showed no interest in exploring it for science, not even in measuring the depth of the ocean. "It was only the Bolsheviks who proved able to meet this task. . . . The task was not just to reach the Pole; one had to set up a scientific station there which would make a complex study of the characteristics of the Central Polar Basin." "In effect an entire scientific institute has been set up on the ice floe," the article boasts, adding that the expedition's task was to "reveal completely the secrets of the pole" (raskroet do kontsa tainy poliusa). "For nine long months four Soviet people waged a struggle against the elements, forcing their secrets out of them." The expedition's principal activity there seems to have been to measure the depth of the ocean at thirty to forty miles deep, setting up a hydrological station. "One would have to spend time in the North oneself," the article comments, "in order to understand how much effort has to be expended to obtain a few cubic centimeters of water from a great depth." Hence the group— veritable Stakhanovites—had to proceed at a feverish pace, working fifteen to sixteen hours a day and scarcely finding any time for sleep.[53]

The Papanin expedition fathomed that which for other nations was unfathomable. But their conquering the sublime was made possible by the direction of Stalin himself, as with the aviators who broke records for long-distance flight. The expedition went beyond its status as an outfit for scientific research. Though its members were in fact engaged in measurement, the account of their work has been transposed to the rhetoric of the sublime. Fathoming the ocean with the Papanin expedition was both about a higher order epistemology obtained in a place of sublime dimensions (extraordinary depth) and about territorial conquest and mastery of physical resources. The national ambitions were both metaphysical and material.[54]

The drama and rhetoric of the sublime intersected with the actuality of the purges. The Papanian four may have reached the Pole just before the Paris Exposition opened, but a closer coincidence with the dates of the expedition would be the repression of Bukharin, who was arrested on February 27, 1937, around the time the expedition conferred with Stalin about their plans (March 13, 1937) and set off (March 22, 1937). In early 1938, during the buildup to the trial of Bukharin and other members of the "rightist-Trotskyite Bloc," and the trial itself, much of the media attention was focused on the expedition. Bukharin was being interrogated even as the expedition was "forcing out" *(vyryvaia)* the pole's secrets. The press reports next year of their dramatic rescue were juxtaposed with those of the Bukharin trial (March 2–13, with the execution on March 14, an event overshadowed by Hitler's march into Austria), at which the prosecutors "revealed completely" the iniquity of Bukharin and his fellow accused, exposing their true identities as bandits and feral animals.

The Papanin narrative complements the material on the purge trial, providing a token, surrogate enactment, as it were, of the sensational drama of narrow escape from ferocious, destructive forces that is implicit in the Great Purge trial transcripts. In *Pravda*'s account, the Papanin expedition involved revelation won by superhuman effort, and virtue (Bolshevik dedication to science) rescued at the eleventh hour. The account here seems almost crafted to transpose the dramas of the NKVD cellars to the Romantic arena of the Arctic. But we will also note that with this displacement the account of how intelligence was wrested from "deep within" dispenses with any need to represent violence but is instead able to invoke it metaphorically.

The dramatic rescue of the Papanin expedition is above all about power. It provides a parable about how Russia/Stalin commands the frozen wastes. As the expedition struggled on the ice, cut off from Soviet Russia by thousands of miles, the Soviet audience (who followed its fate daily in the central press and on the radio) trembled. But a providential Stalin, and Stalin alone, could pull off the drama of rescue in sublime nature. Commentators adduced Scott and the Antarctic as a counterexample to the Papanin group, insisting that his tragedy was that he had one close to care about him (no *blizhnye*), read no Stalin as "caring" head of the Great Family of Soviet peoples.[55]

Stalin did not have to direct events on site because the expedition had a radio link with Moscow. Radio transmitters became cult objects in these years, conferring a special status on those who operated them in remote areas; Ernst Krenkel, the radio operator of the Papanin expedition, was singled out with its leader as a hero and, informants tell me, thereafter young males aspired to become radio operators in remote parts of the country.[56] Radio, wireless and with no material existence in the intervening spaces between the periphery and Moscow, became the link between wild nature and the Kremlin. As the populace waited with bated breath,

Stalin directed the rescue, resolving the geographical dialectic and synthesizing the nation.

The romance of exploration and discovery in places of dramatic nature was very central to Stalinist culture of the late thirties. It could also be seen in the first half of the decade—in fact Tretiakov published in *Pravda* of 1933 an article calling for more writing on this theme—but its heyday was the late 1930s.[57] Many films and novels appeared that sang the romance of adventure in "distant and unknown places," one of the most popular being Sergei Gerasimov's film *Seven Brave Ones* (Semero smelykh) of 1936 about an expedition posted at an isolated Arctic observation station. Another was Vladimir Vainshtok and David Gutman's 1936 film adaptation of *The Children of Captain Grant* (Deti kapitana Granta) by Jules Verne (several of whose novels also appeared in translation).[58] Also popular in these years were films about aviation, such as Dovzhenko's *Aerograd* (1935; set, a sign of the times, in the Soviet Far East, near the border); Yuli Raizman's *Flyers* (Lëtchiki; 1935); Dziga Vertov's *Three Heroines* (Tri geroini; 1938); and Mikhail Kalatozov's *Valerii Chkalov* (1941). But adventure, romance, and discovery were connected to potential economic exploitation. Edward Said in his article "Invention, Memory and Place" remarks that "the mapping, conquest, and annexation of territory in what Conrad called the dark places on the earth. . . . The great voyages of discovery from da Gama to Captain Cook were motivated by curiosity and scientific fervor, but also by a spirit of domination."[59]

A paradigmatic Soviet novel that presents this version of the sublime would be Veniamin Kaverin's *Two Captains* (Dva kapitana) a saga of maturation conflated with the imperial theme of mastery *(osveoenie)* and the romance of the sublime frozen wastes. Kaverin began writing the novel in 1936. Book 1 appeared in the journal of the Pioneer (youth) organization, *Kostër* (the bonfire), over the years 1938–1940 (book 2 appeared in 1944, outside my period so it will not be covered here).[60] Kaverin had been a disciple of the Formalists and author of experimental prose in the 1920s, but in the thirties he had adapted to the demands of socialist realism and produced two novels, which became Soviet classics. The first, *Fulfilment of Desires* (Ispolnenie zhelanii; 1934), concerns recovering a lost chapter of Pushkin's great Russian classic *Eugene Onegin* (Evgenii Onegin). *The*

Two Captains, his second, was wildly successful, in part because his Formalist tutelage had taught him a lot about plot construction.

The novel is told in the first person from the perspective of an orphan,
Sanya, from a provincial town, Ensk, who moves to Moscow as a school-
child, taking as his motto the last line of the English poet Alfred Lord
Tennyson's "Ulysses" (which in turn was derived from Homer and from
Dante's *Inferno*): "To strive, to seek, to find and not to yield." By a series
of coincidences, Sanya becomes involved in solving the mystery of what
happened to a Captain Tatarinov, who had set out in 1911 on a boat to
explore the North Sea route but never returned. Sanya, the narrator, falls
in love with the captain's daughter, Katya, and feels increasingly impelled
to get to the bottom of the captain's fate, but his path is crossed by the
captain's cousin, Nikolai Antonych, who happens to be the principal of
Sanya's school. As it emerges, in a version of *Hamlet,* this cousin had
fallen in love with the captain's wife and had consequently deliberately
provisioned the expedition poorly so that it would fail. When the captain
perished, his cousin took in the captain's family, and eventually beat
down the widow's resistance until she agreed to marry him (when she
subsequently learns the truth, unlike Hamlet's mother, she poisons herself and dies). Much of the novel consists of Sanya progressively collect-
ing material that exposes this villain, though at every turn he is dogged by
him and his accomplice, Romashka, a fellow student of Sanya and later a
rival for Katya's hand. In fact much of the novel also consists, in keeping
with the times, of denunciation and counter-denunciation, denunciations
enacted in domestic space, in meetings at the school, and in the central
press (Nikolai Antonych's veiled denunciation of Sanya in *Sovetskaia
Arktika* is countered by an article in the more authoritative *Pravda* for
which Sanya provides the information). In the end, Sanya triumphs, and
a wavering Katya moves out of her uncle's apartment and into Sanya's life.

As a counterpoint to all the denunciations, the novel is dominated by
the romance of exploration. Sanya and Katya spend much of their childhood together reading about the great explorers who uncovered continents or trekked through the Arctic or Antarctic; they devour books on
Columbus, Cortez, Amerigo Vespucci, Balboa, and such Arctic explorers
as Roald Amundsen, Fridtjof Nansen, and John Franklin and Russians
like Georgy Sedov. They also savor these explorers' diaries and letters, as

well as fictional adventure narratives, especially those of Jules Verne and Defoe's *Robinson Crusoe* (mentioned by Said). These childhood obsessions influence their choices of careers. Sasha grows up to be an aviator who flies out of a base above the Arctic Circle, while Katya becomes a geologist whose expedition ultimately finds gold in the Southern Urals. When Sanya sees a photo of her "on horseback, in men's pants and boots with a carbine slung over her shoulder and a broad-rimmed hat," this "geologist-explorer!" reminds him of Ferdinand Cortez.[61]

Throughout *The Two Captains,* personal dramas are intertwined with an imperial narrative. This is especially so in the sections set in the Arctic. A climactic moment uses many of what had become standard moments in Soviet nonfictional accounts of Arctic aviation,[62] making this novel yet another example of appropriation, of how Western literary models were adapted to Stalinist discourse. In this scene Sanya, now an Arctic aviator, has just been told that Romashka is assiduously courting his beloved Katya and appears about to succeed. At that point, he receives a call from the NKVD (no innocent detail, given that this novel was written at the height of the purges) saying that a local state functionary has been wounded in a suspicious "hunting accident" in a remote region to the north, and they want Sanya to take a doctor there to treat the official and to investigate the real cause of the accident. As they set out, Sanya's anguished thoughts about his desperate love situation are intercut with his glimpses of the frozen wastes. "Below was the Enisei [river]—a broad white ribbon between the white banks along which ran a forest. . . . Then I left the river and the tundra began—flat, infinite, snowy, not a single spot of black and nothing to fasten one's eyes on." "Snow, snow, snow wherever you looked." At this point Sanya decides to go to Moscow to sort things out with Katya, but soon another sublime vision comes into view. "What mountains!" he exclaims. "They stuck up through the clouds, lit by the sun," a description that might have been taken from Wordsworth's *Prelude* (especially by Kaverin, well known to have been an Anglophile). But there is terror to match the joy: "In rare patches of visibility one could see ravines, very long and beautiful ravines, [presaging] certain death if one was forced to land."[63]

Sanya is about to compose a letter to Katya mentally when suddenly a violent snowstorm springs up. He can see nothing and his motor begins to cut out. Then he catches sight of the ravines below, which are "long and absolutely hair-raising [beznadëzhnye]," so he maneuvers away from them and miraculously manages to land with only a mild crash. Once the snowstorm abates, three days later, the crew find themselves near a village of the Nenets, indigenous locals. The plane is damaged, and they need a meter-long plank of wood to repair it, so in a gesture that echoes the practice of the great Pacific navigators and African explorers of the past, they offer the Nenets as barter a primus stove, a wonder of civilization. The villagers are wide-eyed as they see that the primus can heat water so much more quickly than their fires. While searching for timber, Sanya comes across a fragment of Captain Tatarinov's ship, with its name, *Santa Maria,* and he realizes that the boat "drifted" (à la the Papanin expedition) from 1912 until 1914, revealing that a territory that explorers had previously claimed to have "discovered" actually did not exist. Earlier, Sanya had realized that Captain Tatarinov had discovered Severnaia Zemlia half a year before a certain Lieutenant Vil'kitskii claimed it as *his* discovery. Thus, as Sanya comments: "he altered the map of the Arctic."[64].

It goes without saying that maps are important in the foundation of empires. In the thirties, there were several projects to map every corner of the Soviet Union, and maps play a prominent role in this novel, too. Sanya and the crew try to get the Nenets to draw a map telling them how to get to their destination, Vanokan; they are not familiar with maps, and one of them draws a deer. But Moscow can map the space, and eventually the crew work out the location of the nearest town, where a local official surprises them with his knowledge of literature, thanks to training at the Teacher's College (cultural imperialism). Once the wounded official is located and taken to the local hospital, they put every possible light into the makeshift operating room, so that "the room was lit up by a light such as had never been seen in Vanokan."[65]

Though Sanya and his fellows bring a primus, "light," and "maps" to the local populace, still the sublime remains privileged. The dramatic nature outside is adequate to the turbulent psychic drama within. Sanya, while in the air contemplating the endless snowy stretches, resolves to go to Moscow, and his deliberations are intercut with the panoramic view. Sanya's decision to go back to Moscow is connected to his emotional life, but in the event he will be returning to the capital to make the rounds of bureaucratic institutions. The sublime provides a counterpoint to the bureaucratic world, compensating for its grayness. It helps what Schiller called "men of elevated dispositions" break out of the confines of what he dismissed as the "mean and narrow" that characterizes the "dweller in the cities" who applies himself "so readily to trifles."[66]

We will note that both heroes, Sanya and Katya, realize themselves in sublime nature, far from urban centers—he in frozen wastes, among treacherous ravines, she in the Ural Mountains. But then both return to Moscow. Sanya's trip to the capital is a version of an important moment in the standard narrative of the socialist realist novel when the protagonist goes to Moscow on a mission from his far-flung village or work site. There he meets some high official (perhaps even Stalin) and returns to his community recharged and ready to pull off its state-assigned task (meet production targets, finish constructing the dam). In *The Two Captains,* however, Sanya does not encounter a particularly high-ranking official in Moscow, and though he does conduct some administrative business, the plot focuses on the way his visit furthers his love interest and personal mission to expose Katya's uncle. But the drama in the sublime, closely linked as it is to the competing claims of false and true father figures, is ultimately about power.

The sublime in Stalinist culture functioned to naturalize and enhance power relations, and to transpose action from an urban, bureaucratic world with its obvious restrictions and constraining conventions to a dramatic periphery, thereby minimizing the presence of the banal world of apartments and offices. The scientist explorers among the novel's characters went "beyond" literally—beyond the Arctic Circle, as an allegory for going beyond the limitations of the prosaic world. This brings to mind Eagleton's remark about Walter Scott (also prominent at this time) that in his historical novels "romance trades in the marvellous and transgressive, and realism in the mundane; so that by forging a complex unity out of these two literary modes Scott can fashion a form of writing which is true at once to the revolutionary origins and the quotidian life of the early bourgeois epoch."[67]

In Eisenstein's *Nevsky,* similarly, we see an alternation between nature—

such as the broad panoramas of the opening scenes—and urban centers. Once the battle is over, Nevsky switches to a ceremonial role and decamps to Novgorod, where he formally welcomes the victorious warriors as they return, greeted by rejoicing throngs. In this scene, Nevsky recapitulates the standard form of Stalin receiving the members of the Papanin expedition or the aviation heroes on their triumphal return to Moscow. In the film, two warrior-protagonists are singled out for Nevsky's attention. They are more dead than alive from their battle wounds, but he revives them and serves as matchmaker to boot restoring them to the life stream (marriage)—a course that he, and any charismatic leader figure, cannot, according to Freud's analysis in *Group Psychology and the Analysis of the Ego* (1921), take if he is to keep his charisma.

As is evident in this film, the metropolitan center, though offstage for most of the dramas, is far from excluded from Stalinist narratives of the sublime. Moscow might seem to be the antonym to the sublime, but in actuality it was more its twin. Stalin in such narratives as the rescue of the Papanin expedition was inscribed into a sublime landscape without leaving the Kremlin, but this was reciprocal. Rude nature and the metropolitan center were a pair. The metropolitan center (or its medieval equivalent) became a component of dramatic rescue of individuals who have battled in sublime nature and who now stand in for the nation at large. In other words, the cult of Moscow was far from eclipsed in these years. The link involves patronage (Stalin sends and equips his expeditions and communicates with them) but also an ontological affinity between the two privileged spaces. Moscow was both the headquarters directing operations and a space enhanced by the sublime.

In Stalinist culture all spaces were symbolic spaces, in that each one stood for a particular phase of historical development. However, in these years, as the nation's purview was expanding, the earlier binary hierarchy of space—the provincial town as less developed versus Moscow as more advanced—was displaced with a shift out to a third possibility. The drama in the sublime came to overshadow what went on in the provincial setting. Now the principal focus was on twinned spaces—the remote periphery of sublime nature and Moscow—with the provincial center further downgraded in significance. Thus in *The Two Captains*, for example, the original contrast between Moscow and the provincial town of Ensk (by its very title, N-sk, a generic provincial town) from which the protagonist has come is superseded as the hero goes to an area beyond the Arctic circle (to which most of the positive characters have contrived in different ways to decamp).

In *The Two Captains,* the sublime, denunciation, and emotion are all part of the same nexus. In the "blinding" white snows Sanya cannot see clearly and is at the same time blinded by passion. But as W. J. T. Mitchell has remarked, "landscape [as] . . . a potent ideological representation" can "erase history and legibility," rendering "a place of amnesia and erasure."[68] Obviously, there is a degree of "erasure" in this novel (produced as the Stalinist practice of creating "nonpersons" and "nonplaces" was in full force); the scene's bleak and frigid natural setting was a common one for the prison camps, whose captives were more truly confronted by the boundlessness of the Soviet terrain, more literally *beznadezhnyi* to them than to a Sanya surveying it from the air (and the prisoners, more than Katya, were engaged in exploitation of natural resources).

In cultural products of these years the "erasure" in terms of places was linked with an erasure in time. I say this despite the marked Soviet proclivity for using historical precedents for present events and the nation's leaders. So much of the culture in this period has to do with Romantic travel, but travel is, as Paul Fussell has remarked, "an adventure in time as well as distance," in fact, in travel "the figure of time [is] rendered as space."[69] In that an apprehension of the sublime is like an epiphanic moment, and hence about the intensity of the experience, it occludes linear, incremental time (as in the shift to qualitative change in *The Short Course*), even as it also "erases" from the consciousness the surrounding spaces, possibly one reason why the radio, an agency that overcame and thereby annihilated the vast intervening spaces between Moscow and the dramas taking place in the sublimity of nature, was so prominent in the political culture of these years.

Time was, then, entwined with space in a chronotope of sublimity. As with spatial erasure, cultural products that dealt with historical subjects were actually billed as erasing—collapsing—the elapsed time between "then" and the present in a sort of temporal sublime. A striking example would be Koltsov's authoritative review in *Pravda* of Eisenstein's *Nevsky* when it premiered for the Revolution's anniversary in 1938. Here he waxes lyrical about how in the film, Rus' has essentially leaped over the intervening centuries to join with the present times.[70] A *Literaturnaia gazeta* editorial of 1938 recommends to authors a telling cluster of alternative possible topics for them to write on—"the battle on the Kalka or the [present-day] conquerors [zavoevateli] of the Arctic, Alexander Nevsky or a detachment of border guards." the editorial adds: "we must keep a reasonable proportion between past and future."[71] But the distinction between past and future was in effect elided in the interest of a single vision of an imperial sublime that could be represented in alternative ways.

In putting this novel together, Kaverin has essentially taken what Soviets called the *zadanie,* the official assignment or task—"the battle on the Kalka or the conquerors of the Arctic"—and covered many of the bases of the political culture of the late 1930s: denunciations, exploitation of natural resources, a patriotic narrative about claiming new lands for Russia, the secret police, a Komsomol mentor, aviation. Small wonder that the novel was recurrently cited as a classic of socialist realism. And yet, as we saw with what Eisenstein did with his commission from Stalin to make *Ivan the Terrible* (discussed in the introduction), this novel was not defined by its Stalinist features, though it had them. Kaverin's treatment of *osvoenie* might seem to follow the trend to increasing nationalism that many have noted in the culture of the late 1930s, but there are also strong cosmopolitan elements.

Yet again we see an example of translation whereby a mix of literary material, including much from Western sources, is appropriated, and refracted through stock conventions of current political culture. Kaverin placed his story of exploration within the broader world of the great navigators of human history. He also opened this "socialist realist" text up to embrace many precedents from both prerevolutionary Russian and Western literature, especially Dickens, Tennyson, Wordsworth, and Byron (to whom Sanya is compared). Some of these precedents are explicit, and some are to be found in his tropes and plot functions. From Dickens, for example, Kaverin has taken the characteristic plot of orphanhood and included surrogates for a Peggotty *(David Copperfield).* But he has integrated his account of orphanhood into the myth of the Great Family, a master narrative of Stalinist political culture.

A culture that depends on intense, epiphanic moments and is essentially resisting normalcy, a version of millennial pathos, is hard to sustain. The audience experiences the frisson as they contemplate a drama in the sublime, and then order is generally restored. Conventionally, people come upon the sublime as they traverse somewhere outside their normal routes; sustained familiarity would blunt its impact. In actuality Stalinist culture never lost sight of the opposite—privileging everyday life and material progress. The new class was becoming ever more entrenched, their lives ever more prosperous, with consumerism increasingly in evidence.[72] In several films, while some young women visiting the capital set themselves up for encounters with the sublime, others race around the stores gasping at, or scooping up, enticing wares.[73] In painting, a sign of the times would be Yuri I. Pimenov's *New Moscow* (Novaia Moskva; 1937), which features a woman driving a luxurious convertible through daytime central Moscow, dressed in a diaphanous white, suggesting luxury (most of the female pedestrians are also in white). Her short hair suggests a liberated woman, but more likely she is the wife of a high official leading the "new class" existence. And she is heading into the heart of the Soviet establishment as she drives past the square in front of the Bolshoi, toward the House of Unions (where the show trials were held); a huge administrative building and the Hotel Moscow are also visible.

Not all representations of Soviet power were as glamorous or enticing. The main subjects of painting, besides landscapes, had become Party leaders and to a lesser extent such public heroes as Stakhanovites and aviators. Most characteristic was the long line of stolid faces in grey suits that would be hung in an institution or decorate the streets for some national day and bespoke an unimaginative, bureaucratic world, a different version of power. In 1938 as the cult of personality got into high gear, virtually every issue of the cultural journals opened with a full-page picture or photo of Lenin or Stalin. And in an art exhibition of "the achievements of industry" organized in 1939, the majority of the paintings featured the nation's leaders.

The Great Purge is generally said to have ended in early 1939 (in some versions November 1938). As the terror receded (or a little before), a different sort of landscape was favored by painters and writers, one noted

for its "beauty" rather than the sublime. But this did not represent a return to the same cult of beauty that had marked the early thirties. Somewhat as Marx says in the *Eighteenth of Brumaire of Louis Napoleon*—that
history occurs the first time as tragedy, the second as farce—we might say
that the ideal of beauty came initially in the 1930s as an emblem of utopia,
but the second time as kitsch. Now it was a beauty devoid of utopian aus-
terity. This entropic, consumerist tendency toward kitsch is glaringly apparent in a painting project by the leading Soviet artist Alexander
Gerasimov, who had painted *V. I. Stalin and K. E. Voroshilov in the Kremlin* (1938): three paintings of a bouquet of roses.[74] Such subjects were to
be found in Gerasimov's earlier works, especially his prerevolutionary
paintings; now they typified a dominant trend in art.

Landscape remained popular, but it was now more likely to be described in terms conventionally associated with beauty in landscape, such
as an "elegant balance" between component parts, "exquisite gradations," tranquil splendor, or the way a scene was bathed in light.[75] With
landscape increasingly represented as "serene," Isaac Levitan, a favorite
from the nineteenth century, came back into vogue.

These kinds of landscape were now said to define the nation. Alexander Gerasimov was praised in a 1939 review of his new work for having
spent so much time "working on a representation of the national Russian
landscape." The results include *Flowering Gardens, Flowers,* and *Winter
Troika.* But particularly admired is *Spring,* a painting on which Gerasimov had been working for ten years and which captures "the titanic
inexhaustible natural and human forces of our country"—but, as one
reviewer noted, the painting depicts a "garden that has burst into flower;
all covered with a brilliant carpet of assorted flowers; as a mighty green
forest [is] suffused with a joyous light, which lives in the national [or
popular—narodnoe] consciousness as a symbolic image of the spring of a
new life." Now, the review continues to report, Gerasimov has produced
a new canvas, *Comrade Stalin and Gorky at Gorki* (Tovarishch Stalin i
Gor'kii v Gorkakh), where "the landscape is the main component of the
work." An earlier iconic painting of Gorky had shown him at the firing
range, but this one was to be more tranquil. Gerasimov reported that he
rejected his first idea of depicting Gorky and Stalin in a library. His second idea was to have them both walking beside a stream, but that was

abandoned likewise in favor of showing the two in conversation on a dacha porch, open to nature. Stalin and Gorky, then, are not plunged into texts, nor are they beside the running waters (each of these possibilities represents an earlier cultural model), but are having a pleasant conversation comfortably ensconced at the dacha.[76]

The dacha, situated in nature, but also a place for cultivation of gardens, leisure, and relaxation, was far from sublime.[77] In these years it had become an acceptable subject for representation in culture. One example would be Konstantin Iudin's Romantic comedy *Four Stout Hearts* (Serdtsa chetyrekh; 1941). In many respects *Four Stout Hearts* represents a side glance at the Americans, a Soviet appropriation of the plot of *Ninotchka,* with the heroine a humorless mathematician who regards her younger sister's focus on clothes and love life as reprehensibly frivolous and immature—until she herself is smitten by an army officer, even as her sister also finds her true love. In this film you do not see monumental Moscow with its politically resonant landmarks such as the Kremlin and the Bolshoi but rather "intimate," ex-centric Moscow, a Moscow full of sites of assignation: phone booths, Gorky Park, and the dacha. At the end, the two couples, who have been staying at a dacha settlement, go to a local station to buy tickets back to Moscow. By the conventions of socialist realism, this journey to Moscow would be a fitting resolution of the love plot, the moment when the hero, brimming with self-realization, naturally impends toward the nation's "center." But the two couples change their minds and let the train leave. Admittedly, *Four Hearts* was banned when it was released on the very eve of the Nazi invasion, but largely because the principal male character was an army officer and his distraction in love was deemed inappropriate for a military man, too "frivolous" *(legkomyslenno).*[78] Another work of this time set in a dacha settlement, Arkadii Gaidar's beloved *Timur and His Team* (Timur i ego komanda; 1940), also made into a film that year,[79] tells of a group of spirited Pioneers who come together to keep watch over the dachas where the man in the house is off at war, in other words, to preserve personal property, albeit with patriotic fervor.

In 1939, a high point for kitschy landscapes, another World's Fair opened, this one in New York. Newspaper reports on the Soviet pavilion there (again designed by Iofan, this time with Karo Alabian) present a

pointed contrast with those about the Paris pavilion only two years earlier. This time, rivalry was primarily with the United States, which featured in its exhibit the good life to be had in America with its cutting-edge
modern conveniences. The Soviets could not compete. But their artwork
suggested the possibility of lives enhanced in other ways. In the Soviet
reviews, attention is devoted to the paintings displayed, singling out the
Gerasimov portrait of Gorky and Stalin described above and Vasilii
Efanov's *Meeting of Students at the Academy of the Military Air Force with
Actors of K. S. Stanislavsky's Theater* (Vstrecha slushatelei Voenno-
Vozdushnoi akademii s artistami teatra K. S. Stanislavskogo), showing all
those in attendance elegantly attired. But the centerpiece was a gigantic
panel, *Prominent People of the Land of the Soviets* (Znatnye liudi Strany
Sovetov), painted by a brigade of artists led by Efanov, in which an as-
semblage of smiling individuals, many in telltale white, stride forth with
garlands of flowers. The painting celebrates a new category that had entered Soviet parlance, *znatnye liudi,* by which was meant roughly people
of status or distinction, celebrities—production heroes, managers, military officers, sporting heroes, officials—the privileged.[80] And so the *znatnye liudi* on the canvas of that giant panel strode forward, as did the
couple on the Mukhina statue, the emblematic artwork of the 1937 Paris
Exposition, but this time not for an enactment of the sublime.

CHAPTER 9

The Battle over the Genres

(1937–1941)

$\mathbf{F}$ REDRIC JAMESON WRITES in his introduction to Lukács's *Historical Novel:* "Whoever speaks of the historical emergence of a new genre must at the same time take into account the possibility (and perhaps even the inevitability) of the historical decline and death of that same genre, whose idea can no longer exist in some eternal heaven of Platonic or Aristotelian forms but rather in the perpetual mutability of history itself."[1] There was no shortage of "perpetual mutability" in the Stalinist late 1930s, with its purges decimating the political, administrative, and military elites, and yet, or perhaps consequently, the regime fostered the good old-fashioned historical novel, using as its subjects heroes of the prerevolutionary past. But questions of genre were debated more intensely in these years than at any other time, with many participants challenging the "immutability" of socialist realism as thus far instituted, with its highly conventionalized novel enjoying the status of virtually a Platonic form of Soviet culture. Much of the polemical energy was redirected from questions of language, so recently a focus of discussions about what was appropriate for Soviet culture, to questions of genre. Debates swirled around whether the "epic" or the "lyric" was the most fitting genre for cultural forms, with Bakhtin weighing in from the sidelines (banned from publication or residence in the capitals), advocating, rather, the "novel" or, more accurately, "novelness." Meanwhile, the production novel, the mainstay of socialist realism, had come up against Jameson's "perpetual mutability of history itself."

In these years the specter of war hung over the land. *Pravda* introduced a rubric "If There Is War Tomorrow" (Esli zavtra voina) and authorities enjoined cultural producers to undertake themes concerned with war and national consolidation. Rather than Ivan the metalworker, the new heroes of public culture were to be military commanders and national leaders. "We need more literature on our military past," one editorial declared;[2] but the "our" of the military past generally extended to before the Revolution, in part because the Civil War had become more problematical as a subject in the wake of the execution of Marshal Tukhachevsky in 1937 and several others among those formerly considered its heroes.

With the virtual demise of the Popular Front in France and the souring of the international effort in Spain, the Soviet leadership were less concerned with internationalist ideological expansionism, and the country tilted perceptibly in the direction of nationalism. Things Russian—Russia's culture, its language, and even its people—were increasingly depicted as a primus inter pares, the pares being the other ethnic groups within the Soviet Union and their cultures.

The Soviet Union was not alone in this shift. Dudley Andrew and Stephen Ungar have remarked of France in the late 1930s that "the phenomenon of nationalism appealed to those intellectuals who had declared themselves to be post-Enlightenment, that is, to have gone beyond the reassurances of Kant's Critique of Pure Reason." They had turned to such philosophers as Hegel, Nietzsche, and Heidegger, who "tempted intellectuals to calculate the importance of ideas on the basis of their power more than their truth. Hence, nationalism became an acceptable sentiment once it was shown to be a contemporary expression of elemental group feelings. And the rituals of nationalism, including the bombastic rallies being held in Germany, could be taken as a sign of a rejuvenation of experience in a Europe grown stodgy with advanced, liberal ideas."[3]

In the Soviet Union, many Russian works and cultural heroes from tsarist times that had to do with repelling external enemies were co-opted to serve this moment.[4] Even the erstwhile Formalist Viktor Shklovsky found himself writing the scenario "Minin and Pozharsky" (1939) for a film of that name directed by Pudovkin. There were also revivals of tsarist cultural products, the most dramatic being Glinka's opera *A Life for the Tsar* (1836), which is about how in the early seventeenth century Kuzma Minin and Prince Dmitry Pozharsky led the Russians to defeat Polish invaders intent on usurping the Russian throne by planting a pretender (Dmitry) on it. In prerevolutionary times *A Life for the Tsar* had opened each season of the imperial opera, but it disappeared from the repertoire after the tsar's demise in 1917. Renamed *Ivan Susanin* and only slightly amended, the opera was restaged in 1939.[5]

The fact that so much of the national narrative from the tsarist era was revived should not blind us to the differences in the function and interpretation of these individuals and texts in a different historical context—Jameson's "mutability of history." Can we really talk, as does Nicholas Timasheff in his classic text *The Great Retreat,* of a retreat away from revolution and toward tsarist normalcy, while the show trials were going on, and Stakhanovites were being lionized rather than professional managers!? Those involved in the business of literature were appropriating a highly selective version of the past. When, for example, that great Russian writer of the nineteenth century Alexander Pushkin was aggressively promoted as a model writer, those promoting him were not just, so to speak, taking an inert package—Pushkin's works—and plomping it on the table intact, even if as a trophy. Clearly the appropriation of Pushkin was not in the service of returning to Russia the landowning aristocracy from which he came. In fact, among the ludicrous claims made for Pushkin at the time, it was said he would have favored the collective farm system.[6]

Despite increasing political and cultural centralization and homogenization, throughout the 1930s one can find lobbies and interest groups supporting a range of positions. The Central Committee and Politburo directives and editorials pushing for this shift to the national inevitably had a major impact on the direction Soviet culture was taking, but there was also some passive or wily resistance to them, to be seen even at the highest levels of the cultural hierarchy.[7] Divergence from official instructions should not be construed as "dissidence," which did exist in the circumstances of tight control and under the specter of the purges but was rarer than the regime imagined. But intellectuals operated within their caste, which had its own agendas. They drew on material from Russia's past, as instructed, but they commonly used casuistry or reinflected it to serve their own preferences, which were by no means all nostalgic or chauvinist.

There is ample evidence that directives came down from on high that there should be more cultural products about war and national warriors. What is interesting is the response. At a special meeting to discuss one such directive, held in the Writers Union on February 11, 1938, and presided over by Koltsov, he insisted that the theme of a literary work did not have to be war directly in order to meet this mandate. Aleksandr Fadeev, then an emerging leader of the Writers Union, revealed at the meeting that he had been asked to write a stage version of Tolstoy's *War and Peace* but commented that it was not essential to choose military topics in order to inspire patriotism in the populace; Pushkin's novel in verse, *Eugene Onegin,* could also be used for that purpose.[8]

The palpable shift in the Soviet press and culture of the second half of the 1930s to Great Russian nationalism and even to notions of a distinctive "Russian genius" is most evident in *Pravda* and in film (the medium particularly intended for mass consumption).[9] But if you follow periodicals that are more oriented toward intellectuals, such as the newspapers *Literaturnaia gazeta* and *Sovetskoe iskusstvo,* and especially journals such as the cosmopolitan *Literaturnyi kritik* or its bimonthly supplement *Literaturnoe obozrenie,* or *Internatsional'naia literatura,* you will find that as late as 1940, material of a more nationalist or Russian revivalist bent jostles with sympathetic articles about Western figures and trends.[10]

Though a strident Russian nationalism seemed to have crept into the literary world, still a great deal of contemporary Western literature was still being published in translation or reviewed at this time, including Proust.[11] Though after April 1936, when the anti-Formalist campaign (see Chapter 6) was in full swing, *Ulysses* could no longer appear, *Dubliners,* deemed "realist," was published in 1937.[12] What was published in translation was largely, but not exclusively, literature by prominent antifascist writers, not by modernists. But most of the leading European writers of the time were in any case antifascists (though not Joyce particularly), and modernism was less in vogue in Europe generally. *Iskusstvo kino* of the late 1930s, for example, features serious articles on questions of film aesthetics, some by Eisenstein,[13] and many items on American cinema, past and, especially, present (there is some material on French cinema, but it is overwhelmingly on the American).[14] At the same time, the American cinema world had itself become strikingly leftist, heading, as it were, for the confrontations during the hearings of the House Un-American Activities Committee, a body founded in 1938, when it investigated whether the Communist Party had infiltrated the Workers Project Administration (WPA), and especially the Federal Theater Project. This increased attention to America in the Soviet cultural press was also because many of the émigrés from fascism had recently transplanted themselves to New York or Hollywood and the prominent public gatherings of antifascist writers were now held in New York.[15]

Those promoting a cosmopolitan vision had to contend with the rising nationalism and incorporate in their commentaries the new official discourse. Particularly mandatory was the adjective *narodnyi* (peoples') and its noun counterpart *narodnost'*, terms that in these years had effectively replaced "proletarian" as slogans encapsulating Soviet national values and functioned in public discourse as encoded affirmations of loyalty to the state. But *narodnyi* is polyvalent. It can mean "peoples," "folk," or "popular"—"popular" both in the sense of something of the masses and common man and in the term Popular Front (Narodnyi front). *Narodnyi* also can equally be used for "national" or "state" (as in Narodnyi bank: State Bank). And often it was used with strong ethnic, nationalist undertones, referring either explicitly or implicitly to the Russian people *(russkii narod)*.

Narodnost' became a catchphrase in the anti-Formalist campaign of 1936–1938, which decried modernist works as neither accessible to the common man nor of the Russian tradition. A cue to its compulsory use came from its appearance in the *Pravda* "signal" article of January 28, 1936, attacking Shostakovich's opera *Lady Macbeth* (see Chapter 6). For architecture, this meant an end to foregrounding the classical and Renaissance in favor of the Russian national and tracing its provenance not from (Western) Rome but from ancient Greece (associated with Eastern Orthodoxy), though some leading architects resisted jettisoning the Roman cum neoclassical, employing all sorts of casuistry to include it in the Russian national tradition.[16] They were expected to stress Russian architects such as Bazhenov as the moving forces in the national tradition, but characteristically in their accounts of these architects' careers they included some apprenticeship in the European tradition (generally a stint in Italy).

Writers in deploying the term *narodnyi* were able, thanks to its polyvalence, to implicitly lobby, beneath this cover of compliance and affirmation of loyalty to the state, for positions not at that time in favor. Many of those who were effectively critiquing socialist realist practice claimed that their version of Soviet culture was truly a "peoples'" one. A striking example would be Bakhtin in his dissertation on Rabelais (submitted to IMLI in 1940) where he played on the different meanings of *narodnyi* and identified what he called "carnival" with a distinctly eccentric version of "folk culture" *(narodnaia kul'tura).* Here Bakhtin characterizes "carnival" as an antiauthoritarian spirit.

Casuistry was also used in the debates about genre. A good example would be the discussions about the historical novel and historical film, prime vehicles of the national revival.

Lukács and Historical Genres

In *Literaturnaia gazeta* of August 26, 1939, a major editorial on the historical novel, "History and Literature" (Istoriia i literatura), appeared that reiterated an official line that had been standard for some time: "a huge role has been played, and must be played, in inculcating Soviet patriotism by the Soviet historical novel, novella, dramatic work, and film about the past of our country."[17] Though endorsing the folk epics of the national minorities as models for Soviet literature, the editorial is heavily colored by a Russian nationalism as it privileges among the Soviet ethnic groups "the great Russian people who are proceeding in the vanguard of socialist revolution" and "their truly heroic past," reminding readers that "Lenin had in mind this national pride when he wrote his brilliant article 'On the National Pride of the Great Russians.'"

This editorial was one of the most authoritative statements of a trend toward historical subjects that was already entrenched. But, as with so many features of the literary culture of the 1930s, the historical novel received its most comprehensive theoretical coverage in earlier work by Lukács. In 1937–1938 he published in *Literaturnyi kritik, Internatsio-*

nal'naia literatura, and *Literaturnoe obozrenie* a series of articles he had written in 1936–1937 and amalgamated in slightly amended form as *The Historical Novel* (1939).

Though Lukács makes many points in these articles that typify his earlier writings of the 1930s, one can detect significant shifts in his position that one could infer were dictated by the new times and the changes in the Soviet official platform. One such shift could be seen in the way French writers have been largely supplanted by Sir Walter Scott, whose historical novels were also praised in the *Pravda* editorial. Scott was in vogue in the late 1930s, though his translated collected works had been published in fourteen volumes earlier, in 1928–1930 (Mandelstam had worked on them); several of his novels appeared in translation in the mid-1930s in multiple editions with sizable print runs.[18]

In Lukács's account of the historical novel, the principal pairing is Scott and Pushkin, though French writers are discussed (especially Balzac and Stendhal). By contrast, in his earlier essay "Narration or Description?" the positive examples were Balzac and Tolstoy. While this new pairing has its logic, in that Scott was more of a historical novelist than Balzac, another reason for it has to be that Scott was important for Pushkin. Lukács had dismissed Scott in his earlier, pre-Marxist book *Theory of the Novel* (1920) for his "inner emptiness," but here he claims, somewhat controversially, that Scott was no Romantic writer, as generally thought, but provided a "realistic presentation of history" because of his "ability to translate the new elements of economic and social change into human fates," to portray "how historical necessity asserts itself."[19]

Much of the "historical necessity" Lukács points to in his account of the onset of what he sees as the golden age of the historical novel has to do with war, perhaps a sign of the times. To him, this golden age starts with Scott's *Waverly* of 1814, but in listing the events that brought about this golden age, Lukács is careful to include the French Revolution, an iconic moment in Marxist historiography. However, he identifies as crucial for its emergence the way the professional army was replaced by a mass army in the wake of the French Revolution and especially in the Napoleonic campaigns. As the Napoleonic campaigns spread over all of Europe and even to Egypt, "hundreds of thousands and millions of people from different strata of the population coming from virtually all the European countries" fanned out over the continent so that "the theater of military action became all of Europe." He further argues, drawing on the Hegelian model used in the *Short Course,* that this "enormous quantitative expansion" in terrain played "a qualitatively new role, bringing with it an extraordinary broadening of horizons" for the masses who made up the new armies.[20] The Napoleonic campaigns in large measure "destroyed the remnants of feudalism," but above all they "aroused in the masses an interest in history, one moreover on a pan-European scale."[21] This interest in history he sees as leading in turn to "the concrete possibilities for men to comprehend their existence as something historically conditioned," a proto–class consciousness, as it were. A few paragraphs after his remarks about broadened horizons for the masses that now encompass "all of Europe," however, Lukács appears to reverse this cosmopolitan drift. He claims that the impact of the Napoleonic campaigns was felt in "the national idea [natsional'noe myshlenie] becom[ing] the property of the broadest masses"; "a sense of nationhood [natsional'noe chuvstvo]."[22]

Of Scott himself, Lukács asserts "he is a patriot," adding: "this is vital for the creation of a real historical novel." One might ask what it would be to be a patriot for Georgy Lukács, a displaced Hungarian Jew in Soviet Russia who largely identified with the German intellectual tradition. Indeed, little in his account of the early nineteenth-century historical novel suggests the necessity of patriotism. Arguably, however, in the apparent contradiction of "patriot" and "all of Europe" we see an example of the mutual dependence of the national and the international, and of the cosmopolitan patriot, a figure I see as emblematic of these times. Lukács says of Scott that he was "one of the most popular and widely read writers of his time on an international scale. The influence which he exercised over the whole of European literature is immeasurable," extending to Pushkin and Balzac. In other words, Scott was a progenitor of "world literature." Moreover, Lukács pronounces Russia "the most backward country of the time" but allows that "outstanding representatives of tsarism could serve as characters in an historical novel, particularly if they stood for the introduction of Western culture into Russia."[23] Lukács uses the discourse of the nationalist cum retrospectivist drift, then, to lobby for a more "internationalist" position than the one that marked the Soviet cultural policies of the day.

Pushkin, in the Lukács analysis, surpassed Scott, achieving "an art of the ideological level of the entire previous European development."[24] Thus, potentially, we have in Lukács's claim a version of the dynamic that Lotman outlined in *The Universe of the Mind* (discussed in my introduction): a national literature (in this case Russian), having absorbed foreign literature in translation (here Scott), goes on to supersede the achievement of the original and attain international literary hegemony.

In Lukács's book one also finds casuistry, in his deployment of the term *narodnost'*, even claiming that Tolstoy's *War and Peace* presents "an epopée of popular [narodnaia] life."[25] (These terms are rendered in the standard English translation of *The Historical Novel* by Hannah and Stanley Mitchell as "popular," which, while not incorrect as a translation, cannot convey the problematical connotations of *narodnyi* in the Soviet 1930s.)

Lukács could also be seen as responding to the historical moment in this text in the way he engages the problem of the relationship between the ruler figure or hero leader and the common people, a problem particularly pertinent at this time, when the cult of personality was in high gear. In 1939, the year his *Historical Novel* appeared as a book, an obsession of the cultural press, including *Iskusstvo kino,* otherwise so oriented around film developments in America, was "the image of the leader," by which was meant primarily Lenin and especially Stalin. That same year, the Georgian director Mikhail Chiaureli was preparing *The Vow* (Kliatva), which established the paradigm for representing Stalin in the Soviet cinema. The original scenario *(Kliatva narodov)* was edited by Stalin in 1940 and the film was made in a radically amended version.[26]

Lukács, however, praises Scott because in his view he eschews "hero worship" of the sort to be found in Thomas Carlyle. Pushkin and Scott, he contends, were against "placing great men at the center of their historical portrayals," preferring a "middle-of-the-road" hero. The true leader, Lukács contends, is one whose activities "are directly interwoven with the life of the people."[27] We can speculate as to whether such statements represent a whitewashing of Stalin or on the contrary a critique, but this "image" comes up especially in Lukács's discussion of the contemporary antifascist novel, where he most engages the theme of the leader and how the great leader avoids any cult of personality or estrangement from "the people."

Lukács identifies as the most exemplary antifascist novel produced so far Heinrich Mann's *Henry the Fourth* (Die jugend des Königs Henri Quatre, 1935; Die vollendung des Königs Henri Quatre, 1938), about the founder of the Bourbon dynasty who reigned from 1553 to 1610.[28] *Henry the Fourth,* a fictionalized biography of a French king who presided over his country's Renaissance, presents an account of the heroic leader that fits in with standard Soviet historical fiction and films of this time in two key aspects. The prime one would be the theme of national unification. Henry makes the great sacrifice of abjuring his Protestant religion and converting to Catholicism for the sake of national unity and the expansion of the state, despite his bitter experience of the massive slaughter of Protestants by Catholics on St. Bartholomew's Day Eve (1572), an event that in commentary on the novel is generally taken as standing for the burning of the books or of the Reichstag in Nazi Germany. Second, the great leader establishes in France a just and highly cultured society, but he does this only by obdurately engaging in a series of battles in which his military acumen enables his cause to prevail, and by standing up to his many internal and external enemies (in the end Henry has to pay the ultimate sacrifice as he is killed by one of them).

Lukács is not entirely positive about *Henry the Fourth,* but his major criticism is that Mann does not sufficiently show Henry's links with the people. The ruler, Lukács insists, is no more than what the people make him, but Mann shows this only in places. In fact, "the secret of [Henry's] victory, then, as with every important historical figure, is his ability to understand the pressures of popular [narodnyi] life in favor of some historic change, to give consciousness to these pressures and translate them into deeds," a statement reminiscent of the Leninist rationalization of the commanding role played by the Party as a "vanguard of the proletariat," except that in this instance the rationalization is for the extraordinary power assumed by the one ruler.[29]

Henry the Fourth was but one of a selection of contemporary novels by European antifascist writers that were published in the Soviet Union in these years, some of them, such as this novel, with large print runs and avidly read by the populace and thus in effect incorporated into Soviet culture of the late 1930s.[30] Others include Rolland's prewar Bildungsroman *Jean Christophe* (1904–1912) and Thomas Mann's *Magic Mountain*

(Zauberberg; 1924).[31] A sign that these translations had some impact in the Soviet Union, these two novels were (as mentioned in the introduction) cited by the dramatist Afinogenov (who wrote *Salut, Ispaniia*) in his diary entries as he sought to triangulate his identity after he was thrown out of the Party in 1937.[32] Though such novels hardly represent cutting-edge modernism, they are decidedly Western texts and by non-Communist authors. The attention these three novels received in the Soviet Union was due in part, but only in part, to their authors' prominence in the antifascist cause.

Rolland's *Jean-Christophe* is not about national consolidation but rather about a transnational European cultural domain. In this respect, it is similar to Mann's *Magic Mountain,* which is set in a Swiss tuberculosis sanatorium with patients from all over Europe. Jean Christophe, Rolland's eponymous hero, a gifted musician—a Romantic standby—is German but spends much of his life in France, hence transcending the barriers between the two long-standing enemies and creating in his biography an axis at the heart of Europe. Heinrich Mann's *Henry the Fourth* might seem, by contrast, to be focused just on national consolidation. But inasmuch as the author is German, the novel implies transcending the fraught Franco-German boundary; in fact at the time Heinrich Mann idealized Popular Front France as an alternative model to fascist Germany and one that could be used to democratize the Soviet Union.[33]

Soviet historical fiction of this time (a subject, incidentally, left out of Lukács's book because, he says, translations are not yet available and he cannot read the originals) tended to give its parables of the strong leader more nationalist coloring than did European historical fiction. But in most of them this is modulated. This is particularly evident not in a novel but in a film that has been standardly presented as evidence of the vogue for nationalist themes, Eisenstein's *Ivan the Terrible,* part 1.

The subject of this film reflects a shift of the late 1930s in the historical precedents for the national leader. Earlier in the decade, the favorite model had been Peter the Great, a figure standing for modernization. Now it had become Ivan the Terrible, who had proved adept at prevailing over enemies and expanding and consolidating the country in a series of military engagements. His reign is generally considered to mark the beginning of Russian imperial expansionism, one of the themes in Eisenstein's film.

The central theme of the film is the drive to unify the Russian state under a powerful leader. In his initial plans of January 26, 1941, Eisenstein wrote: "a strong state internally is the basis for a strong state internationally."[34] This theme fit in with what was effectively Eisenstein's mandate in making the film—to provide in the story of Ivan's reign, as others also did as the result of similar commissions, an allegory for the career of Stalin, showing his greatness as a unifier of the country.

Ivan, the wild-eyed and grotesque figure in black in the film who is bent over by the cramped, medieval spaces through which he processes, seems the very incarnation of what so recently in the Soviet Union of the 1930s had been dismissed as "obscurantism" *(mrakobesie)*. In many respects, he seems a long way from the head of a great and modernizing state, as the Soviet Union wanted to appear, even allowing for the fact that this state is presented in historical allegory. But in this most complicated of films, the Russian national tradition was not unambiguously present. Much of the trilogy's visual and verbal imagery is derived from the Russian national tradition, and especially from icons and folklore, but other, Western elements are incorporated as well, if more cryptically and less obviously.

The surface plot of *Ivan the Terrible,* part 1, might be seen as crudely étatist and Russian nationalist, with, for example, caricatured images of Westerners at the tsarist court with their starched ruffs, contorted faces, and artificial manner of speech. Yet, as Yuri Tsivian has amply demonstrated, many of the film's key visual motifs (for Eisenstein absolutely crucial) derive from Western sources.[35] In fact, the Kremlin interiors are modeled on sketches for fictitious and atmospheric "prisons" *(Carceri d'invenzione)* made by the Italian artist Giovanni Battisti Piranesi.[36] In addition, Eisenstein was, at the time he began this project, coming off directing a production of Wagner's *Walkyrie* at the Bolshoi, commissioned to mark the Molotov-Ribbentrop Pact, and his stagings for that production colored some of the visual imagery as well.

Here I will be focusing on just one cluster among the several kinds of Western sources (visual and literary) used in the film trilogy. Though space does not permit me to cover the entire range, the examples I will discuss here are connected to a pervasive subtext: the western European

Renaissance as a model or context for Ivan's Russia, or for the contemporary Soviet Union.[37] Visual references to the Renaissance include the appearance in the film of young Basmanov, a founder and leader of the
oprichniki (the infamous special forces of tsar Ivan), an appearance
which is modeled on Botticelli's portrait of Giuliano de Medici.

Such visual cues might seem to be minor details or mere stylization,
but Eisenstein explicitly wanted a Renaissance association for Ivan. Part 1
begins with a text about his rule's Renaissance context. In addition,
Eisenstein titled an important account of his conception of the film, published in 1942, " 'Ivan the Terrible': A Film about the Russian Renaissance of the Sixteenth Century."[38] The main point that he makes there,
and that informs a lot of the imagery in the film, is that the powerful rulers
and patrons of western Europe during its Renaissance were no strangers
to cruel and violent means for dispatching enemies. Thus that Basmanov
is stylized along the lines of the Giuliano de Medici portrait indirectly
points to the fact that the Medici family wielded power by violence and
material wealth rather than by office.[39] In this article Eisenstein places
Ivan in the context of some of the famous western European rulers of the
Renaissance, Ivan's approximate peers, including Catherine de Medici
and Henry VIII,[40] and argues that the use of violence was ineluctable in
these famous Renaissance leaders' pursuit of the twin aims of aesthetic
and political power.[41] It has been an absolute cliché of historiography
about Russia that its Achilles' heel, so to speak, is the fact that it never
experienced a Renaissance and consequently missed out on becoming as
advanced as western Europe (and in the eyes of some is not European at
all). Is Eisenstein, then, seeking to enhance the image of medieval Russia
with Renaissance accoutrements and thereby challenge this cliché? Or is
Eisenstein suggesting an alternative model for the contemporary ruler of
his own country?

One of the more minor and scarcely noticed Renaissance references in
Ivan the Terrible is particularly telling in this connection. Eisenstein stipulates in his scenario, published in 1942, that in the early scenes of Ivan's
precoronation reign, the secretary to one of the foreign ambassadors is to
be made to look like "Erasmus of Rotterdam" (1466/1469–1536), as in the
Holbein portrait.[42] Although in the finished film there is no explicit men-

tion of Erasmus, a trace remains in the secretary's stylized image. In fact Eisenstein draws on artwork by a cluster of artists from the northern European Renaissance, particularly Dürer and Holbein, for his depictions of several characters. Both these artists produced several portraits of Erasmus and were part of his intellectual world. Holbein also, like Erasmus but on a more reduced scale, was a cosmopolitan peripatetic, working in different parts of northern Europe.

Erasmus was that intellectual giant of the Renaissance, a humanist and theologian who, though ordained a Catholic priest, kept up a lifelong assault against church rigidity and its excesses. In Eisenstein's script, by the coronation scene this "Erasmus" figure has been promoted from secretary to ambassador from Livonia, Muscovy's archrival in its territorial ambitions. As the other ambassadors make acerbic comments about how "Europe" will never recognize Ivan as having the status of a tsar, he responds: "if he's strong they will recognize [him]."[43] He then proceeds to undermine Ivan's efforts at unification by conducting a clandestine propaganda campaign that succeeds in persuading Andrey Kurbsky, Ivan's erstwhile friend and now political opponent, to defect to Livonia.

Eisenstein, then, gave a negative character in the film the likeness of a great hero of humanism! One could speculate that for Eisenstein presented a figure in the style of the portraits of Erasmus for purely aesthetic considerations, but this cannot be the whole story, in that in the scenario Eisenstein labels this figure a "humanist," a term especially connected with the antifascist movement. In his writings he includes Erasmus with Rabelais in his list of "the greatest masters of the centuries-long struggle of satire with the Forces of Darkness [Mrak]."[44]

But let us consider the qualities for which Erasmus's life is best known. Erasmus is considered quintessentially an independent spirit. He moved happily from country to country, a veritable citizen of the world, residing now in France, now in Italy, now in today's Belgium, Germany, or Switzerland, and eschewed family ties, honors, and institutional affiliations in the interests of intellectual freedom and independence.

These clichéd qualities of Erasmus could have resonated with Eisenstein himself (as well as Erasmus's possible homosexual proclivities). In the film, however, the Erasmus figure is far from independent; he is the emissary of an ambitious and antagonist state. Furthermore, with his

Realpolitik cynicism, he seems closer to that other Renaissance intellectual giant and opponent of Erasmus, Machiavelli, whose work *The Prince* (1513) was a central text for Eisenstein in preparing his script.[45] The emissary is physically like Erasmus, but his utterances are more like those of Machiavelli.

Why this disparity? An answer is suggested in Joan Neuberger's book on *Ivan the Terrible,* where she points to the many mirror images and semantic inversions in the representation of characters and to a distinct dualism that explains why the one character can represent both a position or an image antithetical to Eisenstein and one he might find ideal. She also suggests that Ivan is not consistently an allegorical representation of Stalin but sometimes stands more for Eisenstein's father and sometimes for Eisenstein himself.[46] One could speculate that Eisenstein is representing himself as Ivan both as a man of vision and as driven to moral lapses by blind ambition, succumbing to Realpolitik, or possibly that here Eisenstein has entered into a dialogue within himself (we will note that in the coronation scene when the Erasmus figure speaks, Ivan cocks his eyes and looks intensely in the direction of "Erasmus," while he shows no response when the other emissaries speak). This Livonian ambassador, then, is both a worthy interlocutor with Ivan, as Erasmus was in effect with Machiavelli, and a cynical opponent.[47]

Eisenstein might well have had Erasmus particularly in mind as a symbolic reference because of another historical novel by a Germanophone antifascist then widely discussed, Stefan Zweig's idealized fictionalization of his biography in *Erasmus* (1934).[48] This seems likely, given that Eisenstein had met Zweig, corresponded with him, and discussed favorably earlier books by Zweig and that Zweig, one of the foreign writers most read by Soviet intellectuals in the 1930s, still had a presence in the Soviet cultural press at this end of the decade.[49]

Zweig had since even before World War I been one of the most prominent opponents of nationalism and advocates of European unification. He presents Erasmus as an emblem of this position, "the first conscious European and cosmopolitan" whose ideal was a "Republic of Letters" facilitated in this instance not by French as the lingua franca but Latin. The republic's antagonist of the time Zweig characterizes, clearly with Nazi Germany in view, as "nationalism" and "terrible movements of mass intoxication." Erasmus was, by contrast, a "humanist," but Zweig defined humanism in terms not likely to be approved by the Soviet officials who advanced "humanism" as a slogan of the Moscow-leaning antifascist movement: "a free and independent mind, which refuses to be bound by any dogma and declines to join any party." Zweig, however, links Erasmus with Rabelais as like-minded and counterposes him to Machiavelli, whose *Prince,* with its advocacy of "the ruthless exercise of power and conquest in the realm of politics," he sees as threatening the Erasmus vision of "European unity as the sublimest ideal to coming generations."[50]

Anatole France, another European writer popular in the 1930s (and whom Eisenstein cites periodically in his writings), in his 1928 biography of Rabelais proposes that Rabelais was drawn to Erasmus and entered into a correspondence with him because Erasmus was considered the "prince" of "that symbolic republic," the republic of letters. This ideal, which took off during the Renaissance, was later adopted by Voltaire (as discussed in Chapter 4), who himself drew on Rabelais's works in his writings. Eisenstein, otherwise enthusiastic about France, was tepid about his account of Rabelais, which Eisenstein found "boring," no doubt because it did not dwell sufficiently on Rabelais's interest in the bodily and scatology.[51] Bakhtin, in his dissertation on Rabelais written at the end of the decade, emphasizes precisely this aspect of *Gargantua and Pantagruel,* but also Rabelais's irreverence and resistance to officially imposed dogma and conventions. In addition, Molière, a writer promoted in the 1930s as a giant of "world literature" but also associated with Rabelais (from whose works he drew), was the subject of Mikhail Bulgakov's play *Molière* (Mol'er; 1933). The production of *Molière* was stopped in 1936, a casualty of the anti-Formalist campaign. In other words, we see here a nexus of Soviet works on Renaissance "humanist" writers that enjoyed a somewhat tenuous existence in the second half of the 1930s. They can be linked with similar interests among western European intellectuals of the interwar period but could also be construed as presenting cosmopolitan biographies of intellectual giants that were part of the return to historical subjects in the 1930s but provided alternative models to those of the military and political leaders promoted in *Pravda* and official speeches.

One should consider here the historical moment in which the scenario for *Ivan the Terrible* was written—the first draft while so much of western Europe had fallen to the Nazi Germans, and later drafts after the Soviet

Union itself had been invaded. In fact, Lukács in *The Historical Novel* discusses Zweig's book on Erasmus but takes exception to the way Zweig "makes humanism and revolution into mutually exclusive opposites." "The really great traditions of European humanism were, on the contrary, always revolutionary," Lukács insists; "the struggle against fanaticism and for tolerance has always stood at the center of humanist ideology both in the Renaissance and particularly in the Enlightenment," and Erasmus in Zweig's account was much too conciliatory, much too into an "abstract pacifism."[52] The central argument of *The Prince,* by contrast, is about the need for a ruler to be strong at all times and to focus on building up the military and being prepared for war, even if this would be to the detriment of the arts and other accoutrements of "civilization".[53] Indeed, *Ivan the Terrible,* with such features as Ivan's establishment in part 1 of the *oprichnina* as a force loyal only to him, could be analyzed as an illustration of the principles outlined in *The Prince,* right down to its dictum "It is much safer to be feared than loved"[54] and its element of paranoia.

At the same time, the Renaissance references in this film trilogy, whether visual or literary, essentially open up the horizon of Russian history, placing it in a pan-European cultural space. They provide a grander context for Ivan, but potentially also a model for a more cosmopolitan purview for Soviet Russia.

In the Erasmus–Machiavelli dialogue, inserted cryptically into the film, we might sense the dilemmas of Eisenstein himself, as on the one hand a cosmopolitan deeply rooted in the European intellectual tradition and immersed in contemporary Western debates and trends and on the other a patriot who dreamed of Soviet intellectual hegemony even as he contemplated the fascist threat to "Europe" and looked to effective ways to combat it. He conceived the film as having a fugue form, a form that, with its theme and counterpoint, he saw as comparable with the dialectic.[55] One could see this form as having provided for Eisenstein a strategy for imbricating the cosmopolitan and the national with each other, while yet permitting both positions individual expression.

In this paradoxical image of Ivan as one who used violence that nonetheless led to a national flowering, one can see parallels between Eisenstein's account of the "Renaissance" leader and Heinrich Mann's *Henry the Fourth.*[56] Among the obvious parallels is the fact that in Mann's novel and Eisenstein's article on the Renaissance they foreground the

St. Bartholomew's Day massacre. But one of the biggest differences to be seen in comparing *Henry the Fourth* with the actual film *Ivan the Terrible* is Mann's salacious love plot, which contrasts with the representation of Ivan's love life; Ivan's wife, Anastasia, appears only in the stereotype of the virginal Slavic maiden cum braided Brunhilde. Though Mann's Henry IV is wise and cultivated, he is no puritan; carnal adventures play a central role in the plot, and presumably titillated the Soviet readers. No model for the puritanical Soviet Union, Henry is consumed by his love for his mistress, who bears him a series of illegitimate children. Rolland's *Jean Christophe,* though less earthy, chronicles a long series of Romantic adventures and misadventures on the part of its eponymous hero.

Romantic love, often tied to war, was, as we have seen, popular at this time in the Soviet Union. The link was so strong that, as mentioned earlier, the authoritative Fadeev, in responding to instructions from on high to produce a work based on Tolstoy's *War and Peace,* suggested Pushkin's *Eugene Onegin* as a substitute, a story of all-consuming Romantic love, albeit a passion ultimately mastered. In *Eugene Onegin,* as so often with Pushkin, the literary model was not from Scott but from another English writer, Lord Byron, whose own life provided a particularly juicy love plot. Pushkin's *Eugene Onegin,* a novel in verse, is generally considered to provide evidence that Pushkin had abandoned his earlier infatuation with the Byronic hero, who is satirized in it. But in the second half of the 1930s, a cult of Byron flourished in the Soviet cultural press.

The cult of Byron in the late 1930s, one of the many revivals of nineteenth-century culture at the time, problematizes such assumptive binaries of Western historiography on this period as national versus international (or westernizing, or cosmopolitan), and official or Party-minded versus dissident. The cult played a central role in a lobby for an alternative model to both socialist realist practice and the vogue for the historical novel, a model centered around a different generic mode, the lyric (favored by Hegel).

The Cult of Byron

In the second half of the 1930s the poets Byron, Pushkin, and Lermontov emerged as emblematic figures for the new times, each presented in his

Romantic aspect (despite Soviet criticism's mandatory insistence on the presentations' "realism"). The three became important as poets of dramatic nature and the sublime, of locales featuring exotic ethnics. Their biographies lent themselves, with more than a little casuistry, to presentation in terms of the love and death theme discussed in Chapter 7, as object lessons in the way the man of true passion defies convention and an oppressive status quo. Of Lermontov, for example, it was said that he preferred death to a dishonorable *(pozornoi)* life.[57]

Of the three, I am focusing here on Byron rather than Pushkin or Lermontov, even though in terms of the number of books published he was a lesser presence in the late 1930s than they were—especially Pushkin. Nineteen million mass editions of Pushkiniana were published in 1937–1938 alone, and he also appeared in the languages of the ethnic minorities.[58] The several editions of Byron released in these years never exceeded a print run of one hundred thousand copies, though that was a lot for a Western writer.[59]

I have chosen to focus on Byron in part because the Pushkin cult has been covered extensively in Western scholarship, but only in part. Another reason is that Byron was so influential in nineteenth-century Russia. In fact the translation of Byron's works into Russian, especially *Childe Harold's Pilgrimage,* was an important moment in the history of Russia's Romanticism, an example of the formative role of translation in cultural evolution that Lotman pinpoints.

I am going to use the cult of Byron as a lens for viewing two disparate but linked aspects of the culture of the late 1930s when the Byron cult was at its height. These aspects can be seen as coming together around "Byron" and the rhetoric the cult generated, though I am proposing the cult neither as cause nor as effect but rather as a phenomenon that throws these aspects into relief. The first of these is the warrior-patriot, the second is the campaign for bringing back "the lyric" to Soviet culture.

Byron—or rather the cult of Byron—was a phenomenon not contained or determined by its ostensible referent, Byron the poet. Byron's primary function was as a symbolic figure, an emblem for a nexus of values. Critics consequently focused on his biography. There was little analysis of his verse (except by Viktor Zhirmunskii, the leading Byronist, and Boris Meilakh) and such analysis of the verse as was produced was largely concerned with biographical aspects. So Byron provided yet another exemplary biography for a culture already overcrowded with them.

Byron seems in many respects an improbable idol for Soviet culture, aristocratic rake that he was. Surely Soviet critics were not promoting the Byron who was "mad, bad and dangerous to know" and a sexual adventurer? But just as recent Western biographical writing on Byron has cast him in terms of trendy preoccupations—Byron the crossdresser, Byron the bi-sexual, Byron the "self-fashioner," Byron who celebrated "anti-modern exoticism" at a time of colonial expansion[60]—Stalinist critics painted a different portrait reflecting their obsessions, picking out aspects that dovetailed with their purposes, and ignoring or denying others. He was said to have been a "political exile."[61] Critics insisted that Western commentators with their "salon version of Byron had "gotten it all wrong" in stressing his "pessimistic inclinations"; they were the inevitable result of a childhood of poverty and humiliation and of his great concern for oppressed peoples.[62] This highly edited biographical portrait is reflected in the selections of poems published in the various Byron anthologies that came out in these years. The contents of these collections varied, but they tended to include some of his politically polemical works, some lyric verse, and some of *Childe Harold*.

One must ask how Byron, even as a "freedom fighter," could be emblematic of the late 1930s when, standard historiography tells us, the dominant trend in Soviet culture was toward establishing hegemony for Russian national culture? The discourse of his cult brings out the ambiguities of these times, which embraced both great Russian chauvinism and cosmopolitanism. Byron was functional for both. Though not a Russian writer, he had strong links with the golden age of Russian literature and particularly with Russia's national poets, Pushkin and Lermontov. The 150th anniversary of Byron's birth on January 22, 1938, was given a lot of media coverage, but it was positioned between the lavish celebrations for the centennial of Pushkin's death in January 1937 and the 125th anniversary of Lermontov's birth on October 15, 1939. Moreover, Byron had already long been incorporated into the account of these two canonical authors.[63] Thus he could be seen as standing on the one hand, for Europe and on the other for the Russian tradition. While he was effectively incorporated into the Russian cum Soviet canon, his assimilation into that canon enabled a de facto new reading of it, taking it beyond the confines of the national chauvinist position. His advocates frequently identified him as a "European" (rather than English) writer.[64]

In Russia, Byron had been a recurrent presence. But in the Soviet era he became particularly prominent in 1936, when two biographies were published: first, a translation of *Byron,* by André Maurois (originally published in French in 1930), and second, a biography by Anatolii Vinogradov, issued by Koltsov's publishing house, Zhurgaz.[65] The Vinogradov text was a response to the Maurois one, which dwelled on Byron's titillating love life; the book so infuriated the Soviet literary establishment that in the Byron anniversary issue of *Literaturnaia gazeta* for 1938, contributors were still obsessively attacking it.

Where Maurois erred on the side of overemphasizing the love life, Vinogradov minimized it; in fact he specifically polemicized against "the majority of biographers of Byron" for their "one-sided" "reduction of the poet's significance to circumstances of a purely personal and even intimate character."[66] Vinogradov mentions most of the poet's best known dalliances, but frequently en passant. The book opens with Byron returning from his first trip to Europe intent on delivering his thundering maiden addresses to the House of Lords (cited copiously) in which he defends the Luddites (local to his seat at Newstead Abbey near Nottingham), whom Vinogradov represents not as antimodernists but as workers suffering at the hands of rapacious capitalist exploiters. Byron's political involvements and the economic and political realities within which he operated then form the dominant narrative thread in the biography. Byron himself is portrayed as a fierce satirist, the restless "genius" who refused to acquiesce to the status quo and became a victim of repeated slanderous press campaigns and secret police informants. His serial love conquests are framed by this extensively documented material and are largely written up as the responses of a noble soul rendered desperate before the specter of postrevolutionary conservatism throughout Europe. Byron's life, we are told, was marked by the way he "sought to contain the chaos of the feelings within, which alternated in Byron with an unstoppable drive to go beyond the limits not only of society's morality but also of those barriers that, in the interests of self-preservation, a normal [zdorovyi] person sets himself."[67]

The Spanish Civil War further vaulted Byron to prominence in Stalinist Russia, and at the Second Congress for the Defense of Culture held in
Valencia, and then Madrid, in the summer of 1937 he was singled out as
the bard of peoples' liberation from despotic regimes or occupying foreign powers. This choice had its own logic, since Byron was, crucially,
not a Russian, and he had been a voluntary exile, like so many writers at
the Congress. Moreover, he had been in Spain in 1808 when the Spaniards had been driving out Napoleon. In actuality, Byron had been enthusiastic about Napoleon, a fact conveniently forgotten (Vinogradov calls
his attitude to Napoleon mixed), but the speakers were in any case able to
focus on Byron's work for the Risorgimento in Italy (the struggle for independence from Austro-Hungary) and above all his sacrifice of dying in
Greece while fighting for the cause of its independence from the Turks
(presented as if it was a heroic death rather than, as in actuality, succumbing to illness).

The cult of Byron outlived the cause of Republican Spain (lost in
March 1939) and the intensely cosmopolitan moment of the Popular
Front. His continued co-optation by Soviet literature could be justified
on many grounds, including the fact that Engels, serendipitously, and as
Soviet commentators pointed out, had noted that Byron was especially
popular among worker readers.[68] Belinsky, at this time the most authoritative nineteenth-century critic, had also endorsed Byron. His line on
Byron was often invoked: "above all Byron's poetry stuns and overwhelms [obomleet], filling one's soul with terror [uzhasom], and wonder
[udivleniem] at the poet's colossal person [lichnosti], his titanic daring,
and the lofty nature [actually gordost'] of his feelings and thoughts."[69]

The imprimatur of Belinsky conveniently places Byron within both
the national canon and Russian revolutionary traditions. But arguably,
even though Belinsky produced this characterization almost a century
earlier, it anticipates important ways that "Byron" resonated with the culture of the late 1930s. In the Belinsky quotation, with such telltale terms as
"terror," "overwhelm," and "colossal," we can see how Belinsky casts Byron the poet as a version of the sublime. Yet Byron also functioned as an
inspirational figure for those who were offended by the more rabid forms
of Russian chauvinism and who were more cosmopolitan in orientation;
Vinogradov emphasizes that Byron had a pan-European perspective.[70]

He was also for many of his advocates the poet of love and war, of all-out engagement in a great cause, and hence often a cipher for Spain. He was also important for writers who wanted to make socialist realism more open to representing characters' inner feelings and aspirations.

Byron's writings probably resonated with the Soviet literati and a public tired of the thin gruel of production novels. The cult of Byron played a role in a campaign to restore to culture the personal and the individual, interior self. A capsule version of Byron often found in the criticism was that of penner of "fiery political satire and tender love lyrics."[71] The political satire was taken to be about rejection of bourgeois society, but the "tender love lyrics" of Byron made him an authorizing referent in a campaign of the late 1930s for a less crudely politicized poetry, what was called "the lyric." In this instance, the debate was not conducted behind closed doors at a high-level meeting in the Writers Union but came out in public, in the press, and especially in *Literaturnaia gazeta*.

"On the Right to the Lyric"

The campaign for "the lyric" evolved progressively, developing partly out of the cult of Mayakovsky that emerged in response to Stalin's pronouncement in 1935 that "Mayakovsky was and remains the best and most talented poet of our Soviet epoch,"[72] which had rescued the poet from the problematic status his reputation had held since 1930, when he had committed suicide.

The canonization of Mayakovsky (actually the only Soviet writer whom Stalin endorsed in such a public and forthright manner) fostered the rise of poetry as the major genre of the late thirties. At Writers Union plenums of March 1935 and 1936, and at a meeting of the Writers Union Presidium in October 1936, spokesmen recommended that Soviet literature pay greater attention to poetry, and this became a recurrent instruction to journals and presses.[73] The percentage of poetry increased in both the literary journals and the publishing house lists, until by 1938 poetry predominated in their literary sections. That same year the string quartet, hitherto marginalized, emerged as a prominent Soviet musical genre, featured at the *dekada* (ten-day festival) of Soviet music, which included quartets by Prokofiev and Shostakovich (his first). In poetry, Mayakovsky's erstwhile associate, Nikolai Aseev—who had also been a mentor to Tretiakov in his early literary career around 1921 in Vladivostok—became a sort of surrogate poet-elder; he periodically pronounced on poetry, and aspiring young poets made pilgrimages to him hoping to get his endorsement for their work.

Mayakovsky was a strange choice for Stalin in 1935, given that his name is particularly associated with the Russian avant-garde, now increasingly discredited. But Mayakovsky was also the author of a long poem on Lenin and of many agitational poems.

Many of the key issues in the campaign for the lyric crystallized in the debate about "political poetry" of early 1937 and also the Writers Union plenum of February 1937, when speakers urged that the lyric be reinstated as a worthy genre. One of the most controversial and central articles contributing to this debate was "On Political Poetry," published in the May number for 1937 of *Literaturnyi kritik* by its leading editor, Usievich. Here Usievich argues against publishing the sort of simplistic poetry that merely translates the political platform directly into verse. "Paradoxical as it might sound," she insists, "in Mayakovsky's cries about love unrequited there was more social content than in many lamentations on political themes written by the minor epigones of populist [narodnyi] poetry." Directly political poems are frequently "prosaic and impersonal [bezlichnost']" and often comprise no more than "hastily rhymed slogans." A worker of today is too sophisticated for this, she contends; he "himself insists on his right to experience the most varied human feelings, including love." "Man is not a machine set up exclusively to 'produce steel' and to express lyrically his love for the factory work bench, 'My darling work bench, I don't want to go home'." Such verse is not "genuine." Poets need to be "sincere."[74]

Key terms of the discourse of 1937–1940 about the lyric, evident in Usievich, are "the authentic (genuine, true [podlinnyi])," and "sincerity" [iskrennost'].[75] These epithets were invoked in the cause of dismantling the facile standard narrative of the production novel, the backbone of Soviet cultural production, in which the love plot was always subordinated to the twin overarching plot that chronicled the hero's fulfillment of the local targets in the national economic plan and of his own political development.[76] In several new novels the agonies and complexities of love are presented in a more realistic vein than in standard socialist realist texts, giving them a greater role in their heroes' lives than that of just auxiliary plots.[77]

A long debate on the lyric and the political in literature ensued over the remaining years of the 1930s, generating dozens of articles like this one from Usievch.[78] One landmark contribution was the article "Notes on Poetry," published by Konstantin Simonov, then a young poet and literary critic, in *Literaturnaia gazeta* of December 28th, 1939. Simonov's first subheading in this article, one that others used in allied articles as a catchphrase, was "On the Right to the Lyric." Simonov asserts here that "an honest lyrical book is always convincing." Such a book, he continues, "tells about a person, but not about a typical person who with a firm, sometimes overly firm, stride progresses through novels and epic poems." Rather "a hero of a true [pravdivyi] lyrical book is an author operating with his own poetic self-perception." "The author does not try to make him a composite person." If he did, the work would become a "poetic falsehood." It is only in time, looking back, that we see in what appears to be an individualized lyric persona the typical traits of his time. But, Simonov observes, in contemporary literature, all too often, if two lovers meet in a work, the boy has to be a "tank driver" and the girl a "parachute jumper." "Some think the task of literature . . . is now just to respond to the events of the day in straight, unmediated agitation," he continues, but this is only a "masked justification for the paltriness [melkovodnosti] of one's talents which are not capable of seeing at a deeper level, beneath the hundreds of daily tasks, the overall movement of the epoch." Though literature should not cease to address burning issues of the day, there should be no "lowering to the lowest common denominator [nivelirovka]." Rather—here implicitly invoking the early Marx—"as we approach Communism in literature there will develop a multifacetedness [mnogogrannost'], a breadth of horizons."

Effectively, behind the front of discussing the lyric, we have in Simonov's article a demand to dismantle the conventions of socialist realism ("the typical," the "composite" character, "unmediated agitation," the focus on current issues, and couples treated not as individuals but as such poster categories as the "tank driver" and the "female parachute jumper"). Simonov's call for "multifacetedness" could be read as a de-

mand for greater pluralism and sophistication, for a less simplistic interpretation of the doctrine of mandatory "Party-mindedness" *(partiinost').*

Understandably, efforts to reinstate a "genuine lyric" in culture recurrently met authoritative opposition, especially likely given that the campaign for the lyric of the 1930s developed in its initial stages more or less
in tandem with the purges. The Writers Union plenum on poetry (the
"Pushkin plenum") of February 1937 finished the day before Bukharin
was arrested (on February 27, 1937), and at its last session the writer Aleksandr Bezymensky, himself a target of the campaign for "the lyric," attacked the speeches made by Bukharin and Radek at the First Congress
of the Writers Union in 1934.[79] Bukharin in his speech had declared that
agitational poetry, which he identified with Mayakovsky, had outlived its
usefulness and proposed as a counter-example the verse of Pasternak.
But Bukharin was purged even as the debate about the lyric was taking
off. Its detractors referred with alacrity to his speech in discrediting the
lobby for the "lyric."

The day after Bukharin's arrest, an unsigned article appeared in
Pravda, "On Political Poetry," which reported that *Pravda* had recently
convened a meeting on this very topic at which speakers had discussed
the dangerous recent tendency to advocate the Bukharinite position on
poetry and claim that poetry need not be directly political.[80] At the Party
plenum, which came shortly after the writers' plenum, Stalin made two
speeches (on March 3 and 5) that provided the official narrative rational-
izing the purges.[81]

The stakes were high and the risks for those advocating a less crudely
politicized poetry palpable.

The "lyric" also had its own powerful lobby. Undeterred by attacks of
early 1937, in late 1937–early 1938 a series of meetings of poets were held
in Moscow to try to foster more lyric poetry.[82] Both lobbies had institutional affiliations. The campaign for the lyric was centered in the journal
Literaturnyi kritik, where Usievich was ensconced, in *Literaturnaia
gazeta,* and in IFLI. Lifshits, an advocate of the lyric, was prominent in all
three.[83]

During the campaign of the late 1930s, both sides of the debate about
the lyric used purge accusations as weapons against their opponents.
While the detractors of the "lyric" had a gift in the current vilification of

Bukharin, Usievich's 1937 article "On Political Poetry" is quite disturbing and distasteful in this regard. Again and again she buttresses her position by denouncing, using stock purge formulations, some writer or group recently purged and attributing to them, often questionably, the position she is arguing against. Similarly, once the leaders of the militant proletarian literary organization RAPP, which had been so powerful in the 1920s, were purged as Trotskyites in 1937, several campaigners for the "lyric" jumped on the bandwagon and (unfairly) attributed "schematicism, varnishing reality," to that organization, alleging that the theoreticians of RAPP's Litfront did not want "human character" depicted but rather "a schema of a human being as a bearer of a social tendency," when in reality Litfront had campaigned for representing the "living man" and showing his inner conflicts.[84]

One should not write such machinations off as only casuistry. The campaign of the late 1930s for "the lyric" could be seen as an integral part of a terror campaign that insisted that citizens not be deceived by external appearances and even apparently impeccable sociological and work profiles but look deep within their fellow citizens to reveal the "true" self within. When classic Russian authors were appropriated in the service of the campaign for "the lyric," accounts of them were often inflected with purge discourse. Lermontov, for example, was characterized as a poet deeply involved in the "personal" and "feverishly sought his own expression for his feelings and thoughts" so that he began to "look intensely [pristal'no]" within himself.

The demand for greater realism, for an end to purely external, superficial representation of characters and to positive heroes who stride through the workplace with seven-league boots, had been recurrent in Soviet literature ever since the early harbingers of what was later codified as socialist realism began to appear. In some instances the critics called for more "lyric."[85] However, some specific terms of this debate, such as "sincerity" and "the authentic (true, or genuine)," were new features.[86] These very qualities were an alleged feature of Romantic style; as Lionel Trilling remarks in his book on Romanticism, *Sincerity and Authenticity,* "these now old-fashioned terms point to a set of stylistic conventions developed by the Romantics to give the illusion of 'spontaneous overflow' to their verse."[87]

The Soviet campaign for the lyric could never be identified with high Romanticism because Romanticism's account of "sincerity," and so on, though as Trilling suggests inevitably grounded in a repertoire of formal strategies, required at least the surface affirmation of individualism and uniqueness. Lovejoy in *The Great Chain of Being* defines Romanticism as a movement that "set the highest value upon the unique, the peculiar, the local."[88] To have advocated for poetry "the lyric" in such senses would have been impossible in the 1930s context, but probably also not desirable to these poets. Simonov pointedly dismissed such notions, asserting: "the right to the lyric is not the right to a propagandistic assertion of one's lyrical 'I'" by poets who "want to be only in themselves."[89] Advocates really only endorsed a less programmatic, less hackneyed poetry that was based on genuine experience, rather than predigested formulas, and more focus on the private lives and personal reactions of the poetic "I." Consequently, most poets and critics at this time promoted what they called "civic lyric" *(grazhdanskaia lirika),* a somewhat oxymoronic genre they claimed to be typical of Byron's work.[90]

Byron also had his detractors, most notably Lukács, who attacked him in *The Historical Novel* for peddling a "lyrical subjectivist absolute," anathema to the Marxist Lukács (he had assessed Byron more favorably in *Theory of the Novel*).[91] But Fadeev promoted Byron. In other words, there were polemics even among the authoritative. It might seem that the old debate of the Romantic era, Byron versus Scott, had somehow resurfaced in the Stalinist 1930s, despite the considerable "mutability" shown by "history" over the intervening one-hundred-odd years. Lukács might, in his take on Byron and the "lyric," seem to have been counterposed to his two allies, Lifshits and Usievich. In point of fact, he was enthusiastic about the lyric, as is seen in his introduction to an edition of Heine's lyrics.[92]

The "campaign for the lyric" was less directed at the historical novel per se than at the epic mode, favored by Lukács, which dominated not just in literature but in Soviet culture of these years broadly conceived. Stalin (more accurately those in power in culture) in effect drew on the imaginative power of the epic as he (they) sought to diminish the divide between the literary and the actual by creating by fiat (or by rhetoric) an epic world. A central feature of public culture was epic stagings. The

rhetoric about the first Stakhanovite, Andrei Stakhanov, created an epic
proletarian, a mythic miner, and then duplicated him in different fields
and different republics, as it were a living complement to the great epics
now being created in literature (not just in novels but also in a series of
pseudo–folk epics). Other examples include the public sagas developed
around long-distance flight and the rescues of the Chelyuskin and Papanin expeditions from the perilous Arctic North (rendered in turn in folk-
style epics).[93] The purges fit in to this epicized world, providing as they
did enemies of a dimension appropriate to epic.

But lyric and epic are not necessarily antagonistic, and especially not
in the historical novel. Some proposed for socialist realism a combination
of "the lyric and the heroic," potentially a generic cross of the lyric and
the epic;[94] Koltsov's *Spanish Diary* was sometimes characterized in these
terms.[95] And, realistically, the socialist realist novel, as the Soviet canonical cultural expression, could never have lost sight of its "epic" nature—
how else could the revolution or military engagement be conveyed as the
originary moment of the new national tradition?

Bakhtin in his essays of the late 1930s entered, in effect, into these
swirling debates, though as a silent participant, in that he could not publish and was condemned to live beyond one hundred kilometers from
Moscow, the standard rule for former exiles such as himself. He argues in
"Epic and Novel" (1941) and elsewhere that the novel, which he counterposes to the epic, and privileges, is a highly fluid genre that potentially
includes in its capacious frame many other genres and subgenres. This
essay contributed *in potentia* to the contemporary critiques of socialist
realist practice. It also implicitly attacked Lukács (his *K istorii realizma* of
1939 is cited in Bakhtin's 1940 dissertation on Rabelais, though the reference is omitted in the published version).[96] Lukács in "Narration or Description?" (1936, discussed in Chapter 3) is careful to distinguish
between the classical epic and the kind of epic forms he is promoting for
present-day fiction, but he stipulates that the contemporary "epic"
should, like its classical antecedent, be characterized by a "wholeness."
Bakhtin, by contrast, identifies "open-endedness," more literally "no-
completedness" *(nezavershënnost')* and the breakup of "epic wholeness"
in the hero as a welcome and defining feature of the novel. He also stresses
the anticanonical stance of his genre-hero, the novel, and is hence effec-

tively at cross-purposes with socialist realism, which had been institutionalized as a set of rigid conventions structured by a "masterplot." He foregrounds the "national epic past," or "national tradition," in his account of the "constitutive features" of the novel's antinomic counterpart, the epic, in effect not only critiquing the anachrony of epic, which he dismisses as a "congealed and half-moribund genre," but also arguing for an "authentic [podlinnyi] profile of the past" no less than the present.[97] With this repeated call for "authenticity," Bakhtin was invoking (though probably not consciously so) a standard term for the advocates of the "lyric."

Even as these debates, which had obvious relevance for current literary practice, were going on, some of the principals in my narrative were succumbing to the purges. Koltsov was among them. In early 1937, when he seems to have been at the peak of his power, his name was everywhere in the press. But on the night of December 13, 1938, just after he delivered a laudatory address at the Writers Union about the *Short Course*, commissioned by Stalin, Koltsov was arrested at his *Pravda* office.

The arrest of Koltsov, a symbol of the Spanish cause at the time, stunned Moscow, and the news spread quickly. The second book of his *Spanish Diary* was being prepared for publication in *Novyi mir*, the page proofs were virtually done, and it was awaited with impatience, but was not to be.[98] There have been several interpretations as to why Koltsov was purged. One of them is that he was one of the several prominent cosmopolitan intellectuals (Meyerhold, Babel) who were arrested and executed at about the same time and who had spent time in the West and hobnobbed with visiting Western antifascists, including Gide, and that Koltsov was particularly associated with the Gide fiasco. In addition, Stalin was not amused that the Spanish effort was by then clearly failing. To compound this, it is said, André Marty, political commissar of the International Brigades in Spain from 1936 to 1938, with whom Koltsov had a fraught relationship, had denounced him.[99] But in any event, Koltsov had always known that the security forces held a thick and growing dossier of material against him and that he could be purged at any time. He underwent 416 days of interrogation before being tried on February 1, 1940, and shot the next day.[100] Apletin replaced him as head of the Foreign Commission of the Writers Union, though Fadeev, who was elevated to secretary of the Writers Union in 1939, ran much of its affairs, liaising with Louis

Aragon in Paris, where the Association for the Defense of Culture still had its headquarters, the two in effect a replacement for the Koltsov-Erenburg axis (Aragon had replaced Erenburg after he resigned in 1937).[101]

Even before his arrest, Koltsov's empire had begun to crumble. In February 1938 he had corresponded with Aragon, but he was out of the Foreign Commission in March.[102] The days of *Das Wort*, which survived on Koltsov's subventions from Zhurgaz, were clearly numbered, and in March 1939 it was closed and amalgamated with *Internationale Literatur*.[103] *Za rubezhom* had already been shut down in 1938, and Zhurgaz itself was liquidated in May 1939, as Erpenbeck reported in a letter of 15 May 1939 to Maria Osten, who had been in Paris running the office of *Das Wort* there since January 1938, adding: "you can show this to Willi [Münzenberg] if you like."[104]

When Maria heard that Koltsov had been arrested, she was so distraught that she decided, against all advice, to go back to Moscow in an attempt to clear his name (one of the accusations in his interrogation was that they were having an affair and she was a Nazi spy). But in vain. When she returned to Paris in May, Hubert, her adopted son from the Saar, realizing that she was in trouble politically, refused to let her into her apartment on the grounds that she was an "enemy of the people" and the apartment was his.[105] Thus her dreams of a transnational, pan-European melded family were shattered. Maria was not immediately arrested. When on May 30, 1941, Brecht left Moscow en route to America via the Soviet Union—a trip organized by the Foreign Commission of the Writers Union under Apletin and partly subsidized by Feuchtwanger's royalties held in Goslitizdat—he was obliged to leave there a dying Margarete Steffin (one of several mistress-collaborators), and Maria cared for Margarete, an old friend, sending Brecht a telegram to inform him of her death.[106] But after Steffin died on June 4, Maria was more vulnerable: she was arrested (on June 24, 1941, two days after the Germans invaded) and was shot on September 16, 1942, in Saratov.[107] The callous Hubert was also arrested, on June 22, and sent to exile in Kazakhstan.[108]

The high point of the traveling mode and European cosmopolitanism, 1935–1937, had passed. Already in 1937 a spate of books had appeared that warned about how foreign governments were sending "spies and diversants" to the Soviet Union, including some "in the guise of actors, directors, and other cultural workers."[109] That the state was losing interest in the émigrés is evident in, for example, the fact that the Club for Foreign Workers, where they had been giving lectures to each other, was closed early in 1938.[110]

Translated works were, however, still the primary obsession of *Literaturnoe obozrenie* as late as 1939. Narrower horizons became evident only starting with number 18 for that year, when a new section—"Around the Regions and Republics" (Po oblastiam i respublikam) was added and the section "Abroad" (Za rubezhom) became shorter and was now mostly concerned with writers from the Soviet orbit, a trend that had been developing over the past few years.

The anticosmopolitan drift did not occur without resistance. Lukács's associate Vladimir Grib, in his published critique of the list of books forthcoming from the state publishing house Goslitizdat in 1939, complains that because of serious omissions, the multivolume Balzac, Heine, Diderot, Schiller, Shakespeare, France, and Goethe will not be complete. In the case of Goethe the multivolume edition will even lack *Faust*. Other exclusions he finds outrageous are volumes 2 and 3 of Hegel's *Aesthetics*, Kant's *Critique of Pure Reason*, Schelling's *Philosophy of Art*, and a few works by Diderot. The translations of Hegel and Schelling are ready and have been lying around for some time in the publishing house (SotsEk-Giz), he adds; and among the poets, many influential ones such as Wordsworth and Verlaine need to be published.[111]

Even as so many cosmopolitan projects and intellectuals were felled in these waning years of the 1930s, a new generation was emerging. With so many established writers purged or cowed, young writers got the opportunity to enter the limelight earlier than they otherwise might have. But this new generation, who were primarily poets rather than prose writers, also had a cosmopolitan bent. And they, not just the older generation of critics such as Lifshits and Usievich, took up the cause of the "genuine lyric"—not coincidentally, perhaps, a short form and hence suitable for moments of change. Many of the emerging poets studied in IFLI or the Literary Institute; Konstantin Simonov, prominent among them, graduated from the Literary Institute in 1938 and was a graduate student at IFLI from 1938 to 1939.

At that time IFLI was located in Sokolniki, in those days the very edge of Moscow and accessible only by a tram from the last metro stop. Memoirists look back on this institution with nostalgia and have painted it as a place where all were caught up in the romance of poetry. Students spurned the tram and walked to class from the metro in order to recite their verses and favorite poems to each other. They crowded into kitchens at night declaiming back and forth. Their literary models included Mayakovsky, and Pasternak, who had earlier been Bukharin's model for postagitational verse, but they were also drawn to some French modernist poets such as Verlaine and Baudelaire who had appeared recently in translation in an anthology of French lyric poetry.[112]

In general IFLI was of cosmopolitan orientation. Legendary from this time are the debates that took place there in auditorium number 15 (standing room only) about an issue hotly contested at the time—Lukács's contention that certain great writers of the nineteenth century were progressive because their commitment to realism meant that they painted an accurate picture of class conditions *despite* their own conservative political positions. His supporters, so called "despitists" *(voprekisty),* were overwhelmingly in the majority there.[113] But "despite" the great support among the student body for the Lukács position, it was not fated to prevail at this time. Nor was his chief Russian-language outlet, *Literaturnyi kritik,* which was closed (November 26, 1940).[114] Its demise had been foreshadowed six months earlier in a memorandum to the Central Committee secretaries of February 10, 1940, "On the Anti-Party Faction in Soviet Literature," by Fadeev and Valery Kirpotin, that attacked *Literaturnyi kritik* as "working from false non-Marxist premises" so that "in their characterizations of Balzac, Shakespeare, Tolstoy, and other writers any element of class characterization is lost." One suspects that this remark has more to do with a reaction against Lukács's highly cosmopolitan account of literary history than specifically with class, but in any event it demonstrates how the Lukács of the 1930s, dubbed by Western criticism a "Stalinist," remained more steadfast in his theoretical positions on literature than did "Stalinism" itself. He was no longer the authority figure of his essay on the novel; a publishing house recruited Shklovsky for a negative internal review of his *Historical Novel.*[115] The next year, on June 29, 1941 (just after the German invasion), Lukács was arrested, though not in his capacity as a literary theoretician but as a member of the Hungarian Communist Party, a politico (he had rejoined only that spring).[116] He was soon released (on August 26) and was evacuated to Tashkent later, in 1941, with a group of Germanophone writers; there he published an anti-Nazi tract, *The Struggle of Humanism with Barbarism* (Bor'ba gumanizma i varvarstva).

The late 1930s are not all about endings, however, or even about the end of cosmopolitanism. The Spanish Civil War held the imagination of Soviet intellectuals long after it had been lost and the Bolshevik leadership turned cold on it. The cult of Byron was linked to an intense Soviet patriotism, one that rejected the *kvasnyi patriotizm* (a term that is difficult to translate but could be very approximately rendered as "redneck patriotism") of many contemporaries. This alternative patriotism involved a reweighting but not an erasure of the international perspective. The new young generation of writers who were coming into Soviet literature more or less as the war in Spain ended, people like Pavel Kogan, Simonov, and Alexander Tvardovsky, took that war as their emblematic inspirational moment.

Simonov and his cohort, inspired by Koltsov's *Spanish Diary,* idealized the ethos of those who fought in the Spanish Civil War, especially the Hungarian Communist writer Mate Zalka, the martyred commander of an International Brigade, there called General Lukács.[117] Simonov, himself an army brat and close to the military, though he trained at the literary Institute and IFLI, wrote in his memoirs later that this war gave him "precise moral criteria," and he produced several poems extolling this military hero.[118]

However, and we have seen this already in his role in the campaign for "the lyric," Simonov was also seriously committed to rejuvenating socialist realism, and this impacted his coverage of war. Like others in his cohort, he was against facile heroism and simplistic poetry where the enemy is routed in just a few days. In the thinking of Simonov's cohort we can see parallels with Bakhtin's account in his essay "Epic and Novel" of the novel's rejection of the heroism of the epic, though of course Bakhtin was operating on a very different level of sophistication, erudition, and theoretical power. Simonov, like Bakhtin in his account of the novel, emphasized grounding the text in "experience." In seeking to give his verse coverage of war an "authentic voice" and to avoid the elevated tone of much socialist realist verse, he used conversational speech in a matter-of-fact style, as was typical in this later moment of those lobbying for "the right to the lyric." Bakhtin emphasized "familiar speech" but went beyond Simonov in including in novelistic discourse "profanation." Simonov also favored a strong autobiographical element in poetry, very striking to those brought up on the austere, ascetic verse of the 1930s.[119]

The cosmopolitan cause received its greatest blow with the signing of the Molotov-Ribbentrop Pact in September 28, 1939. This proved the final straw for many of the leading Western antifascist intellectuals, who had until then held out on condemning the Soviet Union and resisted denouncing the purges in the belief that it was the main bulwark against fascism. Malraux, one of them, had wanted to bring his film on Spain, *Espoir* (see Chapter 7), to Moscow in June 1939 but was enraged by the pact and broke with the Communists.[120] On August 13–14 an antifascist congress was held in Paris, but there were no Soviet attendees, except Erenburg, who went into a deep depression over the pact, so much so that for several months he had trouble eating.

Eisenstein, however, received a windfall from the pact's aftermath, a surprise commission to direct Wagner's opera *The Valkyrie* at the Bolshoi. The production was to be a Soviet gesture in recognition of the pact; the Germans were staging Mussorgsky's *Boris Godunov* in Berlin. Eisenstein began work on the production in March 1940, and the opera premiered in November. However, he reacted to this commission somewhat idiosyncratically, to say the least. In his work on it, he was particularly interested in the Wagnerian idea of the synthesis of the arts, a topic he had just pursued in his article "Pride" (Gordost'), which proclaimed cinema the highest art form precisely for its ability to synthesize.[121] He also included short film pieces in the opera that presented visually Siegfried's narrative about his father. But to the consternation of the critics, he used this project to indulge his interest in the prelogical and the premodern world of myth (discussed in Chapter 5).[122] As for the Germans, they did not appreciate the fact that their Wagner was being staged by a Jew.

After the Molotov-Ribbentrop Pact, correspondence with the antifascist émigrés ceased. Translations and publications of Western literature tapered off in cultural journals, but never disappeared.[123] In fact, antifascist material had diminished sharply earlier, after Litvinov was replaced by Molotov as minister of foreign affairs on May 3, 1939.[124] An example of the changes is that in August 1937 Karmen, on returning to Moscow from Spain, was given a hero's welcome at the Kiev Station.[125] However, by the time Shub and Vishnevsky had turned a selection of his newsreel footage into a film and it premiered in Moscow on August 20, 1939, the Molotov-Ribbentrop Pact was about to be signed, ensuring that the film was virtually never screened. By then, as Iuliia Markovna Zhivova has reported to me, her father, a dismissed cultural journalist from *Izvestiia* and literary scholar, was like many at that time scared to possess foreign books. He offered his collection to the Foreign Languages Library, but its director Margarita Rudomino, was also apprehensive and refused them, and so Zhivov burned them.[126]

Several writers of the German diaspora, such as Asja Lacis's husband, Bernhard Reich, were still able to publish in the cultural press, especially in *Literaturnaia gazeta,* perhaps another sign that literary journals had some, if very limited, independence. The cult of the Spanish Civil War continued to be reflected in these journals' pages, especially the cult of its martyr-hero General Lukács (now referred to by his real name, Mate Zalka). Nazi works or predilections were not promoted, and it remained possible to cover American culture (the United States did not enter the war until December 1941); *Iskusstvo kino* continued to publish on American cinema, though palpably less beginning with the last two issues of 1939.

In the aftermath of the Molotov-Ribbentrop Pact, the Soviet Union invaded and annexed Western Ukraine and Western Belorussia and a year later the Baltic countries and Southern Finland (Karelia)—"liberating" them from their "landowning class" and "exploitative bourgeoisie." Simonov and other poets of his generation, captivated by the romance of the Spanish Civil War, had yearned to go to Spain as volunteers, but they ended up having to fight in the Finnish war instead.[127] Simonov himself did not, for health reasons, participate in that war, but many of the young firebrand lyric poets of his cohort signed up as "volunteers," and several of them were killed in individual tragedies that were often represented as following the example of Byron.[128]

Meanwhile, in western Europe World War II was in progress. In June 1940 the Nazis took Paris. Münzenberg fled the French capital, realizing what fate would await him there because of his anti-Nazi stance. His flight ended in the woods in southern France, where, it is widely held, an NKVD assassination squad caught up with him and hanged him from a tree. Benjamin fled the Nazis and headed for Spain, but after being turned back at a border crossing in the Pyrenees, he committed suicide at the nearby town of Port Bou. Erenburg, deeply shaken after witnessing the Nazi triumph in Paris, returned to the Soviet Union permanently. There he wrote *The Fall of Paris* (Padenie Parizha; 1941–1942), which essentially gives the prehistory of the city's fall and his analysis of its causes. The novel emphasizes the degree to which French intellectuals, lily-livered or venal, were the pawns of the right and the Nazis but also suggests that their fatal step was not sufficiently supporting the Republicans in Spain.

Germany invaded the Soviet Union on June 22, 1941, as Erenburg feared they would. In Moscow a meeting was called of leading Jewish intellectuals charged with organizing a cultural response; the attendees included Erenburg, Eisenstein, the violinist David Oistrakh, Mikhoels, who had played Lear in the famous Yiddish production of 1935, and Boris Iofan, who had designed the Palace of Soviets and the Soviet pavilion for the Paris Exposition of 1937.[129] Eisenstein reported that it was only with the Nazi invasion that he realized he was actually a Jew.[130] Contact was reestablished with the Germanophone émigrés, many of them now in Hollywood, and Harcourt Brace began publishing in translation some of Eisenstein's critical early essays on film.[131]

The war provided ample demonstrations of Jameson's "perpetual mutability of history itself." In terms of genres, the unwieldy historical novel was left in the dust in favor of the short satirical or impassioned propagandistic sketch or article for the newspapers. Erenburg played the central role in the Soviet anti-German propaganda effort. Writing largely for the army paper *Red Star*, he penned some of the most vitriolic attacks on the Germans and quickly became legendary, the single most read journalist of the war, idol of the masses and a persona very grata with the leadership. But the "tender" lyric also flourished. The most famous literary piece from the war is "Wait for Me, and I Shall Return" (Zhdi menia, i ia vernus'), by Simonov. The poem in actuality addresses Valentina Serova, the actress who played the humorless mathematician who succumbs to Cupid in the comedy *Four Stout Hearts* (the 1941 Soviet analogue to *Ninotchka,* discussed in Chapter 8), but it struck a chord with millions of Soviet citizens, as did *Four Stout Hearts* when it was rereleased during the war.

In terms of Soviet cosmopolitanism, however, the "wait" was to be very long.

Epilogue

I N 1947 MOSCOW celebrated the eight-hundredth anniversary of its founding. As part of the celebrations, foundation stones were laid for eight new high-rise buildings (the so-called wedding cakes), which were to circle Moscow and transform its skyline. They were construed as modernizing the capital,[1] but accounts of them were colored by a Soviet national triumphalism that dominated the official rhetoric of this anniversary year.[2] Some compared the buildings with the seven hills of Rome. But in assessing the buildings' importance in his "Greeting" published in *Pravda* to mark the anniversary, Stalin declared to the city: "above all else, . . . Moscow's historic contribution is that she was, and remains, the basis and initiator for forming a centralized state on the Russian lands [na Rusi]."[3]

This image of Moscow had, of course, already been presented by Eisenstein in *Ivan the Terrible,* part 1. To mark the anniversary, he drafted plans for a new film, *Moscow 800* (Moskva 800), in part a reworking of his 1933 ideas for *Moscow* and, like its predecessor, a project that would not even get as far as a full scenario. This film was to extend the timeline further forward than its predecessor, ending with the Soviet triumph in World War II; the victory was to be cast, in a common theme of public rhetoric that year, as the third time Russia had saved Europe (after driving out the Tatars in the medieval period and Napoleon in 1812).[4]

Eisenstein also intended the film to develop a common theme of the many panegyrics that appeared in the press during the anniversary year: the construction under Stalin of an entire system of interior waterways centered around Moscow. Nature had been tamed and channeled. Eisenstein in his predictably eccentric reworking of this standard trope for an enhanced and centralized state expanded the mythic dimensions to include elements of the Russian tales of Sadko and the lost city of Kitezh.[5] The film, moreover, was to have been his first major sally into color (after a small first foray in 1945 with the dance of the *oprichniki* in *Ivan the Terrible,* part 2). Eisenstein did not live to make this film. On February 11, 1948 (shortly after his fiftieth birthday), he died of a heart attack. Though he died in his Moscow apartment, his death is generally seen as having been brought on by the anxieties and pressures of a difficult moment in Soviet cultural history.

That the cultural climate would be bleak had become clear in 1946, when Zhdanov, whose official speech to the First Congress of the Writers Union in 1934 had provided the canonical definition of socialist realism, had attacked the writers Anna Akhmatova and Mikhail Zoshchenko. This speech signaled a return to socialist realist orthodoxy and in effect put an end to any hopes intellectuals might have had of a cultural liberalization.[6] Hence the years up to Stalin's death in 1953 are generally dubbed the Zhdanov era. As the decade wore on, there emerged what was called the anticosmopolitan campaign, which was anti-Western, making it difficult to publish material about Western writers, but also anti-Semitic; Jews lost their jobs in droves. Mikhoels, who in 1935 had acted the role of King Lear (in Yiddish) and during the war had been head of the Soviet Jewish Anti-Fascist Committee and thus effectively the head of Soviet Jewry, was assassinated in 1948.

During the same period, America, too, was far from immune from conservatism and paranoia. In 1947 the Hollywood blacklist was instituted and the Hollywood Ten were accused of being members of the Communist Party. Both Brecht and Eisler, who had taken refuge in America from Nazism, were summoned before the House Un-American Activities Committee. Eisler was deported. For Brecht's appearance the committee had commissioned a special translation of *Measures Taken,* and the questioning revolved around that text as evidence of his Communism. The wily Brecht parried the questions, but after his interrogation he left the country, first for Switzerland, then settling in East Berlin. Feuchtwanger, his fellow editor on *Das Wort,* remained in California until his death in 1958; Thomas Mann moved from America to Switzerland in 1952, where he died in 1955, while his brother Heinrich died in Santa Barbara in 1950, shortly before he was to return to the GDR and become the president of the Prussian Academy of the Arts. Lukács returned to Hungary in 1945 and though his record with non-Party intellectuals during the Cold War is not unblemished, he did in 1956 become a minister of the brief communist revolutionary government of Imre Nagy, which opposed the Soviet Union. He narrowly avoided execution when the Soviet Union invaded, was deported to Roumania, then returned and recanted, but was to criticize the Soviet Union again for its repression of the Prague Spring of 1968.

Europe, and the Germanophone emigration with it, were split in two by the Cold War. The year 1947 marks a milestone in the process with the promulgation of the Truman doctrine of containment, and the establishment of the CIA and the Marshall Plan. The fault line in Europe hardened, locking Brecht into the GDR. It endured until the wall came down in 1989, over forty years later. There were to be two Europes and two Germanys. Meanwhile, in East Germany an entire cohort of German intellectuals who had weathered the 1930s and the war in the Soviet Union returned in the wake of the Soviet victory in 1945. Once back in Germany, they began implementing their plans for a cultural revolution in what became the GDR that had been hatched on September 25, 1944, at a meeting of writers in Moscow's Hotel Lux. This group included the de facto main editor of *Das Wort,* Willi Bredel, and Fritz Erpenbeck, who had stood in for Bredel as an editor while Bredel had served as a commissar in an International Brigade in the Spanish Civil War. Other former Moscow exiles who played important roles in GDR culture include Johannes Becher, who had served as editor of *Internationale Literatur—Deutsche Blätter;* Becher was to become, inter alia, the GDR's minister of culture from 1954 to 1958, and his poem "Risen from the Ruins" (Auferstanden aus Ruinen; 1949), set to music by Eisler, became the GDR's national anthem. But many of these writers assumed important political and administrative roles alongside their contributions to cultural life. Also among the prominent returnees were Friedrich Wolf's two sons—Konrad, who had trained at VGIK and was to become a leading East German film director, and Markus, who was to become the great GDR spymaster for foreign operations.

In the Soviet Union, some measure of cosmopolitanism returned after Stalin died in 1953. Erenburg, the only one of the four main figures in this book to escape Stalinist repressions relatively unscathed (he died of cancer in 1967), was to play a prominent role in the post-Stalin era. His publications were among a spate of influential writings that pressed the pace of de-Stalinization. In fact his *Thaw* (Ottepel'; 1954, 1956), which argues for a less paranoid attitude toward contacts with Westerners, gave the Khrushchev thaws their name. The first, the 1954 thaw, was a prelude to such events as the 1955 founding of the journal *Inostrannaia literature* (Foreign literature), a descendant of *Internatsional'naia literatura*, which had been closed in 1943, and Moscow's International Youth Festival of 1957, where a new generation of young Soviets fraternized with Western delegates. The subsequent publication in the Soviet Union of Erenburg's memoirs, *People, Years, Life* (Liudi, gody, zhizn'; 1960–1965/ 1967), with their accounts of hobnobbing with the likes of Picasso in the Café Rotonde in Paris, restored to the Soviet public sphere the names of many figures and texts that had been stricken from Russian cultural memory. The memoirs were also inflected by Erenburg's long-standing passionate commitment to the Spanish Civil War and the ideals he identified with its Republican cause. In fact the cult of that war experienced a resurgence in the Khrushchev years, especially among the young, with the novels of Hemingway and the songs of the war returning to popularity. In Konrad Wolf's 1967 autobiographical film *I Was Nineteen* (Ich war neunzehn), when a former exile returning to Germany with the invading Soviet army is dropped off to run a recently occupied district, as he contemplates the enormity of the task, the sound track plays Ernst Busch (the main singer for *Measures Taken* and longtime collaborator of Eisler) singing his German adaptation of "Am Rio Jarama," a favorite song of Spanish Civil War veterans that commemorates the huge sacrifices in a battle, and the audience knows he will rise to the occasion. Even during the Brezhnev years, Andrei Tarkovsky in his autobiographical film *The*

Mirror (Zerkalo; 1974) felt compelled, in representing his Moscow child-hood, to include documentary footage (from Karmen's *Spain*) of a shipload of refugee Spanish children being evacuated to the Soviet Union as defeat loomed. And Karmen himself, responding to the renewed cult of the Spanish Civil War, collaborated with Simonov in producing the documentary film *Grenada, Grenada, Grenada Moia* (1968).

On April 16, 1953, just six weeks after Stalin died, Olga Berggolts published in *Literaturnaia gazeta* a programmatic article, "A Conversation about the Lyric" (Razgovor o lirike), which essentially revived the "campaign for the lyric," with which Simonov had also been associated in the 1930s. The new "campaign" used several of the same arguments and the same code terms that had marked the campaign in the thirties; there was also some continuity among the "lyric's" advocates. But it was part of a broader movement to liberalize an ossified Stalinist literary practice,[7] a movement that can be detected in public sources already starting from the early 1950s, before Stalin's death.[8]

Simonov, considered a "Westernizer" *(zapadnik)*,[9] was, however, no longer among those spearheading the campaign. In fact, from the perspective of Western scholarship his postthirties literary career up to his death in 1979 presents a variegated pattern that includes nationalist and anti-American works, such as his 1947 novel *Dym otechestva* (Smoke of the fatherland), which blames America for starting the Cold War; in 1949, as deputy head of the Writers Union he was assigned to draw up plans for anti-American propaganda in culture.[10] He also attacked Erenburg's *Thaw* in *Literaturnaia gazeta* as presenting too black a picture of Soviet life. But from 1954 to 1958 he edited the leading literary journal *Novyi mir*, at a time when most of the works pressing the pace of de-Stalinization appeared there (including the 1956 bombshell *Not By Bread Alone* [Ne khlebom edinym], by Vladimir Dudintsev); due to this record, he was dismissed in the less liberal climate following the Hungarian uprising of late 1956. Simonov later headed the Writers Union from 1967 to 1979, in other words during the so-called period of "stagnation" under Brezhnev that saw a resurgence of xenophobia and a literary vogue for "village prose" with distinct *Blut und Boden* coloration. In 1968, however, he refused to sign a statement of official support for the Soviet invasion of Czechoslovakia.

Simonov's record, then, is hard to categorize. But this is in part because we tend to retroject our own categories, to apply our own intellectual cum political matrices, into our understanding of Soviet intellectuals' mentalities and motives. Simonov's contemporaries did not think in the same terms as we do, and while their actions were inevitably affected by the contingencies and exigencies of particular moments, they were also acts of self-translation into an intellectual force field. The same is no less true of the four intermediaries who have featured in this book, but they were operating in a different historical moment from Simonov's.

These four—Koltsov, Tretiakov, Erenburg, and Eisenstein—were extraordinary figures in extraordinary times. But they were also of a particular generation. Although Simonov entered the cultural world in the late 1930s, with Koltsov his idol and the Spanish Civil War an emblematic inspiration, he was essentially of a different one. His generation's sense of internationalism was no longer informed by a dream of some pan-European fraternity.

Cosmopolitanism, as my introduction has pointed out, is a vague term, and there are different versions of it. Whatever their motives, the cosmopolitan patriots studied here were working with a distinctive version of cosmopolitanism as they sought to institute a transnational fraternity of leftist intellectuals, a republic of letters that stretched over Europe, possibly extending to the United States, and was inspired by Marxism or, minimally, the antifascist cause. Starting around March 1946 with Churchill's "Iron Curtain" speech, however, the politics deployed by the superpowers left the continent with an Eastern bloc and a Western bloc. To a marked degree, Soviet imperialist energies in culture were now directed toward the Third World, anyway—a direction celebrated later in the Tashkent Conference of Afro-Asian Writers of 1958.

Moscow had not become a "fourth Rome." The slight mathematical mismatch of the claim that the eight ("wedding cake") skyscrapers announced in 1947 represented the seven hills of Rome could be taken as symptomatic of the slight mismatch of the Soviet internationalizing ambitions with historical reality.[11] But the failure should not blind us to the intensity with which Soviet intellectuals pursued this ideal, or to the extent to which a distinctive *Soviet* cosmopolitanism informed so much cultural activity in the 1930s.

Notes

Acknowledgments

Index

Notes

All citations are presented in abbreviated format as .../.../.../..., which presents, in order, the archive number (in Russian F.), inventory number (in Russian op.), file number (in Russian d., or ed/kh), folio number or numbers (in Russian l, or ll.).

The following acronyms are used:

GARF:	Gosudarstvennyi arkhiv rossiiskoi federatsii (State Archive of the Russian Federation)
OR IMLI:	Otdel rukopisei, Institut mirovoi literatury imeni Gor'kogo (Manuscript Division, Institute of World Literature Named for Gorky)
RGALI:	Rossiiskii gosudarstvennyi arkhiv literatury i iskusstva (Russian State Archive for Literature and Art)
RGASPI:	Rossiiskii gosudarstvennyi arkhiv sovremennoi politicheskoi istorii (Russian State Archive of Contemporary Political History)
TsGAISP:	Tsentral'nyi Gosudarstvennyi Arkhiv Istorii Sankt Peterburga (Central State Archive of the History of Petersburg)

INTRODUCTION

1. " 'Ivan groznyi.' Kinostsenarii S. M. Eizenshteina," *Novyi mir,* 1943, no. 10–11, 67. This scene actually comes later in the draft script. Eisenstein had planned to have the film

open with the traumatic scene where Ivan's mother is murdered, intended to be a key scene for understanding Ivan's psyche, but this was disallowed. Later Eisenstein incorporated much of it in his opening to part 2.

2. Sergei Eizenshtein, "Moskva vo vremeni," *Literaturnaia gazeta,* 11 July 1933, 3.

3. The traditional historiography has it that he set out this doctrine in a series of letters, though the number, addresses, and dates of the letters are the subjects of controversy.

4. "Poslanie o zlykh dnekh i chasekh," ed. by Vladimir V. Kolesov, in Lev A. Dmitriev and Dmitri S. Likhachëv, eds., *Pamiatniki literatury drevnei Rusi. Konets XV—pervaia polovina XVI veka* (Moscow: Khudozhestvennaia literatura, 1984), 452. For a fuller discussion of these letters see Aleksandr L. Gol'dberg, "Tri 'poslaniia Filofeia' (opyt tekstologicheskogo analiza)," *Trudy otdela drevnerusskoi literatury* 29 (1974), 68–97; N. V. Sinitsyna, *Tretii Rim: Istoki i evoliutsiia russkoi srednevekovoi kontseptsii (XV–XVI vv.)* (Moscow: Izd-vo "Indrik," 1998).

5. "Poslanie o zlykh dnekh i chasekh," 452.

6. My account here is largely based on Marshall Poe, "Moscow, the Third Rome: The Origins and Transformation of a 'Pivotal Moment,'" *Jahrbücher für Geschichte Osteuropas* 49, no. 3 (2001), 412–442. For a dissenting interpretation that raises the possibility that Filofei had in mind Novgorod see Donald Ostrowski, *Muscovy and the Mongols: Cross-cultural influences on the steppe Frontier* (Cambridge: Cambridge University Press, 1998), 219–243, esp. 225, 235, 237, 239, 243.

7. Ju. M. Lotman and B. A. Uspenskij, "Echoes of the Notion of 'Moscow as the Third Rome' in Peter the Great's Ideology," trans. N. F. C. Owen, in Ann Shukman, ed., *The Semiotics of Russian Culture* (Ann Arbor; Michigan Slavic Contributions, 1984), 55; Daniel Rowland, "Moscow: The Third Rome or the New Israel," *Russian Review* 55, no. 4 (1996), 591–614; Judith Kalb, *Russia's Rome: Imperial Visions, Messianic Dreams, 1890–1940* (Madison: University of Wisconsin Press, 2008), esp. 16–33.

8. "'Ivan groznyi.' Kinostsenarii S. M. Eizenshteina," 67.

9. Yuri Tsivian, *Ivan the Terrible* (London: BFI, 2002), 66.

10. Nicholas S. Timasheff, *The Great Retreat: The Growth and Decline of Communism in Russia* (New York: Dutton, 1946); David Brandenberger, *National Bolshevism: Stalinist Mass Culture and the Formation of Modern Russian National Identity, 1931–1956* (Cambridge, Mass.: Harvard University Press, 2002), esp. 2.

11. Tsivian, *Ivan the Terrible,* 7.

12. S. M. Eizenshtein, "'Ivan Groznyi'. Fil'm v russkom renessanse XVI veka" (1942), reprinted in *Izbrannye proizvedeniia,* vol. 1 (Moscow: Iskusstvo, 1964), 193–194.

13. Liah Greenfeld, *Nationalism: Five Roads to Modernity* (Cambridge, Mass.: Harvard University Press, 1992), 14.

14. Pheng Cheah, *Spectral Nationality: Passages of Freedom from Kant to Postcolonial Literatures of Liberation* (New York: Columbia University Press, 2003), 8, see also 2.

15. See for example Immanuel Wallerstein's discussion of the interdependence of "national," "universal," and "cosmopolitan": "The National and the Universal: Can There

Be Such a Thing as World Culture?," in Anthony D. King, ed., *Culture, Globalization and the World System: Contemporary Conditions for the Representation of Identity* (Minneapolis: University of Minnesota Press, 1997), 90–103.

16. Kristin Ross, "On Jacques Rancière," *Artforum*, March 2007, 255; see e.g. Steven Rosefielde, *Red Holocaust* (London: Routledge, 2009).

17. Mark Mazower, "Old Europe: The Struggle to Understand How Even a United Continent Is Far from a Place at the Centre of the World," *Times Literary Supplement*, 2 May 2008, 4, 5.

18. Mikhail Agursky, *The Third Rome: National Bolshevism in the U.S.S.R.* (Boulder, Colo.: Westview Press, 1987), xiii.

19. Karl Schlögel, *Terror und Traum. Moskau 1937* (Munich: Karl Hanser Verlag, 2008), 30–31.

20. Arkhitektor B. Iofan, "Na ulitsakh gorodov Evropy i Ameriki (iz zapisnoi knizhki)," *Pravda*, 13 March 1935.

21. In this respect it could be seen as distinct from the record of Peter the Great and other tsarist predecessors who likewise sought to "appropriate" Western culture on a large scale.

22. Agnes Lugo-Ortiz, "Framing a Forum," *Publications of the Modern Language Association* 122, no. 3 (May 2007), 806.

23. Vilashini Cooppan, *Worlds Within: National Narratives and Global Connections in Postcolonial Writing: Cultural Memory in the Present* (Stanford: Stanford University Press, 2009), 11.

24. David Ferris, "Indiscipline," in Haun Saussy, ed., *Comparative Literature in an Age of Globalization,* American Comparative Literature Association annual report for 2004 (Baltimore: Johns Hopkins University Press, 2006), 83–84.

25. Margaret Cohen, "Traveling Genres," *New Literary History* 34 (Summer 2003), 482, 481.

26. O. V. Khlevniuk, *Politbiuro. Mekhanizmy politicheskoi vlasti v 1930-e gody* (Moscow: Rosspen, 1996), 42, 112. Initially, in 1932, this had been the charge of V. M. Molotov, Stalin's deputy in the Party (67).

27. Interview of Katerina Clark with Maia Turovskaia (who was a Moscow teenager in the 1930s), May 2006.

28. *Pervyi vsesoiuznyi s"ezd sovetskikh pisatelei. Stenografcheskii otchët* (Moscow: Ogiz, 1934), 5.

29. "Privetstvie I. V. Stalinu," *Pervyi vsesoiuznyi s"ezd sovetskikh pisatelei.* Stenograficheskii otchët (Moscow: Ogiz, 1934), 19.

30. Catriona Kelly, "Kak predstavliali angliiskuiu literaturu sovetskomu shkol'niku i massovomu chitateliu 1930-kh godov," paper delivered at a conference on *Schrift und Macht* held at the University of Konstanz, 20 July, 2007.

31. I will not engage here the issue, much debated in recent years, as to whether the Soviet Union was a version of empire or a nation, or, as some have called it, an "empire-state." See Mark I. Beissinger, "The Persisting Ambiguity of Empire," *Post-Soviet Affairs* 11 (1995), 162. See also Ron Suny, "Ambiguous Categories: States, Empires and Nations," *Post-Soviet Affairs* 11 (1995), 185–196; and Terry Martin, *Affirmative Action Empire:*

Nations and Nationalism in the Soviet Union, 1923–1939 (Ithaca: Cornell University Press, 2001), 22.

32. Greg Woolf, "Inventing Empire in Ancient Rome," in Susan E. Alcock et al., eds., *Empires: Perspectives from Archeology and History* (Cambridge: Cambridge University Press, 2001), 311. See also V. I. Lenin, "Theses on the National and Colonial Questions Adopted by the Second Comintern Congress," 28 July 1920, in Jane Degras, ed., *The Communist International, 1919–1943: Documents*, vol. 1, *1919–1922* (London: Frank Cass, 1956), 138–144.

33. Michael Hardt and Antonio Negri, *Empire* (Cambridge, Mass.: Harvard University Press, 2000).

34. Boris Groys made a similar but not identical point in *The Total Art of Stalinism: Avant-Garde, Aesthetic Dictatorship and Beyond*, trans. Charles Rougle (Princeton: Princeton University Press, 1992), 9, 23, as does Evgeny Dobrenko, *Political Economy of Socialist Realism*, trans. Jesse M. Savage (New Haven: Yale University Press, 2007), especially chapter 1.

35. Josef Chytry, *The Aesthetic State: A Quest in Modern German Thought* (Berkeley: University of California Press, 1989), xi–xii.

36. Ibid., xi–xii.

37. G. Lukach, "Shiller kak estetik" in Fridrikh Shiller, *Stat'i po estetike*, trans. A. G. Gornfel'd, (Moscow-Leningrad: Academia, 1935), vii–lxxxiii.

38. Eric Michaud, *The Cult of Art in Nazi Germany* (Stanford: Stanford University Press, 2004), 1, 2.

39. Katerina Clark and Karl Schlögl, "Mutual Perceptions and Projections: Images of Stalin's Russia in Nazi Germany; The Soviet Image of Nazi Germany," in Sheila Fitzpatrick and Michael Geyer, eds., *Beyond Totalitarianism: Stalinism and Nazism Compared* (Cambridge: Cambridge University Press, 2008), 396–441.

40. Régis Debray, "Socialism: A Life Cycle," *New Left Review*, July-August 2007, 5–28.

41. Michaud, *Cult of Art in Nazi Germany*, 13.

42. Ibid., 5.

43. Yuri M. Lotman, *Universe of the Mind: A Semiotic Theory of Culture*, trans. Ann Shukman (London: Tauris, 1990), 194.

44. Nancy Condee, *The Imperial Trace* (Oxford: Oxford University Press, 2009), 13.

45. Martin, *Affirmative Action Empire*, 415.

46. Lotman, *Universe of the Mind*, 145–147.

47. Antoine Berman, *The Experience of the Foreign: Culture and Translation in Romantic Germany*, trans. S. Heyvaert (Albany: State University of New York Press, 1992), 11.

48. Ibid., 11–12; Lawrence Venuti, "Local Contingencies: Translation and National Identities," in Sandra Berman and Michael Wood, eds., *Nation, Language and the Ethics of Translation* (Princeton: Princeton University Press, 2005), 189.

49. Haun Saussy, *Great Walls of Discourse and Other Adventures in Cultural China* (Cambridge, Mass.: Harvard University Asia Center, distributed by Harvard University Press, 2001), 78.

50. Berman, *Experience of the Foreign*, 11, 13, 12.

51. Azade Seyhan, "German Academic Exiles in Istanbul: Translation as the *Bildung* of the Other," in Berman and Wood, *Nation, Language and the Ethics of Translation*, 278, 279, 279. See also Venuti, "Local Contingencies," 180.

52. Brian Baer, "Literary Translation and the Construction of the Soviet Intelligentsia," *Massachusetts Review* 4, no. 73 (Fall 2006), 539.

53. F. Rable, *Gargantiua i Pantagriuel'*, dlia detei, obrabotal N. Zabolotskii (Leningrad: Detgiz, 1935); F. Rable, *Gargantua i Pantagriuel'*, trans. V. A. Piast (Leningrad: Goslitizdat, 1938), print run 20,300; "Novye izdaniia na iazykakh narodov SSSR," *Literaturnoe obozrenie*, 1937, no. 15, 57.

54. On *Ulysses:* Omry Ronen, "On the Subject of 'The Poem to the Unknown Soldier,'" in *Word and Fate: Osip Mandelstam* (Oxford: Bodley Head), 196; on *Childe Harold* and Hegel, John Mackay, *Inscription and Modernity : From Wordsworth to Mandelstam* (Bloomington: Indiana University Press, 2006), 216–17.

55. See also Jochen Hellbeck, *Revolution on My Mind: Writing a Diary under Stalin* (Cambridge, Mass.: Harvard University Press, 2006), 314.

56. For example, Ilya Erenburg's *Second Day* (*Den' vtoroi*, 1933), and *Without Pausing for Breath* (*Ne perevodia dykhaniia*, 1935), and Vasilii Grossman's *Stepan Kol'chugin* (1937–1940).

57. Poe, "Moscow, the Third Rome," 423; Kalb, *Russia's Rome*, especially 18, 25–30.

58. This comes in the last section, "A Soldier, and Brave" of chapter 6; Thomas Mann, *The Magic Mountain*, trans. H. T. Lowe-Porter (New York: Vintage, 1999), 517.

59. I. V. Stalin, *Voprosy leninizma*, 6th ed. (Moscow-Leningrad: Giz, 1929), 200, 201, 203.

60. Rowland, "Moscow," 597; Lotman and Uspenskii, "Echoes of the Notion 'Moscow as the Third Rome,'" 55.

61. Denis Feeney, *Literature and Religion at Rome: Cultures, Contexts, and Beliefs* (Cambridge: Cambridge University Press, 1998), 52–53.

62. Greg Woolf, "Inventing Empire in Ancient Rome," in Alcock et al., *Empires*, 317, see also 315–16.

63. Paul Zanker, *The Power of Images in the Age of Augustus*, trans. Alan Shapiro (Ann Arbor: University of Michigan Press, 1988), 9.

64. Woolf, "Inventing Empire in Ancient Rome," 317–18.

65. One edition alone, Henri Barbusse, *Stalin. Chelovek cherez kotorogo raskryvaetsia novyi mir* (Moscow: Roman-gazeta, 1936), had a print run of three hundred thousand copies.

66. See e.g., G. Geine, *Polnoe sobranie sochinenii*, vol. 1, *Lirika*, n.p.: M. Goslitizdat, 1938); O. Bal'zak, "Utrachennye illiuzii" (Moscow-Leningrad: Academia, 1937); Gëte, I. V., *Stradaniia molodogo Vertera*, trans. A. Eiges (Moscow-Leningrad: Academia, 1937).

67. Franco Moretti, *Modern Epic: The World System from Goethe to Garcia Marquez*, trans. Quintin Hoare (London: Verso, 1996), 49.

68. Gomer, *Iliada*, trans. N. I. Gnedich (Moscow-Leningrad: Academia, 1935); Gomer, *Iliada*, trans. N. M. Minskii (Moscow: GIKhL, 1935); Gomer, *Odisseia*, trans V. A.

Zhukovskii (Moscow: GIKhL, 1935); *Odisseia Gomera,* trans V. A. Zhukovskii (Moscow-Leningrad: Academia, 1935); Vergilii, *Eneida,* trans. Valerii Briusov and Sergei Soloviëv (Moscow-Leningrad: Academia, 1933).

69. Woolf, "Inventing Empire in Ancient Rome," 315.

70. David Quint, *Epic and Empire: Politics and Generic Form from Virgil to Milton* (Princeton: Princeton University Press, 1992), 7.

71. Ibid., 8, 13.

72. "Doklad N. I. Bukharina o poezii, poetike i zadachakh poeticheskogo tvorchestva v SSSR," in *Pervyi vsesoiuznyi s"ezd sovetskikh pisatelei,* 483.

73. Kalb, *Russia's Rome,* 10; F. T. Griffiths and S. J. Rabinowitz, "*Doctor Zhivago* and the Tradition of National Epic," *Comparative Literature* 32, no 1 (Winter 1980), 63–79.

74. V. N. Toporov, "Italiia v Peterburge," in *Italiia v slavianskom mire, sovetsko-ital'ianskii simpozium* (Moscow: 1990), 73.

75. Kalb, *Russia's Rome,* 6, 9, 16–18, 26, 51; Chytry, *Aesthetic State,* xlvi.

76. E.g. "Advokat fashistskogo iskusstva" [unsigned], *Sovetskoe iskusstvo,* 11 May 1937.

77. "The Fellow-Travelers Revisited: The 'Cultured West' through Soviet Eyes," *Journal of Modern History* 75, no. 2 (June 2003), 300–335.

78. RGASPI, 495/30/1076/16.

79. Woolf, "Inventing Empire in Ancient Rome," 322.

80. Dominic Lieven, *Empire: The Russian Empire and Its Rivals* (New Haven: Yale University Press, 2002), 9–12. The quotation is on 10.

81. Michael W. Doyle, *Empires* (Ithaca: Cornell University Press, 1986), 106, 107, 110.

82. Stephen Howe, *Empire: A Very Short Introduction* (Oxford University Press, 2002), 84.

83. RGASPI, 541/1/113/1.

84. Boris Frezinskii, *Pisateli i sovetskie vozhdi. Izbrannye siuzhety 1919–1960 godov* (Moscow: Ellis Lak, 2008), 273–475.

85. Part 5, "Impostures," in Sheila Fitzpatrick, *Tear Off the Masks! Identity and Imposture in Twentieth-Century Russia* (Princeton: Princeton University Press, 2005), 263–300.

86. Schlögel, *Terror und Traum,* 29.

87. Boris Wolfson, "Fear on Stage: Afinogenov, Stanislavsky and the Making of the Stalinist Theater," in Christina Kiaer and Eric Naiman, eds., *Everyday Life in Early Stalinist Russia: Taking the Revolution Inside* (Bloomington: Indiana University Press, 2006), 92–118.

88. Romy Golan, *Modernity and Nostalgia: Art and Politics in France between the Wars* (New Haven: Yale University Press, 1995).

89. Michaud, *Cult of Art in Nazi Germany,* 13.

90. Tim Benton, "Speaking without Adjectives: Architecture in the Service of Totalitarianism," in Dawn Ades, ed., *Art and Power: Europe under the Dictators, 1930–1945* (London: Thames and Hudson, 1995), 53.

91. Burckhardt, 9, 222.

92. See part 2 of Katerina Clark and Yevgeny Dobrenko, eds., *Soviet Culture and Power: A History in Documents, 1917–1953* (New Haven: Yale University Press, 2007).

93. After coming up with this term I discovered that Kwame Anthony Appiah uses it in "Cosmopolitan Patriots," in Pheng Cheah and Bruce Robbins, eds., *Cosmopolitics: Thinking and Feeling beyond the Nation* (Minneapolis: University of Minnesota Press, 1998).

94. Joseph Roach, *Cities of the Dead: The Circum-Atlantic Performance* (New York: Columbia University Press, 1996).

95. Agnes Lugo-Ortiz, "Framing a Forum," *Publications of the Modern Language Association* 122, no. 3 (May 2007), 806.

96. Note I. Erenburg, "V dzhongliakh Evropy," *Izvestiia,* 19 April, 6 May 1934, 11.

97. Biographical information on the early life of Fridliand is available at TsGAISP, 2/9788/ 1–42 ("Moisei Khaimovich Fridliand"). His father, Khaim Movshov Fridliand, is listed as having been a merchant of the Second Guild with a shoe store in Kiev and a leather warehouse in Byalystok. Koltsov was born in Kiev, but the family moved to Byalystok, where he studied in the Belostoksoe Real'noe Uchilishche from 1906 to 1915, pp. 6, 16, 21). I am grateful to John Mackay for sharing this research with me.

98. Oksana Bulgakova, *Sergej Eisenstein—drei Utopien. Architekturentwürfe zur Film-theorie* (Berlin:Potemkin Press, 1993), 103, and introduction to *Eisenstein und Deutschland: Texte, Dokumente, Briefe* (Berlin: Akademie der Künste, 1998), 1.

99. Oksana Bulgakova, *Sergei Eisenstein: A Biography,* trans. Anne Dwyer (Berlin: Potemkin Press, 2001), 4.

100. G. Vasil'kovskii, "Kol'tsov-publitsist," *Literaturnaia gazeta,* 11 July 1932, lists his many publications up to that date, including over twelve hundred feuilletons; Efim Zozulia, "Kol'tsov-redaktor," *Literaturnaia gazeta,* 23 May 1933.

101. Katerina Clark, "Eisenstein's Two Projects for a Film about Moscow," *Modern Language Review* 101 (2006), 188–204.

102. OR IMLI, 318/1/27/19.

103. Il'ia Erenburg, "Siurrealisty" (in his series "Na zapadnom fronte"), *Literaturnaia gazeta,* 17 June 1933).

104. TsGAISP 115/2/9788/6–10, 13, 15, 20–23, 29, 39, 40. After completing the Preparatory Faculty, he transferred to the Medical Faculty, hoping to become a doctor, but sent a request to withdraw in 1918 from Kiev, where he was already active as a political journalist.

105. Boris Efimov, *Sud'ba zhurnalista* (Moscow: Izd "Pravda," Biblioteka Ogonëk no. 35, 1988), 4.

106. Zozulia, "Kol'tsov—redactor."

107. David Iosifovich Zaslavskii, "Pervaia skripka. Iz vospominanii," RGALI, 2846/1/77/21, 23, 25, 26, 28; A. Rubashkin, *Mikhail Kol'tsov. Kritiko-biograficheskii ocherk* (Leningrad: Kudozhestvennaia literatura,1971); Gleb Skorokhodov, *Mikhail Kol'tsov. Kritko-biograficheskii ocherk* (Moscow: Sovetskii pisatel', 1959).

108. Efimov, *Sud'ba zhurnalista,* 12. Note that in his Kabul essay "Vmestilishche spokoistviia," *Pravda,* 3 October 1930, he says of the progressive emir who had been assassinated that he was like Peter the Great in seeking to modernize the country but, unlike Peter, had not learned the efficacy of the executioner's block *(plakha).*

109. "Pervyi god 'Ogon'ka'," [unsigned], *Ogonëk*, 1 April, 1924, 21.
110. "Desiat' let zhurnala 'Ogonëk,'" *Izvestiia*, 23 April 1933.
111. Anne Nesbet, *Savage Junctures: Sergei Eisenstein and the Shape of Thinking* (London: Tauris, 2003), 214.
112. Joan Neuberger, *Ivan the Terrible* (London: Tauris, 2003), 7.
113. Frezinskii, *Pisateli i sovetskie vozhdi*, 379.
114. MORP had oversight from three bodies: the Executive Committee of the Comintern (IKKI), Kul'tprop of the Party's Central Committee, and the Organizational Committee of the Writers Union; RGASPI, 495/30/988/17.
115. O. D. Kameneva, "Rabochaia pomoshch' Rossii," *Ogonëk*, 1923, no. 13 (24 June), 10; Villi Miuntsenberg, "Mezhdunarodnaia rabochaia pomoshch'," *Ogonëk*, 1923, no. 19, 5 August, 4.
116. "VOKS v 1930–1940-e gody," publikatsiia A. V. Golubeva i V. A. Nevezhina, in *Minuvshee, Istoricheskii al'manakh* (Moscow-St. Petersburg: Atheneum-Feniks, 1993), 313–367. Other bodies who organized trips included the trade unions, Intourist (after it was founded in 1929), and the Agitprop Department of the Comintern.
117. GARF, 5283/6/d/52/12.
118. M. Kait, "Berlinskoe obshchestvo druzei novoi Rossii," *Ogonëk*, 1923, no. 26 (23 September), 9.
119. GARF, 5283/6/57/87/111.
120. Villi Miuntsenberg, "Mezhdunarodnaia rabochaia pomoshch,'" *Ogonëk*, 1923, no. 19 (5 August), 4; Ludmila Shtern, *Western Intellectuals and the Soviet Union: From Red Square to the Left Bank* (London: Routledge, 2007), 5–69.
121. See e.g., GARF, 5283/6/57/189; GARF 5283/6/84/1.
122. Viktor Fradkin, *Delo Kol'tsova* (Moscow: Vagrius, 2002), 344; Frezinskii, *Pisateli i sovetskie vozhdi*, 310, 327.
123. RGALI, 631/14/5.
124. Efimov, *Sud'ba zhurnalista*, 11.

1. THE AUTHOR AS PRODUCER

1. GARF, 5283/6/22/139, 140, 141. See also, GARF 5283/6/129/104–108. Benjamin was contracted before leaving for Moscow to write the entry on Goethe for the multivolume *Soviet Encyclopedia*. Radek rejected the draft on the grounds that it mentioned class struggle too often, but sections of it did appear in a multiauthored version of the entry (Mikhail Ryklin, personal communication, 30 October 2009).
2. Walter Benjamin, *Moscow Diary*, trans. Richard Sieburth (Cambridge, Mass.: Harvard University Press, 1986), 72–73.
3. It is not certain that the talk was actually delivered. See Walter Benjamin, *Selected Writings*, vol. 2, *1927–1934*, trans. Rodney Livingstone et al. (Cambridge, Mass: Harvard University Press, 1999), 781.
4. Walter Benjamin, "Paris, the Capital of the Nineteenth Century," in *Selected Writings*, vol. 3, *1935–1938* (Cambridge, Mass.: Harvard University Press, 2002), 40.

5. *Iz istorii mezhdunarodnogo ob"edineniia revoliutsionnykh pisatelei (MORP),* Literaturnoe nasledstvo, no. 81 (Moscow: Nauka, 1962), 17.

6. Johannes R. Becher, "Unsere Wendung: Vom Kampf um Existenz der Proletarisch-Revolutionären Literatur zum Kampf um ihre Erneuerung," *Linkskurve,* 1931, no. 10, 1–18. Reference to Kharkov: 4.

7. Walter Benjamin, "The Author as Producer," in *Selected Writings,* 2:771.

8. Karl Schlögel, *Berlin Ostbahnhof Europas. Russen und deutsche in ihrem Jahrhundert* (Berlin: Siedler Verlag, 1998).

9. Louis Althusser, "Ideology and Ideological State Apparatuses (Notes Towards an Investigation)" (1970) in *Lenin and Philosophy and Other Essays,* trans. Ben Brewster (New York: Monthly Press, 1971), pp. 127–186. The list of outlets includes the newspapers *Rote Fahne, Berlin am Morgen,* and *Berlin am Abend,* and the journals *Rote Aufbau, Das neue Russland, Die Linkskurve,* and *Der Arbeiterfotograf.* Most of them came under the umbrella of Internationale Arbeiter Hilfe (IAH; i.e., Mezhrabpom) and Willi Münzenberg.

10. Liudi odnogo kostra in *Strana perekrëstok. Dokumental'naia proza* (Moscow: Sovetskii pisatel', 1991), 376.

11. RGASPI, 495/30/9930.

12. GARF 5283/6/60/188; GARF 5283/6/77/48.

13. GARF 5283/6/81/44, 88, 90, 92, 94; GARF 5283/6/83/11, 18, 26. S. Tretjakoff, "Der Schriftsteller und das sotsialistische Dorf. Vortrag gehalten in Berlin 21 Januar 1931 in der Gesellschaft der Freunde des neuen Russland's," *Neue Russland,* 1931, no. 2/3, 39–53; an extract, "Die Herausforderung," was also published in *Berlin am Morgen,* 23 January 1931; Fritz Mierau, *Erfindung und Korrektur: Tretjakows Ästhetik der Operativität* (Berlin: Akademie-Verlag, 1976), 21, English trans., "The Writer and the Socialist Village," *October* 118 (Fall 2006), 63–70.

14. Among the communes it incorporated was Red Beacon, Krasnyi maiak, mentioned in Benjamin's essay, to which he had been assigned in 1928; Tretiakov, *Strana perekrëstok,* 560.

15. Benjamin, "Author as Producer," cites a book by Tretiakov on the *kombinat* called *Die Feld-Herren* [Commanders of the field], trans. Rudolf Selke (Berlin: Malik Verlag, 1931), which actually refers to a German publication of Tretiakov in German translation that combines two of Tretiakov's books on the *kombinat, Vyzov. Kol'khoznye ocherki* (Moscow: Izd-vo Federatsiia, 1930), and sections of what was later published as *Tysiacha i odin trudoden'* (1001 Labor Days; Moscow: Sovetskaia literatura, 1934).

16. For a discussion of Tretiakov's visit and the Benjamin essay see also Maria Gough, *The Artist as Producer: Russian Constructivism as Revolution* (Berkeley: University of California Press, 2005), and chapter 1 of Elizabeth Astrid Papazian, *Manufacturing Truth: The Documentary Moment in Early Soviet Culture* (De Kalb: Northern Illinois University Press, 2009).

17. GARF 5283/6/82/124; GARF 5283/6/60/11, 15; "In der Hamburger Ortsgruppe," *Neue Russland,* 1931, no. 4/5 (May-June), 75.

18. S. Tretiakov, "Slovo, kotoroe slomano," *Smena,* 1934, no. 3, 18–19.

19. GARF 5283/6/77/48.

20. Susan Buck-Morss, *Dreamworld and Catastrophe: The Passing of Mass Utopia in East and West* (Cambridge, Mass.: MIT Press, 2000), 164–172.

21. At the end he also discusses two figures from Paris: Aragon—Brik's brother-in-law and, like Tretiakov, on the Executive Committee of MORP—and André Maublanc.

22. Gottfried Benn, "Die neue literarische Saison," *Die Weltbühne,* 1931, no. 37 (15 September), 404.

23. "Über die neueste Literatur," *Das neues Deutschland,* 1930, no. 1/2, 79; "Russische Debatte auf Deutsch," *Die literarische Welt,* 7 April 1930.

24. *Die Feld-Herren. Der Kampf um eine Kollektiv-Wirtschaft,* trans. Rudolf Selke (Berlin: Malik Verlag, 1931); *Tausendundein Arbeitstag* (Zürich: Ringverlag, 1935); *Den Schi Chua. Ein junger Chinese erzählt sein Leben. Bio-Interview,* trans. A. Kurella (Berlin: Malik Verlag, 1932); *15 eiserner Schritte: Ein Buch der Tatsachen aus der Sowjetunion,* a collection of writings by shock workers with a foreword by Tretiakov (Berlin: Universum Bücherei für Alle, 1932).

25. S. Tret'iakov, "Prodolzhenie sleduet," in *Literatura fakta,* ed. Nikolai Chuzhak (Moscow: Federatsiia, 1929), 263–267; "To Be Continued" and other key Tretiakov essays are published in English in *October* 118 (Fall 2006); this reference: 52.

26. Benjamin, "Author as Producer," 770.

27. Ibid., 774.

28. Bertolt Brecht, Hanns Eisler, and Slatan Dudow, *Die Massnahme. Das Exemplar eines Kritikers von der Uraufführung am 13.12.1930* (Berlin: Weidler Buchverlag, 1955).

29. Otto Bikha, "Revoliutsionnyi teatr Germanii," *Internatsional'naia literatura,* 1932, no. 7/8, 110.

30. "Die Zensurmaschine arbeitet. Filmzenen in 'Tai Yang' verboten," *Berlin am Morgen,* 20 January 1931.

31. "The Political Groupings of Russian Writers" (1927), in *Selected Writings,* 2:8.

32. A.F., "'Rychi Kitai' v Evrope, Amerike i Azii," *Internatsional'naia literatura,* 1932, no. 4, 125.

33. Bertolt Brecht, *Die Massnahme: Zwei Fassungen, Anmerkungen* (Frankfurt am Main: Suhrkamp, 1998), parallel 1930 and 1931 versions, 65–85; Bertolt Brecht, *Measures Taken,* in *The Jewish Wife and Other Short Plays by Bertolt Brecht,* trans. Eric Bentley (New York: Grove Weidenfeld, 1992), 99–102, 106–108.

34. S. Tret'iakov, "Bert Brekht," *Literaturnaia gazeta,* 12 May 1932, says that "Vysshaia mera" is very heatedly debated in the press, and though of course it has many mistakes, it is still good.

35. E.g. Alfred Kurella, "'Vysshie mery' Bert Brekhta," *Literatura mirovoi revoliutsii,* 1932, no. 1, 70; [unsigned] "Rabochii Kongress v Khemnitse," Ogonëk, 11 November, 1923, 2.

36. Martin Esslin, *Brecht: A Choice of Evils* (London: Methuen, 1980), 144.

37. Ia. Posel'skii, director, *Protsess po delu Prompartii* (1930); GARF 5283/6/84/14.

38. RGASPI 495/30/99/32; GARF 5283/6/81/103; GARF 5283/6/84/2; "Was geht in der Sowjetunion vor?," *Die rote Fahne,* 7 December 1930 (on one such meeting presided over by K. A. Wittfogel); special number of *Neues Russland* of 2 January 1931;

Spione und Saboteure vor dem Volksgericht in Moskau (Berlin: Neue Deutsche Verlag, 1931).

39. Michael Kolzow, "Geständnisse, Geständnisse und Poincaré," *Neues Russland,* 1931, no. 1, 32–33.

40. GARF 5283/6/83/27.

41. See for example Fredric Jameson's *Brecht and Method,* where he argues that in *Measures Taken* Brecht did not endorse the young agitator's literal self-sacrifice (London: Verso, 1998, 62–63).

42. Brecht, *Die Massnahme,* 18–21; *The Jewish Wife and Other Short Plays,* 81–82.

43. E.g. Julie A. Cassiday, *The Enemy on Trial: Early Soviet Courts on Stage and Screen* (De Kalb: Northern Illinois Press, 2000), 52, 189.

44. Brecht, *Die Massnahme,* 20–21; *Jewish Wife and Other Short Plays,* 82.

45. A. Kurella, "'Vysshaia mera' berta brekhta," *Literatura mirovoi revoliutsii,* 1932, no. 1, 71.

46. Benjamin, "Author as Producer," 769–770.

47. Ibid., 776.

48. A. Stupel', *Gans Eisler, 1898–1962* (Leningrad: Muzyka, 1970), 56.

49. V. Nazarova, *Gans Eisler-Bertol't Brekht. Tvorcheskoe sotrudnichestvo* (Leningrad: Sovetskii kompozitor, 1970), 26–37, 47–53.

50. M. Druskin, *Gans Eisler i rabochee muzykal'noe dvizhenie v Germanii* (Moscow: Gos. Izd. Muzykal'noe iskusstvo, 1934), 52.

51. Brecht, "The Modern Theatre Is the Epic Theatre," in *Brecht on Theatre,* trans. and ed. John Willett (New York: Hill and Wang, 1992), 33–42; Durus, "Arbeitergesang und Agitprop," *Die rote Fahne,* 2 June 1931.

52. M. Druskin, *Gans Eisler i rabochee muzykal'noe dvizhenie v Germanii* (Moscow: Gos. Izd. Muzykal'noe iskusstvo, 1934), 20.

53. Sergei Tretiakov, "Liudi odnogo kostra," in *Strana perekrëstok,* 335. In 1932 during one of his visits to Moscow Brecht talked to Tretiakov about a plan to organize in Berlin a series of theatrical performances that would reenact the most interesting trials in the history of mankind; "Bert Brekht," in B. Brekht, *Epicheskie dramy* (Moscow-Leningrad: GIKhL, 1934).

54. *Brecht on Theatre,* 33–42.

55. Benjamin uses the term "alienation" in his essay on photography, written before Tretiakov's visit. Perhaps he got it from Brik.

56. M. Druskin, "Gans Eisler i ego gruppa," *Sovetskii muzykant,* 1933, no. 4, 61, 63.

57. Bert Brekht, "Vysshaia mera (instruktivnaia p'esa)," trans. I. Barkhali and S. Tret'iakov, *Literatura mirovoi revoliutsii,* 1932, no. 1, 38–45.

58. There had been two performances in Berlin while Tretiakov was there—the premiere took place on 13/14 December 1930 at the Berlin Philharmonic, and the text was slightly revised for a second performance on 18 January in the Grosses Schauspielhaus, more likely the one Tretiakov saw.

59. GARF 5283/ 6/80/88–92, 96, 101–103; GARF 5283/82/86–103; , RGALI,645/1/165/ 46–47.

60. GARF 5283/6/80/86–103; Tretiakov provided a transcript in S. Tretiakov, "Muzyka krasnogo Veddinga," *Sovetskoe iskusstvo,* 3 August 1932.

364 ⟋ Notes to Pages 62–66

61. As examples of attacks on Rodchenko see for example, "Pionery iz lageria Tret'ego, reshaiushchego," *Proletarskoe foto*, 1932, no. 1, 12–13, and G. Boltianskii, "Na putiakh bor'by za tvorcheskii metod," *Proletarskoe foto*, 1932, no. 2, 1.

62. Brekht, *Epicheskie dramy;* Sergej Tretjakov, *Brülle China! Ein Spiel in 9 Bildern.* Einzig autorisierte Übertragung von Leo Lania. (Berlin: Ladyschnikow, 1929).

63. "S fotoapparatom po Rossii!," *Sovetskoe iskusstvo*, 3 September 1932.

64. Erika Wolf, personal communication, 22 August 2008.

65. Note also "Na Cheku. Otryvok iz oratorii. Tekst Erikha Veringerta. Perevod S. Tret'iakova. Muzyka Gansa Eislera," *Sovetskoe iskusstvo*, 27 July 1932.

66. Morus, "Der Zug nach Osten," *Berlin am Morgen*, 9 June 1931; Stephen C. Foster, ed., *Hans Richter: Activism, Modernism and the Avant-Garde* (Cambridge, Mass.: MIT Press, 1998), 86–88, 114–116.

67. Friedrich Wolf, "Gruss am Moskau," *Berlin am Morgen*, 10 June 1931.

68. This appears to have been a mandated topic: Vsevolod Vishnevskii wrote a play, *Germaniia*, about a workers' uprising there in response to the appeal of comrade Lozovsky, head of Profintern (Vsevolod Vishnevskii, "Otkrytoe pis'mo Vs. Meierkhol'du," *Sovetskoe iskusstvo*, 1932, no. 6, 4).

69. S. Tret'iakov, "Brekht—Eisler," *Pravda*, 13 May 1932.

70. "'Komu prinadlezhit mir,'" *Literaturnaia gazeta*, 12 May 1932.

71. S. Tret'iakov [under the rubric] "Pisateli—Krasnoi Armii," *Literaturnaia gazeta*, 29 July 1932.

72. S. Tret'iakov, "'Mat' Bert Brekhta," *Literaturnaia gazeta*, 29 January 1933.

73. A. Stupel', *Gans Eisler, 1898–1962* (Leningrad: Muzyka, 1970), 56–57.

74. B. Brekht, Eisler, Veisborn, "'Mat','" *Internatsional'naia literatura*, 1933, no. 2, 35–59; S. Tretiakov, "Dramaturg i didakt (o p'ese B. Brekhta 'Mat')," *Internatsional'naia literatura*, 1933, no. 2, 116–118.

75. S. Tret'iakov, "Rapport proletarskogo khudozhnika, boitsa bratskoi kompartii" (a version of an article published in several places), *Proletarskoe foto* 1932, no. 3, 16–18; Vl. Kostin, "Iazyk klassovoi nenavisti," *Proletarskoe foto*, 1932, no. 3, 21; [Aleksei] Fedorov-Davydov, "Dzhon Khartfil'd—proletarskii khudozhnik," *Brigada khudozhnikov*, 1932, no. 2, 35–37; S. Tret'iakov, *Dzhon Khartfil'd* (Moscow: Izogiz, 1936).

76. The attacks come under the rubric "Na pervom etape tvorcheskoi diskussii. Gruppa 'Oktiabr' dolzhna nemedlenno perestroitsia . . . ," *Proletarskoe foto* 1932, no. 1, 10.

77. E.g. materials under the rubric "Vospitat' fotoreporterov sotsialisticheskoi pressy," *Sovetskoe foto*, 1929, no. 22 (November); "Opyt peredovikov prodvinut' v massy," *Sovetskoe foto*, 1930, no. 4 (February), 99–102.

78. "Za bol'shevistskuiu perestroiku fotografii" (ed.), *Proletarskoe foto* 1931, no. 1 (September), 1.

79. "Arbeiter-fotograf—organizator mezhdunarodnoi proletarskoi fotosviazi," *Sovetskoe foto*, 1930, no. 7, 198.

80. "Chto pishet 'Der arbeiter fotograf,'" *Sovetskoe foto*, 1931, no. 10 (May).

81. "Berlin-Moskva Mezhdunarodnoe ob"edinenie rabochikh fotografov vsekh stran," *Sovetskoe foto*, 1930, no. 3–4, 98.

82. Erika Wolf, personal communication, April 3, 2009.

83. Erika Wolf, *USSR in Construction: A Modernist Propaganda Magazine for the Stalinist Regime*, forthcoming; Emma Widdis, *Visions of a New Land: Soviet Film from the Revolution to the Second World War* (New Haven: Yale University Press, 2003).

84. RGASPI 538/3/158/4, 10, 23, 144, 152, 158, 180, 190, 201, 232.

85. A. Shaikhet and M. Al'pert, "Kak my snimali Filippovykh," *Proletarskoe foto*, 1931, no. 4 (December), 46–47. For this section and some other material in this chapter I am heavily indebted to Erika Wolf, who generously shared her archival findings with me.

86. N. F. Filippov, "Fotopropagandu—na vysshuiu stupen'," *Proletarskoe foto*, 1931, no. 4 (December), 12.

87. Shaikhet and Al'pert, "Kak my snimali Filippovykh," 46–47 (Tretiakov's principles were followed, p. 46).

88. "24 Stunden aus dem Leben einer Moskauer Arbeiterfamilie," *A-I-Z*, 1931, no. 38 (September), 749–767.

89. B. Zherebtsov, "Kak smontirovana seriia 'Sem'ia Filippovykh,'" *Proletarskoe foto*, 1932, no. 9, 8–10.

90. "Dve sem'i—dva mira. Filippovy i Furnes," *Proletarskoe foto*, 1932, no. 6, 35.

91. "Das 'Arbeiterparadies' in Sowjetrussland! Ein plumpes Schwindel-Manoever der *A-I-Z*," *Reichsbanner. Illustrierte Zeitung*, 10 October 1931.

92. "A-I-Z sagt die Wahrheit! Deutsche Sozial Demokraten besuchen Filipows," *A-I-Z*, 1931, no. 45, 903.

93. "24 chasa iz zhizni moskovskoi rabochei sem'i, Arbeieter illiustrirte tseitung (A-I-Z)," *Pravda*, 24 October 1931.

94. L. Mezhericher, "Za operativnuiu bol'shevistskuiu fotoseriiu. Ovladet' seriinoi s"ëmkoi—politicheskaia zadacha fotografii," *Proletarskoe foto*, 1931, no. 4, 3.

95. S. Tret'iakov, "Ot fotoserii k dlitel'nomu fotonabliudeniiu. V poriadke obsuzhdeniia," *Proletarskoe foto*, 1931, no. 4, 20–21, 45 (the Filippov photos are printed on the intervening pages).

96. S. Tretiakov, "The Writer and the Socialist Village," *October* 118 (Fall 2006), 68.

97. I. V. Stalin, "Novaia obstanovka—novye zadachi khoziastvennikov na stroitel'stvakh. Rech' na soveshchanii khoziastvennikov, 23 iunia, 1931," in *Sochineniia*, vol. 12 (Moscow: Gos. Izd. Polit. Lit, 1951), 55–59.

98. See chapter 3 in R. G. Pikhaia, ed., *I. V. Stalin, istoricheskaia ideologiia v SSSR v 1920–1950-e gody: Perepiska s istorikami, stat'i i zametki po istorii, stenogrammy, vystupleniia*, part 1, *1920–1930-e gody* (Saint Petersburg: Nauka, 2006), 113–182.

99. I. V. Stalin, "O nekotorykh voprosakh istorii bol'shevizma. Pis'mo v redaktsiiu zhurnala, 'Proletarskaia revoliutsiia'," *Molodaia gvardiia*, 1932, no. 1, 5, 9, 10.

100. Sergei Tret'iakov, "Prodolzhenie sleduet," in N. Chuzhak, ed., *Literatura fakta* (Moscow: Federatsiia, 1929), 70, English trans: "To Be Continued," *October* 118 (Fall 2006), 55–56.

101. Laszlo Sziklai, *After the Proletarian Revolution: Georg Lukacs's Marxist Development, 1930–1945* (Budapest: Akademia Kiado, 1992), 158–159, 163.

102. Space does not permit me to cover Lukács's earlier attack on Willi Bredel, the future editor of *Das Wort* (see Chapter 5), and his novel *Maschinenfabrik N & K* of 1931 (Georg Lukács, "Willi Bredels Romane," *Die Linkskurve*, 1931, no. 11 [November],

23–27). This novel was widely praised in Soviet journals before the Lukács article and received a more reserved treatment thereafter (e.g., P. S. Kogan, "Proletarskaia literatura v Germanii," *Inostrannaia kniga,* 1931, no. 3–4, 81–82; [unsigned], "Germanskaia proletarskaia kritika o romanakh Villi Bredelia," *Literatura mirovoi revoliutsii,* 1932, no. 2, 107–110, also criticizes the Lukács article).

103. Georg Lukács, *Essays on Realism,* trans. David Fernbach (Cambridge, Mass: MIT Press, 1981), 50, 59; Georgi Lukács, "Reportage oder Gestaltung. Kritische Bemerkungen anlässlich des Romans von Ottwalt," *Linkskurve* 4, no. 7 (July 1932), 27, no. 8 (August 1932), 28.

104. Georg Lukach, Reportazh ili obrazotvorchestvo? Kriticheskie zamechaniia po povodu romana Otval'ta," and Ernst Otval't, "Roman fakta (otvet Georgu Lukachu)," *Internatsional'naia literatura,* 1933, no. 2, 91–104, 105–109.

105. E.g., G. Sandomirskii, "Denn sie wissen was sie tun (ein deutscher Justiz-Roman)," *Inostrannaia kniga,* 1932, no. 2, 62–63.

106. E.g., a discussion in the German Länderkomission of the Writers Union: RGALI 631/12/50/ 2, 6, 9 (Tretiakov), 10.

107. Lukács, "Reportage oder Gestaltung," *Linkskurve* 4, 23–30 (reference on 30); 5, 26–31.

108. G. Gauzner, "Kollektivnaia rabota pisatelei 'Belomorstroia,'" *Istoriia zavodov,* vols 3–4 (1934), 111–113.

109. Iuz, "'Kule Vampe,'" (review), *Literaturnaia gazeta,* 23 May 1932. (The first revolutionary film. Of course it does not reach the standard of *Blue Angel* or *Var'iete,* but a significant step forward.)

110. "Presledovanie revoliutsionnogo iskusstva v Germanii," *Inostrannaia kniga,* 1932, no. 6, 82–83; Iuz, "'Kule Vampe.'"

111. E.g., V. Kataev, *Vremia, vperëd!* [Time, forward!] n.p.: 1932), and M. Shaginian, *Gidrotsentral'* (n.p.: Hydrocentral, 1929).

112. Simone Barck and Klaus Jarmatz, eds. *Exil in der UdSSR,* vol.1/1, 433–435; "Das russische Hollywood," *Rote Fahne,* 5 July 1931; , GARF 5283/6/80/84, 85.

113. For example, George Orwell's *Down and Out in Paris and London* (1933) or Benjamin's "Little Essay on Photography" (1931).

114. "O 'Moëm Parizhe.' Iz vyskazyvanii Il'i Erenburga," *Sovetskoe foto,* 1934, no. 4–5, 34; Il'ia Erenburg, *Moi Parizh* (Moscow: Izogiz, 1933), 8–9.

115. Benjamin, *Moscow Diary,* 55.

116. Il'ia Erenburg, "Bel'vil'," *Prozhektor,* 1932, no. 5, 15; S. Tret'iakov, "Gamburg," *Prozhektor* 1932, no. 6, 22–24.

117. Arkh. Mai (Germaniia), "Plan Moskvy dolzhen stroit'sia s vozrastaiushchim mezhdunarodnym znacheniem," *Stroitel'stvo Moskvy,* 1930, no. 6, 31; "Sozialistischer Städtebau in der UdSSR. Vortrag von Stadtbaurat Ernst May," *Die rote Fahne,* 7 June 1931; Ernst May, "Das sozialische Bauen in Sowjetrussland, *Welt am Abend,* 6 June 1931; "Bruno Taut baut in Moskau," *Neues Russland,* 1932, no. 1/2 (February), 30; Hannes Meyer, "Der Architekt im Klassenkampf," *Der rote Aufbau,* 1932, no. 13, 614–619.

118. GARF 5283/6/86/63, 99; GARF 5283/85/58; Bruno Taut, "Plan i zhizn'. O general'noi planirovke bol'shoi Moskvy," *Sovetskoe iskusstvo,* 27 August 1932; "Gross Moskau wird gebaut. Unterredung von Bruno Taut," *Berlin am Morgen,* 12 February 1932.

119. Margaret Bourke-White, *Eyes on Russia* (New York: Simon and Schuster, 1931), 22; "Magnitogorsk. Fotoetiud amerikanskogo fotografa," *Prozhektor,* 1932, no. 18, cover. In addition, in *SSSR na stroike,* 1932, no. 10, there is a photo of Stalin by the American James Abbe.
120. Le Corbusier, *Towards a New Architecture,* trans. Frederick Etchells (Oxford: Butterworth Architecture, 1989), 11.
121. Ibid.
122. Benjamin, *Moscow Diary,* 67, 112; Jean-Louis Cohen, *Le Corbusier and the Mystique of the USSR: Theories and Projects for Moscow, 1928–1936,* trans. Kenneth Hylton (Princeton: Princeton University Press, 1992).
123. Le Corbusier, *The City of Tomorrow and Its Planning,* trans. Frederick Etchells (London: Architectural Press, 1971), 287; Le Korbuz'e, *Planirovka goroda,* trans. S. M. Gornyi (Moscow: OGIZ-Izogiz, 1933).

2. MOSCOW, THE LETTERED CITY

1. *Putevoditel' po novoi Moskve,* sost. M. S—v (Moscow: Avrora, 1923), 37–39.
2. Pushkin Square was so named by order of the Moscow Soviet on 28 July 1931, i.e., one month after the plan to reconstruct Moscow was announced. Mayakovsky Square was so named after Stalin endorsed him as the great Soviet poet in a statement of 1935.
3. "Skul'pturnye pamiatniki," *Stroitel'stvo Moskvy,* 1937, no. 12, 32.
4. A. F. Rodin, "Pushkinskaia ploshchad'," *Stroitel'stvo Moskvy,* 1937, no. 2, 13–14.
5. If we are to believe the recollections of I. M. Gronskii, at the time head of the Organizational Committee of the Writers Union, Stalin had the greatest hand in coining the term and the meeting to endorse it took place in his study; see Katerina Clark and Evgeny Dobrenko, eds., *Soviet Culture and Power: A History in Documents* (New Haven: Yale University Press, 2007), 163–165.
6. O. V. Khlevniuk, *Politbiuro. Mekhanizmy politicheskoi vlasti v 1930-e gody* (Moscow: Rosspen, 1996), 65–68.
7. "Rech' U.M. Molotova," *Pravada,* 21 June 1936.
8. "Opyt literatury—v kino" (editorial), *Literaturnaia gazeta,* 17 June 1933.
9. However, Eisenstein wrote the script for the *Ivan the Terrible* trilogy himself.
10. S. Fridliand, "Zametki o tvorcheskoi praktike," *Proletarskoe foto,* 1933, no. 3, 26.
11. B. Zherebtsov, "Montazh fotograficheskoi serii. O serii 'Sem'ia Filippovykh,'" *Proletarskoe foto,* 1932, no. 9, 6; L. Mezhericher, "Za operativnuiu bol'shevitskuiu fotoseriiu. Ovladet' seriinoi s"emkoi—politicheskaia zadacha fotografii," *Proletarskoe foto,* 1931, no. 4 (December), 18–19.
12. Elizabeth Astrid Papazian, *Manufacturing Truth: The Documentary Moment in Early Soviet Culture* (De Kalb: Northern Illinois University Press, 2009), 19, 63–65.
13. Evgeniia Ginzburg, *Krutoi marshrut* (Milan: Arnaldo Mondadori Editore, 1967), 231.
14. E.g., "K. E. Voroshilov na IX s"ezde VLKSM," *Pravda,* January 22, 1931, 2.
15. See e.g. "Pervomaiskaia vystavka arkhitektury i planiroki v Moskve," *Arkhitektura SSSR,* 1934, no. 4, 76.

16. G. P. Gol'ts, "Uroki maiskoi arkhitekturnoi vystavki," *Arkhitektura SSSR*, 1934, no. 6, 10, 8–9.

17. Angel Rama, *The Lettered City*, trans. and ed. John Charles Chasten (Durham, N.C.: Duke University Press, 1996).

18. "O rabote IMEL po vyiavleniiu publikatsii literaturnogo nasledstva K. Marksa," Rech' tov. Adoratskogo na Sobranii TsK, TsKK, VKP(b), TsIK, i SNK SSSR, Ispolkoma Kominterna i MK VKP(b), posviashchënnom 50-letiiu so dnia rozhdeniia K. Marksa," *Izvestiia*, 16 March 1933.

19. "O chistke partii. Postanovlenie TsK I TsKK VKP(b) ot 28 aprelia 1933 g.," in *O chistke partii* (Moscow: Partiinoe izdatel'stvo, 1933), 4; Em. Iaroslavskii, *Chego partiia trebuet ot kommunista*, izdanie vtoroe, ispravlennoe (Moscow: Partizdat TsK VKP(b), 1936), 13–18.

20. There are numerous examples of this in Andrei Artizov and Oleg Naumov, comps., *Vlast' i khudozhestvennaia intelligentsiia. Dokumenty TsK RKP (b)—VKP(b), VChK—OGPU—NKVD o kul'turnoi politike. 1917–1953 gg.* (Moscow: Mezhdunarodnyi fond "Demokratiia," 1999).

21. "O postanovke partiinoi propagandy v sviazi s vypuskom 'Kratkogo kursa istorii VKP (b).' Postanovlenie TsK VKP (b)," *Literaturnaia gazeta*, 1938, no. 64 (20 November).

22. Benedict Anderson, *Imagined Communities: Reflections on the Origin and Spread of Nationalism*, rev. ed. (London: Verso, 1991), 25, 24.

23. *Portret I. V. Stalina* (1928) and *Iosif Vissarionovich Stalin* (1931). In *Portret I. V. Stalina* of 1937, other newsprint has been added (*Izvestiia, Prozhektor, SSSR na stroike*, and other unidentified titles). In Brodsky's *I. V. Stalin* (1932), he has a newspaper in his hand (reproduced in *Iskusstvo*, 1933, no. 1–2, 74). See also Stalin's portrait of 1939 by A. M. Gerasimov, in which he is in military uniform but has one hand on books and papers.

24. *Istoriia Vsesoiznoi kommunisticheskoi partii (bol'shevikov). Kratkii kurs* (Moscow, 1938).

25. Mikhail Yampolsky, "The Rhetoric of Representation of Political Leaders in Soviet Culture," *Elementa*, no. 1, (January 1993),103.

26. E.g., G. M. Shegal's painting *Vozhd', uchitel', drug. I. V. Stalin na II s"ezde kolkhoznikov-udarnikov v fevrale 1935 goda* (1937). In visual depictions of ordinary people, there is generally little sign of books and writing, unless they are depicted with Stalin or writing to him.

27. Anderson, *Imagined Communities*, 19.

28. Yampolsky writes: "in Stalin's emblematic, thinking replaces oratory" (Yampolsky, "The Rhetoric of Representation," 103), but I would maintain that it was texts that bore witness to this thinking, which was otherwise largely invisible and only implied.

29. Victoria E. Bonnell, *Iconography of Power: Soviet Political Posters under Lenin and Stalin* (Berkeley: University of California Press, 1997), fig. 4.17, 187.

30. Igor Golomstock, *Totalitarian Art in the Soviet Union, the Third Reich, Fascist Italy, and the People's Republic of China* (New York: Harper Collins, 1990), 224.

31. Jacques Derrida, "Des Tours de Babel," trans. Joseph T. Graham, in Rainer Schulte and John Biguenet, ed., *Theories of Translation: An Anthology of Essays from Dryden to Derrida* (Chicago: University of Chicago Press, 1992), 218.

32. Iurii Murashev, "Prestuplenie pis'ma i golos nakazaniia: O medial'noi reprezentatsii pokazatel'nykh protsessov 1930-kh godov," in Khans Giunter and Evgenii Dobrenko, eds., *Sotsrealisticheskii kanon* (Saint Petersburg: Akademicheskii proekt, 2000), 729–739.

33. Evgenii Bordiugov, ed., *Uznik Lubianki. Tiuremnye zapisi Nikolaia Bukharina. Sb dokumentov,* 2nd enl. ed. (Moscow: AIRO-XXI, 2008).

34. On the close connection between literature and the purges and their confessions see Thomas Lahusen, *How Life Writes the Book: Real Socialism and Socialist Realism in Stalin's Russia* (Ithaca: Cornell University Press, 1997), and Vitaly Shentalinsky, *Arrested Voices: Resurrecting the Disappeared Writers of the Soviet Regime,* trans. John Crowfoot (New York: Free Press, 1996), 24, 111.

35. Edward Braun, "Vsevolod Meyerhold: The Final Act," in Katherine Bliss Eaton, ed., *Enemies of the People: The Destruction of Soviet Literary, Theater and Film Arts in the 1930s* (Evanston, Ill.: Northwestern University Press, 2002), 152–159.

36. As Sheila Fitzpatrick has established in her archival research (communication of 4 May, 2011), Stalin's corrections to literary texts were far from always ideological in nature and often were for grammatical errors or mistakes in representing Party procedure—symptomatic of his pedantic nature; see for example his corrections of 23 May, 1940 to the script for Mikheil Chiaureli's film *Kliatva narodov* (RGASPI 558/11/167).

37. "O postanovke partiinoi propagandy v sviazi s vypuskom 'Kratkogo kursa istorii VKP (b).'"

38. "Po stranitsam inostrannykh zhurnalov," *Arkhitektura SSSR,* 1934, no. 3, 73–74; "Planirovka novogo Antverpa," *Arkhitektura za rubezhom,* 1934, no. 1, 2–6; P. Gol'denberg, "Proekt rasshireniia Amsterdama (Gollandiia)," *Arkhitektura za rubezhom,* 1937, no. 1, 33; Prof. A. Eingorn (Khar'kov), "Proekt planirovki 'Bol'shogo Parizha' [of 14 May 1932]," *Arkhitektura za rubezhom,* 1936, no. 6, 8–14.

39. "Vperëd k novym pobedam! Vyderzhki iz doklada tov. Kaganovicha L. M. o rabote moskovskogo oblastnogo i gorodskogo komitetov VKP (b) na moskovskoi partkonferentsii," *Stroitel'stvo Moskvy,* 1932, no. 1, 2–5.

40. "Sotsialisticheskaia Moskva" (editorial), *Arkhitektura SSSR,* 1935, no. 10–11, 2.

41. Clark, *Petersburg,* chapter 11.

42. S. Dinamov, "Moskva—boevaia tema tvorcheskoi perestroiki" and S. Eizenshtein, "Moskva vo vremeni," articles published under the rubric "Proletarskaia Moskva zhdët svoego khudozhnika," *Literaturnaia gazeta,* 11 July 1933.

43. Katerina Clark, "Eisenstein's Two Projects for a Film about Moscow," *Modern Language Review* 101 (Spring 2006),188–204.

44. "Arkhitektor derzhit politicheskii ekzamen," *Stroitel'stvo Moskvy,* 1932, no. 3, 23. See also "Tvorcheskie zadachi sovetskoi arkhitektury i problema arkhitekturnogo nasledstva," *Arkhitektura SSSR,* 1933, no. 2, 38, no. 3–4, 4–25.

45. "O general'nom plane rekonstruktsii gor. Moskvy. Postanovlenie SNK SSSR i TsK VKP(b)," *Stroitel'stvo Moskvy,* 1935, no. 7–8, 1.

46. E.g., I. A. Fomin in "Tvorcheskaia diskussiia Soiuza sovetskikh arkhitektorov i problema arkhitekturnogo nasledstva," *Arkhitektura SSSR*, 1933, no. 3-4, 15.

47. M. Ia. Ginzburg in "Tvorcheskaia diskussiia Soiuza,"13–14.

48. "Ploshchad' Dvortsa sovetov," "Arkhitektura komsomol'skoi ploshchadi," *Arkhitektura SSSR*, 1934, no. 2, 12, 18, 19; Alabian in "Tvorcheskaia diskussiia Soiuza," 24.

49. B. Iofan, "Dvorets sovetov," *Arkhitektura SSSR*, 1933, no. 5, 31.

50. B. M. Iofan and V. A. Shchuko, "Ploshchad' dvortsa sovetov," *Arkhitektura SSSR*, 1933, no. 2, 12; A. Bunin and M. Kruglov, "Arkhitekturnaia kompozitsiia ploshchadi," *Arkhitektura SSSR*, 1933, 18–19; D. Arkin, "Vichentsa," *Arkhitektura SSSR*, 1936, no. 6, 55.

51. Aleksandra Latur, *Rozhdenie metropolii. Moskva 1930–1950. Vospominaniia i obrazy* (Moscow: Iskusstvo XXI vek, 2002), 131.

52. G. Gol'ts and S. Kozhin, "Brunelleski," *Arkhitektura SSSR*, 1934, no. 4, 66.

53. B. M. Iofan, "Kak ia rabotal nad proektom dvortsa sovetov," *Arkhitektura SSSR*, 1933, no. 5, 31; D. Arkin, "Bazhenov," *Arkhitektura SSSR*, 1937, no. 2, 3.

54. "Podgotovka arkhitekturnykh kadrov," (editorial), *Arkhitektura SSSR*, 1933, no. 3-4, 1–3; "Zadachi nauchno-issledovatel'skoi raboty," (editorial), *Arkhitektura SSSR*, 1933, no. 6, 1–3; "Pervaia sessiia kabineta teorii i istorii arkhitektury," *Akademiia arkhitektury*, 1934, no. 1–2, 7.

55. I. V. Zholtovskii, "Vstupitelnoe slovo k chitateliam," in Andreia Palladio, *Chetyre knigi ob arkhitekture*, trans. Akad. Arkh. I. V. Zholtovskii, vol. 1 (Moscow: Akademiia Arkhitektury, 1936), 13. Other treatises published by Vsesoiuznaia Akademiia Arkhitektury include Vitruvius, *Desiat' knig ob arkhitekture*, trans. F. A. Petrovskii (Moscow: Akademiia arkhitektury 1936), and Leon Battista Al'berti, *Desiat' knig o zodchestve*, vol. 1, trans. V. P. Zubov (Moscow: Akademiia arkhitektury 1935). See also "Novye knigi. Teoriia arkhitektury," *Arkhitektura SSSR*, 1937, no. 2, 78; "V izdatel'stve Akademii arkhitektury," *Akademiia arkhitektury*, 1934, no. 1–2, 128; also the list provided in Branko Mitrovic´, *Studying Renaissance Architectural Theory in the Age of Stalinism* (Florence: Olschki, 2009), 233–263.

56. Latur, *Rozhdenie metropolii*, 30, 75.

57. "Prakticheskie meropriiatiia po uluchsheniiu i razvitiiu moskovskogo gorodskogo khoziaistva. Postanovlenie Moskovskogo oblasnogo i gorodskogo sovetov VKP(b)," *Pravda*, June 25, 1931, 3.

58. See e.g., "Sotsialisticheskaia Moskva," (editorial), *Arkhitektura SSSR*, 1935, no. 10–11, 2.

59. I. Stalin, "Otchëtnyi doklad semnadtsatomu s"ezdu partii o rabote TsK VKP(b)," *Arkhitektura SSSR*, 1934, no. 1, 2.

60. Varvara Stepanova, comp., *Moskva konstruiruetsia* (Moscow: 1938), 1.

61. "O general'nom plane rekonstruktsii gor. Moskvy. Postanovlenie SNK SSSR i TsK VKP(b)," *Stroitel'stvo Moskvy*, 1935, no. 7–8, 1.

62. L. Leonov, "Padenie zariad'ia," in *Moskva. Sbornik* (Moscow: Rabochaia Moskva, 1935).

63. Timothy J. Colton, *Moscow: Governing the Socialist Metropolis* (Cambridge, Mass.: Harvard University Press, 1995), 111–115, 229–230, 233.

64. "Arkhitekturno-Planovochnyi komitet Mossoveta," *Stroitel'stvo Moskvy,* 1932, no. 2, 27; this was announced before the resolution creating a single writers' organization; "Arkhitekturno-Planirovochnoe upravlenie Mossoveta," *Stroitel'stvo Moskvy,* 1932, no. 3, 44; "Ne stroit' bez razresheniia Mossoveta," *Stroitel'stvo Moskvy,* 1932, no. 4, 32. Previously, in 1931, a temporary Arkhitekturnyi komitet had been formed with several leading architects on it, including members of the avant-garde ("Sozdan arkhitekturnyi komitet Moskvy," *Stroitel'stvo Moskvy,* 1931, no. 7, 24).

65. "General'naia skhema rekonstruktsii Moskvy," *Akhitektura SSSR,* 1933, no. 5, 55.

66. See "Organizatsiia arkhitekturnoi i planirovochnoi raboty" (editorial), and "Organizatsiia proektirovaniia zdanii, planirovki goroda i otvoda zemel'nykh uchastkov v Moskve," *Arkhitektura SSSR,* 1933, no. 5, 2–3, 60.

3. THE RETURN OF THE AESTHETIC

1. *Moskva rekonstruiruetsia. Al'bom diagram, toposkhem i fotografii po rekonstruktsii Moskvy,* text by Viktor Shklovskii, design by A. Rodchenko and V. Stepanova (Moscow, 1937).

2. L. M. Kaganovich, "Rech' na iubileinom plenume TsK VLKSM 29 oktiabria 1933 g.," cited in L. Perchik, "Gorod sotsializma i ego arkhitektura," *Arkhitektura SSSR,* 1934, no. 1, 3.

3. See e.g., D. Arkin's keynote address to the Union of Architects, "Tvorcheskaia diskussiia Soiuza sovetskikh arkhitektorov i problema arkhitekturnogo nasledstva," *Arkhitektura SSSR,* 1933, no. 3-4, 6.

4. James C. Scott, *Seeing Like a State: How Certain Schemes to Improve the Human Condition Have Failed* (New York: Yale University Press, 1998), 56.

5. Walter Benjamin, *Illuminations: Essays and Reflections,* ed. Hannah Arendt, trans. Harry Zohn (New York: Schocken Books, 1968), 241, 242.

6. Unsigned (editorial), "Sozdadim arkhitekturu, dostoinuiu velikoi epokhy sotsializma," *Arkhitekturnaia gazeta,* 1934, no. 1, 1.

7. Valerian Pereverzev, Aleksandr Voronsky, Vladimir Friche, Yury Libedinsky, Trotsky, and other formulators of the major theoretical positions of the twenties tended to use such terms as literaturovedenie (the title of Pereverzev's collection of writings published in 1928); see "Khudozhestvennaia platforma RAPP'a" (Libedinsky's main theoretical treatise for the organization, likewise published in *Na literaturnom postu,* 1928, no. 1, 1–19) or Voronsky's "Iskusstvo videt' mir," likewise of 1928.

8. Peter Demetz, *Marx, Engels and the Poets: The Origins of Marxist Literary Criticism,* trans. Jeffrey L. Sammons (Chicago: University of Chicago Press, 1967).

9. Vol. 1 of 1931 contains the correspondence of Engels with Paul Ernst; vol. 2 of 1932 contains that between Engels and Margaret Harkness; vol. 3 of 1932 contains that of Marx and Engels with Ferdinand Lassalle about his play Franz von Sickingen (the most complete version of this published to that date); and vols. 7–8 of 1933 contains Engels's letters to Minna Kautsky about her novel *The Old and the New.*

10. V. F. Asmus, ed., *Antichnye mysliteli ob iskusstve* (Moscow: Izogiz, 1937).

11. Oksana Bulgakova, "Teoriia kak utopicheskii proekt," *Novoe literaturnoe obozrenie,* no. 88 (2007).

12. "Klassiki esteticheskoi mysli," *Literaturnaia gazeta,* 1933, no. 38 (17 August). Books published include G. Lessing, *Laokoon ili o granitsakh zhivopisi i poezii,* ed. M. Lifshits with an introduction by V. Grib (Leningrad: 1933); I. Vinkel'man, Is- toriia iskusstva drevnosti (Leningrad: 1933); and Fridrikh Shiller, *Stat'i po estetike* (Moscow-Leningrad, 1935), with an introduction by Lukács, "Shiller kak estetik," vii–lxxxiii.

13. Lukach, "Shiller kak estetik," xxxvii, xxx.

14. Ibid., lxxxi, lxxxii.

15. See also Jochen Hellbeck's discussion of this shift in the Party's and the workers' out- look: *Revolution on My Mind: Writing a Diary under Stalin* (Cambridge, Mass.: Har- vard University Press, 2006), 241–247, 254, 258–261.

16. "Samyi krupnyi odarënnyi ideolog i praktik noveishei zapadnoei arkhtitektury." D. Ar- kin, "Tvorcheskie puti sovetskoi arkhitektury i problema arkhitekturnogo naslediia," *Arkhitektura SSSR,* 1933, no. 3–4, 6.

17. "Krestovyi pokhod L. Korbiuz'e," *Arkhitektura SSSR,* 1934, no. 3, 70.

18. Initially, certain Constructivists, such as the Vesnin brothers and M. Ginzburg, con- tinued to enjoy prominence and to participate in the architectural debates. However, the anti-Formalist campaign of 1936 delivered the coup de grâce to their dwindling stature.

19. Boris Barkin recalls that when the Bauhaus architect Hannes Meyer came to Moscow in 1932 and spent a semester at the Moscow Architectural Institute (MAI) with the in- tention of imparting the experience of Bauhaus functionalism, the atmosphere in that institution had changed radically, and he received little attention. "Boris Barkin," in Aleksandra Latur, *Rozhdenie metrolpolii. Moskva 1930–1950. Vospominaniia i obrazy* (Moscow: Iskusstvo XXI veka, 2002), 57.

20. P. Bolokhin, "Planirovka zhilykh kvartalov, sotsgoroda," *Arkhitektura SSSR,* 1933, no. 5, 4.

21. "Nashi goroda, ulitsy, zdaniia dolzhny byt' krasivy" *Stroitel'stvo Moskvy,* 1932, no. 5, 6.

22. I. Cherkasskii, "Arkhitekture—reshaiushchuiu rol'," *Stroitel'stvo Moskvy,* 1932, no. 5, 2–8.

23. "Khronika," *Arkhitektura SSSR,* 1933, no. 2, 38.

24. [Arkin], "Tvorcheskaia diskussiia Soiuza sovetskikh arkhitektorov i problema arkhi- tekturnogo nasledstva," 5.

25. Ibid., 5.

26. See e.g., S. E. Chernyshev, "Arkhitekturnoe litso novoi Moskvy," *Arkhitektura SSSR,* 1935, no. 10–11, 11.

27. "Dvorets sovetov," *Stroitel'stvo Moskvy,* 1937, no. 19–20, 14.

28. "V Akademii arkhitektury," *Arkhitektura SSSR,* 1934, no. 4, 75.

29. "O nekotorykh voprosakh sovetskoi arkhitektury," stenogramma vystupleniia tov. An- garova na obshchemoskovskom soveshchanii arkhitektorov 27 fevralia, 1936 g., *Arki- tektura SSSR,* 1936, no. 4, 9.

30. Cherkasskii, "Arkhitekture—reshaiushchuiu rol'," 4.

31. Ibid.

32. I. Fomin, "Protiv fetishizatsii materiala," *Arkhitektura SSSR,* 1934, no. 4, 28–29.

33. V. Nikolaev, "Konstruktsiia Dvortsa Sovetov na stal'nom karkase," *Arkhitektura SSSR,* 1937, no. 2, 67.

34. D. Arkin, "Zametki ob amerikanskoi arkhitekture," *Arkhitektura SSSR,* 1934, no. 1, 42, 48.

35. See e.g., ibid., 42–51; A. Urban, "Vnutreniaia arkhitektura obshchstvennykh zdanii na zapade," *Arkhitektura za rubezhom,* 1935, no. 3, 1–8.

36. See e.g., "Rokerfeler tsentr," *Arkhitektura SSSR,* 1935, no. 2; "Po stranitsam inostrannykh zhurnalov," *Arkhitektura SSSR,* 1933, no. 3–4, 63.

37. "Zapadno-evropeiskaia arkhitektura. Vpechatleniia ot poezdki (iz soobshchenii D. E. Arkina na 3-i sessii Vsesoiuznoi Akademii arkhitektury 22 dekabria 1935 g.)," *Arkhitektura za rubezhom,* 1936, no. 2, 43; D.A., "Dve mezhdunarodnye vystavki (Chikago-Milan)," *Arkhitektura SSSR,* 1933, no. 3–4, 57.

38. Martin Jay, "Scopic Regimes of Modernity," in Scott Lash and Jonathon Friedman, eds., *Modernity and Identity* (Oxford: Blackwell, 1993), 182.

39. Khudozhnik Bela Uitz, [under the rubric] "K voprosu o monumental'nom iskusstve," *Iskusstvo,* 1934, no. 4, 11.

40. See e.g., Igor' Grabar', "Aktual'nye zadachi sovetskoi skul'ptury," *Iskusstvo,* 1933, 1–2, 156; Akademik A. V. Shchusev, [under the rubric] "K voprosu o monumental'nom iskusstve," 19.

41. [I. A. Fomin, contribution to] "Tvorcheskaia diskussiia Soiuza sovetskikh arkhitektorov i problema arkhitekturnogo nasledstva," 16.

42. "Arkhitekturno-Planovochnyi komitet Mossoveta," Stroitel'stvo Moskvy, 1932, no. 2, 27.

43. "Rech' sekretaria TsK VKP(b) A. A. Zhdanova," in *Pervyi vsesoiuznyi s"ezd sovetskikh pisatelei. Stenograficheskii otchët* (Moscow: Ogiz, 1934), 5.

44. Katerina Clark, *The Soviet Novel: History as Ritual,* 3rd ed. (Bloomington: Indiana University Press, 2000), especially the introductory chapter, "The Distinctive Role of Socialist Realism in Soviet Culture."

45. Katerina Clark, "'The History of the Factories' as a Factory of History," in Jochen Hellbeck and Klaus Heller, eds., *Autobiographical Practices in Russia—Autobiographische Praktiken in Russland* (Göttingen: V & R Unipress, 2004), 251–278.

46. "Socialist Realism *with* Shores: The Conventions for the Positive Hero," in Thomas Lahusen and Evgeny Dobrenko, eds., *Socialist Realism without Shores* (Durham, N.C.: Duke University Press, 1997), 27–50.

47. *Moskva rekonstruiruetsia,* [1].

48. Clark, *Soviet Novel,* especially the introductory chapter, "Distinctive Role of Socialist Realism in Soviet Culture."

49. For example, K. Alabian and V. Simbirtsev, writing in 1933, "Proekt ulitsy Dmitrovka v Moskve," claim that the reconstructed street will be "edinyi tselostnyi arkhitekturnyi ansambl'," which will not be "chaotic" but "spokoen" and "prost"; *Arkhitektura SSSR,* 1933, no. 3–4, 39.

50. In *Soviet Novel,* chapter 3, I also establish links between these epithets and literary conventions of Russian hagiography (58–59).

51. My general account of neoclassicism is taken from Hugh Honor, *Neo-classicism* (Harmondsworth, England: Penguin Books, 1977), 20, 40, 113, 123.

52. See "Imperial Petersburg, 1913," chapter 2 of Clark, *Petersburg: Crucible of Cultural Revolution, 1921–1931* (Cambridge, Mass.: Harvard University Press, 1995).

53. See e.g., "Arkhitekturnoe nasledie," *Arkhitektura SSSR,* 1935, no. 7, 45–52; "Rossi i nikolaevskaia Rossiia," *Arkhtitektura SSSR,* 1935, no. 12, 55–56.

54. Gannes Meier in "Tvorcheskaia tribuna. Kak ia rabotaiu," *Arkhitektura SSSR,* 1933, no. 6, 34; (Taut) GARF, 5283/6/519/13.

55. See chapter 2 of Clark, *Petersburg: Crucible of Cultural Revolution.*

56. Akad. Arkh. I. A. Fomin, "Printsipy tvorcheskoi raboty arkhitekturnoi masterskoi no 3," *Akademiia arkhitektury,* 1934, no. 1–2, 83–84, 92.

57. Peter Gay, *Enlightenment: An Interpretation,* vol. 1 (New York: Vintage, 1968), x–xi.

58. Quoting Renée Descartes, *Discourse on Method,* trans. Donald A. Cress (Indianapolis: Hackett, 1980); Scott, *Seeing Like a State,* 111–112.

59. Terry Eagleton, *The Ideology of the Aesthetic* (Oxford: Blackwell, 1990), 3.

60. Ibid., 17.

61. Ibid., 14.

62. Ibid., 17.

63. Ibid., 20.

64. Régis Debray, "Socialism: A Life Cycle," *New Left Review* 46 (July–August 2005), 15.

65. Erich Auerbach, *Mimesis: The Representation of Reality in Western Literature,* trans. Willard R. Trask (Princeton: Princeton University Press, 2003), 268–270.

66. Giulio Argan, *The Renaissance City,* trans. Susan Edna Bassnett (New York: Braziller, 1970), 13–17.

67. The list includes More's *Utopia* and Étienne *Cabet's Travels in Icarus* (1840).

68. "Vyderzhki iz doklada tov. Kaganovicha, L. M. o rabote Moskovskogo oblastnogo i gorodskogo komitetov VKP(b) na moskovskoi partkonferentsii," *Stroitel'stvo Moskvy,* 1932, no. 1, 4.

69. Northrop Frye, "Varieties of Literary Utopias," in *Utopias and Utopian Thought,* ed. Frank Edward Emanuel (Boston: Houghton Mifflin, 1966), 25–49.

70. "Doma dlia spetsialistov," *Stroitel'stvo Moskvy,* 1932, no. 4, 32.

71. I am grateful to Irina Paperno for this observation.

72. "Moskva rekonstruiruetsia," reproduced in Emma Widdis, *Visions of a New Land: Soviet Film from the Revolution to the Second World War* (New Haven: Yale University Press, 2003), 167.

73. GARF 5283/6/519/1–15. Taut had been commissioned to design an Intourist hotel and had been sent to Germany to buy materials for it, but then the order had been canceled (13), possibly a reason for his rancor.

74. Eagleton, *Ideology of the Aesthetic,* 15.

75. Benedict Anderson, *Imagined Communities; Reflections on the Origin and Spread of Nationalism,* rev. ed. (London: Verso, 1991), 15, 16–17.

76. L. M. Kaganovich, "Rech' na iubileinom plenume TsK VLKSM 29 oktiabria 1933 g.," cited in L. Perchik, "Gorod sotsializma i ego arkhitektura," *Arkhitektura SSSR*, 1934, no. 1, 3.

77. Andrea Palladio, *Chetyre knigi ob arkhitekture v dvukh tomakh, v perevode akademika I. V. Zholtovskogo*, vol. 1 (Moscow: Izdatel'stvo vsesoiuznoi akademii arkhitektury SSSR, 1938).

78. Katerina Clark and Evgeny Dobrenko, eds., *Soviet Culture and Power: A History in Documents, 1917–1953* (New Haven: Yale University Press, 2007).

79. "Letter from A. M. Gorky to I. V. Stalin," of 28 February, 1933; "Letter from I. V. Stalin to A. M. Gorky" of [no earlier than March 1, 1933], in ibid., 184.

80. M. Mertsanov, "Institut mirovoi literatury im. Gor'kogo pri TsIK SSSR," *Arkhitektura SSSR*, 1936, no. 12, 22–23.

81. Hellbeck, *Revolution on My Mind*, 260–261.

82. Clark, *Petersburg: Crucible of Cultural Revolution*, 149–150, 188, 236, 274.

83. *Moscou 1918–1941: De "l'homme nouveau" au bonheur totalitaire*, directed by Catherine Goussef (Paris: Editions Autrement, 1993), 9.

84. Lifshits originally had worked in art history but shifted to literary theory. The passion for the Renaissance was so strong in his case that he gave his daughter an Italian name from the Renaissance, Vittoria (interview with Vittoriia Mikhailovna German, 29 July 1997).

85. See their correspondence in Mikh. Lifshits i D. Lukach, *Perepiska, 1931–1970* (Moscow: Grundrisse, 2011).

86. Mikh. Lifshits, "Chelovek tridtsatykh godov," *V mire estetike* (Moscow: Izobrazitel'noe iskusstvo, 1985), 255–258.

87. See e.g., Mikhail Lifshits, *K voprosu o razvitii vzgliadov Marksa ob iskusstve* (Moscow: GIKhL, 1933), *Voprosy iskusstva i filosofii* (Moscow: Goslitizdat, 1935), and *K. Marks i F. Engel's ob iskusstve* (Moscow-Leningrad: Iskusstvo, 1937); *Lenin o kul'ure i iskusstve* (Moscow, 1938); Ernst Fisher, *Engel's kak literaturnyi kritik* (Moscow: GIKhL, 1933), and Anatolii Lunacharskii, *Lenin i literaturovedenie* (n.p., 1934); *Marks i Engel's o literature. Sbornik statei*, with commentaries by F. Shiller and G. Lukach (Moscow: Literaturnoe nasledstvo, published by Zhurgaz, 1933); "O tendentsioznosti i realizme" (on·an Engels letter), and F. Shiller, "Fridrikh Engel's i roman Minny Kautskogo," both in *Sovetskoe iskusstvo*, 1932, no. 59 (27 December).

88. "Rasskaz ili opisanie" (translated from the German manuscript by N. Vol'kenau), *Literaturnyi kritik*, 1936, no. 8, 44–67; German version, "Erzählen oder beschreiben?," *Internationale Literatur*, 1936, no. 11/12, 100–118, 108–123.

89. "Rasskaz ili opisanie," 65.

90. Ibid., 48.

91. Actually, there were also some surviving sex scenes in Panfërov's novel of collectivization, *Ingots (Bruski)*, but it was attacked by Gorky.

92. The novel is also in its own way metaliterary, containing several implicit discussions of literature. Compare his approach to Bakhtin's dissertation on Rabelais (first submitted in 1940), especially the chapter on St. Bartholemew's Eve.

93. Eagleton, *Ideology of the Aesthetic*, 15.

94. Olga Matich, *Erotic Utopia: The Decadent Imagination in Russia's Fin-de-Siècle* (Madison: University of Wisconsin Press, 2005).

95. L. Beregovoi, "Institut vtoroi zhizni," *Pravda,* 1937, no. 4; "Konferentsiia po perelivaniiu krovi," *Vecherniaia Moskva,* 1935, 5 February; P. Chepov, "Promyvanie organizma i ochishchenie krovi," *Vecherniaia Moskva,* 1935, 1 June; "Nikogda ne pozdno pomolodet'," *Vecherniaia Moskva,* 1935, 29 June. This trend also left its mark on literature; see e.g., Mikhail Zoshchenko, *Youth Restored* [Vozvrashchёnnaia molodost'] [n.p., 1933]).

96. Lukach, "Rasskaz ili opisanie," 55.

4. THE TRAVELING MODE AND THE HORIZON OF IDENTITY

1. This account is from a recreation in Bertrand de Jouvenel, *Vie de Zola* (Paris: Librarie Valois, 1931), 161, 163.

2. "On Imagery" (lecture delivered at the State Film Institute), in Richard Taylor, ed., *The Eisenstein Collection* (London: Seagull, 2006), 28. Jay Leyda dates this lecture 1933, and though Taylor speculates that it was more likely later, it is perfectly possible that it was indeed 1933.

3. Eisenstein had signed a contract with Paramount for it (Naum Kleiman, "Neosushchestvlёnnye zamylsi Eizenshteina," *Iskusstvo kino,* 1992, no. 4, 12–13).

4. This film is also known as *The General Line* [General'naia liniia].

5. Katerina Clark, *Petersburg: Crucible of Cultural Revolution* (Cambridge, Mass.: Harvard University Press, 1995), 175–176.

6. M. M. Vladimirova, *Vsemirnaia literatura i rezhissёskie uroki S. M. Eizenshteina* (Moscow: Moskovskii gosudarstvennyi institut kul'tury, 1990).

7. Uot Karman, Literaturnyi N'iu-Iork, "*Literaturnaia gazeta,* 11 November 1932; this column, for example, is about the John Reed Clubs.

8. See e.g., D. Mirskii, "Intelligentsiia i literatura Anglii," *Literaturnaia gazeta,* 29 October 1923, in which he singles out H. G. Wells.

9. Elliot Pol'," Vstrecha s Dzhoisom," *Literaturnaia gazeta,* 25 September 1932 "an exceptional person. Poor. Knows many languages. Those who like *Ulysses* usually compare it to Rabelais. Knows the epics of many peoples").

10. Epton Sinkler, "O Dzhone Dos Passose," *Literaturnaia gazeta,* August 5, 1932 (placed in the position generally used for editorials).

11. A. Ia Tairov, "Iskusstvo na zapade. Sokrashchёnnaia stenogramma doklada na sobranii pisatelei v redaktsii 'Literaturnoi gazety,'" *Literaturnaia gazeta,* 17 October 1932, includes a section on Picasso with a photograph of one of his paintings.

12. "Vozzvanie siurrealistov" [Against the war], *Literaturnaia gazeta,* 5 August 1932. A Moscow art exhibition of 1933 includes George Grosz, Pablo Picasso, Fernand Leger RGASPI, 541/1/128/47).

13. S. Dinamov, "O stile sovetskogo iskusstva," *Pravda,* 29 April 1935. My emphasis.

14. On these various presses see Simone Barck and Klaus Jarmatz, eds., *Exil in der UdSSR: Kunst und Literatur im antifaschisten Exil 1933–1945,* vol. 1/1 (Leipzig: Reclam, 1989), 271–302.

15. See e. g., "Khudozhniki u A. S. Bubnova. Vtoroi den' soveshchaniia," *Sovetskoe iskusstvo,* 9 March 1932.

16. Some of this novel appeared in Russian translation in 1933: Andre Mal'ro, "Usloviia chelovecheskogo sushchestvovaniia [otryvok iz romana]," trans. N. Gabinovskii, *Internatsional'naia literatura,* 1933, no. 4, 38–43.

17. "Teatr im. Meierkhol'da," *Sovetskii teatr,* 1935, no. 1; interview with Naum Kleiman, director of the Eisenstein Museum, July 1999.

18. Michael David-Fox, "The 'Heroic Life' of a Friend of Stalin's: Romain Rolland and Soviet Culture," *Slavica* 2, no. 1 (April 2005), 20; Ludmila Stern, *Western Intellectuals in the Soviet Union, 1920–1940: From Red Square to the Left Bank* (London: Routledge, 2007).

19. See e.g., Andre Zhid, "My idëm, ustremiv vzory na vas," his letter to MORP, 21 January 1933, *Literaturnaia gazeta,* 5 February 1933; Andrei Zhid, "Strannitsy iz dnevnika," *Literaturnaia gazeta,* 5 October 1932.

20. RGALI, 631/14/5/18.

21. Pascale Casanova, *The World Republic of Letters* (Cambridge, Mass.: Harvard University Press, 2000), 24.

22. See the introduction and article by Alan Wood in Pheng Cheah and Bruce Robbins, eds., *Cosmopolitics: Thinking and Feeling Beyond the Nation* (Minneapolis: University of Minnesota Press, 1998).

23. Also important was Pierre Bayle's *Nouvelles de la Republique des lettres* (1684–1687).

24. Robert Darnton, "A Euro State of Mind," *New York Review of Books,* 28 February 2002, 30.

25. Mikh. Kol'tsov, "Sovetskii patriotizm," *Pravda,* 5 August 1925.

26. "Doklad N. I. Bukharina o poezii, poetike i zadachakh poeticheskogo tvorchestva v SSSR," in *Pervyi vsesoiuznyi s"ezd sovetskikh pisateli. Stenograficheskii otchët* (Moscow: Ogiz, 1934), 493, 498.

27. Darnton, "Euro State of Mind," 30.

28. *The Journals of André Gide,* vol. 3, trans. Justin O'Brian (New York: Knopf, 1949), 180; Viacheslav Popov, ed., *Il'ia Erenburg. Dela i dni (v dokumentakh, pis'makh, vyskazyvaniiakh, i soobshcheniiakh pressy i svidetel'stvakh sovremennikov)* (Saint Petersburg: Biblioteka rossiiskoi Akademii nauk, 2001), 37; I. Erenburg, *Liudi, gody, zhizn'. Kniga tret'ia i chetvërtaia* (Moscow: Sovetskii pisatel', 1963), 462.

29. Erenburg, *Liudi, gody, zhizn',* 462.

30. Boris Bek, "Chërnye i belye. K priezdu negritianskikh grupp kinorabotnikov," *Sovetskoe iskusstvo,* 1932, no. 30 (3 July).

31. Boris Bek, "Iskusstvo negrov," *Sovetskoe iskusstvo,* 1932, no. 35 (3 August); Lengston Kh'iuz, "Moskva i ia," *Internatsional'naia literatura,* 1933, no. 5, 78–82. See also chapter 2 in Kate A. Baldwin, *Beyond the Color Line and the Iron Curtain: Reading Encounters between Black and Red, 1922–1963* (Durham, N.C.: Duke University Press, 2003).

32. *Iz istorii mezhdunarodnogo ob"edineniia revoliutsionnykh pisatelei (MORP).* Literaturnoe nasledstvo, no. 81 (Moscow: Nauka, 1962), 17.

33. RGASPI 495/30/988/17.

34. "Opustoshënnost' burzhuaznoi literatury. Beseda s I. Erenburgom," *Literaturnaia gazeta,* 29 August 1932.

35. RGASPI 541/1/6/17.

36. "MORP na novom etape," *Literaturnaia gazeta,* 23 August 1932; Bela Illesh, "Put' Mezhdunarodnogo ob"edineniia revoliutsionykh pisatelei," *Literaturnaia gazeta,* 29 December 1932. The resolution for a "perestroika" was passed by the Secretariat on July 15 (RGASPI 495/1/96/60).

37. RGASPI 495/1/96/62; RGASPI 495/1/96; RGASPI 495/1/96/60–95; "Perestroika mezhdunarodnogo literaturnogo fronta" and "novyi sostav sekretariata MORP," *Literaturnaia gazeta,* 5 August 1932.

38. RGASPI 495/1/96.

39. "MORP na novom etape."

40. "Dnevnik Sekretariata MORP," *Internatsional'naia literatura,* 1933, no. 1, 158.

41. "Rabota MORP," *Literatura mirovoi revoliutsii,* 1932, no. 9/10, 149–150.

42. Diane Koenker, "The Proletarian Tourist in the 1930s: Between Mass Excursion and Mass Escape," in Diane Koenker and Anne E. Gorsuch, eds., *Turizm: The Russian and East European Tourist under Capitalism and Socialism* (Ithaca: Cornell University Press, 2006).

43. I. R. Groza and P. S. Dubenskii, eds., *Slavnym zavoevateliam Arktiki* (Moscow : Ogiz-Sotsekgiz, 1934).

44. Paul Fussell, "Travel and the British Literary imagination of the Twenties and Thirties," in Michael Kowalewski, ed., *Temperamental Journeys: Essays on the modern literature of travel* (Athens: University of Georgia Press, c1992), 81.

45. Darnton, "Euro State of Mind," 30.

46. Angela Huss-Michel, *Die moskauer Zeitschriften "Internationale Literatur" und "Das Wort" wahrend der Exil-Volksfront (1936–1939). Eine vergleichende Analyse* (Frankfurt am Main: Peter Lang, 1987), 17.

47. Listed in "Knigi M. Kol'tsova," *Literaturnaia gazeta,* 11 July 1932.

48. For example, Koltsov in a feuilleton exposed the "counterrevolutionary group Riutin-Pavlov"; Mikh. Tseitlin, "S tochnym adresom. Novaia kniga fel'etonov M. Kol'tsova (Dusha bolit)," *Literaturnaia gazeta,* 17 October 1932.

49. See Katerina Clark, chapter 5 of *The Soviet Novel: History as Ritual,* 3rd ed. (Bloomington: Indiana University Press, 2001).

50. Mariia Osten, *Gubert v strane chudes. Dela i dni nemetskogo pionera,* predislovie Georgiia Dimitrova, avtorizovannyi perevod s nemetskogo I. Gorkinoi (Moscow: Ogonëk, 1935).

51. Joris Ivens with a Gustav Regler script, *Saarabstimmung und Sowjet Union* (1934), a lost film.

52. RGALI 2263/1/99/6.

53. "Maksim Gor'kii," *Literaturnaia gazeta,* 23 September 1932; "Stroim gigant—samolët 'Maksim Gor'kii," *Sovetskoe iskusstvo,* 21 September 1932; Evg. Kriger, "Eskadril'ia "bolshevitskikh tribun," *Izvestiia,* 8 May 1933.

54. Makrushenko, "V gosti na samolëte," *Pravda,* 18 March 1935; L. L. Kerber, *Stalin's Aviation Gulag: A Memoir of Andrei Tupolev and the Purge Era* (Washingto, D.C.: Smithsonian Institution Press, 1996), 99.

55. Scott W. Palmer, *Dictatorship of the Air: Aviation Culture and the Fate of Modern Russia* (New York: Cambridge University Press, 2006), 212.

56. "Samolët-agitator 'Maksim Gor'kii,'" *Literaturnaia gazeta*, 28 September 1932.

57. "Imia Gor'kogo. Eskadrilia samolëtov," *Sovetskoe iskusstvo*, 9 October 1932.

58. A. Kut, "Fil'ma—boevoi doklad. Kino poezd vyderzhal ekzamen," *Sovetskoe iskusstvo*, 27 July 1932. See also Emma Widdis, *Visions of a New Land: Soviet Film from the Revolution to the Second World War* (New Haven: Yale University Press, 2003), 43–45.

59. In Scott Palmer's interpretation, the flights were intended to expedite grain procurement at this time of famine in rural areas (*Dictatorship of the Air*, 216).

60. Kerber, *Stalin's Aviation Gulag*, 98, 104.

61. Palmer, *Dictatorship of the Air*, 219.

62 RGALI 2263/1/100/3–26; Koltsov's rationalization in terms of Nazi Germany, 18; Peter Fritsche, *A Nation of Flyers: German Aviation and the Popular Imagination* (Cambridge, Mass.: Harvard University Press, 1992), 186.

63. A special edition of Koltsov's journal, *Za rubezhom*, no. 15, 15 August 1934, contains materials on the *Brown Book;* Mikhail Kol'tsov, "Pomoshch' zhertvam germanskogo fashizma," *Pravda*, 3 November 1933; RGASPI 538/3/154; Kond., "Pokazaniia svidetelei na londonskom protsesse," *Pravda*, 17 September, 1934; David Pike, *German Writers in Soviet Exile* (Chapel Hill: University of North Carolina Press, 1982), 95–96.

64. Rudol'f Braun, "Rot Front, tovarishch Tel'man," *Pravda*, 3 March 1935.

65. "Erfolg des Dimitrov Films in New York," *Deutsche Zentral-Zeitung*, 3 October 1936.

66. See e.g., Maks Brod, "Stolitsa mirovoi kul'tury," *Sovetskoe iskusstvo*, 5 January 1935.

67. See e.g., G. Ryklin, "Zdrastvuite, tridtsat' piatyi," *Ogonëk* , 1935, no. 1.

68. Braun, "Rot Front, tovarishch Tel'man."

69. N. Bukharin, "Pochemu my pobedim?," *Izvestiia*, 1 May 1934; Karl Radek, "Kuda idët Germaniia," *Izvestiia*, 22 March 1933.

70. Darnton, "Euro State of Mind," 30.

71. RGASPI 538/3/163/139; Georgi Dimitroff, "Die revolutionäre Literatur im Kampfe gegen den Faschismus," *Internationale Literatur*, 1935, no. 5, 10–11.

72. Karl Radek, "Vysshe znamia sotsialisticheskoi kul'tury," *Izvestiia*, 13 May 1933.

73. David Caute, *The Fellow-Travellers: Intellectuals and Friends of Communism* (New Haven: Yale University Press), 53; "Antifa," *Internatsional'naia literatura*, 1933, no. 3, 141.

74. See e.g., Bernard von Brentano's collection of reportages *Der Beginn der Barbarei in Deutschland* (Berlin: Rohwolt, 1932), reviewed by Hans Günther: "Chto novogo v nemetskoi literature," *Literaturnaia gazeta*, 22 November 1932.

75. The title for the first edition (Amsterdam: Querido Verlag, 1933) was *Die Geschwister Oppenheim.*

76. Adapted for the screen by Wolff, Adolf Minkin, and Herbert Rappoport and directed by Minkin and Rappoport for Lenfilm.

77. "Vecher v gosudarstvennom politekhnicheskom muzee. Rech' Liona Feikhtvangera," *Pravda*, 9 January 1937.

78. Barck and Jarmatz, *Exil in der UdSSR*, vol. 1/1, 322. Editions of Feuchtwanger include a complete works *(Polnoe sobranie sochinenii)*, multiple, journal, and provincial editions of *Uspekh, Lzhe-Neron, Evgenii Ziuss,* and *Sem'ia Oppengeim; Sem'ia Oppengeim*

was adapted for the screen by Serafima Roshal' and directed by Grigorii Roshal', Mosfilm, January 1939.

79. Barck and Jarmatz, *Exil in der UdSSR,* vol. 1/1, 320, 322.

80. They also claimed to have more German books in their pavilion at the 1937 Paris Expo than did the Germans in theirs (Stormann, "Brief aus Paris," *Das Wort,* 1937, no. 9, 78); Barck and Jarmatz, *Exil in der UdSSR,* vol. 1/1 , 271–302.

81. Johannes R. Becher, "Im Zeichen des Menschen und der Menschheit," *Internationale Literatur,* 1935, no. 9, 29.

82. Alfred Kurella, "Sowjet-Humanismus," *Internationale Literatur,* 1934, no. 5.

83. For more on the topic of the Germanophone diaspora see Katerina Clark, "Germanophone Exiles in Stalin's Russia: Diaspora and Cultural Identity in the 1930s," *Kritika* 2, no. 3 (Summer 2001), 529–551.

84. Ernst Ottwalt, "Der Aufstand der Fischer," *Internationale Literatur,* 1934, no. 6, 151–156; "Portoviki kaspiiskogo basseina," *Vecherniaia Moskva,* 1935, July 9.

85. RGALI 631/14/5/5–7.

86. RGALI 631/14/5/30.

87. Terry Eagleton, *The Idea of Culture* (Oxford: Blaxwell, 2000), 59.

88. Greta N. Slobin, "The 'Homecoming' of the First Wave Diaspora," *Slavic Review* 60, no. 3 (Fall 2001), 515.

89. Ernst Toller, "Unser Kampf um Deutschland," *Das Wort,* 1937, no. 3, 52–53.

90. James Clifford, *Routes: Travel and Translation in the Late Twentieth Century* (Cambridge, Mass.: Harvard University Press, 1997), 251; see also R. Radhakrishnan, *Diasporic Mediations: Between Home and Location* (Minneapolis: University of Minnesota Press, 1996), xxvii.

91. RGALI 631/15/14/38–41; RGALI 631/15/271/45–75.

92. RGALI 631/14/5/30.

93. RGALI 631/15/14/41.

94. Bertolt-Brecht-Archiv, Berlin, Box 477, 101, 111, 112;, RGALI 631/14/47/26.

95. RGASPI 538/3/143/31–33;, GARF, 5283/6/82/53-85.

96. Darnton, "Euro State of Mind," 31.

97. RGASPI 495/1/96.

98. It was published in *Internatsional'naia literature,* nos. 1–3, 9–12, 1935, and 1–4, 1936, and small sections of a translation by Valentin Stenich appeared in other journals in 1934 and 1935. See Ekaterina Genieva, ed., *"Russkaia Odisseia" Dzheimsa Dzhoisa* (Moscow: Rudomino, 2005), 140.

99. In *Pervyi vsesoiuznyi s"ezd sovetskikh pisatelei,* 315–318.

100. Lui Ferdinand Selin, *Puteshestvie na krai nochi,* trans. El'za Triole (Moscow: Goslitizdat, 1934), print run fifteen thousand.

101. RGALI 631/14/5/26.

102. Vsevolod Vishnevskii, " in Genieva, *"Russkaia Odisseia" Dzheimsa Dzhoisa,* 87–88.

103. Vsevolod Vishnevskii, "V Evrope. Iz putevogo dnevnika," *Znamia,* 1936, no. 10, 239.

104. Fridrikh Vol'f, "Do kontsa razoblachit' vraga," *Sovetskoe iskusstvo,* 5 February 1937.

105. Darnton, "Euro State of Mind," 31.

106. RGALI 631/14/1313/74; RGALI 631/15/14/41.

107. Interview with Iuliia Markovna Zhivova, 19 July 2001. In addition, at a combined meeting of 9 August 1938 of the Board of the Writers Union and members of the Union's German Section, the Germanophones who spoke required a translator, but apparently not Lukács (RGALI 631/15/271/45–57).

108. "Doklad A. M. Gor'kogo o sovetskoi literature," in *Pervyi vsesoiuznyi s"ezd sovetskikh pisatelei*, 6.

109. A revised version appeared as G. Lukach, "Roman kak burzhuaznaia epopeia," *Literaturnaia entsiklopediia*, vol. 9 (Moscow: 1935), 795–832.

110. RGALI 631/12/50/15.

111. "Problemy teorii romana. Doklad G. Lukacha v sektsii literatury Instituta Filosofii Kommunisticheskoi Akademii (avtoreferat)," and "Institut filosofii Komakademii. Pravlennaia stenogramma diskussii po dokladu G. Lukacha 'Problemy teorii romana,'" *Literaturnyi kritik*, 1935, no. 2, 214–249, no. 3, 231–254. This version omits some material including in particular the contributions of Shklovskii and Igor Sats. A fuller version of these texts appeared in German in *Disput über den Roman: Beiträge aus der SU 1917 bis 1941*, ed. M. Wegner et al. (Berlin, 1988). For a more extended coverage of the debate see chapter 6 of Galin Tikhanov, *The Master and the Slave: Lukacs, Bakhtin and the Ideas of Their Time* (Oxford: Clarendon Press, 2000).

112. "Problemy teorii romana. Doklad G. Lukacha . . . ," *Literaturnyi kritik*, 1935, no. 2, 214–215.

113. Ibid., 217–219, 216.

114. Ibid., 217–219, 216, 219, 217, 219, 210, 219, 220, respectively.

115. Mikhail Lifshits in ibid., 240.

116. Tov. Aristova in ibid., 232; Lifshits calls the classical epic "folklore."

117. "Problemy teorii romana," no. 2, 215.

118. Tov. Mirskii in "Preniia po dokladu," *Literaturnyi kritik*, 1935, no. 2, 222.

119. V. F. Pereverzev in ibid., 230.

120. Kemenov in "Problema teorii romana (Okonchanie diskussii)," 241, 242, Lifshits, 248.

121. Usievich in "Problema teorii romana (Okonchanie diskussii)," 239; Hegel in *Literaturnyi kritik*, nos. 10, 11, 1934, 1, 2, 6, 8 for 1935, nos. 3, 5, 7 for 1936, 4, 5 for 1937, and 1, 7, 8 for 1938.

122. Lifshits in "Problema teorii romana (Okonchanie diskussii)," 246.

123. A. N. Dmitriev, *Marksizm bez proletariata: Georgii Lukach i raniaia Frankfurtskaia shkola 1920–1930-e gg.* (Saint Petersburg–Moscow: Letnii sad, 2004), 105, 147.

124. Lukach in "Problemy teorii romana," no 2. 216.

125. Ibid., 218.

126. Karl Marx and Friedrich Engels, *On Literature and Art* (Moscow: Progress, 1978), 91.

127. Tov. Focht in "Problema teorii romana (Okonchanie diskussii)," 235.

128. Usievich in ibid., 237.

129. Pereverzev in ibid., 236–37.

130. F. Shiller, *Istoriia zapadno-evropeiskoi literatury novogo vremeni*, vol. 1, *XVII–XIX 30–40 gg.* (Moscow: Goslitizdat, 1935);vol. 2, *Rukovodstvo po istorii realizma* (Moscow: Goslitizdat, 1936); vol. 3 (Moscow: Goslitizdat, 1937).

5. "WORLD LITERATURE"/"WORLD CULTURE"

1. RGALI 631/13/65/21; Frezinskii, *Pisateli i sovetskie vozhdi. Izbrannye siuzhety 1919–1960 godov* (Moscow: Ellis Lak, 2008), 389. Note also Koltsov's *Den' mira,* for which writers from all over the world contributed pieces on the one day, 27 September 1935 (RGALI 631/15/4/30).

2. The first version was written in September to October 1935, the second in December 1935 to February 1936, and the third in 1939.

3. Walter Benjamin, "Paris, Capital of the Nineteenth Century," in *Selected Writings,* vol. 3, trans. Edmund Jephcott, Howard Eiland, et al., ed. Howard Eiland and Michael W. Jennings (Cambridge, Mass.: Harvard University Press, 2002), 39–40.

4. Walter Benjamin, "The Work of Art in the Age of Its Reproducibility," in *Selected Writings,* 3:103.

5. Ibid., 106.

6. Julian Jackson, *The Popular Front in France: Defending Democracy, 1934–38* (Cambridge: Cambridge University Press, 1988), 23–36.

7. Benjamin, "The Work of Art," 39.

8. *Dimitrov and Stalin: Letters from the Soviet Archives,* ed. Alexander Dallin and F. I. Firsov (New Haven: Yale University Press, 2000), 11–13; Georgi Dimitrov, "The Fascist Offensive and the Tasks of the Communist International in the Struggle of the Working Class against Fascism. Report before the Seventh World Congress of the Communist International, delivered on August 2, 1935," in Dimitrov, *Selected Works,* vol. 1 (Sofia: Foreign Language Press, 1967), 561–639, 582.

9. Simone Barck and Klavis Jarmatz, eds., *Exil in der UdSSR. Kunst und Literatur im antifschistischen Exil 1933–1945,* vol. 1/1 (Leipzig: Reclam, 1989), 126.

10. See the correspondence in RGALI 1204/2/1701.

11. G. Lukacs, "Erzählen oder Beschreiben?" *Internationale Literatur,* 1936, no.11, 100–118, no. 12, 108–123; G. Lukach, "Rasskaz ili opisanie," *Literaturnyi kritik,* 1936, no. 8, 44–67.

12. M. Vertsman, "Gegel' ob arkhitekture," *Arkhitektura SSSR,* 1936, no. 6, 65–70.

13. I. Stalin, S. Kirov, and A. Zhdanov, "Zamechanie o konspekte uchebnika 'Novoi istorii,'" 9 August 1934; I. Stalin, A. Zhdanov, and S. Kirov, "Zamechanie po povodu konspekta uchebnika po 'Istorii SSSR,'" 8 August 1934.

14. Mikhail Kol'tsov, "Otchët sovetskoi delegatsii na kongresse zashchity kul'tury v Parizhe. Rasshirënnoe zasedanie pravleniia SP SSSR ot 21 iunia 1935 g.," RGALI 631/15/47/24: RGALI 1204/2/668.

15. Deni Didro, *Sobranie sochinenii v 10-ti tomov,* 1935–1947 (Moscow-Leningrad: Academia/Goslitizdat), ed. I. K. Luppol; Deni Didro, *Plemiannik Ramo,* trans. M. V. Lind (Moscow: Goslitizdat, 1936); Deni Didro, *Mysli ob iskusstve,* vols. 1 and 2 (Moscow-Leningrad: Iskusstvo, 1936); I. K. Luppol, *Deni Didro. Zhizn' i tvorchestvo* (Moscow-Leningrad: Sotsekgiz,1934); D. I. Gachev, *Esteticheskie vzgliady Didro* (Moscow: Goslitizdat, 1936).

16. Ursula El-Akramy, *Transit Moskau. Margarete Steffin und Maria Osten* (Hamburg: Europäische Verlagsanstalt, 1998), 170.

17. RGALI 631/14/5/12; Erenburg to Koltsov, 5 April 1936, RGALI 1204/e/kh. 668, l. 12; June 26, 1936, l. 25; Viacheslav Popov, ed., *Il'ia Erenburg. Dela i dni (v dokumentakh, pis'makh, vyskazyvaniiakh, i soobshcheniiakh pressy i svidetel'stvakh sovremennikov)* (Saint Petersburg: Biblioteka rossiiskoi Akademii nauk, 2001), 29, 51–52; Boris Frezinskii, *Pisateli i sovetskie vozhdi,* 408–409, 411, 413, 417–18.

18. The Schutzverband deutscher Schriftsteller put together a book on the influence of the French Revolution on German intellectual life (RGALI 631/13/64).

19. Robert Darnton, "A Euro State of Mind," *New York Review of Books,* 28 February 2002, 30.

20. Jackson, *Popular Front in France,* 41.

21. See e.g., "Polkovodtsy Krasnoi armii," *Pravda,* 21 November 1935; "Instsenirovka perekopskogo boia," *Pravda,* 25 November 1935.

22. The biographical series, *Istoriia grazhdanskoi voiny* eclipsed *Istoriia zavodov* in prominence.

23. Mikhail Kol'tsov, ed., *15 let Pervoi konnoi armii* (Moscow: Zhurgaz, 1935).

24. L. Anninskii, introduction to Nikolai Ostrovskii, *Sobranie sochinenii v trëkh tomakh,* vol. 1 (Moscow: Molodaia gvardiia, 1989), 12.

25. S. Tregub, *Nikolai Aleksandrovich Ostrovskii (1904–1936), Zhizn' zamechatel'nykh liudei* (Moscow: Molodaia gvardiia, 1950), 300, 302; S. Tregub, *Zhivoi Korchagin* (Moscow: Sovetskaia Rossiia, 1973), 7.

26. L. Kait, "Publichnoe sozhzhenie knig. Germanskoe srednevekov'e," *Izvestiia,* 12 May 1933.

27. Marc Fumaroli, "La Coupole," in Pierre Nora, ed., *Realms of Memory,* trans. Arthur Goldhammer (New York: Columbia University Press, 1996–1998), vol. 2, *Traditions,* 300–304.

28. Jackson, *Popular Front in France,* 54–57, 65, 140, and the illustrations between 176 and 177.

29. Boris Frezinskii, "Velikaia illiuziia—Parizh, 1935 (Materialy k istorii Mezhdunarodnogo kongressa pisatelei v zashchitu kul'tury)," in *Minuvshee,* Istoricheskii al'manakh, no. 24 (Petersburg: Atheneum-Feniks, 1998), 166–239.

30. Much of my information on the Congress comes from Frezinskii, *Pisateli i sovetskie vozhdi,* 273–289.

31. RGASPI 495/30/1076/12, 15; RGALI 1204/2/1701/6; RGALI 631/15/14/62.

32. RGASPI 495/30/1076/74–75; When Malraux visited Moscow in March 1936, Koltsov was still insisting, at a Writers Union meeting, that the anti-Fascist Association was not founded to further the Soviet cause (RGALI 631/15/15/3).

33. RGASPI, 495/30/1076/77.

34. For the twenty brief passages where Goethe deals with this concept see the appendix to Fritz Strich, *Goethe and World Literature* (London: Routledge and Kegan Paul, 1945), 349–351.

35. RGASPI 17/163/1080/122.

36. RGASPI 88/1/606/3–7, 12, 13; Frezinskii, *Pisateli i sovetskie vozhdi,* 375.

37. RGALI 631/12/138(1).

38. RGALI 631/12/142; RGALI, 631/12/143/341; Barck and Jarmatz, *Exil in der UdSSR,* vol. 1/1, 221.

39. RGALI 631/12/142/109, 117, 172, 315; RGALI 631/13/65/7.

40. RGALI 631/12/143/321, 323, 336, 341.

41. RGALI 631/13/65/7.

42. Andrea Huss-Michel, *Die Moskauer Zeitschriften "Internationale Literatur" und "Das Wort" während der Exil—Volksfront (1936–1939)* (Frankfurt am Main: Peter Lang, 1987).

43. RGALI 631/12/142/389-402; RGALI 631/12/143/305; RGASPI 495/30/988/16.

44. RGALI, 631/13/13/140; RGALI 631/12/141/80, 81; OR IMLI 324/1/4.

45. Walter Benjamin, "Pariser Brief. Andre Gide und sein neuer Gegner," *Das Wort,* 1936, no. 5, 86–95.

46. RGALI 631/12/141/71, 73, 74, 75, 83, 104, 10 ; RGALI 631/12/146/346; RGALI 631/13/64/103, 107, 114.

47. RGALI 631/13/64/102, 107, 108, 112, 114.

48. B. Poole, "Bakhtin and Cassirer: The Philosophical Origin of Bakhtin's Carnival Messianism," *South Atlantic Quarterly* 97, no. 3-4 (1998), 537-578.

49. The term "carnival" is actually sparingly present in the early chapters of the dissertation, but its use increases from chapter to chapter until it becomes the dominant term for his analysis in chapter 4. Before then, especially in chapter 1, his main term is "Gothic realism." The final draft of the dissertation was probably begun no earlier than November 1938, but some work on Rabelais may have been begun earlier in the decade. One might therefore speculate that Bakhtin adopted the term "carnival" only at some point after it became central to Soviet official cultural practice in 1935, but this could only be speculation; "Istoriia 'Rable': 1930-1950-gody," in M. M. Bakhtin, *Sobranie sochinenii,* vol. 4 (1), ed. I. L. Popova (Moscow: Iazyki slavianskikh kul'tur, 2008), 841, 846, 858).

50. Dudley Andrew and Steven Ungar, *Popular Front Paris and the Poetics of Culture* (Cambridge, Mass.: Harvard University Press, 2005), 143; Jackson, *Popular Front in France,* 39–41.

51. Katerina Clark, *Petersburg: Crucible of Cultural Revolution* (Cambridge, Mass.: Harvard University Press, 1995), 117, 329 n. 70.

52. Denis Hollier, ed., *Le Collège de Sociologie, 1937–1939* (Paris: Gallimard, 1995), 645–690.

53. M. M. Bakhtin, "Fransua Rable v istorii realizma (1940 g.)," in *Sobranie sochinenii,* vol. 4 (1), 257; OR IMLI, 427/1/19/366-367.

54. Bakhtin, "Fransua Rable v istorii realizma," 211; OR IMLI, 427/1/19/270.

55. Bakhtin, "Fransua Rable v istorii realizma,"191, 210; OR IMLI, 427/1/19/239, 268.

56. Bakhtin, "Fransua Rable v istorii realizma," 262, see also 241; OR IMLI, 427/1/19/343b, 314.

57. Bakhtin, "Fransua Rable v istorii realizma," 479; OR IMLI, 427/1/19/629.

58. Bakhtin, "Fransua Rable v istorii realizma," 242; OR IMLI, 427/1/19/267.

59. See e.g., "Bol'she shekspirovat'!," *Literaturnaia gazeta* 23 April 1933.

60. "Kakoi Shekspir nam nuzhen," (editorial), *Sovetskoe iskusstvo,* 1933, no. 46 (8 October), 1.

61. I. A. Aksënov, "Shekspir podlinnyi i Shekspir dosochinënnyi," *Literaturnaia gazeta,* 29 June 1933.

62. Boris Pasternak did not begin his translation of *Hamlet,* the first of a series of his translations, until the beginning of 1939, but he also believed in a vernacular rendition of Shakespeare. His resistance to a literal translation and use of contemporary, colloquial Russian in the name of conveying the "vital power" of the original was widely criticized; Anna K. France, *Boris Pasternak's Translations of Shakespeare* (Berkeley: University of California Press, 1978), 8–9.

63. "Shekspirovskaia konferentsiia," *Pravda,* 29 November 1935.

64. O. Litovskii, "Zhivoi Shekspir," *Sovetskii teatr,* 1935, no. 4, 7; see also "Kakoi Shekspir nam nuzhen," (editorial), and Prof. A. A. Smirnov, "Bor'ba za Shekspira," in *Sovetskoe iskusstvo,* 1933, no. 46 (8 October).

65. A. A. Smirnov, "Na putiakh izucheniia Mol'era (O rabotakh S. S. Mokul'skogo)," in V. Zhirmunskii, ed., *Zapadnyi sbornik,* vol. 1 (Moscow-Leningrad: Akademiia nauk, 1937), 149, 153, 152.

66. Bakhtin clearly read *Zapadnyi sbornik;* he polemicizes in his dissertation against N. Berkovskii's account there, inter alia, of Rabelais and Renaissance literature; N. Berkovskii, "Realizm burzhuaznogo obshchestva i voprosy istorii literatury," in Zhirmunskii, ed., *Zapadnyi sbornik,* 53–86; Bakhtin, "Fransua Rable v istorii realizma,"19–25.

67. Andrew and Ungar, *Popular Front Paris,* 155.

68. Katerina Clark, "Grigory Aleksandrov's 'Volga-Volga,'" in Igal Halfin, ed., *Language and Revolution: The Making of Modern Political Identity* (London: Frank Cass, 2002), 215–234.

69. "Rabota Anglo-Amerikanskoi kommissii MORP," *Literatura mirovoi revoliutsii,* 1932, no. 9/10, 150–151; "V Dzhon-rid klubakh," *Literaturnaia gazeta,* 1 November 1932; Michael Denning, *Cultural Front: The Laboring of American Culture in the Twentieth Century* (London: Verso, 1998).

70. See e.g., Sender Gardin, "Epton Sinkler—reaktsionnyi utopist," and David Al'fer Sikveros, "Kontrrevoliutsionnyi put' Rivery" (both reprinted from *New Masses*), *Internatsional'naia literatura,* 1934, no. 5, 132–135, 142–146.

71. Presumably the reference is to Copeland's "Into the Streets for the First of May" (1934); "Khronika iskusstv," *Sovetskoe iskusstvo,* 1935, no. 32 (11 July); Gans Eisler, "Unichtozhenie iskusstva," *Sovetskoe iskusstvo,* 1935, no. 35 (29 July); "Gans Eisler v Moskve," *Sovetskoe iskusstvo,* 1935, no. 30 (29 June).

72. [Unsigned], "Novosti teatra i kino," *Pravda,* 27 January 1936; RGASPI 493/30/988/14.

73. "Liga amerikanskikh pisatelei," *Literaturnaia gazeta,* 15 October 1935.

74. "Khronika. Podgotovka k s"ezdu amerikanskikh pisatelei," *Internatsional'naia literatura,* 1935, no. 2, 155; Alan M. Wald, Exiles from a Future Time: The Forging of the Mid Twentieth Century Literary Left (Chapel Hill: University of North Carolina Press, 2002), 78; D. Aaron, *Writers on the Left: Episodes in American Literary Communism* (New York: Harcourt, Brace and World, 1961), 283.

75. GARF 5283/1/298/39; see also Edmund Vil'son, "Pis'mo sovetskim chitateliam o Khemingue," *Internatsional'naia literatura,* 1936, no. 2, 151–153.

76. "Vystuplenie Stefana Spendera protiv T. S. Eliota," *Internatsional'naia literatura,* 1934, no. 1, 128; "Revoliutsionnoe kul'turnoe dvizhenie rastët," *Internatsional'naia*

literatura, 1934, no. 5, 147–148; "Klub levoi knigi," *Internatsional'naia literatura,* 1936, no. 6, 178.

77. A. Kr-v, "Vsesoiuznoe tematicheskoe kinosoveshchanie," *Sovetskoe iskusstvo,* 1935, no. 58 (17 December); GARF 5283/1/371/6.

78. "Amerikanskie fotografii," *Ogonëk,* 1936, nos. 11–17, 19–23; "Doroga v N'iu Iork," *Pravda,* 24 November 1935; "Amerikanskaia vstrecha," *Pravda,* 5 January 1935.

79. Erika Wolf, ed., *Ilf and Petrov's American Road Trip,* trans. Anne O. Fisher (New York: Architectural Press, 2007), 89–92, quotation 136.

80. Ibid., 27.

81. "Sovetskie fil'my v N'iu-Iorke," *Pravda,* 2 March 1935.

82. A. Erlikh, "Disnei na ekranakh soiuza," *Pravda,* 29 November 1935.

83. One of the achievements was the animated film *Novyi Gulliver,* also shown at the festival; B. Shumiatskii, "Otvechaem delom. O kartinakh 'Lëtchiki' i 'Novyi Gulliver,'" *Pravda,* 23 March 1935.

84. GARF 5283/8/242.

85. O. Litovskii, "Korol' Lir," *Pravda,* 27 February 1935; Benjamin Harshav, *The Moscow Yiddish Theater: Art on Stage in a Time of Revolution* (New Haven: Yale University Press, 2008), 90.

86. "Gordon Kreg edet v Moskvu," *Sovetskoe iskusstvo,* 17 March 1935; Gordon Kreg v Moskve," *Literaturnaia gazeta,* 29 March 1935. He arrived 27 March 1935.

87. S. Mikhoels, "Moia rabota nad 'Korolëm Lirom,'" in *Mikhoels: Stat'i, besedy, rechi* (Moscow: Iskusstvo, 1964), 94–123.

88. George Steiner, *After Babel: Aspects of Language and Translation* (Oxford: Oxford University Press, 1998), 24.

89. Wolf, *Ilf and Petrov's American Road Trip,* 65, 115–127.

90. "Sovetskie fil'my v N'iu-Iorke," *Pravda,* 2 March 1935. *Three Songs of Lenin* was re-edited in 1938 and 1970. John Mackay, "Allegory and Accommodation: Vertov's *Three Songs of Lenin* (1934) as a Stalinist Film," *Film History* 18 (2006), 383. My information here comes from this article and from John Mackay, personal communication, 12 August 2008.

91. "'I Am at Home' Says Robeson at Reception in S.U.," *Daily Worker,* 15 January 1935.

92. Negotiations with Eisenstein about a variety of roles for Robeson continued during his later visit of May 1937 GARF 5283/1371/70.

93. Interview with Naum Kleiman, 10 July 2008.

94. GARF 5283/4/211/1–24. The transcript of this encounter was published in *Iskusstvo kino* in 1992; "Zhivye impul'sy iskusstva," no. 1, 132–139. The Swedish scholar Lars Kleberg, who published the transcript, had earlier (in 1986) written a theatricalized projection of this encounter, *Ucheniki charodeia,* as part of his trilogy of plays about Soviet intellectual life, "Zvezdopad" (Swedish: *Staernjall*).

95. Min Tian, "'Alienation-Effect' for Whom? Brecht's (Mis)interpretation of the Classical Chinese Theatre," *Asian Theatre Journal* 14, no. 2 (Autumn 1997), 201–202.

96. GARF 5283/8/267/115. The visit is covered on 1, 3, 5, 103, 108–110, 113–117, 124, 127, 145, 149, 152, 156, 161–162, 165–166, 169, 179. Also GARF 5283/1/298/22.

97. GARF 5283/8/267/124, 149.

98. Karl Radek, "Staryi Kitai govorit o novom," *Izvestiia*, 23 March 1935; D. Cherniavskii, "Mei Lan'-Fan," *Literaturnaia gazeta*, 24 March 1935; B. Vasil'ev, "Mei Lan'-Fan i kitaiskii teatr," *Izvestiia*, 12 March 1935; N. Volkov, "Spektakli Mei Lan'-Fana," 29 March 1935.

99. S. Tret'iakov, "Polmilliarda zritelei. K gastroliam Mei Lan'-Fana v SSSR," *Literaturnaia gazeta*, 15 March 1935; S. Eizenshtein, "Charodei grushevogo sada," in *Mei Lan'-Fan i kitaiskii teatr. K gastroliam v SSSR* (Moscow-Leningrad: VOKS, 1935), 17–26.

100. Sergei Eisenstein, "To the Magician of the Pear Orchard," in Eisenstein, *Selected Works*, vol. 3 (1934–1947), ed. Richard Taylor, trans. William Powell (London: British Film Institute, 1996), 59.

101. S. Tret'iakov, "Aziatskii teatr. (Ot nashego spetsial'nogo pekinskogo korrespondenta)," *Prozhektor*, 1924, no. 21, 30.

102. S. Tret'iakov, "Mei Lan'-Fan—nash gost'," *Pravda*, 12 March 1935.

103. Bertolt Brecht, "Alienation Effects in Chinese Acting," in *Brecht on Theatre*, trans. and ed. John Willett (New York: Hill and Wang, 1992), 94.

104. "Privet sobrat'iam. Beseda s doktorom Mei Lan'-Fanom," *Sovetskoe iskusstvo*, 17 March 1935.

105. Haun Saussy, *Great Walls of Discourse and Other Adventures in Cultural China* (Cambridge, Mass.: Harvard University Press, 2001), 167.

106. S. Tret'iakov, "Velikoe masterstvo," *Pravda*, 23 March 1935. A similar argument is made in S. Tret'iakov, "Polmilliarda zritelei. K gastroliam Mei Lan'-Fana v SSSR," *Literaturnaia gazeta*, 15 March 1935.

107. Brecht, "Alienation Effects," 93.

108. Gordon Craig, *The Theatre Advancing* (Boston: Little, Brown, 1919), 105; Sang-Kyong Lee, "Edward Gordon Craig and Japanese Theatre," *Asian Theatre Journal* 17, no. 2 (Autumn 2000), 221.

109. GARF 5283/8/267/5; Sergei Kapterev, communication of 2 June, 2011..

110. "Porazhaet rost kul'tury. Beseda s doktorom Mei Lan'-Fanom," *Vecherniaia Moskva*, 13 April 1935; GARF 5283/8/267/1. Min Tian tries to refute the notion that Mei's acting has to do with the alienation-effect by citing from writings by Mei of 1981 and 1990, but one should be cautious about retrojecting attitudes: Min Tian, " 'Alienation-Effect' for Whom," 212, 214.

111. Eisenstein, "To the Magician," 66; Brecht, "Alienation Effects," 95.

112. Brecht, "Alienation Effects," 91, 92, 94, 93, 93.

113. Min Tian, " 'Alienation-Effect' for Whom," 204–214.

114. Brecht, "Alienation Effects," 93; Eisenstein, "To the Magician," 66.

115. Brecht, "Alienation Effects," 92. Both "making strange" *(ostranenie)* and "automatization" feature in Shklovsky's essay "Iskusstvo kak priëm" [Art as technique] (1915–1916), first published in *Sborniki po teorii literaturnogo iazyka, vol. I (Petrograd: Tip. Sokolinskogo, 1917), 3-14,* the de facto manifesto of early Formalism. It is generally assumed that Brecht became apprised of the Formalist concept of *ostranenie* during this Moscow visit of 1935, but he may have learned of it from another Formalist, Osip Brik, when he lectured in Berlin in 1930 or through his long association with Tretiakov, dating from the same year.

116. Sergei Eisenstein, "The Dramaturgy of Film Form (The Dialectical Approach to Film Form)" (originally written in 1929 in German), in *The Eisenstein Reader,* ed. Richard Taylor, trans. Richard Taylor and William Powell (London: BFI, 1998), 94.

117. Lee, "Edward Gordon Craig and Japanese Theatre," 216.

118. Sergei Eizenshtein, "Za kadrom," in N. Kaufman, ed., *Iaponskoe kino* (Moscow: Teakinopechat', 1929), 72–92.

119. For example, in Eisenstein's major theoretical text of the late 1930s–1940s, *Nonindifferent Nature* (trans Herbert Marshall [Cambridge: Cambridge University Press, 1987]) especially in chapter 3, which he wrote after 1945, "The Music of Landscape and the Fate of Montage Counterpoint at a New Stage."

120. See e.g., Ernest Fenollosa (with Ezra Pound), "The Chinese Written Character as a Medium for Poetry," in Fenollosa, *Investigations of Ezra Pound* (Freeport, N.Y.: Books for Libraries Press, 1920), 386.

121. Marcel Granet, *La Pensée chinoise* (Paris: La Renaissance du livre, 1934), 46.

122. Brecht, "Alienation Effects," 97.

123. Eisenstein, "To the Magician," 66.

124. Ibid., 61.

125. Walter Benjamin, "Problems in the Sociology of Language," in Benjamin, *Selected Writings,* vol. 1 (Cambridge, Mass.: Harvard University Press, 2002), 74.

126. Ibid., 75.

127. N. Ia. Marr, "K proiskhozhdeniiu iazykov," *Krasnaia gazeta,* no. 247 (2 October 1925); N. Ia. Marr, *Iafeticheskaia teoriia: Programma obshchego kursa o iazyke* (Baku, 1927), 64.

128. N. Ia. Marr, "Pochemu tak trudno stat' lingvistom teoretikom," in Marr, ed., *Iazykovedenie i materializm* (Leningrad: ILIaZV RANION, 1929), 33. For a fuller account of Marr's theories see Clark, *Petersburg,* 212–223. Marr assigns language a place in the superstructure rather than the base (a position that later got him a bad name and even incurred a rebuttal by Stalin).

129. Marr, "Pochemu tak trudno stat' lingvistom teoretikom," 33; N. Ia. Marr, "O Iafeticheskoi teorii," *Iafeticheskaia teoriia,* 4.

130. Benjamin, "Problems in the Sociology of Language," 85.

131. Elena Luriia, *Moi otets A. R. Luriia* (Moscow: Gnosis, 1994), 124.

132. Lev Vygotsky, *Thought and Language,* trans. and newly rev. and ed. Alex Kozulin (Cambridge, Mass.: MIT Press, 1986), originally published as *Myshlenie i rech'* (1934), 236, 244–248; L. S. Vygotskii and A. R. Luriia, *Etiudy po istorii povedeniia. Ob"eziana. Primitiv. Rebënok* (Moscow-Leningrad: Gos. Izd., 1930), 63, 192–194.

133. Granet, *La Pensée chinoise,* 33, 54, 82, 82.

134. Eisenstein, "To the Magician," 65.

135. Ibid., 64, 66.

136. Ibid., 61, 62.

137. Sergei Eisenstein, *Immoral Memories: An Autobiography,* trans. Herbert Marshall (Boston: Houghton Mifflin, 1983), 209–211; "Eizenshtein v arkhive A. R. Lurii," *Kinovedcheskie zapiski,* no. 8 (1990), 79–81.

138. "Riadom s Eizenshteinom . . . Bela Balash vo VGIKe. Zasedanie kafedry rezhissëry," *Kinovedcheskie zapiski,* no. 25 (1995), 236, 237.

139. S. M. Eizenshtein, "Gogol' i kinoiazyk," *Kinovedcheskie zapiski,* no. 4 (1989), 94.

140. M. M. Vladimirova, *Vsemirnaia literatura i rezhissërskie uroki S. M. Eizenshteina* (Moscow: Moskovskii gosudarstvennyi institut kul'tury, 1990), 25–34.

141. Eisenstein, "To the Magician," 61, 62.

142. "Vystuplenia i zakliuchitel'noe slovo na Vsesoiuznom tvorcheskom soveshchanii rabotnikov sovetskoi kinematografii" (1935), in Sergei Eizenshtein, *Izbrannye proizvedeniia v shesti tomakh,* vol. 2 (Moscow: Nauka, 1963), 113, 116, 119, 120–121; Eisenstein, *Selected Works,* 3:32, 36–37, 38.

143. N. Volkov, "Spektakli Mei Lan' Fana," 29 March 1935. Roland Barthes makes a similar point in *Empire of the Signs,* trans. Richard Howard (New York: Hill and Wang, 1982], 54.

144. Eisenstein, "To the Magician," 66.

145. David Bordwell, "Eisenstein's Epistemological Shift," *Screen* 15, no. 4 (Winter 1974–1975), 29–46.

146. Eisenstein, "To the Magician," 64.

147. See also Jacques Derrida's discussion in Derrida, *The Pit and the Pyramid: Introduction to Hegel's Semiology,* in *Margins of Philosophy,* trans. Alan Bass (Chicago: University of Chicago Press, 1982), 77.

148. Eisenstein, "To the Magician," 68, 58.

149. A. Angarov, "O rabote teatra nad obrazom," *Sovetskii teatr,* 1936, no. 4–5, 5.

6. FACE AND MASK

1. Ludmila Shtern, *Western Intellectuals and the Soviet Union, 1920–1946: From Red Square to the Left Bank* (New York: Routledge, 2007), 104, 155–156.

2. Reinhard Mueller, ed., *Die Säuberung: Moskau 1936: Stenogramm eines geschlossenen Parteiversammlung. Georg Lukacs, Johannes Becher, Friedrich Wolf* (Reinbeck bei Hamburg: Rowohlt, 1991); RGASPI, 495/30/1120, and 1121.

3. [Unsigned], "Sumbur vmesto muzyki," *Pravda,* 28 January 1936, 3.

4. The debate began with responses to two essays published in the September 1937 number of *Das Wort* by Klaus Mann and Alfred Kurella, under the pseudonym Bernhard Ziegler, "Nun ist dies Erbe zuende"; Georg Lukacs, "Grösse und Verfall des Expressionismus," *Internationale Literatur,* 1934, no. 1, 153–173.

5. See *Die Expressionismus Debatte. Materialen zu einer marksistisch Realismuskonzeption* (Frankfurt am Main: H. J. Schmitt, 1973).

6. RGALI, 631/12/141-142. See also 143, 144, 173.

7. Ernst Bloch und Hanns Eisler, "Avantgarde-Kunst und Volksfront," *Die neue Weltbühne,* 1937, no. 50 (9 December), 1568–1573, esp. 1568; Hans Günther, "Antwort an Ernst Bloch," *Internationale Literatur,* 1936, no. 8, 112–134. Other contributions to the debate include Ernst Bloch, "Diskussionen über Expressionismus," *Das Wort,* 1938, no. 6, 103–112; Georg Lukács, "Es geht um Realismus," *Das Wort,* 1938, no. 6, 112–138, published as "Spor idët o realizme," *Internatsional'naia literatura,* 1938, no.

12; Ernst Bloch and Hanns Eisler, "Die Kunst zu erben," *Die neue Weltbühne*, 6, January 1938, 13–18.

8. For the correspondence see RGALI 631/13/64/46, 52, 57, 64, 72, 88, 91, 105. See also RGALI 631/12/142/389, 402; RGALI 631/12/143/305; RGALI 631/13/88/9, 13; RGASPI 495/30/988/16.

9. "Bor'ba za masterstvo," (editorial), *Arkhitektura SSSR*, 1936, no. 5, 2; Karl Schlögel, *Terror und Traum. Moskau 1937* (Munich: Hanser Verlag, 2008), 305–306, 313.

10. See e.g., "Rech' tovarishcha Stalina na pervom vsesoiuznom soveshchanii stakhanovtsev," *Literaturnaia gazeta*, 24 November 1935, 1; Katerina Clark, *The Soviet Novel: History as Ritual*, 3rd ed. (Bloomington: Indiana University Press, 2001), chapter 5.

11. Katerina Clark, "Utopian Anthropology as a Context for Socialist Realism," in Robert Tucker, ed., *Stalinism: Essays in Historical Interpretation* (New York: Norton, 1977), 180–198.

12. Stalin's speeches were published in *Pravda* slightly later, on 29 March and 1 April 1937.

13. Exposition Internationale des Arts et Techniques Appliqués à la Vie Moderne.

14. D. A[rkin], "Sovetskii pavil'on," *Arkhitektura SSSR*, 1937, no. 9, 6, 8.

15. A similar iconography was used in the finales of two Soviet films of 1936, Grigorii Alexandrov's *The Circus* (Tsirk), and Efim Dzigan's *We Are from Kronstadt* (My iz Kronstadta; discussed in Chapter 8).

16. See e.g., A. Efros, "Monumental'naia statua parizhskoi vystavki," *Arkhitektura SSSR*, 1937, no. 5, 16.

17. Ibid.

18. See e.g., Aleksandr M. Gerasimov, *Lenin on the Tribune* (1929). The Mukhina statue was allegedly based on three precedents in the classical style—Harmodius and Aristogeiton of 514 BC Athens, the *Winged Victory of Samothrace* (of the Greek goddess Nike) from the second century BC, and François Rude's *Départ des volontaires de 1792* (also known as La Marseillaise), executed for the Paris Arc de Triomphe in 1833–1836; Igor A. Kazus, "The Great Illusion: Architecture," in Dawn Ades et al., eds., *Art and Power: Europe under the Dictators 1930–1945* (London: Thames and Hudson, 1996), 193.

19. This description is based on photographs of the statue taken from different angles and published in *Arkhitektura SSSR*, 1937, no. 5, 7, 13, 15.

20. A. Efros, "Monumental'naia statuia parizhskogo pavil'ona," *Arkhitektura SSSR*, 1937, no. 5, 16.

21. Ibid., 16.

22. See chapter 1 in Clark, *Soviet Novel*.

23. Zholtovsky's advocacy of the palazzo was attacked, without mentioning him by name, in the *Pravda* article on architecture that signaled the extension of the anti-Formalist campaign to that branch of the arts ("Kakafoniia v arkhitekture," *Pravda*, 20 February 1936), and by name by the head of the Architects Union, K. S. Alabian, in his attack on Formalism in architecture ("Protiv formalizma, uproshchenchestva, eklektiki," *Arkhitektura SSSR*, 1936, no. 4, 10, 11); "Tematicheskii plan izdanii akademii na 1937 g," *Akademiia arkhitektury SSSR. Vnutrennii informatsionnyi biulleten'*, 1936, no. 4, 13.

24. K. Dzerzhinskaia, "Sovetskaia opernaia klassika," *Pravda*, 1938, no. 1; G. Polianovskii, " 'Bronenosets Potemkin.' Novaia postanovka Bol'shogo teatra SSSR," *Pravda*,1938, no. 3.

25. "Rech' L. M. Kaganovicha na soveshchanii po voprosam stroitel'stva," *Pravda*, 21 December 1935; "Konstruktsiia gorodov, zhilishchnoe stroitel'stvo i zadachi arkhitektora. Rech' tov N. A. Bulganina na I Vsesoiuznom s"ezde sovetskikh arkhitektorov," *Arkhitektura SSSR*, 1937, no. 9, 17. See also D. D. Bulgakov, "Opyt arkhitekturnoi rekonstruktsii zhilogo doma," *Arkhitektura SSSR*, 1935, no. 12, 46, 47; Arkhitekt, "Kakafoniia v arkhitekture," *Pravda*, 20 February 1936.

26. "Podniat' stroitel'nuiu industriiu. Rech' tov. A. I. Mikoiana," *Pravda*, 21 December 1935.

27. "Konstruktsiia gorodov, zhilishchnoe stroitel'stvo i zadachi arkhitektora," 17.

28. Efros, "Monumental'naia statuia parizhskogo pavil'ona," 16.

29. Walter Benjamin, *Moscow Diary*, trans. Richard Sieburth (Cambridge, Mass.: Harvard University Press, 1986), 55, 73, 85.

30. Jochen Hellbeck, *Revolution on My Mind: Writing a Diary under Stalin* (Cambridge, Mass.: Harvard University Press, 2006), 86.

31. A. Vlasov,"Arkhitekturno-tekhnicheskii proekt dvortsa sovetov soiuza SSSR," *Arkhitektura SSSR*, 1937, no. 6, 28–30.

32. Konstantin Stanislavsky (1863–1938) is the pseudonym of Konstantin Sergeevich Alekseev.

33. N. Volkov, "Khudozhnik-myslitel'," *Pravda*, 17 January 1938, 4.

34. This was the end result of a long struggle conducted not directly between these two, but more between their supporters. This is, for example, evident in the transcript of the Writers Union plenum of 1935.

35. The Russian title means *An Actor's Work on Himself*, but the text has generally been published in English translation together with other Stanislavsky materials under the title *An Actor Prepares*.

36. Veronique Garros, Natasha Korenevskaya and Thomas Lahusen, eds., *Intimacy and Terror* (New York: New Press, 1995), 22.

37. Robert Bechtold Heilman, *Tragedy and Melodrama: Versions of Experience* (Seattle: University of Washington Press, 1968), 81–82.

38. Robert Lang, *American Film Melodrama: Griffith, Vidor, Minelli* (Princeton: Princeton University Press, 1989), 49–50.

39. Ibid., 8.

40. See chapter 5 of Clark, *Soviet Novel*.

41. Mikhail Kol'tsov, "Ubiitsa s pretenziiami. Iz zala suda," *Pravda*, 7 March 1938, 3.

42. See e.g., Volkov, "Khudozhnik-myslitel'," 4.

43. K. Stanislavskii, Rabota aktëra nad soboi v tvorcheskom protsesse perezhivaniia. Dnevnik uchenika, 2nd. ed. (Moscow: GIKhL, 1938), 541.

44. Ibid., 197.

45. Ibid., 13, 14, 13, 15 (my emphasis).

46. K. Stanislavskii, "Ob aktëre," *Pravda*, 17 January 1938, 4.

47. Peter Brooks, *The Melodramatic Imagination* (New York: Columbia University Press, 1984), 2.

48. K. S. Stanislavskii, *Moia zhizn' v iskusstve* (Moscow: Iskusstvo, 1983), 226–227.

49. L. N. Tolstoi, *Polnoe sobranie sochinenii,* series II, ed. V. D. Bonch-Bruevich, I. K. Luppol, and M. A. Savel'ev: *Dnevniki i zapisnye knizhki,* vol. 47 (Moscow: GIKhL, 1937), Dnevniki vol. 54 (Moscow: GIKhL, 1934), vol. 55, vol. 56 (Moscow: GIKhL, 1937), vol. 58 (Moscow-Leningrad: GIKhL, 1934); A. Gertsen, *Byloe i dumy v 5-ti tomakh* Goslitizdat, 1937–1938); Irina Paperno, *Stories of the Soviet Experience: Memoirs, Diaries, Dreams* (Ithaca: Cornell University Press, 2009), 10–15.

50. See e.g., Volkov, "Khudozhnik-myslitel'," 4.

51. Stanislavskii, Rabota aktëra nad soboi, 63, 65.

52. Ibid., 63.

53. Sheila Fitzpatrick, "Ascribing Class," *Journal of Modern History,* vol. 65, no. 4 (December 1993), 745–770.

54. "O nedostatkakh partiinoi raboty i merakh likvidatsii trotskistkikh i drugikh dvurushnikov. Doklad tovarishcha Stalina na Plenume TsKVKP(b) 3 marta 1937 g.," Prilozhenie, *Stroitel'stvo Moskvy,* 1937, no. 4, 6.

55. Ibid., 3.

56. "Utrennee zasedanie 11 marta 1938 goda," in *Sudebnyi otchët po delu antisovetskogo 'pravo-trotskistskogo bloka'* (Moscow: Iuridicheskoe izdatel'stvo narodnogo komissariata iustitsii SSSR, 1938), 561.

57. Stanislavskii, "Ob aktëre," 4.

58. Mel Gussow, "Demystifying the Method: Once-Exclusive Actors Studio Reaches out to the Public," *New York Times,* May 20, 1997, C11.

59. Stanislavskii, *Rabota aktëra nad soboi,* 39.

60. Ibid., 40.

61. Ibid., 40–41.

62. Ibid. 45.

63. Ibid., 46.

64. Ibid., 47.

65. Hellbeck, *Revolution on My Mind.*

66. Stanislavskii, *Rabota aktëra nad soboi,* 15; my emphasis.

67. Ibid., 14.

68. Ibid., 539–541.

69. Ibid., 348.

70. Hannah Arendt in her *Origins of Totalitarianism* notes the curious phenomenon that in Nazi practice and in the Bolshevik show trials people would confess to the most far-fetched sins, yet their confessed misdeeds were often the same as those in the confessions of countless others. (New York: Meridian Books, 1958), 352. However, she takes her analysis of this in different directions from mine.

71. Staniskavskii, *Rabota aktëra nad soboi,* 130.

72. Ibid., 224.

73. Ibid., 341.

74. Versions of this position can be found in Oleg Kharkhordin, *The Collective and the Individual in Russia: A Study in Practices* (Berkeley: University of California Press, 1999), and Hellbeck, *Revolution on My Mind.*

7. LOVE AND DEATH IN THE
TIME OF THE SPANISH CIVIL WAR

1. Interview with Maya Turovskaya, 9 September 2007; Jochen Hellbeck, *Revolution on My Mind: Writing a Diary under Stalin* (Cambridge, Mass.: Harvard University Press, 2006), 92.

2. A. N. Afinogenov, *Stat'i, dnevniki, pis'ma, vospominaniia* (Moscow: Iskusstvo, 1957).

3. Daniel Kowalsky, *Stalin and the Spanish Civil War,* available at http://quod.lib.umich .edu/cgi/t/text/text-idx?c=acls;idno=heb99012.0, provides further information on this series and clips from the newsreels and the Soviet films screened in Spain. See paras. 433–445.

4. *Dimitrov and Stalin 1934–1943: Letters from the Soviet Archives,* ed. Alexander Dallin and F. I. Firsov (New Haven: Yale University Press, 2000), 48.

5. See chapter 12 of Jean-François Lyotard, *signed, MALRAUX,* trans. Robert Harvey (Minneapolis: University of Minnesota Press, 1999); Frederick Benson, *Writers in Arms: The Literary Impact of the Spanish Civil War* (New York: New York University Press, 1967), 99.

6. David Iosifovich Zaslavskii, "Pervaia skripka (iz vospominanii)," RGALI, 2846/1/77.

7. Kowalsky, *Stalin and the Spanish Civil War,* para. 457; Anatol Goldberg, *Ilya Erenburg: Writing, Politics and the Art of Survival* (London: Weidenfeld and Nicholson), 161.

8. G. Skorokhodov, *Mikhail Kol'tsov. Kratko-biograficheskii ocherk* (Moscow: Sovetskii pisatel', 1959), 158–159; see Koltsov's dispatches "Komitet oborony Madrida," *Pravda* 15, 16, 17, 24 November 1936; Kowalsky, *Stalin and the Spanish Civil War,* para. 457; Goldberg, *Ilya Erenburg,* 161.

9. Ronald Radosh, Mary R. Habeck, and Grigory Sevostianov, eds., *Spain Betrayed: The Soviet Union and the Spanish Civil War* (New Haven: Yale University Press, 2001), 23–31.

10. The original by I. D. Volkov was further adapted by V. I. Nemirovich-Danchenko, and V. G. Sakhnovskii acted as codirector.

11. Alisa Koonen, "Emma Bovari," *Sovetskoe iskusstvo,* 17 September 1937.

12. "Iz stenogramm repetitsii spektaklia 'Anna Karenina,'" in *Vl. I Nemirovich-Danchenko. Tvorchestvo aktëra. Khrestomatiia,* comp. V. I. Vilenkin (Moscow: Iskusstvo, 1984), 338; N. D. Volkov, "Dramaturgiia Anny Kareninoi," in *Anna Karenina v postanovke Moskovskogo ordena Lenina khudozhestvennogo akademicheskogo teatra* (Moscow: Izdanie MKhAT, 1938), 197.

13. Anna Muza, The Tragedy of a Russian Woman *Anna Karenina* in the Moscow Art Theater, 1937," *Russian Literature* 65, no. 4 (May 2009), 495.

14. Koonen, "Emma Bovari"; A. Kut, "Balet 'Romeo i Dzhulietta,'" *Sovetskoe iskusstvo,* 22 January 1936; "Khronika," *Sovetskoe iskusstvo,* 29 August 1937; Iz pis'ma V. G. Sakhnovskomu," in *Vl. I. Nemirovich-Danchenko,* 303.

15. "Iz stenogram repetitsii spektaklia 'Anny Kareninoi'," in *Vl. I. Nemirovich Danchenko,* 266.

16. "Pervye vpechatleniia L. Feikhtvangera o sovetskom iskusstve," *Sovetskoe iskusstvo* 1937, no. 1; G. Roshal', "'Sem'ia Oppengeim,'" *Sovetskoe iskusstvo,* 1937, no. 9.

17. See Dudley Andrew and Steven Ungar, "*Esprit* in the Arena of Extremist Politics," in Andrew and Ungar, *Popular Front Paris and the Poetics of Culture* (Cambridge, Mass.: Harvard University Press, 2005), 109–141. I am indebted to the analysis of de Rougement there for some of the ideas in this chapter.

18. De Rougement, *Love in the Western World,* trans. Montgomery Belgion, rev. and augmented ed. (New York: Harper Colophon, 1956), 21, 41.

19. Ibid., 15.

20. See e.g., Koonen, "Emma Bovari."

21. A. Iablochk, "Posle spektaklia," *Sovetskoe iskusstvo,* 5 May 1937.

22. See e.g., I. Sidorov, "Moskva v 1938 godu," *Pravda,* 27 March 1938.

23. Fridrikh Vol'f, "Propaganda razboia i ubiistv," *Sovetskoe iskusstvo,* 29 July 1937.

24. Andrew and Ungar, *Popular Front Paris,* 131.

25. De Rougement, *Love in the Western World,* 51.

26. I. V. Göte, *Stradaniia molodogo Vertera,* trans. A. Eige, Vstupitel'naia stat'ia G. Lukacha (Moscow-Leningrad: Academiia, 1937).

27. "O teatre Vs. Meierkhol'da," *Sovetskoe iskusstvo,* 17 December 1937.

28. De Rougement, *Love in the Western World,* 51.

29. See e.g., "Nashi zadachi bor'by s inymi vrediteliami diversantami i shpionami," *Sovetskoe iskusstvo,* 23 April 1937, 3–4, is followed by M. Tverskoi, "Anna Karenina," 5.

30. Cited in Hugh Thomas, *The Spanish Civil War,* rev. ed. (New York: Modern Library, 2001), 333.

31. Anthony Aldgate, *Cinema and History: British Newsreels and the Spanish Civil War* (London: Scolar Press, 1979, 105–194).

32. A partial exception would be *Spain,* whose ultimate director, Esfir Shub, never went to Spain, though the film is largely based on footage shot by Roman Karmen in 1936–1937.

33. Erik Barnouw, *Document: A History of Documentary Film,* rev. ed. (Oxford: Oxford University Press, 1983), 136.

34. Paul Virilio, *War and Cinema: The Logistics of Perception* (London: Verso, 1989), 8.

35. Sidney Meyers and Jay Leyda, "Joris Ivens: Artist in Documentary," in Lewis Jacobs, ed., *The Documentary Tradition,* 2nd ed. (New York: Norton, 1979), 158.

36. De Rougement, *Love in the Western World,* 51.

37. Andre Stufkens, "Lust for Life: An Introduction to Joris Ivens and the Twentieth Century," in Andre Stufkens, ed., *Cinema without Borders: The Films of Joris Ivens* (Nijmegen, Netherlands: European Foundation Joris Ivens, 2002), 13.

38. Frederick Benson, *Writers in Arms: The Literary Impact of the Spanish Civil War* (New York: New York University Press, 1967), 66.

39. Gustav Regler, *The Owl of Minerva,* trans. Norman Denny, with a preface by Ernest Hemingway (New York: Farrar, Straus and Cudahy, 1960), 196.

40. Enrique Esperabé de Arteaga, "La Guerra de reconquista," in Noel Valis, ed., *Teaching Representations of the Spanish Civil War* (New York: MLA, 2007), 45–47.

41. Thomas, *Spanish Civil War,* 285–286.

42. Skorokhodov, *Mikhail Kol'tsov,* 157.

43. Jean-Francois Lyotard, *signed, MALRAUX,* 178.

44. Mikhail Kol'tsov, *Ispanskii dnevnik,* book 2 (entry of 16 February 1937), *Novyi mir,* 1938, no. 6, 74.

45. Gustav Regler, *The Great Crusade,* trans. Wittaker Chambers and Barrows Mussey (Toronto: Longmans, 1940), 70.

46. *Roman Karmen. Une Légende rouge* (Paris: Seuil, 2002), 55.

47. Tatiana Tess in *Roman Karmen v vospominaniiakh sovremennikov* (Moscow: Iskusstvo, 1983), 90; Daniel Kowalsky, "The Role of Soviet Cinema," avaiable at http://quod.lib .umich.edu/cgi/t/text/text-idx?c=acls;idno=heb99012.0, para. 396.

48. Dzhorzh Bernanos, "Bol'shoe kladbishche v lunnom svete," *Internatsional'naia literatura,* 1938, no. 9.

49. See e.g., Arthur Koestler, *Dialogue with Death,* trans. Trevor and Phyllis Blewitt (New York: Macmillan, 1942), 30, 43, 101, 106.

50. Denis Hollier, *Absent without Leave: French Literature under the Threat of War* (Cambridge, Mass.: Harvard University Press, 1997), 184, 187.

51. Ibid., 150.

52. See Lucien Goldmann, *Pour une sociologie du roman* (Paris: Gallimard, 1964), 232–233, and Susan Suleiman, *Authoritarian Fictions: The Ideological Novel as a Literary Genre* (New York: Columbia University Press, 1983), 135, 138–139, 182, 187.

53. Andre Malraux, *Days of Hope,* trans. Stuart Gilbert and Alastair Macdonald (London: Hamish Hamilton, 1968), 335.

54. Mikh. Kol'tsov, "Lëtchik Antonio," *Pravda,* 16 November 1936; *Ispanskii dnevnik,* part 1 (Moscow: Izdatel'stvo politicheskoi literatury, 1987), 205.

55. *Ispanskii dnevnik,* book 2, 255–256, 263, 265, 275.

56. N. Poszhol'skii, comp., *"Kryl'ia Ispanii." Ocherki i rasskazy o lëtchikakh respublikanskoi Ispanii* (Moscow: Molodaia gvardiia, 1938). Louis Fischer mentions Tarkhov's aviation prowess in his intelligence debriefing of 31 December 1936, , in Radosh et al., *Spain Betrayed,* 111.

57. Regler, *Great Crusade,* 185–200.

58. Koestler, *Dialogue with Death,* 64–65.

59. Cervantes is also featured in Kol'tsov's *Spanish Diary.*

60. Regler, *Great Crusade,* 262, 257, 287, 364–365.

61. Ibid., 4–5.

62. Kol'tsov, *Ispanskii dnevnik,* part 1, 281.

63. Ibid., 271.

64. The two main places where Stalin is invoked are Stalin's telegram to Jose Diaz, sent to express solidarity with the Republicans (in part 1), and at the very end in a long discussion about the Stalin constitution (see also the diary installment in *Novyi mir,* 1938, no. 8, 35).

65. *Ispanskii dnevnik,* part 1, 219.

66. Il'ia Erenburg, *No Pasaran! Grazhdanskaia voina iul'-dekabr' 1936 goda* (Moscow: Ogiz-Izogiz, 1937), 42.

67. Viacheslav Popov, ed., *Il'ia Erenburg. Dela i dni (v dokumentakh, pis'makh, vyskazyvaniiakh, i soobshcheniiakh pressy i svidetel'stvakh sovremennikakh)* (Saint Petersburg: Biblioteka rossiiskoi Akademii nauk, 2001), 89, 99, 101, 103.

68. Daniel Kowalsky, "The Soviet Cinematic Offensive in the Spanish Civil War," *Film History* 19 (2007), 9–10; Il'ja Erenburg, *No Pasaran!* (London: Malik Verlag, 1937), 75–78, 91.

69. André Gide, *Return from the U.S.S.R*, trans. Dorothy Bussy (New York: Knopf, 1937), 32.

70. "Oboronnye pisateli, vperëd!," *Literaturnaia gazeta*, 15 October 1937.

71. Vs. Vishnevskii, "90 dnei v Evrope," *Sovetskoe iskusstvo*, 17 July 1936.

72. Quotation from [unsigned], "Vishnevskii—ordenosets," *Znamia*, 1937, no. 2, 271. On Koltsov's reports from Spain see in the same issue V. Shklovskii, "O Mikhaile Kol'tsove," 276–281.

73. Naum Kleiman, "Ne osushchestvlënnye zamysly Eizenshteina," *Iskusstvo kino*, 1992, no. 4, 17.

74. Kol'tsov, *Ispanskii dnevnik,* part 1, 164–167 (entry of 16 October); Koestler, *Dialogue with Death*, 20; Il'ia Erenburg, *Ispanskii zakal. Fevral-iul' 1937* (Moscow: Goslitizdat, 1938), 11, 13, 14; Erenburg, *No Pasaran!*, chapters 17 and 20, and 119–121; Ilja Erenburg, *No Pasaran! (Sie kommen nicht durch). Vom Freiheitskämpfer der Spanien* (London: Malik Verlag, 1937), 75–77, 91.

75. Malraux, *Days of Hope*, 208.

76. Regler, *Great Crusade,* reference to Chapaev 26, 55; to General Paul's speech, 112.

77. Kowalsky, *Stalin and the Spanish Civil War*, paras. 427–430.

78. *Ispanskii dnevnik,* book 3 (entry of 17 June 1937), *Novyi mir*, 1938, no. 8, 18.

79. RGALI 631/13/88/8.

80. Both the novel *For Whom the Bell Tolls* and especially the play *The Fifth Column* and his later story "The Denunciation," set in Madrid.

81. The film was partly produced by Ivor Montagu, a Communist and associate of Eisenstein.

82. The real events and the ramifications of this narrative are discussed in Catriona Kelly, *Comrade Pavlik: The Rise and Fall of a Soviet Boy Hero* (London: Granta Books, 2005).

83. RGALI 1923/1/403/1–4.

84. RGALI 1923/1/403; "Vse teatry staviat Pushkina. Moskovskie vpechateleniia. Beseda s Lionom Feikhtvangerom," *Sovetskoe iskusstvo*, 5 February 1937; "Memorandum from B. Z. Shumiatsky to V. M. Molotov" in Katerina Clark and Evgeny Dobrenko, eds., *Soviet Culture and Power: A History in Documents, 1917–1953* (New Haven: Yale University Press, 2007), 245.

85. GARF,5283/5/745/20-22.

86. For more on the visits of Gide and Feuchtwanger see Boris Frezinskii, *Pisateli i sovetskie vozhdi. Izbrannye siuzhety 1919–1960 godov* (Moscow: Ellis Lak, 2008), 421–433; Michael David-Fox, *Showcasing the Great Experiment: Cultural Diplomacy and Western Visitors to Soviet Russia, 1921-1941* (Oxford/New York: Oxford University Press, 2011); and Ludmila Stern, *Western Intellectuals and the Soviet Union, 1920–40: From Red Square to the Left Bank* (London: Routledge, 2007).

87. Frezinskii, *Pisateli i sovetskie vozhdi*, 277.

88. David Cesarani, *Arthur Koestler: The Homeless Mind* (New York: Free Press, 1998), 148.

89. Frezinskii, *Pisateli i sovetskie vozhdi,* 425; *Ispanskii dnevnik,* book 2, 299–300.

90. Hollier, *Absent without Leave,* 177.

91. Lion Feuchtwanger, *Moscow 1937: a visit described for my friends,* trans. Irene Josephy (New York: Viking, 1937). Originally published as *Moskau 1937. Ein Reisebericht für meine Freunde);* Viktor Fradkin, *Delo Kol'tsova* (Moscow: Vagrius, 2002), 290.

92. Reports of D. Karavkina, assigned by VOKS to work with him, are in GARF 5283/1/354, with his comments on the trials, 7–8.

93. Picasso's response, his tableau *Guernica,* commissioned for Republican Spain's pavilion at the Paris Exposition and famous today, was apparently largely ignored in the literature of the time; James D. Herbert, *Paris 1937: Worlds on Exhibition* (Ithaca: Cornell University Press, 1998), 33.

94. *Ispanskii dnevnik,* book 2 (entry of 23 May 1937), *Novyi mir* 1938, no. 7, 33.

95. Vs. Vishnevskii, "Respublikanskaia Ispaniia segodnia," *Sovetskoe iskusstvo,* 5 August 1937.

96. Fradkin, *Delo Kol'tsova,* 305.

97. RGALI 1204/2/668/33–34.

98. Frezinskii, *Pisateli i sovetskie vozhdi,* 460–466.

99. K. A. Zalesskii, *Imperiia Stalina. Biograficheskii entsiklopedicheskii slovar'* (Moscow: Veche, 2000).

100. Kowalsky, *Stalin and the Spanish Civil War,* para. 439.

101. Goldberg, *Ilya Erenburg,* 162.

102. S. Eizenshtein, *Izbrannye proizvedeniia v 6-i tomakh,* vol. 6 (Moscow: Iskusstvo, 1971), 500.

103. Simon Morrison, *The People's Artist: Prokofiev's Soviet Years* (New York: Oxford University Press, 2009), 32–40.

104. V. F. Koliazin, ed., *"Vernite mne svobodu!" Deiateli literatury i iskusstva Rossii i Germanii—zhertvy stalinskogo terrora* (Moscow: Medium, 1997), documents 48–68, narrative 51, wife's rebuttal, 373.

8. THE IMPERIAL SUBLIME

1. See e.g., Iurii Krymov's *The Tanker Derbent* (Tanker "Derbent"; 1938).

2. Tim Barringer, "The Course of Empires: Landscape and Identity in America and Britain, 1820–1880," in Andrew Wilton and Tim Barringer, *American Landscape: Landscape Painting in the United States, 1820–1880* (Princeton: Princeton University Press, 2002), 39.

3. See e.g., Harsha Ram, *The Imperial Sublime: A Russian Poetics of Empire* (Madison: University of Wisconsin Press, 2003), 8.

4. A treatise on the sublime by Longinus, *On the Sublime,* received attention from European intellectuals after it was translated by Nicolas Boileau in 1674. Also appearing in the eighteenth century were Edmund Burke's *Philosophical Enquiry into the Origins of Our Idea of the Sublime and Beautiful* (1757), Kant's sections on the sublime in his *Critique of Judgment* (1790) and *Observations on the Feeling of the Beautiful and the Sublime* (1764), and Hegel's in his *Aesthetics: Lectures on Fine Art* (put together by his

students from their lecture notes and published posthumously in 1835). Also important was Friedrich von Schiller, "On the Sublime" (1801) and "On the Pathetic" (1794).

5. Edmund Burke, *A Philosophical Enquiry into Our Ideas of the Sublime and the Beautiful* (Oxford: World's Classics, 1990), 59–61.

6. The quotation comes from a description of Rosa's paintings by the painter Henry Fuseli (1741–1785), cited in Andrew Wilton, "The Sublime in the Old World and the New," in Wilton and Barringer, *American Sublime*, 12.

7. Marjorie Hope Nicolson, *Mountain Gloom and Mountain Glory: The Development of the Aesthetics of the Infinite* (Ithaca: Cornell University Press, 1959).

8. Burke, *Philosophical Enquiry*, 67.

9. *The Prelude*, canto 13, lines 35–91.

10. See also *The Prelude*, book 6, lines 533–536.

11. G. W. F. Hegel, *Aesthetics: Lectures on Fine Art*, trans. T. M. Knox, vol. 1 (Oxford: Clarendon Press, 1975), 372.

12. Thomas Weiskel, *The Romantic Sublime: Studies in the Structure and Psychology of Transcendence* (Baltimore: John Hopkins University Press, 1976), 4.

13. Terry Eagleton, *Holy Terror* (Oxford: Oxford University Press, 2005), 41.

14. See also the encounter with Stalin in Mikhail Kalatozov's film *Valerii Chkalov* (Red wings; 1941) where the hero-aviator is reduced to a quivering figure.

15. Burke, *Philosophical Enquiry*, 67.

16. Friedrich Schiller, "Upon the Sublime," in *Aesthetic Letters, Essays and Philosophical Letters of Schiller*, trans. J. Weiss (Boston: Charles and Little, 1845), 62–63, 246.

17. Eagleton, *Holy Terror*, 53–54.

18. Gegel', *Sochineniia*, t. XII. Lekstii po estetike. Kniga pervaia, trans. B. S. Stolpner (Moscow: Insitut filosofii Akademii nauk, 1938). Stolpner's translations of sections of Hegel's *Aesthetics* were also published in *Literaturnyi kritik*, nos. 10, 11, 1934; nos. 1, 2, 6, 8, 1935; nos. 3, 5, 7, 1936; nos.4, 5, 1937; nos.1, 7, 8, 1938. See Mikh. Lifshits, "Estetika Gegelia," *Sovetskoe iskusstvo*, 28 August 1938.

19. L. Spokoinyi, "Estetika Kanta," *Literaturnyi kritik*, 1935, no. 3, 17–37.

20. See e.g., Rostislav Ju. Danilevskii, *Schiller in der russischen Literatur. 18. Jahrhundert–erster Hälfe 19. Jahrhundert* (Dresden: Dresden University Press, 1978); V. F. Pustarnakov, ed., *Filosofiia Shellinga v Rossii* (Saint Petersburg: Izd. Russkogo Khristianskogo Gumanitarnogo Instituta, 1998); Victor Terras, *Belinskij and Russian Literary Criticism* (Madison: University of Wisconsin Press, 1974). It is to be noted that Belinsky was not always a Schiller enthusiast and attacked him for a few years in the late 1830s.

21. Hegel, *Aesthetics*, 518, 363, 520, 518.

22. Ibid., 525.

23. Schiller, "Upon the Sublime," 259.

24. Ibid., 254–255, 259, 253.

25. Ibid., 256.

26. Evgenii Gavrilov, "Preobrazovatel' prirody," *Pravda*, 29 November 1938.

27. Tikh. Kholodnyi, "Trofim Denisovich Lysenko," *Pravda*, 7 December 1938. Lysenko has been one of the negative characters in Western narratives of Soviet science; his struggle in the late 1930s against the supporters of Nikolai Vavilov, before the revolu-

tion a collaborator of William Bateson, the founder of genetics, was resolved in 1940 when Lysenko was made head of the Institute of Genetics of the Soviet Academy of Sciences and Vavilov was arrested.

28. James Kirwan, *Sublimity: The Non-rational and the Rational in the History of Aesthetics* (London: Routledge, 2005), 161.

29. "Derzat' v nauke," (editorial), *Pravda*, 21 November 1938.

30. Yale University Press in its Annals of Communism series is bringing out a facsimile of a *Short Course* manuscript showing Stalin's changes throughout.

31. *Istoriia Vsesoiznoi kommunisticheskoi partii (bol'shevikov). Kratkii kurs* (Moscow, 1938), 99–127.

32. Ibid., 101.

33. Ibid., 102–106.

34. Danilevskii, *Schiller in der russischen Literatur*, 38.

35. Sergei Eisenstein, "O stroenii veshchei," *Iskusstvo kino*, 1939, no. 6, 7–20.

36. Ibid., 15.

37. [Unsigned], "Lëtchiki u K. S. Stanislavskogo," *Sovetskoe iskusstvo*, 23 December 1935.

38. Schiller, "Upon the Sublime," 254.

39. Ibid., 254. This association with the masculine is especially marked in Burke, and in Kant's *Observations Concerning the Beautiful and the Sublime*.

40. Ram, *Imperial Sublime*.

41. N. Naumov, "Ukrepit' sviaz' s natsional'nymi literaturami," *Literaturnaia gazeta*, 20 August 1938, chronicles a series of moves to foster and supervise a literature of the ethnic minorities equipped with copious translations of Russian literature to guide it.

42. Frank J. Miller, *Folklore for Stalin* (Armonk: M. E. Sharpe, 1990).

43. Lev Kassil', "Govorit Krasnaia ploshchad'," *Literaturnaia gazeta*, 2 May 1937.

44. W. J. T. Mitchell, ed., *Landscape and Power*, 2nd ed. (Chicago: Chicago University Press, 2002), 10.

45. Barringer, "Course of Empires," 60.

46. Here one might also consider the sublime potential that was exploited in the famous mountain films of Fanck and Riefenstahl and that attracted the attention of Goebbels.

47. N. Undasynov, "Pervyi kazakhskii fil'm," *Iskusstvo kino*, 1939, no. 5, 28–29. See also the film *Muzhestvo*, involving a perilous battle in the cockpit of a plane above the Pamirs near the Soviet border between a loyal pilot and a bandit trying to force him to take the plane over the Soviet border, a situation saved when he makes a perilous forced landing: G. Chakhorian, "Novella o muzhestvennom lëtchike," *Iskusstvo kino*, 1939, no. 9, 21–22.

48. Examples of the Arctic theme in fiction of the late 1930s include V. Gorbatov, in the periodical *Obyknovennaia Arktika, Oktiabr'*, 1937, no. 12.

49. See e.g., Konstantin Simonov, "Ledovoe Poboishche (Poema)," *Znamia*, 1938, no. 1.

50. RGALI 1966/1/344/3.

51. John McCannon, *Red Arctic: Polar Exploration and the Myth of the North in the Soviet Union, 1932–1939* (New York: Oxford University Press, 1998), 78. For more information on this expedition see 74–78.

52. Redakteur-konstrukteur Sergej Tretjakow, *Tjeljuskin. Ein Land rettet seine Söhne* (Moscow-Leningrad: VEGAAR, 1934).

53. G. A. Ushakov, "Besprimernyi podvig," *Pravda,* 22 February 1938, 4.

54. A good example of this linkage with exploitation of natural resources and the enigmatic nature of the Arctic is to be seen in M. Vodop'ianov, "Na vershine mira," *Literaturnaia gazeta,* 26 November 1938.

55. S. Marvich, "S geroiami vsia strana," *Literaturnaia gazeta,* 20 March 1938.

56. Interview with Elena Moiseevna Rzhevskaia (first wife of Pavel Kogan who trained at IFLI as a German scholar), June 1999.

57. S. Tret'iakov, "Belye piatna," *Pravda,* 13 July 1933.

58. Vern, Zhiul', *Iz pushki na lunu* (Leningrad: Detizdat, 1936); Vern, *80 dnei vokrug sveta* (Leningrad: Molodaia gvardiia, 1936). The plot of *The Children of Captain Grant,* inasmuch as it involves the search for a lost father in a remote place (in this case the Pacific) bears some comparison with Kaverin's *Two Captains,* discussed below.

59. "Invention, Memory and Place," in W. J. T. Mitchell, ed., *Landscape and Power,* 2nd ed. (Chicago: University of Chicago Press, 2002), 147.

60. *Kostër,* 1938, nos. 8–12; 1939, nos. 1, 2, 4–6, 9–12; 1940, nos. 2–4. Book 2 appeared in *Oktiabr',* 1944, nos. 1–2, 7–8, 11–12. Part 1 was first published as a book with Detgiz, the children's publishing house, in 1940, and part 2 with the same press in 1945.

61. V. Kaverin, *Dva kapitana, Kostër,* 1939, no. 10, 38.

62. E.g., M. Vodop'ianov, *Polët na zemliu Frantsa Iosifa* (Moscow-Leningrad: ONTI, 1937), 54–55, 59, 75–78, 86, 88–90, 115, especially 48–40 (a forced landing), 44 (the Nenets), and 121 (the primus); G. Baidukov, *Zapiski pilota* (Moscow: GIKhL, 1938), 54, 124–126, 138–139, 178, 238–239, 247–149.

63. Kaverin, *Dva kapitana, Kostër,* 1939, no. 11–12, 29–30.

64. Ibid., 30–31.

65. Ibid., 36.

66. Schiller, "Upon the Sublime," 256.

67. Eagleton, *Holy Terror,* 61.

68. Mitchell, "Israel, Palestine, and the American Wilderness," in *Landscape and Power,* 262.

69. Paul Fussell, "Travel and the British literary Imagination of the Twenties and Thirties," in Michael Kowalewski, ed., *Temperamental Journeys: Essays on the Modern Literature of Travel* (Athens: University of Georgia Press, 1992), 87.

70. Mikhail Koltsov, "Narod Bogatyr'," *Pravda,* 7 November 1938. See also N. Krutikov, "Aleksandr Nevskii," *Pravda,* 4 December 1938.

71. "V poiskakh temy" (editorial), *Literaturnaia gazeta,* 19 April 1938. The Battle of Kalka (1223) was a tragic event in Russian history when the Russians lost to the Mongols and several Russian princes lost their lives.

72. M. Chertkov, "Fundament zazhitochnoi zhizni," *Pravda,* 6 November 1936; chapter 4, "The Magic Tablecloth," in Sheila Fitzpatrick, *Everyday Stalinism: Ordinary Life in Extraordinary Times: Soviet Russia in the 1930s* (New York: Oxford University Press, 1999).

73. See e.g., *Devushka s kharakterom* (dir. K. Iudin, Mosfil'm 1939); Ivan Pyr'ev, *Swineherd and the Shepherd* (Svinarka i pastukh, 1941).

74. A. Lebedev, "V masterskoi A. M. Gerasimova," *Sovetskoe iskusstvo,* 25 January 1939.
75. Andrew Wilton, "The Sublime in the Old World and the New," 12–13. See also Hegel, *Aesthetics,* 141,157.
76. Lebedev, "V masterskoi A. M. Gerasimova."
77. Less officially, the dacha was also a place where people kept literature they thought risky to keep in their Moscow apartments and where more risky conversations and meetings might take place.
78. See documents nos. 64, 65, 66, in Andrei Artizov and Oleg Naumov, comps., *Vlast'i i khudozhestvennaia intelligentsiia. Dokumenty TsK RKP (b)—VKP (b)—VChK—OGPU—NKVD o kul'turnoi politike 1917-1953 gg.* (Moscow: Mezhdunarodnyi fond "Demokratiia," 1999), 470–473.
79. *Timur i ego komanda,* scenario by Arkadii Gaidar, with a reworking by the director A. Razumnyi (1940).
80. Natal'ia Syslova, "Zametki o vystavke," *Sovetskoe iskusstvo,* 16 April 1939; *Sovetskoe iskusstvo,* 1 May 1939, has on its front page a photograph of "Znatnye liudy strany Sovetov," together with "Pavil'ion SSSR na mezhdunarodnoi vystavke v N'iu-Iorke."

9. THE BATTLE OVER THE GENRES

1. Fredric Jameson, introduction to Georg Lukacs, *The Historical Novel,* trans. Hannah and Stanley Mitchell (Lincoln: University of Nebraska Press, 1983), 2.
2. "Mobilizatsionnaia gotovnost'," *Literaturnaia gazeta,* 10 May, 1938.
3. Dudley Andrew and Steven Ungar, *Popular Front Paris and the Poetics of Culture* (Cambridge, Mass.: Harvard University Press, 2005), 133.
4. For a fuller coverage see David Brandenberger, *National Bolshevism: Stalinist Mass Culture and the Formation of Modern Russian National Identity, 1931–1956* (Cambridge, Mass.: Harvard University Press, 2002); David Brandenberger and Kevin M. F. Platt, *Epic Revisionism* (Madison: University of Wisconsin Press, 2006).
5. T. Pavlov, "Novaia redaktsiia spektaklia 'Ivan Susanin,'" *Sovetskoe iskusstvo,* 6 April 1939.
6. N. L. Brodskii, *A. S. Pushkin. Biografiia* (Moscow: GIKhL, 1937), 891.
7. "Obshchemoskovskoe sobranie pisatelei. Doklad tov. A Fadeeva ob itogakh XVIII s"ezda VKP (b)," *Literaturnaia gazeta,* 1939, no. 22.
8. RGALI, 631/15/275/10, 14.
9. See e.g., B. Volin, "Velikii russkii narod," *Bol'shevik,* 1939, no. 8, 26–37.
10. See e.g., in *Literaturnoe obozrenie,* 1940, no. 1, material on the visit of Auden and Isherwood to China ("za rubezhom. Puteshestvie na voinu," 62), and Stephen Spender in no. 8, 63; in no. 2, reviews of books by Steinbeck and Oscar Wilde; in no. 4, announcements of the publication of books by Carlo Goldoni, Victor Hugo, Charles Dickens, Gustave Flaubert, and Anatole France (63). Simonov in his memoirs suggests that in *Literaturnaia gazeta* there was resistance to the mandated line, though this could be self-serving.

11. "Novyi tom Prusta, tom v, 'V poiskakh utrachennoi vremeni,'" *Literaturnaia gazeta*, 20 August 1938.

12. Dzhems Dzhois, *Dublintsy*, trans. I. A. Kashkin (Moscow: Goslitizdat, 1937), Ia. Rykachev, "'Dublintsy,'" *Literaturnoe obozrenie*, 1937, no. 1, 50.

13. Prof. S. Eizenshtein, "Vertkal'nyi montazh," *Iskusstvo kino*, 1940, 1941; "Montazh 1938," *Iskusstvo kino*, 1939, no. 1, 37–49; "O stroenii veshchei," *Iskusstvo kino*, 1939, no. 6, 7–20.

14. See e.g., "Frank Kapra," *Iskusstvo kino*, 1940, no. 12, 62–63; Bett Devis, "Kinoaktrisa rabotaet nad rol'iu," *Iskusstvo kino*, 1941, no. 1, 26–28; "Chetyre luchshikh amerikanskikh fil'ma" (includes *A. Lincoln in Illinois*), *Iskusstvo kino*, 1940, no. 1, 55-56.

15. "Privetstvie sovetskikh pisatelei lige amerikanskikh pisatelei," *Literaturnaia gazeta*, 1939, no. 22; Tomas Mann, "Svoboda, spravedlivost', sovest'. Iz rechi proizvedënnoi na Vsemirnom kongresse pisatelei v N'iu-Iorke," *Literaturnaia gazeta*, 1939, no. 32.

16. See e.g., Akademik arkhitektury I. V. Zholtovskii, "Traditsii narodnogo iskusstva," *Sovetskoe iskusstvo*, 5 March 1937.

17. "Istoriia i literatura" ed., *Literaturnaia gazeta*, 26 August 1939.

18. The list includes *Rob Roy* (Rob Roi), *Ivanhoe* (Aivengo), and *The Talisman* (Richard L'vinoe serdtse).

19. Georg Lukács, *The Theory of the Novel*, trans. Anna Bostock (Cambridge, Mass.: MIT Press, 1971), 115; Lukács, *Historical Novel*, 58, 59.

20. Lukács, *Historical Novel*, 24.

21. This is my translation from Georg Lukach, "Istoricheskii roman," *Literaturnyi kritik*, 1937, no. 7, 50; Lukács, *Historical Novel*, 23.

22. Lukach, "Istoricheskii roman," 52, 52, 53; Lukács, *Historical Novel*, 24, 25, 25.

23. Lukács, *Historical Novel*, 53, 63, 71.

24. Ibid., 73.

25. Ibid., 86.

26. "V Tbliskom kinostudii," *Iskusstvo kino*, 1939, no. 7, 62–63; Stalin's suggested corrections made on 23 May, 1940 (RGASPI 558/11/167). I am grateful to Sheila Fitzpatrick for this information.

27. Lukács, *Historical Novel*, 38, 72, 72, 37, and 38.

28. A version of this coverage appeared as G. Lukach, "'Iunost' Genrikha IV' (roman Genrikha Manna)," *Literaturnoe obozrenie*, 1937, no. 16, 31–35.

29. Ibid., 315, 319.

30. See e.g., G. Mann *Iunost' korolia Genrikha IV*, trans. N. M. Krymova (Moscow: Vsemirnaia literatura of Zhurgaz, vypusk I and II of 1937 and in *Internatsional'naia literatura* 1937, nos. 9, 10; *Zrelost' korolia Genrikha IV*, tr. N. Kasatkina, *Internatsional'naia literatura*, 1939, no 3–4.

31. Among several editions: Romen Rollan, *Zhan-Khristof*, ed. A. A. Smirnov (Leningrad: Goslitizdat, 1937), vol. 1 and vol. 2 each with a print run of fifty thousand.

32. Jochen Hellbeck, *Revolution on My Mind: Writing a Diary under Stalin* (Cambridge, Mass.: Harvard University Press, 2006), 314.

33. RGASPI, 495/30/1076/17.

34. RGALI 1923/1/530/2.

35. Yuri Tsivian, *Ivan the Terrible* (London: BFI, 2002).

36. Neuberger, *Ivan the Terrible* (London: Tauris, 2003), 100.

37. I elaborate this point in greater detail in "Sergei Eisenstein's *Ivan the Terrible* and the Renaissance: An Example of Stalinist Cosmopolitanism?," forthcoming in *Slavic Review*, Spring 2012.

38. Sergei Eizenshtein, " 'Ivan Groznyi.' Fil'm o russkom renessanse XVI veka," *Izbrannye proizvedeniia v shesti tomakh, vol I* (Moscow: Iskusstvo, 1964), 189–195.

39. Another reason for pointing to Giuliano specifically was because he was stabbed to death in the cathedral, as was Ivan's simpleton cousin Vladimir in Part II of Eisenstein's film (Tsivian, *Ivan the Terrible,* 67).

40. Eizenshtein, " 'Ivan Groznyi'. Fil'm o russkom renessanse," 189, 190, 191.

41. Ibid., 193–194.

42. RGALI 1923/1/572/35, 36; RGALI 1923/1/554/86.

43. The ambassadors here refer to "Europe," as was unlikely in the early sixteenth century, one of many probable indications of references to contemporary times.

44. Sergei Eizenshtein, "Charlie the Kid" (1943–1944), in *Izbrannye proizvedeniia v shesti tomakh,* vol. 5 (Moscow: Iskusstvo, 1965), 521.

45. Neuberger, *Ivan the Terrible* 71.

46. Ibid., 3, 78, 81.

47. Another possibility: the emissary is given spectacles, often a sign that he represents Trotsky.

48. Stefan Zweig, *Triumph und Tragik des Erasmus von Rotterdam* (Vienna: Verlag Herbert Reichner, 1934); G. Lukach, "Novelly S. Tsveiga," *Literaturnoe obozrenie,* 1937, no. 8, 22–27.

49. Iuliia Markovna Zhivova, personal communication, 19 July 2001. Stefan Tsveig, " 'Motsart' Bela Balasha," *Sovetskoe iskusstvo,* 24 August 1939 (i.e. just before the Molotov-Ribbentrop Pact).

50. Stefan Zweig, *Erasmus of Rotterdam,* trans. Eden and Cedar Paul (New York: Viking Press, 1934), 16, 18, 100, 22, 203, 218, 221.

51. Sergei Mikhailovich Eizenshtein, *Memuary,* vol. 1 (Moscow: "Trud," 1997), 231. It should be noted that Eisenstein was commenting on the lectures on Rabelais that France gave in Buenos Aires in 1909 and that were published posthumously as the book on Rabelais.

52. Lukács, *Historical Novel,* 266, 268.

53. Machiavelli, *The Prince,* trans. Quentin Skinner (Cambridge: Cambridge University Press, 1988), esp. 51–52 (chapter 14), 89–90 (chapter 26).

54. Ibid., 59 (chapter 17).

55. Sergei Eisenstein, *Nonindifferent Nature: Film and the Structure of Things,* trans. Herbert Marshall (Cambridge: Cambridge University Press, 1987), 324–325.

56. This novel appeared in two parts and their English translations are frequently titled *Young Henry of Navarre* and *Henry, King of France.*

57. Nik. Volkonskii, "On smert' predpochpël pozornoi zhizni," *Sovetskoe iskusstvo,* 1939, commemorative issue of 14 October, no. 74.

58. Brandenberger, *National Bolshevism,* 79 n. 14.

59. See e.g., Dzhordzh Bairon, *Izbrannye proizvedeniia,* various translators (Moscow: Goslitizdat, 1938); in the same year, 1938, another one-volume selection came out in

Biblioteka "Ogonëk," with a print run of fifty thousand; Dzhordz Bairon, *Poemy*, vols. 1 and 2, trans. Georgii Shengeli (Moscow: GIKhL, 1940), with a print run of twenty thousand.

60. Saree Makdisi, *Romantic Imperialism: Universal Empires and the Culture of Modernity* (Cambridge: Cambridge University Press, 1998), 123, 8, 10.

61. B. Zozulia, "Predislovie," in Dzhordzh Gordon Bairon, *Stikhi* (Moscow: Biblioteka "Ogonëk," 1938).

62. A. Elistratova, "Predislovie," in Dzhordzh Bairon, *Izbrannye proizvedeniia* (Moscow: Goslitizdat, 1938), 4.

63. P. Antokol'skii, "Lermontov," *Literaturnaia gazeta*, 1938, no. 56 (October); see also Leonid Grossman, "Lermontov i mirovaia kul'tura," *Sovetskoe iskusstvo*, 1939 (October 14).

64. See e.g., P. Antokol'skii, "Dzhordzh Gordon Bairon," *Literaturnaia gazeta*, 20 January 1938.

65. Anatolii Vinogradov, *Bairon (1788–1824), Zhizn' zamechatel'nykh liudei* (Moscow: Zhurgaz, 1936).

66. Ibid., 110.

67. Ibid., 62.

68. I. Anisimov, "Bairon (k 150-letiiu so dnia rozhdeniia)," *Pravda*, 22 February 1938.

69. All this material is in Mikhail Zabludovskii, "Poemy Bairona," in Dzhordzh Bairon, *Poemy*, trans. Georgii Shengeli, vol. 1 (Moscow: GIKhL, 1940), 7, 10.

70. See e.g., M. Zagorskii, "Bairon i teatr," *Sovetskoe iskusstvo*, 22 January 1938 (the issue for the 150th anniversary of his birth).

71. Elistratova, "Predislovie," 3.

72. "Vladimir Maiakovskii," *Pravda*, 5 December 1935.

73. See e.g., RGALI 634/1/177/4–83.

74. E. Usievich, "K sporam o politicheskoi poezii," *Literaturnyi kritik*, 1937, no. 5, pp. 70, 87, 90, 89, 90 and 102, respectively.

75. See e.g., A. Evgen'ev, "Proshchanie s liubimym. O chetyrëkh sonetakh S. Kirsanova," *Literaturnaia gazeta*, 1938, no. 57.

76. See e.g., M. Gus, "A gde zhe liubov'?," *Literaturnaia gazeta*, 13 October 1940.

77. See e.g., R. Fraerman, *Dikaia sobaka dingo* (1940), about first love between adolescents, a love complicated by divorce and step-siblings. Kaverin also wrote about the need to restore the love plot to its due place in Soviet literature so that readers would have "pravdivye knigi" (V. Kaverin, "Nenapisannye knigi," *Literaturnaia gazeta*, 1939, no. 45).

78. E. Usievich, "V zashchitu politicheskoi poezii," *Literaturnyi kritik*, 1937, no. 5, and the response, Dzhek Al'tauzen, "V zashchitu politicheskoi poezii," *Literaturnaia gazeta*, 1 November 1937. In no. 63 there is a whole page of criticism in which, inter alia, she is accused of peddling the Bukharin line; E. Usievich, "K sporam o politicheskoi poezii," *Literaturnyi kritik*, 1937, no. 5, 70, 87, 90, 89, 90, 102.

79. "Plenum pravleniia Soiuza pisatelei," *Literaturnaia gazeta*, 27 February 1937; "Doklad N. I. Bukharina o poezii, poetike i zadachakh poeticheskogo tvorchestva v SSSR," in *Pervyi Vsesoiuznyi s"ezd sovetskikh pisatelei. Stenograficheskii otchët* (Moscow: Ogiz, 1934), 479–503.

80. "O politicheskoi poezii," *Pravda,* 28 February 1937.
81. The publication of these speeches in *Pravda* was delayed, and they appeared on 29 March and 1 April, respectively.
82. See, e.g., "Satira i lirika," *Literaturnaia gazeta,* March 1938.
83. Grigorii Pomerants, "Zapiski gadkogo utenka," *Znamia,* 143.
84. "Vykorchevat' bez ostatki," (editorial), *Literaturnaia gazeta,* 18 May 1937.
85. See e.g., A. Voronskii, "Literaturnye zametki," *Prozhektor,* 1925, no. 5, 25.
86. Katerina Clark, " 'Wait for Me and I Shall Return': The Initial Post-Stalin Thaw as a Reprise of Late 1930s Culture?," in Eleonory Gilburd and Denis Kozlov, eds., *The Thaw: Soviet Society and Culture during the 1950s and 1960s,* forthcoming with the University of Toronto Press.
87 Lionel Trilling, *Sincerity and Authenticity* (Cambridge, Mass.: Harvard University Press, 1972), 63.
88. Arthur O. Lovejoy, *The Great Chain of Being: A Study of the History of an Idea* (Cambridge, Mass.: Harvard University Press, 1974), 31.
89. K. Simonov, "O prave na liriku," *Literaturnaia gazeta,* 28 December 1939.
90. B. Meilakh, *Bairon i russkii romantizm* (Moscow-Leningrad: Izdatel'stvo Akademii nauk, 1937), 217.
91. Lukács, *Historical Novel,* 33–34; Lukács, *Theory of the Novel,* 59.
92. G. Geine, *Polnoe sobranie sochinenii,* vol. 1, *Lirika,* vstupitel'naia stat'ia G. Lukacha (Moscow: Goslitizdat, 1938).
93. Especially favored were the classic Russian epic *The Lay of Igor's Host* (Slovo o polku Igoreve) and the classic Georgian *Knight in Tiger's Skin* (Vitiaz' v tigrovoi shkure), by Stalin's fellow Georgian Shota Rustaveli, trans. N. Zabolotskii, (Moscow-Leningrad: Detizdat,1937); Stalin edited the translation himself, anonymously (Evgeny Dobrenko, personal communication, March 2007).
94. Boris Pasternak's *Doctor Zhivago* (1957), a novel substantially set in Moscow, though written in the postwar years, seems in many respects to belong to this period and provides a somewhat idiosyncratic example of this.
95. RGALI 2846/1/77.
96. M. M. Bakhtin, "Fransua Rable v istorii realizma (1940 g.)," in *Sobranie sochinenii,* vol. IV 4/1(Moscow: Iazyki slavianskikh kul'tur, 2008), 47 and see also 41; OR IMLI, 427/1/19, 42, 33. For more on Lukács and Bakhtin see Galin Tihanov, *Master and the Slave: Lukacs, Bakhtin, and the Ideas of Their Time* (Oxford: Clarendon, 2000).
97. Mikhail Bakhtin, "Epos i roman," in *Voprosy literatury i estetiki. Issledovaniia raznykh let* (Moscow: Khudozhestvennaia literatura, 1975), 480, 481, 457, 444; English versions in M. M. Bakhtin, *The Dialogic Imagination: Four Essays,* trans. Caryl Emerson and Michael Holquist (Austin: University of Texas Press, 1981), 37, 38, 14, 30.
98. Konstantin Simonov, "Glazami cheloveka moego pokoleniia," in Mikhail Kol'tsov, *Vostorg i iarost'. Ocherki. Fel'etony. Stat'i. Vospominaniia sovremennikov* (Moscow: Izdatel'stvo "Pravda," 1990), 472.
99. B. Sopel'niak, "Vy ne sobiraetes' zastrelit'sia?," *Ogonëk,* 1935, no. 13, 42–43.
100. Mikhail Kol'tsov, "Velikii avtor Iosif Stalin," *Literaturnaia gazeta,* 5 December 1938.
101. RGALI 631/1/298/138, 141, 172–173, 194, 225
102. RGALI 631/11/298/127.

103. RGALI 631/12/154/181–182; RGALI 631/13/88/9–13; Feuchtwanger's reaction in RGALI 631/11/435/14–15.

104. RGALI, 631/13/88/14–16.

105. Viktor Fradkin, *Delo Kol'tsova* (Moscow: Vagrius, 2002), 169.

106. RGALI 631/14/459/1, 3, 7, 13, 17, 18, 19, 21; Simone Barck and Klavis Jarmatz, eds., *Exil in der UdSSR. Kunst und Literatur im antifaschistischen Exil 1933–1945,* vol. I, part I (Leipzig: Reclam, 1989), 344–345.

107. Frezinskii, *Pisateli i sovetskie vozhdi,* 391–393; the interrogation transcript is published in Fradkin, *Delo Kol'tsova,* 171–194.

108. Fradkin, *Delo Kol'tsova,* 166.

109. A list of these sources appears in E. Muromets, "Budem bditel'ny!," *Sovetskoe iskusstvo,* 23 July 1937 (i.e. shortly after Tretiakov was arrested).

110. Barck and Jarmatz, *Exil in der UdSSR,* vol, I, part I.

111. Vladimir Grib, "Obsuzhdenie plana Goslitizdata na 1939 god," *Literaturnaia gazeta,* 20 October 1938.

112. *Frantsuzskie liriki XIX i XX vekov,* sost. Benedikt Lifshits (L: Goslitizdat, 1937); the anthology includes works by Alphonse de Lamartine, Hugo, Paul Verlaine, and Charles Baudelaire.

113. Elena Moiseevna Rzhevskaia (Kogan's first wife), personal communication, June 1999.

114. Katerina Clark and Evgeny Dobrenko, eds., *Soviet Culture and Power: A History in Documents, 1917–1953* (New Haven: Yale University Press, 2007), 210–215, citation from 211.

115. RGALI 562/1/126/1–18.

116. V. Sereda and A. Stykalin, eds. and comps., *Besedy na Lubianke: Sledstvennoe delo Dërdia Lukacha. Materialy k biografii* (Moscow: Rossiiskaia akademiia nauk, 1999).

117. Konstantin Simonov, "Glazami cheloveka moego pokoleniia," in Kol'tsov, *Vostorg i iarost',* 472.

118. L. I. Lazarev, *Konstantin Simonov. Zhizn' i tvorchestvo* (Moscow: Moskovskii rabochii, 1990), 17. Simonov in his self-serving memoirs, "Glazami cheloveka moego pokoleniia," claims: "I wrote my first poem when I heard of General Lukacs' death in Spain"; in actuality his first major long poem was about reforging class enemies on the Belomor Canal (15).

119. Lazarev, *Konstantin Simonov,* 15, 20.

120. Frezinskii, *Pisateli i sovetskie vozhdi,* 475.

121. Prof. S. Eizenshtein, "Gordost'," *Iskusstvo kino,* 1940, no. 1–2, 22.

122. RGALI 1923/1/352/21, 24, 31, 32, 35; RGALI 1923/1/3/19, 28, 39, 46, 51, 65, 68; RGALI 1923/1/4, 14, 16, 41, 50, 57; D.R., "Prem'era 'Val'kirii,'" *Sovetskoe iskusstvo,* 24 November 1940.

123. An article on Brecht's *Galileo* and another by Stefan Zweig appeared in *Sovetskoe iskusstvo* shortly before the ratification of the Molotov-Ribbentrop Pact, announced 26 August 1939 (M. Gel'fand, "'Zhizn' Galileia.' O novoi p'ese Bertol'da Brekhta," *Sovetskoe iskusstvo,* 18 August 1939; Stefan Tsveig, "'Motsart' Bela Balasha."

124. Frezinskii, *Pisateli i sovetskie vozhdi,* 468.

125. Patrick Barberis and Dominique Chapius, *Roman Karmen: Une legende rouge* (Paris: Éditions Seuil, 2002), 76.
126. Iuliia Markovna Zhivova, personal communication, 19 July 2001.
127. Vishnevskaia, *Konstantin Simonov*, 8, 10.
128. Iu. P. Sharapov, *Litsei v Sokol'nikakh. Ocherk istorii IFLI* (Moscow: Aero, 1995), 68–71.
129. "Miting predstavitelei evreiskogo naroda," *Sovetskoe iskusstvo*, 28 August 1941.
130. Naum Kleiman, personal communication, July 2006.
131. GARF 5283/14/98 ; GARF 5283/14/83/5, 8–9.

EPILOGUE

1. See "Zakladka mnogoetazhnykh zdanii," *Pravda*, 8 September 1947; "Vsenarodnoe torzhestvo," *Pravda*, 8 September 1947; "Moskovskie neboskreby. Beseda s avtorom inzhenernoi chasti proektov 26 i 32 etazhnykh zdanii V. I. Nosovym," *Literaturnaia gazeta*, 24 September 1947.
2. I. Vlasov, "Moskva, natsional'naia gordost' sovetskogo naroda," *Pravda*, 2 September 1947; Pavlo Tychina, "Tsentr mirovoi kul'tury," *Literaturnaia gazeta*, 6 September 1947.
3. "Privetstvie tov. I. V. Stalina," *Pravda*, 7 September 1947.
4. Ibid.; he lists four. See also e.g., "Narodnoe torzhestvo," *Pravda*, 8 September 1947.
5. S. Eizenshtein, "Tsvet i muzyka. Tsvetovaia rodoslovnaia 'Moskvy 800,'" in *Mosfil'm. Stat'i, publikatsii, izobrazitel'nye materialy*, Vypusk vtoroi (Moscow: Iskusstvo, 1961), 244.
6. "Doklad t. Zhdanova o zhurnalakh 'Zvezda' i 'Leningrad,'" *Literaturnaia gazeta*, 21 September 1946.
7. The list includes Ol'ga Berggol'ts, "Protiv likvidatsii liriki," *Literaturnaia gazeta*, 28 October 1954. Compare Margarita Aliger, "Vo ves' golos," *Literaturnaia gazeta*, 1940, no. 31.
8. "K itogam poeticheskogo goda. V sektsii poezii Soiuza sovetskikh pisatelei," *Literaturnaia gazeta*, 10 January 1953, reports that at a recent meeting "Olga Berggolts reproached contemporary lyricists with 'fear of themselves' [samoboiazni], with a fear of expressing all the complexity, the unrepeatable particularity of the lyric persona"— While "the young poet E. Evtushenko" attacked N. Gribachëv for the very "fear of the self" Berggolts discussed. M. Aliger spoke in the same vein.
9. Interview of Maia Turovskaia, September 2005.
10. RGASPI 17/139/81, 47–61.
11. Actually there ended up being seven "wedding cakes," in that all these buildings projected in 1947 were completed, except one of twenty-six stories that was to have been erected on the site later occupied by the Hotel Rossia.

Acknowledgments

I would like to thank the National Endowment for the Humanities whose Fellowship enabled me to spend a year on research and writing, and the Humanities Research Center of the Australian National University and its National Europe Center, which supported me for a semester in residence. In addition, many individuals assisted me during this long-term project, and I am sure I will have left out some of the names, for which I apologize. Those who helped either with research tips or by commenting on chapters include Dudley Andrew, Warren Breckman, Dymphna Clark, Sebastian Clark, Nancy Condee, Rossen Djagalov, Evgeny Dobrenko, Sheila Fitzpatrick, Gregory Freidin, Anastasia Gacheva, Michael Holquist, Peter Holquist, Naum Kleiman, Ilya Kliger, John Mackay, Richard Maxwell, Joan Neuberger, Stephen Norris, Scott Palmer, Irina Paperno, Kevin Platt, Constantine Rusanov, Svetlana Semenova, Greta Slobin, Bill and Jane Taubman, Galin Tihanov, and Erica Wolf. Especially profound gratitude is due to Michael David-Fox and Katie Trumpener, who commented on the entire manuscript. And last but not least, I would like to thank the many members of my family who have supported me during this time, including Pete, Diana, Ben, Carol, Josh, Martha, Nick, Sara, and Bas Holquist.

Index